Edward B. Segel

D0389457

POWER, FREEDOM, *and* DIPLOMACY:

The Foreign Policy of the United States of America

POWER, FREEDOM, *and* DIPLOMACY

The Foreign Policy
of the United States of America

PAUL SEABURY

UNIVERSITY OF CALIFORNIA

RANDOM HOUSE   NEW YORK

Sources of all quoted material are cited in the footnotes. The author and publisher are particularly grateful for the use of the following materials:

Pages 261-262: from *Listen, Yankee* by C. Wright Mills. Copyright © 1960 by C. Wright Mills. Reprinted by permission of Ballantine Books, Inc.

Pages 296, 297: from *The Pattern of Responsibility* by McGeorge Bundy. By permission of Houghton Mifflin Company.

Page 301: from *Duel at the Brink* by Gaston Coblentz and Roscoe Drummond. By permission of Doubleday & Company.

Page 35: from "Geography of This Time" by Archibald MacLeish. Copyright 1942 by Archibald MacLeish. Reprinted from *Act Five and Other Poems*, by permission of Random House, Inc.

Page 283: from "The Managers" by W. H. Auden. Copyright 1949 by W. H. Auden. Reprinted from *Nones*, by permission of Random House, Inc.

Pages 77-78, 301, 307, 313: from *The Memoirs of Harry Truman*, Volume II. By permission of Life. © 1956 Time, Inc.

Pages 240-241: from an unpublished manuscript by Arthur Goodfriend. By permission of the author.

Pages 375-376: From F. S. C. Northrop, "Neutralism and U.S. Foreign Policy," *Annals of the Academy of Political and Social Science*, July, 1957, p. 58. By permission of the Academy of Political and Social Science.

FIRST PRINTING

© *Copyright, 1963, by Random House, Inc.*

All rights reserved under International and Pan-American Copyright Conventions. Published in New York by Random House, Inc., and simultaneously in Toronto, Canada, by Random House of Canada, Limited.

Library of Congress Catalog Card Number: 63-8272

Manufactured in the United States of America by THE COLONIAL PRESS INC., CLINTON, MASS.

TO MY TWO SONS,

David and John

PREFACE

Books about politics necessarily bear heavy marks of the special place and time of their writing. The ideas expressed in the following pages took shape during the course of several years, but they were for the most part written during the late summer, fall, and early winter of 1961, in Washington, D. C. This was the time of the building of the Berlin wall, of the Soviets' resumption of thermonuclear tests, and of the death of Dag Hammarskjöld, the United Nations Secretary General, during his Congo mission.

Whether or not this unique context stamps too heavy an impress of gloom upon the general problems with which this book deals, the reader must himself decide. Nearly all books about foreign policy and world politics today become quickly obsolete, if not irrelevant. This is not just because so many people now write political books, which pile like effluvial layers upon earlier ones; nor is it because of the continuous development of newer or more remarkable techniques and insights of the social sciences. It is chiefly because conditions and problems in world politics seem swiftly to change their essential nature or relative importance even as we look at them. If we cannot find or establish durable geodetic markers to delineate the problems with which policy must cope, we face the frustration or futility which comes when problems seem kaleidoscopically to change their essences before our very eyes—especially so, when immediate crisis clamors that this, or that, is what now must be most important, most critical, most needful of action. To write in crisis, then, is to be made aware of the necessity of choice, of the consequences of not choosing and of making wrong choices; but most of all, to be made aware of the essential need for standards by which problems may be measured, and action taken. If choice is not made, political processes tragically act with predetermined or automated guidance, as did the Schlieffen Plan in the summer of 1914. Things, not men, are in the saddle.

While flashes of international crisis electrified and illumined these thoughts, the author can hardly thank them for the favor. More benevolent institutions and friends deserve expression of my gratitude here: the John Simon Guggenheim Memorial Foundation, upon whose grant of precious time and leisure I heavily drew during these months; the Brookings Institution of Washington, D. C., and especially its Director of Foreign Policy Studies, H. Field Haviland, Jr., for congenial, tolerant company and comfortable surroundings during the months I spent with them; Mr. Charles Lieber of Random House, for his relentless, ebullient curiosity about the kind of book I might write; Mrs. Harriet Cobbe, who deciphered and typed most of this book from palimpsestic pages; Mr. Richard Ashcraft, who tersely indexed a prolix manuscript; Messrs. David Williams and Arthur Goodfriend, and Mrs. Violet Gunther, of Washington, D. C., who serve as example and reminder that critical citizens and civil servants can effectively act with conscience and wit, to govern what politicians and statesmen think and do; finally, my wife, who also lived through these things which I then experienced, and whose concern for the non-political needs of civilized life is matched by her severe appraisal of the conditions which make a book such as this necessary to write.

Berkeley, California   PAUL SEABURY

Contents

Contents

POWER, FREEDOM, *and* DIPLOMACY:

The Foreign Policy of the United States of America

CHAPTER

I

POLICY AND THE NATIONAL COMMUNITY

T HE SOCIETY OF NATIONS, of which America is a part, consists of more than one hundred sovereign states. Although they differ greatly in size, strength, culture, and political form, we regard them collectively as the chief actors in world politics. Their interests, aspirations, conflicts, and the many networks of relationship among them and their people comprise the primary subjects of international politics.

The study of American foreign policy focuses upon only one of these nation-states; in the chapters which follow, problems of world politics will be approached from within the political universe of America, its unique purposes and concerns. America today possesses wide-ranging influence in world politics; the subject matter of its foreign policies is virtually coextensive with the study of international politics. Since World War II, American diplomacy has been confronted with political and social crises in nearly all parts of the world. The shattering of the old European society of nations during World War II, coupled with the rising influence of totalitarian Communist states, led the United States toward global responsibilities, dilemmas, and choices wholly unknown to American statecraft two generations ago. This universal crisis of world politics in which America finds itself is aggravated by great military vulnerability from possible thermonuclear war, a vulnerability which Americans share with humanity as a whole.

This book attempts both to define and analyze the sources of American conduct in world affairs and the manner in which American interests, conduct, and purposes fit into the broader patterns of world politics. When Robert Benchley was a student at Harvard, he was once asked to write an examination essay on the international regulation of the whaling industry from the viewpoint of Britain, France, or the United States. He wrote in his answer that since he was not familiar with any of these viewpoints he preferred to discuss it from the viewpoint of the whale. The reader is asked to imitate Benchley. Observing American foreign policy from the point of view of American politics is the best way to understand the various interests, values, and pressures out of which American aspirations, commitments, and claims in foreign affairs arise today. But our foreign policy must also be studied from a more comprehensive and universal vantage point in world politics if we are to see how American actions and policies interact with those of other states. Thus the reader should observe American foreign policy from a civic station within the American community of which he may be a part; but it must also be seen from a summit where these national policies and actions become engaged in a broader system of international politics. An understanding of only the sources of American conduct—the historical and cultural milieu out of which national interests have arisen and the clusters of contemporary interests and influences which bear upon contemporary policy—cannot illumine the nature of the crises which America today confronts. Nor can any deep understanding of the external theater of world politics in which American policies today engage explain either the texture or the vigor of these policies nor explain why, so often, they appear mistaken, inconsistent, or inappropriate or, for that matter, why policies often seem to persist long after the original context within which they arose—and which they might have served efficiently —has disappeared.

SOME DEFINITIONS OF POLICY

When we speak of a nation's foreign policy, we are speaking of many things and of one thing at the same time. Policy is often taken to mean some settled course of action adopted and followed by a government. It usually means concerted, purposive action arising out of rational deliberation among rational men. Policy can mean this and often does. Some of the great foreign policies of the United States in the recent past such as the Marshall Plan for European recovery were products of such rational, purposeful thought, the product of a concert of judgment among men responsible for actions in the realm of international affairs.

But this definition is too narrow. Relying on it exclusively we run the danger of misjudging and oversimplifying the nature of the political processes out of which policies normally spring. All too often policy is the product of random, haphazard, or even irrational forces and events. Equally often it is the result of deadlocked judgments, an uneasy compromise formula. Often what appears on the surface as a nation's settled course of action may be due to indecision, unwillingness or inability to act. It may be no policy at all but simply a drift with events. Sometimes foreign policies are products of statesmen's passive compliance with strong domestic political pressures—and thus products of contending political forces within the nation itself. Finally policy may be due to statesmen's abdication of choice and rational judgment in the face of ruthless and strong external pressures.

Walter Lippmann once said that policy must be taken to

mean the harmonious balancing of a nation's external commitments with the resources and power capable of sustaining them.[1] This concept of policy is essential if we are to regard foreign policy as the art of matching means to ends. Ambitious or imaginative policy suited to some great end will flag unless sustained by adequate resources; purposes, in this sense, are useless without power. This ideal conception of policy, so necessary to purposive action, also constricts the meaning of policy too narrowly. The foreign policies of a nation often embody commitments, purposes, or desires which greatly exceed the resources a nation is able or willing to put behind them; and to suggest that when great imbalance of purpose and power exists policy does not exist, would be to make the study of foreign policy merely a pathological tale of human shortcomings. Lippmann may be right in saying that between the era of McKinley's imperialism and the Second World War, American overseas commitments were not matched by resources adequate to back them up. If so, it may well have been a grievous error of American policy-makers and the American public as a whole that this gap between objectives and resources was not perceived in time. Nevertheless there were American policies. James Reston of the New York *Times* once poignantly illustrated in fable the tragic disparity between resources and purposes which often confronts policy-makers. After frivolously wasting the summer in riotous living, an indolent grasshopper, alarmed by the approaching winter, asked his friend the ant for advice. "I advise you to turn yourself into a cockroach," said the ant. "Then, move into town and spend the winter comfortably under a radiator in a nice warm apartment." "But that is impossible," said the grasshopper, "for I am a grasshopper." "Be that as it may," said the ant, "I was only giving you policy-guidance."

In an ideal sense, policy may also be regarded as the reasoned product of creative leadership, the conscious, rational, un-

---

[1] See Walter Lippmann, *U.S. Foreign Policy: Shield of the Republic.* Boston: Little, Brown, and Co., 1943.

remitting attempt to harmonize influence and power with political goals, and to respond continuously to new problems. Seen thus qualitatively, foreign policy is the result of statesmen's conscious choice among alternative courses of action involving the matching of resources to goals. This qualitative conception still overlooks the many limitations and constraints upon policy-makers, for there are some problems which transcend in complexity and severity any human resources and intelligence. In American politics, adverse events in the outside world are often blamed upon "failures" of policy or of policy-makers but, all too often, even powerful men have very little control over events. There never has been an omnipotent nation governed by omniscient men.

Foreign and Domestic Policies

In any event, American foreign policies comprise the totality of purposes and commitments by which the United States, through its constitutionally designated authorities, seeks by means of influence, power, and sometimes violence to deal with foreign states and problems in the international environment. For purposes of clarity, we might draw an illustrative distinction between a government's foreign policies and its domestic ones. In constitutional democracies in particular, a sharp distinction must be made between the realm of domestic and foreign policies. The former is a constitutional polity, a national community, and policies and acts of governments if constitutionally undertaken, come to represent the law of the community.

In America, Congress and President, together with a massive bureaucracy, "make" policy which is universally applicable within the confines of the United States. But the realm of foreign policy is radically different. Here American policies do not become law or fiat. There is no international community with a recognizable constitutional authority, and there are sharp limits on American policy's influence. Domestic policy may become law through appropriate and known legal procedures. Foreign policy, on the other hand, amounts to a perpetual attempt by constitutional authorities of the United States to attain purposes and ends in an arena in which *many* states and nations contend. But as the United States is not the ultimate arbiter of international law or of world politics, foreign policy involves par excellence something which is essentially subsidiary in domestic politics: the continuous negotiation between and among powerful state entities to achieve purposes which, however beneficial or benevolent they may be, are justified *in terms of* the United States itself, its interests and aspirations.

When speaking of a touchstone against which domestic policies are often weighed, we frequently speak of a "public interest," meaning by this the interest of the entire community which is affected by law and policy. When speaking of the touchstone against which foreign policies are judged, we often speak of the "national interest," as though it were the opposite side of the coin of the public interest. And yet a sharp distinction should be made between these two terms. The idea of public interest supposes an identity between the scope of the community and the scope of measures undertaken on its behalf, but the idea of national interest assumes no such identity. Policies undertaken by the American government on behalf of the national community in world politics may, and often do, adversely affect the interests of other communities of men in very dramatic ways. The idea of the general welfare, as a constitutional conception, has been an important point of reference for policies designed to benefit all Americans. Yet in the international arena not only is there no constitutional procedure by which such a transcendent general welfare might be arrived at for all men, but there is barely a rudimentary consensus among nations about what that general welfare might comprise. The point of reference of American foreign policy, then, is the welfare of the American public, its prosperity, its security from external attack, its manifold political and cultural interests in a world of many nations. This is not to say that American foreign policies do not on some occasions serve interests and causes more extensive than those of the American public alone, but rather that the primary reference point is the American public.

The Art and Science of Foreign Policy

Foreign policy may mean, then, many things at any one particular moment in time. For instance, the foreign policy of the United States may be said to consist of a bundle of major principles and purposes which are never of equal importance nor even necessarily harmonious with each other. Such principles serve as points of reference and as standards against which the activities of American statesmen and policy-makers may be judged and criticized. Whatever these principles, there may be said to be a higher law of American foreign policy, that of the public welfare in an international environment: the national interest. This supreme principle may be difficult to define in specific circumstances, but it arises nevertheless from the historical fact that an American national community exists and that this community wishes to survive as a community in world politics without destroying its own image of itself in the process. That these two wishes are quite separate might be illustrated by one dilemma of American diplomacy in the first years of the atomic age, when America had a monopoly of nuclear weapons. These weapons could easily have been used then, as a Hitler surely would have used them, to obliterate all possible foreign military threats to the United States. The United States as a political entity might perhaps have survived such a preventive war physically undamaged, but American civilization might have been spiritually corrupted beyond recognition: the "image" of America might well have been irreparably destroyed in the process by such an unprecedented act of international murder. Thus the idea of an American national interest may be said to go far beyond the purpose of mere biological or communal survival, for it embraces the many purposes of a vigorous society unconstrained by a single, purposive totalitarian rule.

But foreign policy means more than the principles and collective interest that supposedly govern the actions of American diplomacy. It also embraces all of the purposeful and random interactions that take place between the American nation and its international environment. Regardless of what bearing these actions and relationships may have upon the principles mentioned above, they contribute to the substance of America's foreign relations. In the day-to-day conduct of foreign policy, actions and events often appear to occur in a haphazard way, at times with no discernible bearing upon broad national purposes; equally often they occur in seeming contradiction with them, and not surprisingly so. For the conduct of foreign relations is not a formal, monolithic process. If there were fewer sides to American diplomacy, we might say that often the left hand did not know what the right hand was doing, but this metaphor would be inaccurate. America is not just a nation; it may also be seen as a great constellation of cultural, corporate, and group forces, private and governmental, many of which not only have extensive domestic and foreign interests of their own but even entertain their own private conceptions of what a desirable national interest should be. Often in the past, the realm of foreign policy has served as an arena in which domestic groups have struggled amongst themselves to achieve particular ambitions and goals. Often, too, such groups have by virtue of their own foreign activities involved the nation in enterprises bearing no apparent relation to any national interest.

It might, then, be useful to distinguish between the art and the science of foreign policy. In the first sense, we might regard the study of American foreign policy as the art of fashioning order, congruence, and purpose out of these many relationships between our nation and the outside world—the art of harmoniously relating private and governmental actions to broader national purposes. In a sense, the mastery of this art (the art of

accommodating means to ends, purposes to resources) is chiefly
the responsibility of statesmen and requires high intellectual capacities. Yet in democracies, where the discretion and power of
policy-makers is limited by political and constitutional restraints,
and where political power is broadly shared, this art is one that
must be widely diffused throughout the nation. If large numbers
of Americans were greatly to misconceive the purposes of American diplomacy or to misjudge the environment in which these
purposes must operate, great dangers might ensue.

However, we must also study foreign policy as a science, not
as artistic, statesmanlike creation of order, purpose, and action
but as discernment of patterns of political behavior and order
as they already exist. Here we should observe the broad impulses
which arise out of American society and which express themselves
in American purposes in the outside world; we seek to discern the
broader historical trends of American behavior in world politics
which lend consistency even to incongruity. Finally we seek to
discover the patterns of relationships which have been established
between the United States and the rest of the world over the
course of nearly two centuries.

Our Present Crisis

The point of departure for this study of American foreign
policy lies in a diagnosis of the contemporary world of politics,
not in history. We must see where we are before finding out
where we have been. We must diagnose the crisis of present-day
world politics as a whole before we analyze America's particular
place in this crisis. In many ways, the environment of world
politics is radically different from that which existed throughout
most of America's past. In fact, it is radically different from that
which has prevailed at any previous time in the history of mankind. And most significant of all, it is far more unstable and
dangerous than ever before.

The uniqueness of our present crisis is often said to arise

from two historically unique conditions: the threat to the "free world" posed by Communist totalitarian expansion in many parts of the world, and the threat to nations and to human life posed by the existence of very powerful nuclear weapons. Without these two unprecedented twentieth-century circumstances, international relations would be safer and more congenial than they unfortunately are. Yet both of them are already familiar features of the world we live in. The Bolshevik Revolution has endured for more than forty years; while its collapse was often prophesied, its power has increased in ways that even Lenin and Stalin could scarcely have imagined. Nuclear weapons have existed for a decade and a half; having failed either to abolish or regulate them internationally, we are on the threshold of an era in which many nations, not just three or four powerful ones, will have the skills both to make and use them.

Communist totalitarianism and nuclear weapons can both be regarded as symptoms of a more fundamental derangement of the international community. Were either or both of them absent, the forces that gave rise to them would raise equally disturbing problems in their place. Scarcely twenty years ago, the great threat to Western civilization came not from Communism but from Nazi, Fascist, and Axis expansion. In some ways this earlier revolution was far more savage and nihilistic than is that of the Soviet Union today. It is not difficult to imagine some new constellation of revolutionary power, bearing little resemblance to either Communism or Fascism, which might pose an equally serious danger to American security in the future. In some ways, the spectacular qualities of Communism have obscured equally significant tendencies in international affairs which exist independently of it; the passing of a "Communist threat" might only serve to bring them more clearly to light. Likewise, were nuclear weapons somehow done away with, science would undoubtedly very soon place in our hands other, equally lethal methods of destruction and terror (as, for example, bacteriological and chemical weapons). Human ingenuity and military science being what they are, there is more than one way to skin a cat, or a whole civilization.

American Stability and World Change

Americans are accustomed to taking for granted most of the basic features of the domestic political order in which they live; here there appears to be both historical continuity and permanence. No matter how greatly the American landscape has changed over the past half century, no matter how startling the changes that have taken place in the American economy, the constitutional order as well as the agencies of politics through which it operates closely resemble those that existed long before the first World War.

Yet, when Americans look at the contemporary state of world politics, we perceive the very opposite. In this larger dimension of our national life there is such a bewildering array of novel features that it seems impossible even to reduce them to terms which the human mind can rigorously and systematically grasp. If what was "new" in the international order gave promise of permanence and if political and social change slowed to a rate which would permit us to hold various features of contemporary world politics as "givens," our search for regularities might hold out some hope. Yet massive upheavals in international politics seem, in each decade, to swiftly change basic patterns of relationships amongst nations, while groundswells of social and technological change—now occurring everywhere throughout the world —contribute to power constellations that are ever changing. Our great difficulty in predicting the shape of things to come is nowhere better seen than in the field of weapons technology where, it is said, technological change is so swift that often the length of time from drawing-board to mass production of a new weapon is equal to the useful life-span of the weapon being produced. As a result, by the time a particular weapon becomes operational, it has already been rendered obsolete by some newer instrument of war.

This kaleidoscopic quality of world politics today leads many to simply accept with fatalism the dizzy turn of events. How can they control events they cannot even comprehend? To cope only with the immediate and the tangible seems the easiest way out. Why plan ahead when one cannot know the shape of the newer "new world" for which plans are to be designed?

The unprecedented power at the disposal of nations and the speed and magnitude of contemporary social and political change throughout the world today make the purposeful conduct of foreign relations intellectually hazardous. Social scientists often speak of a culture lag, the seeming inability of ideologies, political systems, and social behavior to keep pace with scientific and technological change. But the reverse is often true; cultures may change so swiftly that technology and science cannot keep pace with them. This is particularly true in many of today's underdeveloped countries, where powerful elite groups, together with broad masses of the people, hold expectations of great scientific and technological improvements for themselves, expectations which often greatly exceed the ability of science and technology to keep pace.

A New Relationship to the World

The most striking change that Americans have experienced in world politics during the past decade and a half has been their nation's recent global involvement in world politics and the great costs and risks this has entailed. Barely two decades ago, isolationism not only meant a sentimental aspiration and policy; it described the condition of America's actual relationship to world politics. As great as American power in world politics has been through all of the twentieth century, the conscious, purposive exercise of that power and influence was confined chiefly to the

Western hemisphere until World War II. As recently as the New Deal era, the chief governing principle of American foreign policy was that of a *unilateral* security policy which, avoiding alliances with non-Western hemisphere nations, sought to minimize American commitments in all other parts of the world. To be sure, this meant that America's capacity purposefully to influence political events abroad was voluntarily inhibited until moments of very great international crisis, such as the Nazi conquest of Europe in 1940. It was nonetheless a respectable tradition of American policy, based upon a popular confidence that the United States could defend itself against any probable coalition of aggressors. Throughout the nineteenth century this condition and policy of isolation had as corollary the belief that the American political system was separate and distinct from that of Europe and the European-dominated world. Doubtless this American aloofness and isolation contributed to the political cohesiveness of American society and to a deepening sense of national identity; continuous involvement in European affairs might well have meant continuous European involvement in America and could have produced deep divisions within European nationality groups in the United States. The human resources spent during a century and a half of American isolation upon the internal development of North America could conceivably have been dissipated in costly enterprises abroad.

The end of isolationism marked an irrevocable break with tradition which American political attitudes have had difficulty adjusting to. The change from aloofness to domination of world politics is often equally difficult for Americans to accept. In the past, American political thinkers often resisted more active U.S. involvement in world affairs, fearing it would mean a loss of American autonomy and the subjection of American interests to the purposes of more powerful European states. Ironically, however, the point in history at which America relinquished its isolation coincided with the sudden collapse of all the traditional world powers of Europe (Russia excepted) during the second World War. The historic distaste of many Americans for "power politics," their liberal uneasiness about expedient alliances, balance-of-power strategies, and the sustained, calculated use of military power, these attitudes gradually took shape during a century of American history in which world politics had been dominated by Europe. Moving from the periphery to the center of world politics during a period of scarcely five years and remaining there produced an intellectual shock in American thought which has even now not wholly subsided.

This changing relationship to the world should also be perceived in a far broader international context. Both in the long phase of isolation and in the ensuing, still brief, period of central involvement, American attitudes toward world politics took form within a climate of popular confidence in American strength and mastery over events. Aside from such frustrating stalemates as the costly and inconclusive war in Korea, the era of the cold war has not lessened this popular confidence in American strength to any great extent. The United States has never been successfully invaded, much less defeated in war. In an age of intercontinental missiles, its interior has never suffered more than trivial physical damage from enemy attack in time of war. For more than a century, no serious threat to the continental United States was staged from the entire Western hemisphere. From the Civil War up until the time of the Cuban crisis of 1962, civilian America had only experienced the terrors of revolution, civil war, or international conflict vicariously. Americans shared this national immunity from large-scale conflict and terror with very few other peoples. America had been a unique exception in the modern world.

SUGGESTED READING

Lippmann, Walter, *U.S. Foreign Policy: Shield of the Republic*, Boston, Little, Brown and Co., 1943.
Morgenthau, Hans J., *In Defense of the National Interest*, New York, Alfred A. Knopf, 1951.

Niebuhr, Reinhold, *The Irony of American History*, New York, Scribner's, 1952, chaps. I-IV.

Tannenbaum, Frank, *The American Tradition in Foreign Policy*, Norman, Okla., University of Oklahoma Press, 1954.

Wolfers, Arnold, and Martin, Laurence W., eds., *The Anglo-American Tradition in Foreign Affairs, Readings from Thomas More to Woodrow Wilson*, New Haven, Yale University Press, 1956.

POLICY AND THE INTERNATIONAL ENVIRONMENT

Two SEEMINGLY contradictory yet quite radical changes in the nature of world politics have occurred during our lifetime: first, international politics has become universalized, and second, power and political influence in world politics have seemingly become bipolarized. By the universalization of politics we mean the coming into being of a multi-continental, multi-cultural society of nations which, though governed by no universal authority or laws, must still be seen as a political system of juridically independent states, global in scope. Bipolarity describes, if somewhat crudely, the gravitation of political power in this society of nations toward two polar points: the United States and the Soviet Union. One might more generally speak of this global division as one between the Western world and a Communist bloc of states, with an uncommitted, unstable, and in many ways powerless world lying in between. Yet even here, the respective positions of influence possessed by America and Russia today still are for the most part unquestioned. Despite this concentration of power and influence there is not a concentration of authority, if by authority we mean the capacity to evoke obedience and compliance with law without recourse to violence, by virtue of unquestioning monopoly of ideological influence over the masses. As Reinhold Niebuhr points out in *The Irony of American History*, both the United States and the Soviet Union have "traditionally" rejected imperialism as a mode of political rule. The Jeffersonian doctrine of the consent of the governed as the basis of political order finds its counterpart in Soviet-Marxist doctrines of the universal triumph of the party-led proletariat.

THE NEW NATION-STATES AND THE TWO SUPER POWERS

In several ways, these two developments—the universalization of world politics and the polarization of power—seem both incongruous and contradictory. The first of them can be seen in the constantly growing number of sovereign states in the society of nations: nearly half the population of the world has gained its nominal political independence within the past fifteen years. This proliferation of new nation-states seems to fragment the community of man into more and more formal units. Moreover, while many of the new states are integrating old societies and creating wholly new ones through social and economic changes, one price of this political revolution has been the destruction of a traditional, Europe-oriented world. Scarcely half a century ago, world politics was European world politics. The society of nations (namely, the juridically independent states which collectively governed international affairs) was, before the first World War, almost exclusively European or at least Western, if we include the United States and the Latin American republics. Until the twentieth century only the Ottoman Empire and, more recently, Japan were non-Western nations of any importance and influence in world politics. For nearly two centuries before 1914 the non-Western world had been the object of European expansion, colonization, exploitation, and imperial rule. The empires of France, Britain, Russia, Italy, the Netherlands, Portugal, Germany, and Spain had forged what measure of political integration existed in this non-Western world. In their wake has risen a vast community of new nation-states in Asia and Africa.

One legacy of Western dominion over these non-European peoples was the spirit and ideology of nationalism which Europe left behind as it retreated, a quickened popular sense of loyalty to and identification with these new states among the dominant political and intellectual elites which European influence had nurtured.[1] Borrowing a biological term, we might speak of this creation of new nations as a process of binary fission, the splitting up of older empires and the fragmentation of the society of nations into ever smaller parts. In many ways the world of the 1960's is far smaller than it was fifty years ago; yet the birth of new nations suggests that it is in some ways even further from the ideal of a politically integrated world civilization (so attractive to some humanist philosophers) than it seemed to be to many Europeans before the first World War.

At first glance, the growth of these new nation-states appears to be a process moving in quite the opposite direction from the gravitation of political power to the U.S. and Russia. Today these two super-powers appear as nuclei toward which other states within the society of nations are drawn. Despite their many political dissimilarities, Russia and America today both command influence and power over a theater of politics which would have staggered the imagination of a Caesar. Both possess a global influence which has brought some semblance of political and economic integration to large parts of the world, even if their rivalry has created grave international tensions. Soviet Marxists confidently describe this bipolarization of world politics as the tem-

---

[1] Rupert Emerson, *From Empire to Nation*. Cambridge, Mass.; Harvard University Press, 1960.

porary division of the world into two camps, a socialist and a
capitalist one. They see this political cleavage as merely the final
stage in an uncompleted process of history which culminates in
the triumph of socialism throughout the world and its replace-
ment by a new Communist order. Many Westerners, all of whom
lack such doctrinal certainty in historical processes, prefer to see
this bipolarization as an unstable, even tragic schism between a
"free" world and a "totalitarian" one. Yet regardless of what
name we give to this condition, its global dimensions are historically unprecedented. Even the ancient schism between Christian
and Moslem worlds was never so great.

The Death of the Old Order

Contemporary politics can often deceive men about the nature of both politics and history. The present polarity between
America and Russia was neither inevitable nor is it of long
standing; there is no more reason to assume that it will remain
indefinitely the chief distinguishing feature of world politics
than that the opposite condition of fragmentation described
above is permanent. There are significant countervailing tendencies at work offsetting both of them. The steady growth of
regional organizations in Africa and Asia; the political recovery
and economic integration of Western Europe; the sudden emergence of Communist China as a major world power—each of
these recent changes suggests the possibility that a new, global,
multiple system of political power is in the making. The threat
of nuclear war between Russia and the West conceivably could
alter the distribution of power and influence beyond anyone's
imagination. (A thermonuclear war between Russia and the
West could conceivably shift the center of world civilization
overnight into the Southern Hemisphere, since most nuclear target
areas lie in the Northern Hemisphere.) Yet both fragmentation and bipolarity heighten our awareness of the very great
differences between our present world, its possibilities for change,
and the earlier world of European politics out of which the

modern state system has grown. Not only did the older society of nations have the European continent as its central theater and focus, while ours today has no such focal point; this European society of nations for a very long time included in itself a number of influential states, each of which possessed roughly equal or commensurate capabilities, prestige, and influence. From the mid-seventeenth century until 1939, international politics was governed by these great powers: Britain, Russia, Prussia (Germany), France, Spain and, until 1918, Austria-Hungary. While the fortunes of each of them fluctuated considerably during this three-hundred-year period, none of them was ever able to control the political system of Europe for any considerable period of time. None alone could dominate it; none managed to command power greater than that of a countervailing coalition of states brought to bear against it; nor did any two of them ever succeed in dividing Europe between them for very long. Thus for centuries a multiple balance of power appeared to be a mechanical law governing the relationships amongst the great European powers. While this fluid system of alliances and alignments in no way kept the peace of Europe, and while its operation worked many overt injustices upon various peoples of the continent, it nevertheless prevented any one state from achieving permanent hegemony over the whole society of nations. Because of it, Europe remained both politically and culturally plural.

During the latter years of Europe's preeminence this system not only dominated the world of politics; it also governed it. The new nation-states of Africa and Asia were its colonial progeny, its political step-children. The emerging ideological character of their politics today testifies to the decisive imprint which these European empires exerted on their non-European subjects during their span of political control. The swift passing of European authority in the non-Western world may chiefly be attributed to the two great World Wars of 1914-1918 and 1939-1945. For these together tore European society apart, deflected Europe's political concerns toward its own internal civil war, reduced the European nations' effective control over their outlying possessions, and irreparably destroyed Europe's prestige and authority overseas. It is interesting that those European colonies in Southeast Asia which were either overrun or threatened by Japanese occupation between 1941 and 1945 were those most speedily to gain formal independence after World War II. For here the early Japanese victories over European powers smashed the traditional image of European colonial invincibility.

Yet these wars probably only hastened an inexorable process of independence. Europe's decline as the center of world politics was more fundamentally prompted by Europe's profound cultural and technological impact upon these areas. The leaders of successful revolt against Europe were nationalists who had been most closely touched and affected by Westernization. As it had been earlier with the American colonies, Westernization led to liberation from Europe. Thus the price paid by the former colonial peoples of Asia and Africa for their national independence was the emulation and adoption of the political ideologies and systems, the technology and ethical values of their former colonial oppressors.

In scarcely half a century then, a once familiar order of world politics disappeared. Of the five great powers which dominated the society of nations barely forty years ago, three of them —France, Germany, and Italy—are today third-rate powers at best. One, Austria, is today a tiny neutralized enclave in central Europe. Another, Britain, has retained some measure of global political influence by virtue of its constantly diminishing role in the Commonwealth, its close relationship with other nations in the English-speaking world, and its prudent decision, after 1945, to liquidate most of its overseas empire. Today Western Europe, politically and culturally cut off from the Soviet Empire in Eastern Europe, remains one of the world's three great industrial centers; its present cultural vitality has defied Oswald Spengler's predictions of its decline. But its authority and dominion over the rest of the non-European world seems to have passed irrevocably.

Economics and Politics in the Nation-State

Second only in significance to this passing of the old European order is the manner in which the nation-state, as building-block of the international society of nations, has changed both in its economic and its political characteristics. Since the time of the French Revolution in 1789, most Europeans have identified the idea of political community with the idea of the nation-state and the idea of democracy with that of nationalism. Human rights were closely associated with *national* rights of men within these new nation-states. This peculiar European model of political society both subverted the older imperial orders of traditional Europe and was widely emulated by non-European peoples as they gained independence from Europe. National self-determination, the right of nations freely to choose their own forms of government, today commands widespread support as an ideal throughout the world. More comprehensive systems of political order, notably the idea of empire, today stand in disrepute; even Soviet Marxists, whose homeland, the Soviet Union, bestrides many subject nationalities, deny the legitimacy of imperialism. Even the United Nations Charter pays tribute to this right of nations, for one of its declared purposes is to "develop friendly relations among nations based upon respect for the principle of equal rights and self-determination of peoples."

Wherever we look in the world of politics we see the common propensity of nation-states to weave ever more elaborate and intricate systems of social organization and power within themselves. The citizens of all the more industrially advanced nations of the world live out their lives in a politico-economic order of astonishing complexity. The modern state, whether it be democratic, authoritarian, or totalitarian, reaches down deep into its national society to order, direct, and control the lives of citizens in mass society in ways which their forebears scarcely could have imagined. Indeed such intricate regulation of mass society appears to be closely related to the very aspirations of modern men: the desire for heightened economic opportunities, for job security, for more dynamic economic growth in consumer industries, and for a more secure and abundant old age. Protection against the vicissitudes of depressions, of uncontrollable changes in the world economy, and of war, all of these have placed heavy burdens upon all governments. Throughout the world, the political power of the State over its own citizens seems to have grown concomitantly with economic and social "progress."

In time of war, the nation-state's authority over society is most dramatically revealed. In time of total war, so it would seem, the whole of society can be mobilized to collective purposes almost overnight. A few men in positions of great authority can make decisions which drastically affect everyone's lives. Most surprising is the fact that such decisions and commands are usually so swiftly and unquestioningly obeyed. No tyrant in history could ever command such allegiance of his subjects as can the modern democratic state in time of war-crisis. Without a doubt, modern war has been the chief spur to this organizational revolution. The defense, the expansion, of the state—acting as the protector or agent of society—has prompted the designing of organizational systems to facilitate prompt obedience all the way down the line in time of crisis. For a medieval ruler to marshal human resources for war often required continuous, protracted negotiations with lesser political authorities—contractual agreements on which obedience depended. The outbreak of World War I in 1914 showed that war would not evoke widespread civil disobedience among the peoples of Europe. Nearly all European Socialists, for instance, immediately identified their own ideological interests with those of their nation-states despite their own previous proclamation of class solidarity among all European workers.

This extraordinary deference to the State in time of war or

of international crisis may seem surprising at first glance. How can the modern state so quickly exact such obedience? There is a certain mystery in the whole matter of civil obedience which cannot be explained away on sociological or psychological grounds. Historically such grandiose obedience is unparalleled. Yet it becomes somewhat more plausible when we consider the beneficent role the modern state has come to play. Even the Soviet state under Stalin, widely despised and feared by many Soviet citizens, was unflinchingly supported by most Russians after the Nazi attack in 1941. The defense of the Russian motherland against German invaders was preferable to national defeat and occupation. The great powers of the modern state—democratic, totalitarian, or other—are not wholly, or even in large part, exploitative and oppressive. The sovereign state in modern times has become an overarching constitutional order which enables most men to live out their lives under at least minimal conditions of public order and rule of law. Most modern states, in addition, are welfare states, providing conditions in which men may live longer, more abundant, and more secure lives. Even the most tyrannous state today normally regards it as a chief duty to maintain civil peace, foster economic and industrial growth, establish equitable or minimal standards of social justice, income, and conditions of employment. The claims which modern men assert against the state invariably have their price in the obedience which the state can call for in times of international crisis. Indeed, the more homogeneous the culture upon which the state rests, the more easily this obedience in war seems to be attained. For one supreme responsibility of the modern state is that of protecting its society from foreign attack—and modern war today threatens not only regimes, governments, and armies; it can obliterate whole societies.

There is something supremely ironic in this political condition which all modern men share. For while at least in America, Western Europe, Russia, and a few other prosperous countries men reap great benefits from the secure organizational context of life which the state provides, they are exposed to corresponding dangers and insecurities from the external conditions of world politics. In most nations today, civil peace is very nearly taken for granted. Domestic lawlessness, disorder, overt private brutality and violence are more and more atypical conditions within societies. Few Americans bother to carry or own weapons for their private protection, not just because the police protect men more efficiently than once they did, but because within this civil order men are educated to civility. Yet as this internal peace has both enlarged and deepened within societies, so has international violence become more destructive and threatening than ever before. And so it is that the many advantages which common men derive from the protection of their sovereign state are counterbalanced by the extraordinary threats posed by the destructive power of other states against their own.

THE EUROPEAN ORDER BEFORE WORLD WAR II

While the international society of nations since 1914 has been greatly broadened into a global system, this change in itself has greatly augmented the insecurity of nearly all states within it. Radical improvements in communication and transportation have dramatically shrunk the human scale of the world; but on balance these improvements have done more to dramatize and reveal the wide disparity among cultures and political systems than they have done to modify them. In turn, the emergence of patterns of global economic organization has hastened the improvement of men's living conditions, at least in most industrializing nations. But the uneven pace of industrial change, the ensuing enhancement of inequality among nations, and the loss of national economic independence have in turn bred new fears and new insecurities among men. Many unanticipated technological changes in production have made most nations dependent for their prosperity and economic stability upon the state of the world economy and upon access to markets and supplies lying far beyond the radius of their effective political control. The absence of any great post-war depression after 1945 has meant that the worst vicissitudes of the world economy have been avoided. Still, dependence upon world markets constantly carries with it the seeds of economic vulnerability. This is as true of the more industrialized trading nations of Europe as it has been of the more backward economies of Asia, Africa, and Latin America. Despite spectacular progress towards economic abundance in America in the past two decades, this abundance has been accompanied by a growing loss of economic self-sufficiency, notably in raw materials. The spectacular rise in American living standards, coupled with the increasing disparity of income between America and the underdeveloped nations, has come to create its own problems. Ironically, the increase of communications, the enlarged flow of information from place to place in the world has heightened men's mutual awareness of differences in economic prosperity.

Furthermore, to the extent that technological innovations have been introduced into backward areas of the world they have brought in their train quite radical disruptions of traditional social orders, politics, and customs. In Europe and America, during the eighteenth and nineteenth centuries, the transition from agrarian-rural to metropolitan-industrial society occurred gradually over a very long period of time. By the end of the nineteenth century, America and Europe both had experienced the most significant phases of urbanization and industrialization, spread over more than a century of time. In Europe and America also, the cultural shock of industrialization and urbanization was mitigated in its political effects by the presence of *pre-existing* middle classes, themselves rooted in the civil values and traditions of the older civilization *out of which these changes had come.*

No student of world politics can safely ignore the distinction which must today be made between these earlier processes of industrialization and urbanization in Europe and the whole West and those now transpiring in the non-European world. For today the pace of social change in non-Europe vastly exceeds that which preceded it in the West. Secondly, the impetus to such change in the non-Western world comes not from indigenous cultural sources but from the outside. In Europe, the Western bourgeoisie was the carrier of indigenous ideas about economic change *and* political democracy, but in non-Europe, no such internal agency of cultural stability exists. Liberalism, Marxism, nationalism are unique products of the Western intellectual tradition. Thus while the Afro-Asian world today largely consists of nominally independent states, few of them now exhibit any degree of internal political stability; and it is the very tentativeness of so many of them which today contributes to international instability. Political history teaches one thing, that political order must necessarily precede social justice. The absence of the kinds of long-established conditions which in Europe made constitutional government possible, seriously endangers the viability of many of these new states. Certainly their sudden introduction en masse into the society of nations has created new political problems for world politics which few men, even a decade ago, had contemplated.

The Peace Conferences

Before 1945, it had been customary for men who were concerned with the establishment of world order to look to the center of that traditional order for the political conditions of peace which should follow international war. Since the early seventeenth century and the last years of the great religious wars which wracked Europe, periods of international peace were ushered in by great international peacemaking conferences. European diplomatic history reveals the continuity of these diplomatic acts which invariably followed great upheavals. The Peace of Westphalia in 1648 was the first of these; the Paris Peace Conference of 1919 was the last. The function of such international congresses was not merely to register the new constellation of political power in world politics which had been wrought in the crucible of war. Much more, it was to establish clear understandings and customs and conventions with respect to territories, frontiers, the internal regimes of states, and the kinds of diplomatic machinery to maintain and to enforce the peace, once established. Following the Napoleonic Wars, the Congress of Vienna had established a general groundwork of European public international law among the Great Powers; and the broad patterns of understanding, not merely about the political map of Europe, but about the diplomatic governance of Europe by the Great Powers in concert, remained with surprising durability until 1870 and the Franco-Prussian War. Indeed even until 1914, the broad outlines of the Vienna peace remained discernible over the political landscape of Europe.

This was the European tradition, that world peace and international order depended upon the prior establishment of order and public international law among the European states themselves. Indeed, even at the Paris Conference in 1919 it was generally assumed by all of the European powers, Russia and Germany excepted, that the combined power, prestige, and purpose of the Great Powers in concert could establish and maintain an umbrella of political and economic order in the world outside Europe as well.[2]

It might seem somewhat idle, in the midst of the cold war, to point out the uniqueness of the conditions which followed World War II. If we regard that war as one of the most disastrous in human history, we must also see it as the first major war of European history which was not followed by a comprehensive international act of peace, a treaty of the magnitude and importance of Paris, Vienna, or Westphalia. The great acts of peacemaking in European history had sought to legitimize a new juridical and political order of things by concert among all great powers. And

[2] See Sir Arthur Zimmern, *The League of Nations and the Rule of Law,* and Harold Nicolson, *Peacemaking, 1919,* for a discussion of the theory of the concert of European powers and the concert in the last days of its operation.

while the conditions out of which peace was to arise were ones shaped by war, force alone was not the sole arbiter of peace. Legitimacy arose from a new consensus accepted in covenant by all states. Yet nearly two decades after the end of World War II, no such international act of comparable comprehensiveness has been made to register and legitimize the changes which war produced. The world in which American foreign policy operates today has areas of profound disagreement about the legitimacy of states, political regimes, frontiers, and ideologies. No peace treaty dealing with Germany was ever concluded among the victorious allies after World War II. A series of patchwork treaties, some of them multilateral, some undertaken unilaterally, have established segments of new juridical order in Europe and in the Pacific. (The Treaty of Paris, in 1946, among the European powers, set a new framework for peace in Eastern Europe, yet one which even at that time the Soviet Union itself was undermining; in 1951, the United States and its chief Western allies made unilateral peace with Japan, establishing a new juridical order in the Pacific. The Soviet Union, however, refused to join in the act. In 1955, Western and Soviet negotiators finally completed a state treaty with Austria, the only durable act of peace to be made between East and West since the war.)

The Absence of Political Focus

The absence of any such comprehensive peace settlement may in part be explained by two major historical facts of our times, both of which make it exceptionally difficult to imagine any future attempts to create, by one act, a new international juridical order. Both of them also suggest that in the foreseeable future we must look not so much into the specific juridical conventions and acts among states for our picture of international order, but rather into the informal, non-juridical, and political understandings among states to perceive regularities and patterns of relations among states.

For one thing, this war which was not followed by peace was also a war which temporarily destroyed the heart of the traditional European society of nations, the very European powers which, traditionally, had held the power and authority to reestablish peace. Almost immediately after the war, America and Russia became the nuclei around which new systems of political power began to develop. Indeed, since the Bolshevik Revolution in 1917, the Soviet leadership, suspicious and hostile to the "bourgeois world" which Europe had represented to them, had proclaimed Russia to be the center of an emerging constellation of a new political order in world politics, an alternative nucleus to the "bourgeois, capitalist state system" which, they assumed, would inexorably collapse. In some respects, as historian Daniel Boorstin has pointed out, America too was in some measure "anti-Europe." Like Russia, it had traditionally lain on the peripheries of the European state system, politically isolated from it and, in some respects, contemptuous of the old order of power politics which Europe had appeared to be in American eyes.[3] This sudden reconstellation of political power around two non-European centers thus, almost unexpectedly, wrought a change in the dimensions of the political arena in which order had to be created. At the same time, it juxtaposed two national civilizations which were ideologically hostile to each other, each the self-styled prototype of a new style of politics which was to supplant the old style of Europe itself. It was the political collapse of Europe which brought America and Russia into such sudden political juxtaposition in the heart of Europe. But Europe's collapse had even wider ramifications in that its authority over the non-European world, as we have seen, was also irrevocably broken. In the wake of this older authority emerged the world politics of the underdeveloped world. Henceforth in the 1950's and 1960's, both the sphere of world politics and the number of participating states so greatly increased as to make even

[3] See Daniel J. Boorstin, *America and the Image of Europe*. New York: Meridian Books, 1960.

more difficult and remote the prospects for any future comprehensive peace treaty to govern the whole system of the society of nations. The Europe-centered character of world politics suddenly gave way to a radically new constellation of power in which there was no particular geographic or political focus at all. In this new era of world politics, through bilateral and multilateral diplomacy in the United Nations and elsewhere, nations might seek to cope with the massive conflicts which all of this revolutionary turbulence engendered. Yet any effort to ground a universal political order upon any common historical traditions, common ethical principles and purposes, once present in the much smaller confines of an exceedingly small Europe, came up against an ominous obstacle: none of these necessary bases had any precedent in tradition or in history.

These radical changes in world politics came at a time when American power—economic, political, and military—had risen to unprecedented heights. The end of American isolationism in 1945 coincided both with the achievement of maximum strength and influence in world affairs and with the nearly complete collapse of the old order of world politics. It was not merely the search for national security, in its limited military connotations, which became the obsession of American policy-makers in this confusing world of the cold war, but also the search for new conceptions of political order and new nuclei of political authority compatible with American conceptions of justice and freedom. In this search, neither the lessons of history from America's isolationist past nor the accumulated experiences of the old European society of nations could point in any meaningful direction to guide American purposes.

SUGGESTED READING

Aron, Raymond, *The Century of Total War*, Boston, The Beacon Press, 1955.
Herz, John, *International Politics in the Atomic Age*, New York, Columbia University Press, 1959.

Holborn, Hajo, "The Collapse of the European Political System, 1914-45," in Harold K. Jacobson, *America's Foreign Policy*, pp. 212-232.

Isaacs, H. R., "World Affairs and U.S. Race Relations: a Note on Little Rock," *Public Opinion Quarterly*, XXII, Fall 1958, pp. 364-370.

Myrdal, Gunnar, "National versus International Integration," Harold K. Jacobson, *America's Foreign Policy*, pp. 188-211.

Myrdal, Gunnar, *An International Economy: Problems and Prospects*, New York, Harper, 1956.

von Neumann, John, "Can We Survive Technology?" in Walter Hahn and John C. Neff, *American Strategy for the Nuclear Age*, ch. 3, pp. 32-42.

Toynbee, Arnold, *The World and the West*, New York, Oxford University Press, 1952.

86th Congress, 1st Session, "U.S. Foreign Policy: Possible Nonmilitary Scientific Developments and Their Potential Impact on Foreign Policy Problems of the United States," a Study prepared at the request of the Committee on Foreign Relations, U.S. Senate, by Stanford Research Institute.

CHAPTER

3

THE REMEMBRANCE
OF THINGS PAST

*What is required of us is the rec-
ognition of the frontiers between
the centuries.*

ARCHIBALD MACLEISH

IN OUR TIMES, political power in world politics has suddenly
been transferred from Europe, its historic center, to new frontier
areas. The great revolutionary impulses in international affairs
arise today from ideologies, crises, and revolutions within new
nations and nations new to political influence. Even the two
great world powers today, America and the Soviet Union, are
both political novices in world affairs. Historically, neither of them
lay close to the center of the society of nations; both developed
on the peripheries of Europe. Each owed its rise to power in the
recent era of European imperialism to its acquisition of large,
contiguous land-masses and to the successful adaptation of modern science and technology to the abundant resources which these
land-masses contained. When the great European powers turned
outward upon the world to conquer overseas empires, America

and Russia expanded inwardly and acquired, as a consequence, a self-sufficiency in natural resources attained by no other great powers. This turning inward of national energies brought success earlier to America than to Russia in the nineteenth century, but in both cases it served to make their relationships to Europe and to the society of nations discontinuous and often unpredictable. Their simultaneous rise to global influence in the twentieth century hastened the end of Europe's historic monopoly upon international affairs. After World War I and the Bolshevik Revolution, American and Soviet ideological influences upon Europe, Asia, and Africa hastened the collapse of the older empires and accelerated political and social revolutions which might otherwise still be in their infancy. Nevertheless, both America and Russia have remained European, for they are heirs, respectively, to powerful schools of modern European political thought: Liberalism and Marxism. Curiously enough, their rise to political dominance at Europe's expense has polarized world politics between two ideologies which originated within Europe itself.

Although their swift ascendancy has also meant a common inexperience in the management of international affairs, a mismanagement which Europeans are quick to point out when the opportunity presents itself, they have with great skill and energy shifted quite swiftly from the wings to the center of the international stage. Within only a few decades, they have acquired a span of global interests and responsibilities which no previous world powers ever possessed.

Yet American national interests show a continuity and persistence in world politics sharply contrasting with those of the Soviet Union. Since the late eighteenth century, U.S. political history has been unbroken by revolution or by invasion and defeat in war. America's growth in size, economic power, and influence has been steady and uninterrupted. Since the early nineteenth century its territory has never been invaded or attacked; today no part of the continental United States is territorially disputed by a foreign power. Finally, America was, geographically, far distant from the chief locales of historic great-power rivalry during her growth to power and maturity. This continuity of political history has meant an historical continuity of both attitude and purpose in world affairs which makes the study of American foreign policy in large measure the study of American history. The legacy of past national experiences subtly shapes most men's concept of present national purpose. "History" is a powerful influence on contemporary American foreign policy. Americans often pride themselves upon the newness of their own culture, upon the revolutionary qualities of American civilization, and upon the manner in which America's "freedom from history" has made it less subject to old hatreds and resentments than are many European nations. But in another sense, its unbroken political history, its successful avoidance of defeat and conquest in war, has made possible a continuity of ideological attitudes toward world politics as well as a surprising persistence of basic policies. In these respects, the United States as a nation in the society of nations is quite old indeed.

ISOLATIONISM: AN
AMERICAN TRADITION

Until barely two decades ago, it could have been said that the most outstanding historical fact of America's role in world politics was its isolation. The tradition of isolationism served as the central unifying theme of American diplomatic history. A mystique that grew up around the concept of American isolationism obscured the many strong ties binding America both to Europe and the society of nations as a whole. Yet until the time of World War II and the rise of the totalitarian nations, the United States was not involved in affairs outside of the Western Hemisphere. In fact, from the late eighteenth century until the end of World War II, the United States never allied itself in peacetime with any non-hemispheric nation and never sought to act in protracted concert with other powers to maintain or to recreate an international order. This policy of isolation might better be called unilateralism. It reflected a preference for autonomous action in world politics and a disinclination to be bound by alliances or by any supranational agreements committing the nation in advance to policies which might involve the use of force or war. Only briefly, in its earliest history and under the duress of war crisis, did the United States ever bind itself to engagements such as the Franco-American alliance of 1777-1792 which specifically bound the United States to unite its own national power with that of another Western nation. Thus, we might say that until the second World War, the United States followed the injunctions of George Washington and Thomas Jefferson, who had urged avoidance of "permanent" or "entangling" alliances. Historically, isolationism never resulted in American abstention from any *general* European or international conflict. In fact, from the time of the settlement of the first American colonies in the seventeenth century until today, the colonies and states of the North American continent participated in *every* major European war, both before and after American independence. Historically also, isolationism did not, as policy, mean American political non-involvement in non-hemispheric affairs. This is particularly true of American foreign policy in the Far East after the opening up of Japan in the 1850's. What isolationism did mean as an historic policy was an explicit American commitment—one so consistently followed as to be almost a constitutional understanding—*not* to employ its diplomacy and force persistently and purposefully in explicit concert with other nations, either to maintain international peace, to extend its sphere of influence outside the Western Hemisphere, or to guarantee the integrity, territorial or otherwise, of any European nation or alliance. In this sense, until the mid-twentieth century, the old role of America in world politics, while at times a very substantial one, was to rely chiefly upon its own strength and resources, to act or not to act "at times and places of its own choosing," and to interpret its own national purposes and destiny as distinct and separate from that of any other nation or group of nations.

The consistency with which the doctrine of isolation was applied through such a long period of American history makes us ask what its appeal was and what was its relation to the many national interests of the United States and the social and ideological components of American nationalism. In one sense, isolationism as described above might be said to flow from and depend upon the peculiar geopolitical relationship of the United States to the society of nations before the twentieth-century revolution in economics, weapons, and communications. The nineteenth century was a protracted era of international peace during which, by historical accident, the new American nation was insulated from most potential European enemies by two large oceans dominated by the naval power of Great Britain. In retrospect, too much can be attributed to that, for until the end of the American Civil War the relationship of England to America was hardly cordial or stable, and the dangers of Anglo-American war were quite great at times. Nevertheless, throughout the greater part of the nineteenth century there was no autonomous center of military power other than the United States in the Western Hemisphere and consequently no proximate threat endangering its existence. By historical accident, too, the great theaters of the nineteenth- and twentieth-century wars which absorbed the resources and attention of the great powers were in Europe, the Mediterranean, and the Far East. By way of contrast, the Western Hemisphere (both Latin and North America) was a theater from which the older European imperial powers were in retreat. The resources they were prepared to expend in war were severely limited by the exigencies of their defense in Europe itself. The American diplomatic historian Samuel Flagg Bemis wrote that during this entire period of United States history, "Europe's distresses were America's opportunity." The European power balance, in delicate equipoise for a whole century between

1815 and 1914, made unlikely any substantial European coalition of power against the United States, or any one power's sustained threat to the United States itself. So long as Europe itself remained precariously divided among a number of powers, no serious threat to the security of the American Republic was likely to arise from that direction. In fact, in only one brief period—between 1861 and 1864, when the United States itself was divided in civil war, did this rule not apply. Then, the very weakness and disunity of America served as an invitation to foreign intervention.

So long, then, as American national expansion was directed away from Europe and towards the great frontier zone of the American hinterland, the United States found its own territorial expansion blocked chiefly by nature, by aboriginal tribes, and by its own internal limitations. As in 1917 and in 1941, when serious threats to American security arose, America's relative remoteness from them provided a respite in which to prepare its own defenses and to assist in military operations far removed from the continental United States.

Contingencies such as these sanctioned American policies of non-entanglement in world politics. In the history of the society of nations, most European states had normally depended heavily for their security upon alliances and balance-of-power diplomacy. For most of them, political or diplomatic isolation was a condition to be avoided at all costs. Deliberately to avoid alliances and thus to depend wholly upon one's own autonomous strength would have been to court danger. The shifts and realignments of European balance-of-power politics were a consequence of the political disunity of a system of states, each of which lay geographically close to the others, and none of which could in war have singly withstood a military coalition of all others. Throughout the nineteenth century, however, avoidance of alliances augmented rather than weakened America's own security in world politics. To be sure, during the American Revolution, the independence of the colonies had been won only because of the al-

liance of the United States with France. The war could not have
been fought without the material and military aid she gave to the
colonies. Yet after the Peace of Vienna in 1815, the United States
was a passive beneficiary of the European balance of power for
nearly a century. Europe's disunity and America's remoteness together acted to restrain any European power which might have
launched a major war against the United States. Likewise, both
conditions made alliances almost superfluous for America. Un-
encumbered by political commitments to European powers,
American diplomacy retained a maneuverability and flexibility
within the confines of the Western Hemisphere, while in more
distant areas of the world America's reputation as a neutral, liberal, disinterested observer of world politics served to enhance its
moral influence among nations and peoples who considered themselves victims of the European balance-of-power system. Above
all, this attitude of detachment and remoteness from European
politics meant that, before 1914 at least, America's startling physical and industrial growth was commonly viewed by the European powers with indifference rather than concern.

Isolation and Insulation

Until the first World War a certain strategic rationale underlay, and to a certain extent explained, the political detachment
of America from the international politics of Europe. Yet the appeal of isolationism to generations of Americans cannot be explained on military grounds alone; indeed, the doctrine of isolationism during the nineteenth and twentieth centuries sprang from
so many cultural, economic, and political sources that in some
ways to explain it was at the same time to explore the nature of
American nationalism itself. In some ways, too, isolationism came
to serve as the basis for an American political theory about world
politics. If the United States were *outside* of the traditional system of world politics and the "American System" were geographically and ideologically distinct from that of Europe, then Ameri-

can nationalists could compare the political order of a New World with that of the Old and find the Old World wanting. They regarded their own political order qualitatively better and more perfectible than Europe's. They regarded this American System, comprising the United States and the Latin republics to the South, as a new community of nations which had broken with traditions of European international politics. Thus they were free from European domination and from the periodic European political upheavals which, during colonial times, had involved the Americas in wars and power struggles whose causes were remote from theirs.

The Monroe Doctrine, formulated by the United States in 1823, was an expression of this two-world theory. Despite the many efforts of American statecraft to reformulate it in the light of new circumstance, the substance of the Doctrine has shown surprising vitality even in the mid-twentieth century. To be sure, the Doctrine was a unilateral American declaration. By declaring that the American system would tolerate no further extension of European power, it assured the independence of the nations of the Hemisphere. By making the United States a guarantor of their freedom it also assured the U.S. pre-eminence among them, in *de facto* domination of the entire system.

To be sure, this unilateral declaration of hemispheric solidarity glossed over the deep cultural, economic, and political differences among the sister states of the Americas, whose only affinities were a shared historical experience of colonial subjection to European powers, a certain geographic proximity, and a superficial similarity of republican institutions. Yet the continued strength and appeal of the Doctrine to generations of American nationalists lay in its ideological juxtaposition of a "new" political order to that of an older culture which, in the eyes of many Americans, possessed all of the attributes of cultural senility: aristocratic wealth and domination coupled with widespread poverty and the powerlessness of the people; cultural effeminacy set alongside popular illiteracy and ignorance; and, above all, periodic wars which seemed to bear no relationship to the needs or desires of the European common people. It was widely believed that so long as this American system could be kept separate and distinct in its interests and politics from that of Europe, it could remain free from the political conflicts of Europe itself and from the contaminations of European ideological movements. Remaining thus distinct, the democratic experiments of the Western Hemisphere would be insulated from extra-hemispheric wars and continue to set an example of political order to the rest of the world.

THE ETHNIC CAUSES OF ISOLATIONISM

Whatever other merits the doctrine of isolation may have had for the United States during the first century and a half of its existence, we should bear in mind its salutary effect in relaxing the domestic, ethnic tensions which confronted the American nation from the first years of its independence. The history of the first years of the American republic was chiefly that of transplanted Englishmen colonizing the North American continent, and the grievances of the colonists at the time of the American Revolution were expressed as those of Englishmen protesting the usurpation of their rights by a tyrannical government. Time passed, successive emigrations of new European nationality groups —from Ireland, Scandinavia, and Central and Southern Europe— broke the monopoly of the original colonists upon the political control of the United States. At the same time, these new emigrations helped to sustain the widespread belief that America, as a nation of transplanted Europeans, was a refuge from Europe and its discontents. Most of the immigrants who came to America did so voluntarily. Whatever their motives, they shared in common a cultural shock in their abrupt transfer from an older, static culture to a new and dynamic one. For many of these newly arrived ethnic groups, cultural assimilation was difficult. Some of them, particularly the Irish and the East Europeans, found that they were considered social inferiors in the land of equality. As a result, the tension between a lingering nostalgia for their familiar national culture and a desire for absorption into the dominant English-speaking culture was considerable, creating an unhappy ambivalence toward the homeland they had forsaken.

For many of them, memories of their European background were humiliating reminders of an incomplete assimilation into American culture and a lack of organic connection to the society in which they found themselves. On the other hand, their historic memories and ethnic identifications served to build around them a comforting ethnic subculture within America, lessening their sense of loneliness and isolation from the broader streams of American activities. It is not surprising then that an American nationalism which stressed America's detachment and non-involvement in European affairs, a nationalism neutral towards the European balance of power, served to lessen ethnic tensions within a multi-national America. So long as one's own personal renunciation of Europe coincided with the broader national purposes of America, there was no reason to expect that foreign policy crises would tear apart the seam of American nationalism. Isolated politically from Europe, throughout the nineteenth century the United States often expressed in official pronouncements its moral support for European peoples struggling for independence against oppression. Yet the fact that the United States did not link itself by alliance to any one European nation against another in these power struggles forestalled the day in which European wars and political crises would trigger open conflict among Americans of German, Irish, Polish, Italian, and English origin.

The multi-national background of American society thus served to enhance the country's isolationist impulse toward Europe until the time of the first World War. In particular, it helped thwart the development of close Anglo-American collaboration in world politics. Two American ethnic groups, the Irish and the Germans, found themselves joined by historical accident in this common purpose and, for nearly half a century, from the time of the Spanish-American War until World War II, these two sectors of the American public furnished much of the political opposition to an American alignment with Great Britain against Imperial Germany and, later, against Hitler's Third Reich. Among the Irish-Americans in particular, hatred of Britain as cause of Ireland's degradation and backwardness often prompted them to ignore or underestimate new threats to the security of the United States which Anglo-American collaboration might have checked. Their political influence in American politics was expressed through their preponderance in urban political machines of the Democratic Party in many Northern cities, and their Anglophobia was often indistinguishable from their animus against dominant Anglo-American elements in the society in which they themselves had, traditionally, been regarded as social inferiors.

Within the preponderantly Irish-American hierarchy of the Catholic Church, these Anglophobic isolationist sentiments continued to be forcefully expressed as late as the advent of Hitler, even when the Vatican itself had unequivocally called for American assistance to the European democracies against Nazi totalitarianism. At the time of both World Wars, the bitter public debates in the United States about American intervention in Europe's wars must be seen, in large measure, as a cultural civil war about the relationship between America and Europe.

We should remember that these ethnic disputes in America were those of European-Americans and hence concerned chiefly with American responses toward European crises. The absence of any politically significant or numerous Asian minorities in America gave the United States considerably greater freedom in the twentieth century for an active Asian policy. Large numbers of American isolationists who would have nothing to do with "Europe's wars" had no compunctions at all about American intervention in China and Japan. In one respect, however, ethnic animosity in America toward Great Britain reinforced a traditional animosity against European (i.e., British) imperialism, and thus made it difficult even in the Far East for American policy-makers to collaborate closely with the British.

If American policy toward China and Japan in the twentieth century often appeared to be unilateral and independent of European powers, one explanation may be found in the peculiar political pressures which arose from American isolationists. As late as the famous Truman-MacArthur dispute over American policy in the Korean War, American politics were profoundly shaken by a cultural crisis between two alternatives: a go-it-alone policy in Asia, free from British and Western European assistance, and a collaborative Asian policy which would have blended American purposes with those of its Western European allies. Statesmen like George Marshall and Dean Acheson, who urged close Anglo-American collaboration in the Far East and who recoiled from wholly unilateral American policies in the Korean War, were branded by many neo-isolationists as either traitors or Anglophiles.

There is a touch of irony in all of this, for it would appear that America's very composition of transplanted Europeans intensified American impulses to isolate itself politically *from* Europe. In certain sections of the United States such as the American South, where the white population was English and Scots-Irish in origin and homogeneous rather than multi-ethnic, these impulses to withdraw were far less powerful. In fact, the historic cultural affinity between the wealthier Southern classes and British society made American Southerners disposed to cooperate with England in international affairs. On the other hand, in other areas, notably the Middle West with its blend of Scandinavian, German, and Anglo-Americans and the large Eastern cities with their large Irish populations, exactly the opposite was true. Until World War II, fundamental disagreements about what American foreign policy should be were often regional disagreements. In American political folklore, the Middle West was a regional repository of political isolationism, while among the regions of America, the

American South appeared most favorably disposed to policies of Anglo-American cooperation, support for international organizations, and so forth.

There is a certain symmetry in American-European relationships which bears out this theory of the ethnic causes of isolationism. So long as conflict remained between those very European countries which were countries of origins for most Americans, so long did it remain difficult to establish a domestic American consensus concerning American alliances with European powers and so long did the United States refrain from entering such alliances. Yet after World War II when Europe, exhausted by internecine conflicts and jeopardized by Soviet communism, composed its long-standing national conflicts and turned to America for aid, the United States jettisoned its historic policies of peacetime isolationism. NATO, the first American military alliance since the eighteenth century, was an alliance with *all* of Europe—Catholic and Protestant, English, German, French, and Italian—and thus gave offense to no influential ethnic bloc in American politics. (Nominally, of course, the NATO pact was composed of Western European states, Italy, Greece and Turkey; but since one of its principal purposes was the containment of Communist imperialism, it found favor with American nationality groups of East European origin as well, Czechs, Poles, Serbs, and others whose own homelands had been overrun by the Red Army.)

THE WESTWARD MOVEMENT

In the American political tradition, isolationism did not represent a passive attitude towards politics. Rather it was one aspect of America's aggressive territorial growth and its cultural and economic expansion, which took place within the limits of the Western Hemisphere. The westward and inward course of this expansion progressively attenuated America's once close political ties to Europe. This was particularly true during the period of history which began after the Napoleonic wars and came to a close in

1914. Before Jefferson's Louisiana Purchase in 1803 (a territorial acquisition which opened up two-thirds of the present United States to colonization), the United States was a political appendage of the European society of nations, confined to the Eastern seaboard of North America, its Western frontier of population settlement roughly paralleling the Appalachian mountains. Its culture was English and its trade and commerce carried on within the Atlantic area. At that time, thoughtful Americans assumed that the United States would remain in this posture indefinitely. Some statesmen, like Alexander Hamilton, argued that America could best achieve political and economic power among the nations of Europe by remaining within this finite, territorial framework. Through political centralization, industrial growth, urbanization, and maritime, commercial expansion, the United States could become an active power among the nations of the North Atlantic region. Others like Jefferson wished instead that America could become a power as a prosperous, democratic society of small artisans and free farmers. In his view, political and economic decentralization were an important part of political democracy.

Looking backward, we might hazard the judgment that Jefferson's system was in some ways the more hospitable to the American political and social forces pressing for westward expansion. The Jeffersonians, the party of democracy, found their political strength among small-scale farmers, craftsmen, and rural debtor classes; the political center of gravity of these groups shifted westward as trans-Appalachian America was opened to new settlement. Hamilton's political support came chiefly from conservative and more affluent classes of the Atlantic seaboard cities. The prosperity and growth of these commercial classes and interests of Boston, New York, and Pennsylvania depended in the early eighteenth century upon a flourishing commerce with Europe. The Eastern seaboard therefore remained a more internationalist region of America, its manners and morals attuned more closely to those of Europe and, in contrast to that of the American West, its cultural and political leadership less fascinated by the image of a wholly self-contained America.

Neither the Jeffersonians nor the Hamiltonians could in their time have possibly taken into account the immense possibilities for westward national expansion pursuant to increased immigration from Europe, the development of railroads, and discovery of valuable farm lands and natural resources in the American heartland. Throughout the nineteenth century, this westward movement profoundly affected American thinking about foreign affairs and about world politics in general. As America's cultural center of gravity moved further away from the East and thus also from Europe, America's national culture became ever more remote from its English origins. To nationalists of the Victorian era, America's destiny necessarily involved movement away from the traditional centers of cultural creativity and political power in both Europe and the United States.

In the American language, the rich connotations of the word "frontier" suggest the power which this westward direction of American national growth exerted upon popular thought. The European equivalent of this uniquely American term, the French term, *la frontière*, for instance, had static connotations, denoting as it did a border or fixed line of demarcation, tension, or conflict between two more or less well-established states or cultures. In the United States, however, the idea of the frontier suggested something far different, a dynamic region of life, not a border, a region constantly at odds with and moving away from older traditional centers of civilization and politics, within which a continuous process of national renewal took place.

In a political sense, the concept of the frontier in the hands of historians, poets, and politicians assumed strong nationalistic and egalitarian connotations. The frontier became the crucible of democracy, the milieu in which a unique American national character was shaped. Since it was a zone within which a classless society of Americans was constantly growing, it served to ameliorate economic and social tensions in older areas of the nation. Above all, the frontier was the zone of opportunity. As it moved further west, it opened up more and more free lands to agricultural settlement; it enticed more and more Easterners and Europeans to break their ties with older, more static cultures.

The historian Frederick Jackson Turner believed that the vigor of democracy depended upon the frontier. In the conquest of the wilderness were the principal conditions for human social equality and growth, while in older, established, more static conditions of human life, inequality, aristocracy, and oppression flourished. This idealization of the frontier, whether conscious or unconscious, made many Americans contemptuous of urban life and "civilization"; it profoundly affected attitudes toward conventions of urban life; it elevated and honored the simple, "uncultivated" man in the same way that eighteenth-century romantics had glorified Rousseau's "natural man."

These illusions and impressions of the frontier were often romantic and ill-founded. Frontier life in most parts of America was violent, lonely, painful, and vulgar. The cultural vigor of American life found expression within its cities, as has been the case in all civilized communities, not in its most remote settlements or beyond them in *terra incognita*.

Still, the westward expansion of the United States, coupled with the leveling of social and economic conditions which it intensified, markedly influenced Americans' attitudes toward world politics. It rendered tenuous and remote America's cultural affinities with Europe; it turned most Americans' attention inward upon the North American continent and away from broader affairs of international life; it fostered a national temper which took pride in the growing estrangement of America from Europe. (Carl Becker, the historian, tells that when World War I broke out in 1914, scarcely anyone in his Iowa home town had the slightest idea where its battles were being fought, so remote did France seem from the Middle West.) This cultural remoteness was intensified by the development of an American historiography, which made American history and the American Revolution in particular the starting-point for an understanding of the world in which Americans lived. It exaggerated the autonomous events of American life and diminished the once close dependence of America upon European civilization.

ECONOMIC DEVELOPMENT IN A NATIONAL FRAMEWORK

This internal experience of national development estranged Americans from world politics in economic ways as well. The conquest of the American interior during the nineteenth century carved an immense framework within which the economic development of the nation could subsequently proceed. The absence of internal tariff barriers and restrictions on interstate commerce made possible a gigantic internal market within which industrial and agricultural production could be marketed. The American continent was found to contain most of the natural resources necessary to sustain a constantly enlarging standard of living for the American people.

With the spread of industrial technique and development through Europe, it had become impossible for any European nation to find, within its national boundaries, the requisite resources to supply the needs for its new industries. Searching for them, Europe had had to turn outwards upon the world, to conquer or buy the sources of minerals or other unfabricated commodities in Asia, Africa, the Middle East, and elsewhere. European imperial expansion had been enormously accelerated by this search for raw materials, and industrialization had thus served to enhance the dependence of every European industrial nation upon both foreign markets and foreign supplies. In some cases, notably England, industrialization had been made possible only by the transfer of its rural, agrarian population to new industrial areas; and industrialization thus made the British Isles dependent upon overseas sources for its food.

Economic development necessarily had increased the relative involvement of European nations in world trade, heightening their sensitivity to the international implications of their own economic policies. In America, the consequences of economic growth were just the opposite. Increased agricultural productivity, rendering the United States virtually self-sufficient in foodstuffs, *paralleled* industrial growth; industrial growth was made possible primarily by the exploitation of domestic, not foreign, natural resources; trade and commerce grew within a national framework.

Greater internal opportunities for economic development distinguished America from Europe in another sense as well. The domestic need for investment capital was throughout American history vastly more tempting to American investors than the lure of foreign markets, prompting American capital to turn inward upon the continent rather than outward upon the world. Aside from a few firms with extensive overseas interests, such as the oil industry and some Eastern banking and commercial firms, American big and small business was essentially American-oriented, and tended to conceive the realm of American vital interests as a hemispheric one at most. They feared the outward extension of American political interests in Europe for a wide variety of reasons. For one thing, such a broadening of political interests might also entail abandoning America's traditional policies of high tariffs and economic protection, which had effectively insulated the American economic system from competition with European firms since the Civil War.

More important however, American business feared the unpredictable economic consequences of war. American industrialization throughout the course of American history had taken place in a political climate which permitted a high degree of independence and autonomy to *private* economic decisions. It had been a civilian economy, developing in a political climate congenial to the private corporation and the businessman. In peacetime, the American economy had traditionally been guided by impulses and forces which were relatively free from governmental restraints and from policies arising from considerations of national security and national defense. This in turn had given American industry a surprising degree of freedom from government control and direction. War and protracted international crisis were thus feared because they might well entail an increase in government regulation of business, if not nationalization.

Such crises were feared also because of the economic dislocations of production which war always entailed. War not only meant high taxes but also dangerous and unpredictable disruptions of normal peacetime production and the possibility of postwar depressions and inflation. If the greater part of the American business community thus preferred policies of isolationism and "hemispherism," they did so because of deep convictions about an impregnable hemispheric "fortress America," identical in its geographic dimensions with the American economic system. Even in quite recent times, some of the most prominent spokesmen of American business, the late Henry Ford, Senator Robert A. Taft, General Robert Wood, for instance, held to such views long after the United States had officially abandoned its traditions of isolationism, and their influence over important segments of the Republican Party remained great until the early part of the 1950's.

There were influential segments of American business in the twentieth century which served as critic and as antithesis to the dominant isolationist wing of American business. Certain commercial and industrial interests such as the ship-building industry, export-import firms, a few Eastern banking houses, parts of the oil industry, and firms with extensive overseas investments and plants sought to counteract the political power of the isolationist business community. The locale in which these interests proved most influential was the American Northeast, notably the metropolitan seaboard cities. Conversely, the isolationist business influence lay in the industrial heartland of which Chicago was the center.

Economic Influence Abroad

After World War I, there was a marked incongruity between the nationalist-isolationist aspirations of the dominant parts
of the American economy and the sudden, profound influence it
began to exert upon the world economy as a whole. It seems
strange that a national economy, moved by such compulsions to
withdraw, should at the same time play such a powerful role in
world trade and finance and, hence, significantly affect levels of
world economic activity. Yet this was the case. American protec-
tionist policies and the erratic international movements of American capital and technology powerfully affected the stability and
growth of the European economy; even more did they profoundly
affect the character of economic development in the whole Western Hemisphere. Domestic levels of American business and prices
after World War I exerted a controlling effect on world trade.

Incongruously then, a relatively self-sufficient America came
absent-mindedly to tyrannize a world economy which was vulnerable both to its erratic policies and to its unstable state of health.
The immediate causes of the great world depression of 1930-39
may be traced to the American financial crisis of 1929 and the
domestic depression which followed. There is reason to assume
that, had this crisis been avoided or proved less catastrophic than
it was, the social upheavals of Europe and Asia which produced
the fanatical movements of fascism might have been kept in
check.

The immediate explanations for this incongruous situation
are not hard to find. Throughout the nineteenth century, the
United States was, by European standards, a backward and underdeveloped region, although sensitive observers in Europe had
earlier been aware of the swiftness of its economic growth. By the
end of World War I, the American economy, invigorated by
the war which had devastated Europe, was suddenly seen to have
attained prodigious heights of industrial productivity which

dwarfed the output of all other nations. At that time, and for the ensuing three decades, the annual total output of American industry accounted for more than half of the industrial productivity of the whole world, an extraordinary feat for a nation which occupied only six percent of the earth's surface, and which accounted for only ten percent of the world's population. During World War I, when Britain, France, and Russia had been deadlocked in war against Germany and Austria, this industrial productivity had decisively affected the outcome of the war. Between 1917 and 1919, after the United States had declared war upon Germany, the American hinterland had supplied the Western powers with foodstuffs, raw materials, ships, and weapons of war. Due to this assistance and an expeditionary force in Europe, the balance of power in war had been decisively tipped by 1918 in favor of the Western allies.

After the Armistice, and through the ensuing postwar decade, American relief supplies, loans, and technical assistance made possible Europe's swift, if haphazard, physical recovery from its first "total war." In the decade of the 1920's, between the Versailles Treaty and the economic collapse of Europe, American trade and finance moved in upon the old European world in a spectacular spurt of expansion. American industrial technique, industrial products, and consumer tastes combined to stage a second-wave invasion of the European continent, with profound effects upon it. Signs of this invasion could be found in the introduction of American chewing gum, neon signs, movies, automobiles, jazz, and other artifacts which conspicuously exerted a profound effect upon the consumer tastes of the new European buying public. But the fundamental influences were less conspicuous. Private capital investment and technological expertise, these revealed to some sensitive European and American observers a historic fact: that amongst the Western powers the United States had finally seized the cultural, economic, and technological —although *not* the political—initiative in Western civilization.

This outburst of productive energy, with such effects upon

world trade and economic style, might have been regarded as salutary from several points of view. Before the Great Depression it often was argued by economists and political philosophers that a future American dominion of productive technique, taste, and consumption throughout the world could be justified because of the economic democracy brought in its train. To be sure, the spread of American consumers' tastes among the European buying public after World War I produced a powerful cultural reaction amongst many educated Europeans, revolted in part, by certain "vulgar" American products like chewing gum, soft drinks, movies, etc. But more important was the widespread fear among European intellectuals and monied classes that American mass-production, distribution, and cultivated mass tastes might hasten the demise of traditional European economic systems, notably the small-scale productive unit with its humane emphasis upon craft skills and individual taste.

On the other hand, the American system of production bade well to effect an economic and social leveling of the nations which became exposed to it. Washing machines, vacuum-cleaners, and other paraphernalia of American life might have appeared vulgar to the affluent European minority who never had been compelled to work with their hands and to European businessmen who feared the disruptive effect of large-scale systems of manufacturing and distribution on their competitive position in trade. Under such circumstances, it is not surprising that many American businessmen came to identify the expansion of the American system of economic production—with its attendant emphasis upon industrial technique, managerial efficiency, advantages of size, and competitive spirit—with the spread of humane enlightenment and progress. It had been commonly assumed by many nineteenth- and twentieth-century liberals that higher standards of living eliminated the causes of war, social unrest, and revolution and strengthened, in turn, the democratic aspirations of human beings. In the 1920's, the self-confident self-interest of many American businessmen, intent upon the expansion of American trade overseas, was identified closely with an American national interest in exporting an American way-of-life abroad, and establishing conditions under which the human race could live in prosperity and peace. Agencies of the United States Government, such as the Department of Commerce, had put themselves at the disposal of American firms, to serve as advance agents in establishing footholds for American exports. This was considered justifiable, despite the disruptive consequences which this expansion exerted upon a world economy unable to re-export manufactured goods as repayment to the United States.

These general considerations account in large measure for the curious and awkward relationship of the American economy to the world economy in the twentieth century and help us understand, in part, why two contradictory pictures of the United States foreign economic relations are both substantially correct. From the time of World War I, the United States became deeply involved in the world economy, decisively affecting levels of world trade, economic development, and capital movements. More especially, the American economy, towering over those of all other advanced industrial nations, seemed before the Great Depression to set the pace of world economic development. After the Bolshevik Revolution, even Lenin's Russia was deeply indebted to American technology. Ironically, it borrowed capital, technical expertise, and organizational systems from American industry to facilitate its transition to Communism. Thus the dual picture of America was on one side that of a powerful economic system, crucially affecting the world economy and deeply involved in it, and on the other that of a system surprisingly independent of the outside world, exporting only a small fraction of its domestic capital abroad, selling its industrial and agricultural produce largely within a self-contained hemispheric empire, and following policies of economic protectionism designed to shelter this empire from outside competition. The one picture was that of an international America; the other, of an isolated, self-sufficient America. Both were correct. The solution to the riddle was not hard to find:

In the eyes of American nationalists, America was self-sufficient, but this was a self-sufficiency of a powerful giant sitting amongst pygmies in a crowded room.

American Anti-Colonialism

These features of American geographic expansion and economic growth profoundly affected Americans' thinking about international politics. If America's geographic location, remote from older centers of culture and present threats of enemies, enhanced a national mood of self-sufficiency in the nineteenth century, so did its course of westward geographic expansion enhance a widespread confidence and even naïveté about the processes which facilitated the growth and prosperity of nations. In more crowded areas of the world, national territorial expansion undertaken by a dynamic state inevitably pushes against other cultures and usually also results in friction, animosity, and war. It was the luck of America during the nineteenth century to be spared any major conflict of this sort, comparable, for instance, to the struggle of Germans against Slavs in Central and Eastern Europe.

To be sure, American imperialism, from the time of the Spanish-American War and through the Wilson administration, thrust the political influence of the United States southward into the Caribbean and Central America and generated deep resentment amongst Latin Americans. Between 1898 and 1924, United States protectorates were established by force over most of the Caribbean republics. Some American business firms, benefitting from this turn of events, profited enormously from the resulting political control which enabled them to establish and maintain concessions. Until 1933 United States military and naval force was used to crush revolts against American hegemony in Cuba, Nicaragua, Haiti, Panama, and elsewhere, and local regimes were established to maintain political order consonant with American aims in the area. Yet these developments, important as they doubtless were to Latin Americans, were still not enough to disillusion most Americans about the virtues of America's "anti-imperialist" traditions, nor did they result in any steady augmentation of American imperial control of these regions. Powerful political and economic forces within the United States struggled, for both practical and selfish reasons, against continued American imperial expansion outside of the continental United States.

Permanent American annexation of non-contiguous areas such as the Philippines has often been opposed by important domestic, economic, and cultural interests, notably food and raw-material producers, who feared competition. More important, however, was the domestic opposition to annexation that arose from important segments of the American community which doubted the possibility of assimilating alien populations to American culture or resented the threat of annexation to the traditional policy of extending statehood to new territories. It should be borne in mind that American westward expansion, since the Northwest Ordinance of 1787, had followed a consistent pattern of extending self-government and, ultimately, statehood, to annexed areas, a form of "imperialism" consonant with liberal, Lockean theories of representative self-government.

One powerful, intellectual consequence of the American experience in Western hemispheric growth and expansion was the flowering of a liberal, though nationalistic, distaste for the notion of Empire. In the early years of its existence, the American Republic set the tone and style of modern anti-colonialism by its successful, spectacular revolt against European colonial control. The origins of the American Revolution could be found in the powerful impulse of the original colonies for self-determination, an impulse which became political doctrine. In essence, the American doctrine of self-determination was based upon theories of political representation and participation deriving from English origins. At the time of the American Revolution, Edmund Burke thus correctly interpreted the Revolution as that of Englishmen demanding their rights as Englishmen: the right not to be taxed or coerced without legislative consent and the right of people within a given territory to grant or withhold consent to legislation, expressed through elected representatives.

Not only was this American revolt against colonialism and empire widely emulated throughout the Spanish colonies of Latin America in the early nineteenth century (Bolivar joined Washington as a symbolic leader against older systems of Empire), but the peculiar circumstances of European and world politics in the ensuing century reinforced American prejudices against Empire and imperial control. From the time of the French Revolution through the early 1920's, as various European nationalities struggled against alien domination for national self-determination, the United States appeared to many of them as a sympathetic, if not terribly active, supporter of their aspirations. The stream of émigrés to America from European subject nations—Ireland, Eastern Europe, Italy—made a constantly augmented constituency of exiles who helped keep alive, in the United States, its historic memories of an earlier revolt against imperial control. In the European revolutions of 1848, considerable public sympathy in the United States was produced for the courageous freedom fighters of Central Europe (notably Kossuth in Austria-Hungary) who, so it seemed, were engaged in the same kind of struggle which had earlier won the American colonists their liberties against imperial and monarchic control.

There were limits to national self-determination, as Americans learned in the depressing aftermath of World War I. In many parts of postwar Europe, national self-determination resulted in the establishment of small, vulnerable, nation-states, which later become the prey of German and Soviet totalitarian imperialism. In many parts of Central and Eastern Europe, freedom for one nationality group, the Poles, for example, meant minority status and exploitation for other ethnic groups who were arbitrarily included within territorial limits of their new state and who often resisted with force the efforts of the dominant population to assimilate them into their cultural system.

Many, if not most, of the new states established after the

first World War—Hungary, Austria, the Baltic states, Poland, Bulgaria, Rumania, etc.—were based upon nationality groups settled within a land mass utterly devoid of adequate resources for a balanced economy. All of them, closely situated near historic, ethnic, or ideological enemies, found it impossible to maintain their own independence save through alliances with other states. Consequently, in the 1930's, nearly all of them were swallowed up by giant neighbors with few scruples about imperialism: Nazi Germany and Soviet Russia. The present plight of East European peoples under Soviet rule, as distressing as it may now seem, is not markedly more deplorable than the condition under which many of them lived in the era of Nazi hegemony or earlier, when they possessed a freedom of nationality they were ill able to exercise.

Despite these disillusionments, the American distaste for imperialism remained rooted in popular thought. During World War II, for instance, a deep American suspicion of British and West European colonialism was reflected in the Atlantic Charter—which expressed the right of peoples "freely to choose" their form of government—and in President Roosevelt's prejudice against British imperial policies towards Asia and Africa. In particular, many Americans—thrust for the first time into the cauldron of colonial revolt in Asia and Africa—were repelled by evidences of European-white superiority over subject peoples. Having rarely experienced at home such deep contrasts of poverty and wealth and dominion and subjection, as well as racial superiority, Americans in overseas areas often instinctively blamed imperial powers for such repugnant features of empire. They instinctively lent moral support to nationalist forces which were struggling to overthrow the vestiges of empire. In the years after World War II, this ideological sympathy was considerably dampened by the increasing influence of Communist strength in the revolt of native imperialism against Europe. It was dampened also by the reluctance of many neutralist nations in Asia and Africa to align themselves with the United States in military opposition to Soviet expansion. But on the other hand, the aversion to political domination has persisted, not merely as ideological opposition to Communism, but as an important feature of American foreign policy in the struggles of new peoples for independence. Without doubt, it has greatly helped hasten the movements of national liberation throughout Africa and Asia. For while the United States did not take the lead in colonial liberation (and occasionally, as in Indochina, opposed this on grounds of military security), neither did the United States encourage the European powers to resist colonial revolts. Noticeably few American political figures have publicly expressed sympathy for European colonialism.

Hand in hand with this cultural distaste for imperialism and empire is a dominant strand of American intellectual thought which has looked with favor upon supranational or international systems of political organization. The very remoteness of the United States through much of its history from world politics and the older European society of nations caused a certain detached and critical frame of mind about the nature of the older European system of balance of power and of power politics. To be sure, distance sometimes encourages a fuzzy view of the facts, as the recent example of India's Nehru shows. Remote and detached from Europe's periodic wars and internecine struggles in the nineteenth century, the American liberal outlook on world politics was not without a certain unjustified moralism and a tone of moral superiority which a detached outsider often shows toward bitter family quarrels that can only be fully comprehended from within. Europe's failure, from the mid-nineteenth century onward, to keep pace with the waxing prosperity and economic egalitarianism of America, was attributed by many American observers to European inability to form an integrated common market, as America had done earlier. From World War I to the present, America favored some kind of European economic integration which would make possible the economies of size which the American realm had provided for American mass-production and distribution. Europe's inability to keep the peace of Europe was also contrasted with the civil peace within the United States, where the very nationality-groups at war with each other on the other side of the Atlantic lived in peace.

SUMMARY

We may conclude that certain American traditional modes of thinking emerged from a century and a half of isolation from world politics. America's military security was enhanced by its remoteness from the traditional centers of world politics. Its geographic expansion, which took a westerly course into the North American hinterland, turned the attention of most Americans during the nineteenth century inward upon an American empire and away from Europe. This remoteness and the direction of expansion encouraged an easy public optimism about America's position in world politics. Many Americans regarded the United States as a qualitatively "new" culture by European or Asian standards. Its democratic institutions, its rising standards of living, its relative freedom from class conflicts, and its attainments as a multi-national society were all attributed to this newness. The United States viewed these qualities as export items and hence a certain messianism is to be found in American liberal traditions. American liberals preferred to see America's political influence overseas used for humanitarian purposes. Part of the deep and bitter reaction within the United States to Soviet Communism may be explained by Communism's challenge to the pretensions of America as a new culture and political system and its own claim that Communism has leaped over America in the race to modernity.

SUGGESTED READING

Boorstin, Daniel J., *America and the Image of Europe*, New York, Meridian Books, 1960. A study of cross-cultural ties and tensions.
Carleton, William, *The Revolution in American Foreign Policy*, New York, Random House, 1957, rev. ed.

DeConde, Alexander, *Isolation and Security: Ideas and Interests in Twentieth Century American Foreign Policy*, Durham, N.C., Duke University Press, 1957.
Handlin, Oscar, *The Uprooted*, Boston, Little, Brown, and Co., 1951.
Hayes, Carleton, J. M., "The American Frontier: Frontier of What?", *American Historical Review*, 51, June, 1946, pp. 199-216.
Langer, William and Gleason, S. E., *The Challenge to Isolation 1937-1940*, New York, Harper, 1952, I.
Lubell, Samuel, *The Future of American Politics*, Garden City, Doubleday and Co., 1956, rev. ed.
Woodward, C. Vann, "The Irony of Southern History," *Journal of Southern History*, XIX, Feb. 1953, pp. 3-19.

THE IDEA OF NATIONAL INTEREST

As we see the world today, the interest of the United States, like the national interests of all other nations, can only be fulfilled within an order far wider than its own geographical limits.

PROSPECTS FOR AMERICA: THE ROCKEFELLER PANEL REPORTS, 1961.

WHEN STUDYING WORLD POLITICS, we first see a world filled with innumerable overlapping and interrelated human organizations, movements, and forces. Among these, nation-states are most significant, since at any given time they invest human affairs with political order and are the chief focal points of political power. These nation-states are communities of men organized within a particular political, constitutional order which prevails over some specific geographical terrain. America is one of these complex entities. Nearly every habitable part of the globe today lies within one or another of them.

The term nation-state hyphenates two essential concepts. As a mode of political and social organization, it is of relatively recent origin. Nationalities within the older order of European society are groupings of men based upon common ethnic, linguistic, religious, tribal qualities. The origins of some of these nationalities are obscure; some, like the Magyars, trace their origins to ancient migrant tribes; others, like the Italians, to a particular geographic area embracing many different sub-cultures. Some, like most Israeli Jews, were scattered across the Western world; others, like the French, were confined chiefly to a known geographic area. Until the time of the French Revolution, the political order of Europe was not based upon nationalities but upon empires and dynastic orders. Before Germany was unified in 1870, Germans lived within more than three hundred political entities. The idea of the State is that of a political system. Prussia was a state, not a nation. Germany before 1870 was a nation, not a state. When Prussia unified Germany by force, a nation-state was born.

The fusion of the idea of nation and state creates a juridical-constitutional order but there are many ways in which this fusion occurs. The degree to which a particular state achieves a common conception of shared nationality among its citizens or subjects varies also. Metternich, the Austrian statesman, once referred to Italy as a "geographic expression," nothing more than an agglomeration of principalities and peoples commonly inhabiting a piece of contiguous terrain. To the many nation-states crowding onto the international scene today, Metternich's cynical remark has a bitter relevance.

THE FORMATION OF THE NATION-STATE

In a general sense, this process of fusion whereby nation-states come into being occurs in two quite distinct ways. Territorial states—systems of political authority and power covering specific areas of human habitation—may in time build within themselves complex cultural and social systems and also common human loyalties to the abstract authority of the state. Over the centuries, this is what happened in both France and Britain; for in both instances, a pre-existing dynastic state surviving through time grew in strength and, in so doing, subordinated lesser political loyalties to its own. The territorial state provided conditions of public order, authority, and economic integration. It helped to diffuse within its borders a considerable degree of linguistic homogeneity and cultural uniformity. Both France and French culture, as it were, trickled down. Modern France began as a juridical-political entity, not a cultural one.

Yet nation-states may also be creatures of the nation. In Europe, most of the smaller sovereign states of Eastern Europe, like Hungary, Czechoslovakia, Rumania, and Finland, which came into being after World War I, are rooted in self-conscious nationalities which existed *before* the state came into being. German nationalism, too, preceded the German state. The State of Israel, established in 1948, was created in the name of a pre-existing Jewish nation.

Where "nation" creates "state," a revolutionary act usually takes place which later generations of citizens seek to sanctify. Not violence as such, but patriotism, is exalted. To make the nation, then, is also to capture or destroy an older political order. On the other hand, when the state creates the nation, this process of gestation and development proceeds more gently and ambiguously. Israel was "born" in 1948, in violence. But it would be hard to say when Sweden's or Denmark's birth took place.

When nation precedes state, nationalism provides the human and ideological energy of revolution. Men's loyalties supposedly turn first to it, and with it the state is either captured or constructed. French nationalism *captured* the state in 1789; Czech nationalism *constructed* a state in 1918. In either event, nationalism then seeks to determine the nature of nationality, the criteria by which men are deemed fit to belong to the nation-state. In 1947, when the Indian subcontinent achieved independence from Britain, Indian and Moslem nationalists both deemed that "India" was not to be Moslem and a great civil war ensued. When ethnic nationalism captures state power for the first time, national minorities are born within the territory of the state. When governments are establishing political order they frequently seek to devise political formulae by which other nationalities may be accommodated to the dominant political culture, while retaining their unique culture.

Useful as these processes may be for purposes of clarification, many political communities today do not readily lend themselves to such classifications. The United States of America is one of these. In this instance, it is hard to say which preceded which. In one sense, we may say that not until well into the nineteenth century did any *common* awareness of American nationality emerge. In his *History of the United States*, for instance, Henry Adams notes that even a decade after the American Constitution was drafted, Virginians and New Yorkers and New Englanders rarely spoke of themselves as Americans. The Constitution itself contains no reference to an American nation or an American people. The birth of the United States was thus not a nationalist act as much as it was a common juridical act of state-entities rebelling against British misrule and establishing, by a series of juridical acts, a new system of united states. Pre-existing state entities, by their consent, thus joined themselves together. This was not the fusion of separate national tribes or cultural entities but of state entities. Upon this legal-juridical base, a concept of American nationality was ultimately built. Those who, like the Loyalists, left or were driven into exile at the end of the American Revolution, fled because of their loyalty to the British Crown, not because of clearly distinct ethnic or cultural differences from those who remained to become "Americans." Perhaps because the American nation emerged from such juridical acts, the American conception of nationality and citizenship from the beginning was territorial rather than ethnic or cultural. An American is an American citizen, and vice versa; a person born within the territories and possessions of the United States is, or may become, an American.

This is the idea of *ius solis*, not *ius sanguinis*—soil, not blood, as basis of nationality in law. In Hitler's Third Reich, Nazi law sought to establish the opposite principle, not only *within* the German state, but everywhere in Europe. Thus an ethnic-cultural German anywhere in Europe was regarded as a corporeal part of "Germany," even when he never had been a national of the German state.

This national experience with nation-building has made many Americans overemphasize the purely juridical and constitutional aspects of constructing new nation-states and other political entities, while diminishing the importance of pre-existing cultural disparities and uniformities. Yet clearly, before the American Revolution, there had been in the North American colonies clear signs of ethnic and cultural uniformity and these persisted in time. The omnipresence of the English language, of English juridical and political principles and institutions; the pre-eminence of Protestant sects in all the original colonies save Maryland; the common origins of most of the colonists in England and Ireland— these sociological uniformities made the difference. While the United States developed into a multi-ethnic society in the nineteenth century, it did so by combining European nationality groups in a basic culture which could be understood only as English in origin. Twentieth-century American immigration laws now bear witness to a public consensus that the United States remain ethnically composed principally of Northern and Central Europeans.

POLITICAL POWER AND THE
NATIONAL INTEREST

The fusion of nation and state is a fusion of political power and political community. The state grounds itself upon a national community of men, or to put the matter the other way around, the national community supposedly expresses its wishes and aspirations through the state. The state, possessing power, expresses the interests of the community in its own acts and purposes. It legitimizes these acts and purposes, as well as its possession of power, by linking them philosophically to the presumed interests of the people. As the agent managing the affairs of society *in the name of* society, it acts as trustee of the interests of society in its relations with other nation-states. It manages the affairs of society in relation to its external environment.

The modern nation-state resembles in some respects the old dynastic European state, the juridical-constitutional entity which preceded it in time. The dynastic state, like the new nation-state, was territorial in its dimensions; it was the vehicle for expressing and giving assistance to interests more comprehensive than the particular interests of lesser, more parochial, groupings of men in institutions. *Raison d'état, Staatsraison:* these were the justifications of the dynastic state's power and authority. The management of the affairs of the dynastic state resembled more the management of American corporations today in that, while the corporation was necessarily concerned with the welfare of its employees, it was essentially a managerial interest of an organizational enterprise concerned with the efficient combination and employment of resources, human and material, to serve the interests of the "firm." Frederick the Great of Prussia, a notable management expert, said, "I am the first servant of the State," and he meant it. He was not the first servant of the Prussian people. The efficient management of resources in the interest of the state was designed to augment the power of the state; and if, in turn, this meant that the state concerned itself with the welfare of the people, this was because their livelihood, security, and prosperity were deemed essential to the survival of the state. We see remnants of this older conception of dynastic statehood in some political entities like Saudi Arabia today. Here political power and authority are fused with the familial power and authority of the Saudi dynasty; the management of the affairs of the country are dominated by state familial interests and political power succeeds according to blood-line.

The idea of national interest differs radically, however, from the older idea of *raison d'état* in that the supposed interests of the state were enlarged to encompass the interests of the whole society. At the same time, the very legitimacy of the state *depended upon* the tacit or express approval of the people. This idea finds its most radical expression in Jefferson's words, embodied in the American Declaration of Independence: "Whenever any Form of Government becomes destructive of these ends [Life, Liberty, and the pursuit of Happiness] it is the Right of the People to alter or abolish it, and to institute new Government. . . ." The idea of popular sovereignty thus, in theory, underlies the idea of national interest.

While officials of the dynastic state then were committed to loyalty to the state, which lay above society, power was beholden to state interests. But the elected and appointive officers of the democratic state are supposedly beholden to the interests of the nation. In the United States, all public officers owe fealty not to the nation or "nation-state" as such, but to the Constitution. Yet even here the general welfare principle embodies the concept of popular will.

Thus, the idea of national interest became the metaphysical justification of exercise of power in foreign affairs for modern sovereign states. It was the other side of the coin of the idea of *public* interest, the difference between the two concepts lying in this, that whereas the public interest was expressed in policies pertaining to the domestic welfare of the national community, the *national* interest had to do with the welfare of the whole national community set in the context of world politics among a number of other discrete national entities. The chief distinction, then, between the two concepts lay in this: that the *public* interest, from a philosophic point of view, seemed one which referred ideally to a total interest of a whole community and to policies which could be justified or geared to the collective interests of a society within which they came into force. The *national* interest, playing within the theater of world politics, engaged itself in tension, conflict and cooperation with *other* national interests and could thus claim no higher justification than those particular national interests warranted. This distinction is illustrated by U.S. tariff policies. Under certain circumstances, by sheltering certain domestic industries, a high protective tariff might prove beneficial to the totality of the national economy and thus be justified *in terms of* both a public and national interest. Its effects, however, might prove disastrous to industries in *other* states. Thus while the public interest and the national interest might be served by such legislation, obviously the national interest could excite little enthusiasm from those outside who were harmed.

This necessary means-end relationship between power and national interest raises two special problems: that of conflict of interest in the minds and actions of men wielding power, and the problem of subjectivity in men's conceptions of interest. For if the national interest were to be interpreted and enforced on a day-to-day basis by men who held power, and if this were a necessary condition for the holding of power, wouldn't these men have special affinities for causes, purposes, institutions, and men which would to some considerable measure affect their personal conception of the national interest? He who holds power is for that reason *personally* powerful; to wield public power is to augment personal power as well; to aspire to public power is to aspire also to personal power.

There was never anything self-evident about the national interest. Charles Evans Hughes, Harding's Secretary of State, once had said that "foreign policies are not built upon abstractions" but were "the result of practical conceptions of national interest arising out of some immediate exigency or standing out vividly in historical perspective." To preserve an "American way of life," to defend the nation against outside attack, to preserve its "political and territorial integrity" from foreign control—some people might deem these indisputable principles. However, they leave unanswered the question of how they are to be attained. As Max Weber remarked: *"Interests*—material and spiritual ones—and not ideas, directly govern the relations among men. But the 'pictures of the world' which have been created by ideas all too frequently, like the tracings of a pencil, sketch out the routes along which interests move." [1]

Most statesmen hold in their minds, implicitly or explicitly, certain images of their own nation and its specific interests. Their political decisions may be subtly, even fundamentally, affected by these pictures. Some imagine their own nation-state to be the vehicle for powerful metaphysical or ideological purposes. Sometimes these purposes may include the purpose of transforming part or all of the world in which they live. A deep sense of mission has often informed the minds of American statesmen. Often it has prompted them to espouse particular causes in the name of a national interest which was by no means self-evident to many of their contemporaries. To possess no such abstract, rough guides to purposive action, would be to founder in a sea of events. Whether policy-makers merely find such abstract conceptions of national interest within the political climate of their immediate times and seek to fulfill them, or whether, like Hitler, they *impose* these conceptions as "destiny" upon their fellow countrymen, the fact remains that abstractions do furnish the motive force for the statesman's actions in world affairs.

During any long period of time, the national interests of particular nation-states undergo surprising substantive changes and, in the history of any nation, there come times when men may disagree passionately among themselves about the nature of interests. In the United States of the 1960's, there seemed to be a surprising public and political consensus about certain broad aims of American policy; at other moments of our history, fundamental cleavages of opinion arose. In the early years of the American Republic, for instance, there was a profound rift between those Americans who saw America's destiny as that of a westward-expanding agrarian nation and those who saw it as an eastern seaboard commercial nation involved in world commerce and in world poli-

[1] Weber, quoted in Marianne Weber, *Max Weber*, 1926, p. 347.

tics. Here the Jeffersonian image of an isolationist, decentralized, continental nation clashed with the image of a Hamiltonian, Atlantic nation with strong central authorities. The one pressed inward upon a continent; the other, outward into the world. Both, to be sure, were expansionist, yet each contained within itself the essence of a nation quite divergent from the other. (Obviously, two such different conceptions of national interest found favor with divergent economic and social forces within America. Hamilton's America found enthusiastic response among eastern seaboard commercial and industrial interests; Jefferson's, among western agrarian interests. Yet to say that each was merely a *function of* specific, lesser interests within the nation would be to deny the importance of the substantive choice which their confrontation presented.)

A Question of Goals: Universal or Particular

Perhaps one of the most serious difficulties which the very idea of national interest raises for us arises from two particular sets of problems: the nation and the idea of national interest may both be vehicles for quite universal goals, or goals at least transcending the *immediate* and specific purposes of a society, or they may be vehicles for quite specific interests. Not only despots and tyrants may use the energies of a nation and waste its substance in aggressive enterprises of expansion. Democratic nations have been known to do so as well. The expansionist foreign policies of Louis XIV may have had as their purpose the augmentation of the glory and prestige of the French dynastic state; and this was also true of Frederick the Great's designs. But the armies of the French Revolution, too, were expansionist and, in the name of universal principles, carried the flag of France even further than the Bourbons had done. Thus dynastic France and Republican France were both expansionist, the one, for particular, the other, for universal purposes. In both instances, perhaps, one could say that "France" had "interests." Yet in one case, it would seem that interest was quite specific. It was confined to the aspirations and goals of a dynastic state which was even less than French. In the other, the interests of France were, at the same time, deemed to be the interests of the State, of the French people, and of great universal principles which both of these supposedly represented to the rest of Europe: the Rights of Man.

This asserted identity of popular, state, and universal interests within one national entity is most apparent in modern revolutionary regimes and in movements which seek to seize political power over them. It would be fallacious to say that, as a general rule, states or nation-states pursue only the specific interests of particular communities, just as it would be to say that they pursue only broad, universal objectives. If one took President DeGaulle's word for it, modern France is a contemporary manifestation of a great, yet quite finite, historical idea. The glory of France, to him, should be made manifest in the acts of French statesmen. To him, France, as a specific communal entity, lives in a world of *other* states, pursuing *its* interests by diplomacy and force, just as other states do. To DeGaulle, the national interest of France supersedes all other political concerns, including NATO, the new European Common Market, or any other supranational interest. Yet many Frenchmen today regard DeGaulle's vision as archaic, seeing the survival of their own nation only in terms of much broader communities of men.

On the other hand, after the October Revolution in 1917, Bolshevik Russia was regarded among its ideological supporters as a movement embodying the purposes of a universal revolution, one which was not Russian but supranational. To them, Russia was only a vessel for a great historical ideal, an idea which, as Marx said, "knew no frontiers." The new Bolshevik state's leaders, exhorting comrades elsewhere in Europe to revolt against capitalist and imperialist oppressors, were not asking them to do this on behalf of Russia, but on behalf of Communism. The revolution, however, failed to spread westward. It failed most notably in Germany, even before Lenin's death in 1924. Thereafter under

Stalin, the C.P.S.U. (Communist Party of the Soviet Union) came inexorably to dominate the affairs and policies of the Communist International. Communist parties in so-called capitalist states in the West became pawns of the Soviet party, their leadership dictated by the necessities and interests of a Soviet party which in turn became more and more enmeshed with the diverse interests of the U.S.S.R. In the late 1920's, Stalin spoke of the need to establish "Socialism in one country" before attending to the revolution's business elsewhere. When Trotsky, his rival, accused him of betraying the revolution, Trotsky was removed. By 1932, Karl Radek, then editor of *Izvestia,* was able to write:

> The Soviet Union is strong enough to defend her territorial integrity and her interests. Concentrating her efforts on building up peaceful industries for meeting the needs of her population, keeping aloof from armed interferences with the affairs of foreign [sic] nations, the Soviet Union will seek a peaceful settlement of all conflicts which may arise between her and her neighbors. She will base her policy exclusively on her own interests. . . .[2]

Who was right? Which interest was paramount? Even today such questions are unanswerable. To regard Stalin's and Khrushchev's foreign policies as Soviet or Russian imperialism is to underrate or ignore powerful messianic elements within Soviet Marxism. On the other hand, to regard Russian leaders as unswervingly committed to world revolution, even at the expense of Soviet interests, seems equally absurd. It is not without importance that contemporary Soviet leaders, like their Bolshevik predecessors, assume that the justification of the Bolshevik Revolution lay in the fact that it was one stage, albeit a crucial one, in a much broader, universal upheaval of men in all countries. Thus their idea of interest reconciles, at least to their own satisfaction, the tension between the universal and the particular: the interests of "humanity," of Soviet Communism, and of the people of the U.S.S.R.

[2] Radek, *Foreign Affairs,* July, 1932, p. 557. Quoted in Charles A. Beard, *The Idea of National Interest,* New York: Macmillan, 1934, p. 3.

One might dismiss this particular instance of ambiguity concerning the nature of interest and nation as an unfortunate anomaly due to the presence of an unusual revolutionary power in world politics. But this is impossible. The source of the quandary about national interests is much more fundamental. It lies in the fact, more apparent than ever in the thermonuclear age, that *all* political entities are constantly in the process of flux and change. Radical shifts of power and influence within particular states produce equally radical alterations in definition of "national interests." The Castro Revolution wrenched Cuba out of the orbit of American and Western hemispheric interests and policies, just as the Colonels' Revolt in Egypt earlier had radically redefined Egypt's national interests. Today ideological affinities among men are too various to be forced into the Procrustean bed of exclusive national interests. So too, a community of interest among diverse nations seems to arise from a common perception of global problems which requires concerted action among nations, even though the particular problem bears no discernibly direct relationship to *specific* national or more parochial interests. During the Korean War, for instance, Ethiopian battalions were sent by Emperor Haile Selassie to fight alongside R.O.K. and American forces, even though he would reap no immediate benefits. In this instance, Ethiopia paid tribute to the universal principle of collective security among nations in the society of nations. Had this principle been followed by other nation-states in 1935 following Mussolini's attack upon Ethiopia, aggression might conceivably have been repelled. In his *Memoirs*, former President Truman wrote about the similar problem of Korean aggression—that American intervention on behalf of the U.N. Charter in 1950 had been on behalf of something transcending the national interest:

In my generation, this was not the first occasion when the strong had attacked the weak. I recalled earlier instances: Manchuria, Ethiopia, Austria. I remembered how each time that the democracies failed to act it had encouraged the aggressors to keep going ahead. I felt certain that if South Korea was allowed to fall Communist leaders would be emboldened to override nations closer to our shores. . . . It was also clear to me that the foundations and the principles of the United Nations were at stake unless this unprovoked attack on Korea could be stopped.[3]

Power Versus Community

An inherent difficulty in discussing the nature of the national interest arises from a basic and permanent tension between power and community. The national interest assumes the *existence* of a viable and integrated society. Tied as it is to the idea of popular sovereignty, it is supposedly responsive and responsible to prevailing concepts of interest among dominant groups within a democratic society. In this, it is unlike the older conception of *Staatsraison*, which claimed to serve interests *higher than* and transcending these particular interests of society. The national interest speaks for the nation-as-collectivity, not for the state as a transcendent entity. Yet the national interest, like the public interest, is a product of tension and conflict within a governmental process. The men who formulate national interests themselves are, for this reason alone, men of power.

Political power, at any given time, has always been vested in particular men and institutions. Because this is so, has it not always been the case that power too created interests, just as interest could seek and create power? Because power became manifest in power centers, in "power elites," and in the administrators of power, power itself could command the authority to define interests as it saw them; the national interest could become the servant of the very agencies to which society entrusted the care of its well-being in foreign affairs. In cold war context, this dilemma about power and national interest has become all the more intense. As the problems of foreign affairs have become increasingly complex, the management of the national interest has required a more intricate and specialized knowledge of things, and

[3] Harry S. Truman, *Memoirs*, Vol. 2. New York: Doubleday, 1958, p. 333.

the ordinary man is told he must acknowledge the limits of his own judgment and information.

In modern times, only the totalitarian state has claimed both the ability and the justification to impose a monolithic, overriding conception of total interest upon society, denying that real disagreements exist *within* society about the nature of interest and purpose in foreign affairs. Here two traditional distinctions, always present in Western political thought, have been erased by totalitarian ideology and coercion: the tension between the state and society, and the socio-political tensions within society itself. Denying the presence of necessarily opposed interests in society and eliminating those which did appear, the totalitarian state could, without fear of being contradicted, proclaim a harmony of interests among all "progressive" elements in Socialist society. (In the mid-1930's, Soviet Trotskyites and other opponents of the regime were accused of being agents of foreign imperialism before they were liquidated. To admit that they were indigenous would have been to admit also the possibility that they spoke with authenticity about the direction and purposes of Soviet foreign and domestic policies.)

Of course the free society could not do this. The free society, so it was said, sought openly to express conflicts of interest and power and differing conceptions about the national interest as long as such conflicts took place among those groups and individuals who accepted the constitutional rules of the game, the limits of conflict, *and* the overriding concept of public good: *salus republica suprema lex.* But here we come full circle and the intrinsic difficulty in the idea of national interest appears once more: Is foreign policy a consensus among dominant power elements in society? And how does one *know* that this consensus is in fact congruent with the collective purposes of the community?

Platonists and Realists: Two Views of Society

Thus we see an extraordinary dichotomy in the very idea of the national interest, one which arises from the necessary opposition of two ways of looking at the politics of society. The first is a Platonic point of view which assumes the existence of a *necessarily* harmonious political system with its special needs for social integration. It speaks of the social system's need for a consensus of values and purposes among its members. It emphasizes the system's requirements for stability, permanence, and durability through time. This "on-going" political system, placed within the larger context of world politics, confronts other social systems with their own special needs. According to this view, the American political system should seek in its foreign policies to attain and keep a necessary national unity of purpose. It should seek always a rational congruence *among* different domestic concepts of national purpose and public policy. Thus unity in foreign policy is essential to the stability of the society at home.

Yet set against this metaphysical concept of unity is a realistic metaphysic of power and conflict. Cannot society and the state both equally well be perceived as systems of power and domination, systems of political conflict incessantly subject to processes of change which revise even the substantive meaning of the national interest? Is not the state subject to conflict *among* those holding power and to tension between the holders of power and those seeking power? Do not these obvious, apparent qualities of political life then constantly affect the content of the national interest, and thus minimize its importance and even subjectify it?

A further difficulty to those seriously concerned with the survival and stability of the nation through time, is this: the Platonic concept of society and state as *necessarily* and continuously seeking stability, "integration," and consensus raises nightmarish logical possibilities. The first is that the claims made by society on behalf of its survival and stability, and expressed in part through formulations of national interest, might "of necessity" destroy certain institutions, interests, and values within society itself. The survival of the whole might risk or entail the destruction or transformation of the parts.

In times of international crisis, who is to say what rights and liberties are to be sacrificed or maintained, in order that the "collectivity" might survive? In the name of national security during World War I, American war-resisters had been imprisoned; pro-German elements in society punished; and restraints imposed upon a free press. During World War II, by administrative edict, West Coast Nisei Japanese were arbitrarily deported and imprisoned—some, in fact, stripped of their American citizenship; and this in the name of the American nation. Such have been the latent impulses to preserve the metaphysic of a national interest, seemingly threatened by the defection or disobedience of parts of the public.

There is yet another matter, also related to the Platonic conception of society, namely, that the metaphysic of the national interest and its claims to supremacy run afoul of the interests of *other* social systems. For instance, it had been the business of the national interest in World War II to smash and destroy other systems of power which threatened America. The very existence of Nazism, it was said, was incompatible with the survival of American free institutions and with all of their associated values. Imbedded within German society, the Nazi system was destroyed by American power. With it, a very substantial part of the German community also disappeared. In the cold war, one might say that now a supreme purpose of the national interest is to prevent the recurrence of such a tragic necessity. Yet so long as the national interest remains a touchstone of policy, so long does it assert that the integrity of the nation and its values is the supreme end of public policy. Thus, if circumstances were to arise in which, let us say, the survival of other political entities—Communist states, for instance—proved dysfunctional and threatened the American system with *dis*integration, what then? These have been the crisis questions, which some men prefer to put out of mind in a thermonuclear age; others, by means of policy and attitude, seek to defer or prevent the disaster inherent in the wrong answers.

The National Interest as End Product

If one regards the national interest as a conglomeration of purposes fashioned in a system of political power, change, and conflict, one sees it then as malleable, plastic, provisional, the "step-child" of a governmental process. It is then an end product, not an end; ontological, not teleological. As such, one sees also the redefinitions of essential purposes which themselves are provisional end products of power-relationships. From this point of view, special political forces within the nation have sprung into light, each with its provisional conception of national interest related ideologically to its own conceptions of special interest.

At any given moment in time, particular concepts of national strategy and public policy are deeply entrenched within particular governmental institutions. Inter-service rivalries in the military, couched in strategic terms, could be seen for example to relate to the particular needs and thus interests of particular services. The Pentagon could be viewed as a vast system of power, pyramidal, seeking to fuse component service interests into a large, harmonious whole; a system seeking, in short, an over-arching strategic concept congruent both with specific services and with the national interest. *This* particular system of power radiates in widening circles, embracing other elements of power within American public life. Unless one dismisses as absurd the notion that the nation's security is dependent upon such institutions of power, the difficulty is inherent in the process: agencies of public purpose invariably become vested agencies of power and acquire their own interests. And since this is so, special and private power becomes interwoven with public power, special and private policy with public policy. How does one determine where one begins and the other leaves off? How discern, where one might be incompatible with the other?

Senatorial confirmation hearings for appointive officers of the executive branch often reveal the confusing problem of "conflict of interest" for public servants. John Foster Dulles' private legal interests in German corporations' activities during the 1930's; Dean Acheson's private legal activities on behalf of the Polish government in the 1940's; and John McCone's extensive private holdings of stock in oil companies with Middle Eastern investments were, for instance, sometimes deemed incompatible with objectivity in public policy. When Charles Wilson, up for Senate confirmation in 1953 as Defense Secretary, was asked whether his extensive interests in General Motors were prejudicial to his "disinterested" role as a major defense procurement official, he replied that "what is good for General Motors is good for the country."

Corporate and military power were, insofar as they came into play in decisions essential to national interests in foreign policy, both extensive and powerful, and necessary. Other elements of a political bureaucracy must be added to them; for example, the State Department, the focal point of on-going national interest formulation. All the other agencies of policy and power, inside and outside of government, appear in turn. To greater or lesser degrees, all are subject to the same inherent problem of fusing of public and private motives. All who possess power and influence make use of it: national committees of persecuted nationality ethnic groups, trade unions, peace organizations, trade associations, veterans' societies, political parties, none are exempt. To the extent that interest is institutionalized, particular interest expresses itself with power; and, out of governmental processes, so it is said, national interests emerge, subjectified. The play of pressures make a cockpit of the national interest.

(A classic and unpleasant instance of the play of such pressures could be seen in the late 1940's over American Middle Eastern policies. Here, two specific pressures collided, neither a plausible embodiment of the national interest: American Zionists and the Arabian American Oil Company. The wish of the former, that American policy place itself behind the emerging State of Israel, posed a direct threat to the security and interests of American oil investments in the Middle East. Yet to say that neither interest embodied the national interest was not the same as to say that the American national interest should be unmindful of either. After all, in Hitler's time, it had been Americans of English descent who saw the survival of England essential to America's interests, and American trade unionists who had seen fascism's assault on European trade unions as a threat to their own freedom. Did, then, the expression of these special interests place them outside the pale? Ernest Bevin sardonically remarked in 1948 that American Middle Eastern policy might have been quite different had there been a sizeable Arab population in America: but it might also have been different if American business firms had had no oil interests or aspirations in the Middle East or if oil resources had been of no concern to American policy-makers.)

One American political scientist, David Truman, was led by such speculations to deny the possibility either that the national interest could have any substantive content, or that it could have any conceptual meaning at all. He wrote:

> There is a political significance in assertions of a totally inclusive interest within the nation. . . . Such claims are a tremendously useful promotional device by means of which a particularly extensive group or league of groups tries to reduce or eliminate opposing groups. . . . In themselves, these claims are part of the data of politics. However, they do not describe any actual or possible political situation within a complex modern nation. In developing a group interpretation of politics, therefore, we do not need to account for a totally inclusive interest, because one does not exist.[4]

The dismaying, if interesting, possibility is that *both* approaches to this matter are necessary, incompatible as they are. To make of the national interest an overarching metaphysic which transcends particular interests risks the danger of ignoring the facts of power and conflict in society by simply not mentioning them. In the cold war, for instance, great needs for national

[4] David B. Truman, *The Governmental Process*. New York: Alfred A. Knopf, 1958, pp. 50-51 .

power have resulted in the pyramiding of giant enterprises of power and major reconstellations of influence and authority in American life. To examine them as systems of power is somehow to unmask them, revealing the inherent fusion of private, personal, and public interests and motives which they contain. Not to examine them, merely to assert their necessity, is to avoid the possibilities of political corruption which the workings of this system necessarily entail. Not to examine them critically is also to avoid asking if a differently constellated system of power might possibly lead to a "better" national interest. There is the final risk that an infatuation with an overarching mystique of a national interest might lead to attempts, in the name of a stable, persistent socio-political structure, to cut out or psychoanalyze out those elements of society which are deemed dysfunctional. Who is to be the judge and jury of that?

To view the national interest merely as the play of power, however, is to lose sight of those essential truths which lie in the metaphysic itself. To see the national interest as merely the consequence of process and interplay of power, is to overlook the forest for the trees. To transcend particular interests and powerful private institutions is not necessarily to obliterate them or ignore their existence and involvement in the political process. A metaphysical national interest, as in Plato's *Republic* and Talcott Parson's *Social System*, contains within itself the requirements of a civilized society's survival, as well as the seeds of totalitarianism. The idea of national interest as mere process and interplay of powerful institutions contains within itself the denial of any objective authority or authentic interest. It denies the possibility of concerted, rational action by the nation-as-collectivity in world politics other than what "came out of process." The tension between the two ideas is inescapable.

There are three possible meanings then for American national interest as we use it in this book. The idea of national interest may refer to some *ideal* set of purposes which a nation (here the United States) *should* seek to realize in the conduct of its foreign relations. Wanting a better word, we might call this a *normative*, civic concept of national interest. This normative approach is of special importance to citizens, politicians, and statesmen when deliberating on goals for their nation. A second meaning of equal importance, might be called *descriptive*. In this sense the national interest may be regarded as those purposes which the nation, through its leadership, appears to pursue persistently through time. When we speak of the national interest in this descriptive sense, we move out of the metaphysical into a realm of facts. Hughes himself once remarked carelessly that the Constitution of the United States was "what the courts say it is." It might similarly be said that the national interest is what foreign-policy makers say it is.

A third definition might make the meaning of national interest somewhat clearer. The American national interest has often been an arena for conflict amongst individuals and groups whose conceptions of it (as we will subsequently see) have differed widely. Historians may see long lines of doctrinal consistency in formulations of American national interest through time, such as the Monroe Doctrine: these bear witness to the continuity of specific attitudes about foreign policy. Yet basic conflicts have always been present *within* American society about the purposes it should pursue in world politics and the means to achieve them. During World War II and later, at the time of the Korean war, America was sharply divided about both the aims and the means of policy. Within Congress and the Administration, these disagreements reached acute heights before they were reconciled. Disagreement about policy and action may arise even among men who are essentially in agreement about the general aims of their country in the world. But policy disagreements are usually due to differences among policy-makers about conceptions both of what the United States *is* and what its role in world politics, even its mission, should be. Foreign policies often become subjects of violent debate when Americans hold deeply divergent images of what their nation is, or what it should become in the future.

Like domestic politics, foreign policy may be a theater in which domestic power groups struggle amongst themselves to achieve their own interests or to impose their particular conceptions of broader interests on the nation as a whole. Then the national interest may be seen like a young child in the hands of contentious parents, an object to be moulded to one's particular purposes and advantages.

We might thus conceive of the national interest as a kaleidoscopic *process* by which forces latent in American society seek to express certain political and economic aspirations in world politics through the highest organs of state. To comprehend this process, we must not merely understand something of the formal governmental processes by which foreign policy is made, but also penetrate into the depth of the nation itself to discern the wellsprings of thought, ideology, and smaller interests which feed into the mainstreams of American policy abroad.

Practical men such as Charles Evans Hughes may not speculate deeply about metaphysical, long-range meanings of the national interest, preferring rather to see what it should be from day to day. But speculation is necessary. Every day decisions and actions are undertaken by American policy-makers in the name of national interest; ideally, policy-makers are supposed to develop specific policies within the broader framework of more permanent goals and purposes of the nation. In times of crisis, when debates over foreign policies arise, such deep national purposes come to the forefront of men's minds. In quieter times, they may be hidden or rarely articulated. Today the American national interest is said to be manifest in grand designs: defense of the "free world" against Soviet totalitarianism; defense of Western Europe and Britain as keystones of this free world; fashioning and strengthening of "free societies" in Asia and Africa; prudent avoidance of total, nuclear war. These broad policy designs include many particulars: the maintenance, with the aid of U.S. military forces, of a free Berlin in Germany and a free Korea in Asia; assistance to underdeveloped, non-totalitarian nations to augment their rates of economic growth and productivity, and so forth. Such particular expressions of an American national interest may change through time. While they may be visible signs of the national interest, they are not of its essence. As adaptations to new circumstances, they are historically contingent expressions of interest of quite recent origin.

Searching for this essence of the national interest divested of contemporaneous content, we encounter problems which go to the very heart of political theory. It seems self-evident to some that nations, like individuals, have interests which they seek to protect or pursue. Nations, like individual men, are said to have a basic desire to survive, to escape "extinction." As Nicholas Spykman wrote, "The basic objective of the foreign policy of all states is the preservation of territorial integrity and political independence." For the nation-state and for the individual, self-preservation does not mean merely physical survival; it also means cultural survival. History records instances in which a whole people met with physical destruction at the hands of its enemies. Yet far more frequently, foreign policy failures led to cultural or political extinction. Often nations are willing, as collectivities, to risk biological extinction through war in order to avoid cultural extinction.

New Contexts for National Interests

While national interests may appear on the surface to be self-evident, they are by no means so. The world of international politics is not only a world of sovereign states, each equally committed to its own national interest, with its own autonomous values, seeking to maximize its power-position in the world.

In the first place, in international politics, political power is regrouping itself with great swiftness. Nations and national interest which exist today may not have existed a few decades ago. Many of these nation-states arose from the wreckage of previous ones. Some came into being as a consequence of revolutionary acts against established, sovereign states; others, as a consequence of voluntary and peaceful integration of several smaller national communities. Moreover, as the Soviet-bloc states of Eastern Europe and the Soviet Union show, certain states express in their declared national interest the aspirations and interests of a much more comprehensive collectivity: the empire of Soviet communism. In many parts of the free world, processes of trans-national and supranational political integration are taking place with surprising swiftness. As they do, the idea of an autonomous national interest becomes so blurred and involved in emergent interests of larger communities that we cannot say, as has been said, "Every country operates on the principle that its highest duty is to preserve its identity as a nation." The forcible political and economic integration now taking place within the Soviet empire quite possibly violates the traditional national interests of sovereign states and peoples subject to it; but we must realize that the vigor of this process of political change springs from concepts of political interest and from an ideology which transcend simple national interests. (It could be noted, too, that the spiritual vigor of internal resistance to Soviet tyranny among subject peoples in Eastern Europe springs not merely from national interests and nationalist forces but from interests and commitments which are supranational, if not universal, in scope as, for instance, from the Roman Catholic Church in Poland, Hungary, and elsewhere.)

In Western Europe also, traditional international politics are giving way swiftly to the politics of a broader European community. Interests cut across the territorial lines which divide sovereign states. At no time in its history was Europe unambiguously divided into compact and exclusive nation-state collectivities, yet the high-water mark of European nationalism was reached long ago, possibly between 1914 1939. Few Europeans today would either welcome or anticipate a return to this state of affairs. The major intellectual and ideological currents at work in Europe as a whole now transcend purely national entities. Some European statesmen, like President DeGaulle, profess to see contemporary

Europe in classical form, as a theater in which purely national interests act upon each other. Despite his view, this classical image carried over from the nineteenth century is both nostalgic and archaic. The internal politics of Europe as a whole is played out in a theater in which overlapping, supranational interests compete strongly with traditional, national ones in matters of defense, economic and social policy, and ideological commitments.

The idea of the supremacy of the national interest over other political considerations does violence to ordinary political reality in other ways. In all societies, men are normally loyal to many things: to personal conscience, to family, to political parties, to their church, to ethnic communities, often to causes which transcend their own nation. As a general rule, most Americans tend to assume that loyalty to the United States is harmonious with loyalty to such particular or more embracing commitments and affiliations. American political parties, churches, and nationality groups accept, it is said, a common constitutional framework as a given condition which both guarantees and sets limits upon the exercise of their political power. Some fringe groups may regard important parts of the American community as un-American or as intrinsically disloyal to the nation; but these groups command little public support today. Traditionally, racial or religious minority groups have fought to be accepted in the American community and to share in its constitutional and political rights, rather than aspire to disrupt the political order or be sheltered from it. The absence of hard class lines; the relative ease with which American citizens may move occupationally, geographically, and socially; the low pitch of religious and sectional controversy; the relatively peaceful assimilation of new immigrant groups into American life—all these features of contemporary America have led to a widely-accepted belief that loyalty to nation harmonizes with loyalty to other causes and commitments. In turn, this has given further meaning and substance to the idea of an American national interest. (This is not to say that all Americans have similar images of an American national interest but that most Americans would assume that such an interest did exist and that it was compatible with their other loyalties.)

At earlier times in American history and in many other parts of the world today, such a degree of national cohesiveness did and does not exist. The idea of a national interest as the philosophic yardstick for foreign policies of states makes little sense when the rudiments of political *community* do not exist within a particular state, or when contentious factions within a national society disagree fundamentally about the desirable nature of their political life. In many parts of the world today and throughout modern times, there has been a great tension between loyalty to nation and loyalty to state. Conflicts of loyalties arise inevitably when men do not conceive of their nation as co-extensive with their state. In the Middle East, where Arab nationalism cuts horizontally across the frontiers of territorial states, no particular state, not even the United Arab Republic, can claim to represent the national interest. Often, as in the latter days of the Austro-Hungarian Empire, which was a multi-ethnic state, loyalty to *nation* meant loyalty to a community of men far smaller than the state itself. Thomas Masaryk's loyalty to the cause of Czech national interests was thus disruptive of the state and hastened the collapse of the Empire. Before 1870, German nationalist movements (expressing a "national" interest) within all of the kingdoms, principalities, and city-states of Germany were subversive of the existing constitutional order. Even after unification, the fact that Germany as a territorial entity at no time embraced all ethnic Germans on the European continent was disruptive of the constitutional order and peace of Europe.

Even when we deal with a national community such as the United States, Britain, or France in which the constitutional *state* is co-extensive with *nation* and, in fact, in which the nation grew to self-consciousness within a pre-existing territorial state, there are still considerable hazards in accepting the conception of a metaphysical national interest too unquestioningly. If the idea of national interest is the keystone of the public policy arch, what we wish to know at all times is what various concepts of the national interest exist within the nation. In particular, we want to know who possesses both formal authority and effective power to formulate these particular conceptions. What images of national purpose do such political leaders possess and what kind of practical means to achieve those purposes do they have in mind? In the early 1950's, for instance, men of such stature as Senator Robert A. Taft and President Truman both acknowledged the primacy of the national interest, yet their conceptions of that interest differed sharply, as did their ideas about the means to further it.

The Conflict with Democratic Procedure

Perhaps one of the most perplexing issues posed by the idea of national interest is the relationship of national interest to the constitutional processes of the nation. In the best of times, it is difficult to reconcile the procedural values of a democratic society with the requirements of foreign policy. We like to think that in democracies, public policies are shaped by procedures of free and open deliberation in which the public does not just assent passively but plays an active, creative part. We like also to think that there is a constitutional understanding about the conduct of foreign policy which clearly distributes the powers over the control of foreign relations among constitutional entities—President, Congress, and Court—in a manner resembling the distribution of authority over domestic policy.

Yet during protracted crises such as arise from the cold war, the conduct of foreign relations often does violence to these procedural values of a democratic order. The speed necessary to meet crisis situations often requires that the circle of decision-makers be sharply reduced in size, and official secrecy often masks both deliberation and action.

But even in periods of protracted involvement in international affairs, there are other reasons why the public often waits passively on events, and why this public cannot pass an intelligent judgment on policy. Even in a highly literate nation such as the United States, the general public perceives events in world politics too dimly to respond to them rationally. Normally, the events themselves are too remote; they do not "fit" into the affairs of ordinary life. The public usually glimpses great historical developments in moments of strange lightning-like illumination—when something extraordinary happens. The mass media which document world politics dramatize the sensational and the topical and are rarely capable of more than that.

Under such normal circumstances, influence over political events tends to be centered within narrow strata of American society. How narrow, how representative this "elite" may be, we shall have occasion to discuss later. But we should realize that within this narrow minority in America effective deliberation over the national interest takes place continuously. The power to *apply* the national interest to particular circumstance is exercised within an even narrower stratum of American society. However small a role the general public plays, by its own values and aspirations it sets limits upon the amount and kinds of power which decision-makers feel they may employ. Men of power draw their conceptions of national interest from an intellectual milieu far broader than the narrow limits of their circles of "influentials." The character of their view of national interest comes from their perceptions of the traditions, the aspirations, and the needs of their own civilization.

SUGGESTED READING

Beard, Charles, *The Idea of National Interest, an Analytical Study in American Foreign Policy*, New York, Macmillan, 1934.
Cook, Thomas Ira, and Moos, Malcolm, *Power through Purpose, the Realism of Idealism as a Basis for Foreign Policy*, Baltimore, The Johns Hopkins Press, 1954.
Morgenthau, Hans, *In Defense of the National Interest*, New York, Alfred A. Knopf, 1952.

CHAPTER

5

POWER AND POLICY

*Our age must learn that some
things are beyond "doing."*

KARL JASPERS

Throughout the history of the Western world, the study of international politics has been, in large measure, the study of the great powers. Despite the legal fiction of the sovereign equality of states, each age has seen the pre-eminence of certain states or empires whose power gave them the capacity, and usually the impulse, to regulate or govern the international order. In the traditional society of nations, to be sure, no one power ever succeeded for long in dominating the theater of European politics. At certain times certain states, notably Germany and France, nearly achieved hegemony over the whole European continent; yet at no time was such hegemony actually consolidated; and indeed, it was always inhibited by a countervailing group of other states. There have been occasions when one power sought to dominate the whole society of nations but, in general, international public policy has been determined by great powers acting in concert or in conflict.

At different times, various states in the international community have been regarded as great powers. Immediately before 1914, Britain, France, Germany, Russia, Austria-Hungary, and possibly America and Japan were the great powers. For a brief time after World War II, there were only three: America, Britain, and Russia. At present, it is difficult to say. China and India are obviously powers, as are such European states as France and Western Germany. But there has been no obvious demarcation point between that short period following the war and the present. The United States and the Union of Socialist Soviet Republics remain preeminent in world politics; they are the "super-powers." World politics in many respects appears bi-polarized, with Washington and Moscow the two major centers of world power (see Chapter 1). The most likely new centers of power to compete with Washington and Moscow in international politics are non-European. The age of West-European pre-eminence in international affairs is over.

WHAT CONSTITUTES NATIONAL POWER?

While most of us take for granted a certain ranking of states in order of power and scan the events of each year to discern shifts in power relations among states, we would be hard put either to explain the meaning of power in world politics, or to explain satisfactorily what criteria are used in judging a nation's power. We may also balk at laying such stress upon power as a chief analytic measure for studying world politics. In the past, many Americans found the notion of power politics ethically repugnant and advocated isolation and non-involvement as a means of avoiding the corruption of power which allegedly lay at the heart of the European system of politics. Many liberal Americans sought to devise ideal systems of international order which, once established, might put an end to power politics.

It is difficult to build a theory of international politics exclusively upon a basis of power politics, if by power politics we mean a system composed of states, each of which seeks to augment its own power in relation to other states. It would be equally impossible to ignore power. Individuals and nations alike may use force on occasion in their relations with each other, yet some appear to do so with great reluctance, preferring other less violent means of expressing their influence. Not all states, not even all totalitarian ones, are inherently expansionist. Many, in fact a very great number, have for long periods of time appeared content to avoid deliberate aggressive enterprises. Such avoidance of aggression seems independent of any passive or aggressive attributes of national character. Moreover, as power structures, nation-states differ greatly in the extent to which they turn themselves outward upon the world.

It is nevertheless true that all nation-states, to a greater or lesser extent, seek constantly to influence their external environment and in so doing, draw upon a wide range of national resources. In a sense, national power might be defined as a combination of resources. Military power ranks high among these properties, for a principal objective of nation-states has been to avoid defeat in war and possible extinction as national entities at the hands of enemies.

Classically, national power is regarded as *power tested in war*; yet many nations have greatly augmented their influence in international affairs without possessing a large military establishment or even aspiring to one. Often too, the capacity of a nation to attain international objectives has been weakened by the misuse of, or infatuation with, military power. Finally, national power has often been used with discrimination by statesmen who wish to achieve their objectives *without* war. Hence the crucible of war, the testing ground of power, is avoided.

Even in those states bent upon expanding and augmenting their power at the expense of others, military power is merely one of a number of resources. The vigorous European colonial expansion in the nineteenth century, which led to imperial domination of most of Africa and Asia, cannot be seen merely as military conquest (in fact, remarkably few forces were employed in either the conquest or domination of these new colonial areas). The means of expansion came from every vital area of European life: its technology, its churches and missions, its motley adventurers. At the height of British imperium in India, barely 800 police and 60,000 British soldiers were required to maintain order in a sub-continent of 400,000,000 people. In recent times too, the character of Soviet imperialism has been determined as much by its non-military, revolutionary strength as by the Red Army. "Communist aggression," like the earlier aggression of Jacobin revolutionary forces at the time of the French Revolution, has derived its unique power from a combination of conventional military force and the ideologically-committed revolutionaries.

NATIONAL POWER AS END OR MEANS?

National power is an ambiguous concept largely because of its two contradictory meanings: power may be variously regarded as a means toward an end—or an end in itself. However, it is exceptionally difficult to distinguish between these meanings when we are faced with concrete examples. In recent times, Nazi and Soviet revolutionary totalitarianism sought both to dominate the lives of men within their orbits and to extend the orbits themselves. By its very nature, the totalitarian state seems compelled to destroy, capture, or mute all competing centers of power and to bend the personalities of men wholly to its purposes. Yet even here, we would err grievously in assuming that these purposes were merely the purposes of power alone. Soviet totalitarianism is informed by a monolithic, ideological conception of the "new society" which it seeks to impose upon men by force. Every ideological revolutionary, whether Communist, Nazi, or other, shares one common concern: to force "reality" to conform to its own image or picture. When "reality" resists, he is often constrained to use violence. To interpret his activities *merely* as the effort to achieve limitless power is to overlook the vision which often spurs him to action and which often finds favor with so many other men.

The Power to Make War

National power, in the sense of instrument, remains equally ambiguous. We often think of national power as a composite of resources and skills, which can be symphonically orchestrated into some grand national design. We have generally assumed that this power, when properly synchronized, includes the power either to wage war successfully, or to deter the warlike intentions of other states. This national power need not necessarily comprise "forces in being," the organizational or physical entities which wage war. It may be latent, lying beneath the surface of an overtly peaceful society. In the American experience, national power thus defined has traditionally been latent. In peacetime, the United States maintained until 1950 only skeletal ground forces for waging land war. Its naval strength, while substantial in comparison with other seapowers, imposed no considerable drain upon national resources. The American economy as a whole developed in a climate of civilian rather than military concern. The physical remoteness of the United States from other major military powers provided until quite recently a respite of time in which to prepare after a threat of war became unambiguous. But when war came, as in 1941, America was able to convert its human and material resources in record time from peaceful to military purposes, becoming, in the words of President Roosevelt, an "arsenal of democracy."

If national power is thus viewed as a composite of various resources—a nation's industries, population, geographical location and terrain, natural resources, scientific and managerial skills, etc. —we encounter peculiar difficulties when we try to relate this power to the foreign policy purposes of the society itself. To be sure, in times of total war there is an ironic simplicity of relationship between national power and national purpose. The meaning of power then seems quite unambiguous. It is the capacity to destroy some clearly-defined enemy or to subject him to one's will. Conversely, it is the capacity to protect the national community from him. Thus in times of total war the public clarity and simplicity of political ends (e.g., "total victory" or "unconditional surrender") are matched by a certain clarity in the definition of power. To be sure, there may be strategic difficulties of a very high order involved in arranging and employing the elements of power to best accomplish the ends of total war, but these difficulties are offset by the grandiose simplicities of military purpose.

Power in Peacetime

At all other times however, including the periods of cold war such as we are now experiencing, both national purpose and national power convey no such clear meaning. Since avoidance of total war is today a central objective of international statesmanship, national power may have to be used most intelligently to avoid that very exercise of power in war by which it is most clearly measured.

At other times too, a nation's energies from which its wartime capacities emerge are devoted to many purposes which bear no clear or direct relationship to the nation's foreign policies. One of the great difficulties of comparing the national power of great states in times of peace arises from the different ways in which they allocate both the human and material components of national power. In the 1930's, when Nazi Germany threatened the peace of Europe, and today, when the Soviet Union and Communist China threaten the free world, totalitarian states have managed to divert a greater proportion of their annual gross national product into military channels than have the democratic nations and they have done so without noticeably weakening their authority at home. Today, as in the 1930's, the combined economies of the non-totalitarian world far exceed the total productivity of the totalitarian world. Still, the ratio of military productivity has been far more favorable to the latter. The states of the free world are more sensitive to consumer interests, high standards of living, and non-military capital investment than are totalitarian countries. The annual production of steel in the Soviet bloc today may thus be substantially less than the combined production of steel in Western Europe and the United States, yet Western metallurgical industries are primarily servants of the civilian consumer who wishes more automobiles, deep-freezes, apartment houses, etc. The startling capacity of the relatively underdeveloped Soviet bloc in new-weapons development betrays the inequitable resource allocations within the totalitarian world, where living standards are notoriously lower than in the West. It also testifies to the advantages of totalitarian states in augmenting their military national power.

Foreign Policy

In a more modest definition, national power may be said to consist of those resources which a nation, by its unique constitutional processes, places at the disposal of its foreign policy makers. From this point of view, it would appear that the modern totalitarian state possesses greater capacities for mobilizing such resources than the democratic state. Democratic constitutional processes sometimes seem poorly suited to sustained and purposeful enterprises in foreign affairs. When policies are left to the mercies of random shifts of public opinion, they may shift more drastically than they do in a regime where control (and purpose) is determined more centrally. Some observers, including Walter Lippmann,[1] argue that the Western democracies have been progressively enfeebled by a constitutional derangement of powers over foreign policy, in particular by the authority which the legislature and the broad public often exert over men whose formal responsibility it is to execute public policy. If the nation, here defined as its articulate, politically effective public, chooses to in-

---

[1] Walter Lippmann, *Essays in the Public Philosophy*. Boston: Little, Brown and Co., 1955.

hibit the discretionary power of its executive to respond flexibly to certain foreign policy crises, then Mr. Lippmann's criticism would make a good deal of sense. It would make even better sense if it could be shown that other forms of government, granting greater authority to the executive, exhibit a higher degree of sustained purposefulness in foreign affairs. But such generalizations about the liabilities of democracies in foreign affairs should be carefully examined, particularly as they apply to the United States today.

However, the question raised by Lippmann, George Kennan, and others bears upon the whole issue of the meaning of national power. National power does have a very great deal to do with the internal, constitutional arrangements of a state; and further, it has a great deal to do with prevailing attitudes about constitutional arrangements held by the public within a particular nation. Incorrect inferences are often drawn about the effect of domestic political instability upon a nation's international power. During certain phases of the cold war, many Westerners looked anxiously for signs of tensions and instabilities within the Soviet Union and its satellites, assuming that they would weaken the Soviet Union in relation to the West. Measures were even undertaken during the first years of the Eisenhower administration to foster tensions within captive satellite states in Eastern Europe. Yet domestic instability within a nation may often lead to increased vigor in its international activities and often, to very risky ones. (In "The Dog that Bit People," James Thurber writes how his mother often apologized for the misbehavior of Muggs, attributing it to the fact that the dog "was not well." "He may not have been well," Thurber said, "but he was terribly strong.")

In one respect, the idea of national power has been dramatically altered by developments in the arts of war in the past two decades. If national power includes all of those instruments of war which could protect a nation from external attack, we can see how the idea of power was closely related to one major purpose: to protect the territorial nation from any serious outside attack.

The test of national power was the capacity to repel, remove, or mitigate such threats. As such, it could be augmented by skillful diplomacy, by alliances, by adherence to international organizations, etc. Every viable nation-state, no matter what its standing within the society of nations, justified itself to its public on the grounds that it could adequately protect that society from outside attack. For such reasons, the military, as guardians of society, have been accorded high prestige and influence in most Western societies.

It seems then that the instruments of national power have been those which, at the least, could promise the inhabitants of a nation-state protection, if not immunity, from invasion and devastating attack. Drawn metaphorically around the periphery of the territorial state, the armed forces could be seen as a shell or ring, the purpose of which was to guarantee national military impermeability. Even at the outset of major wars in the past, the wielders of national power could plausibly justify their possession of force on grounds that its presence and employment would ultimately save the nation.

Nuclear Weapons and National Power

Nuclear and other unconventional weapons have created a crisis with respect to this traditional meaning of national power. Without doubt these weapons greatly enhance the importance of national defense in the hierarchy of services which the nation-state seeks to provide, but their excessive power and the growing ease of delivering them to targets has created almost insoluble problems of national security for all major nations. The holocaustic nature of the war they now make possible seems to transcend the purposes for which most wars have been fought in the past. Most important of all, their power and the ease of delivering them to any target area in the world have dealt a deathblow to the traditional arguments of nations that they could protect their inhabitants from devastating military attack in time of war. In the words of John Herz, the historic possibility of achieving military impermeability of the nation-state in time of war is gone. The ring has been broken. The shell has been cracked by the absolute weapon, and the thin hopes for the survival of national societies depend today on the degree of their moral self-restraint, their political prudence, and their common fear, which the weapons themselves have made necessary.

The last few decades have seen an extraordinary growing callousness among civilized men with respect to instruments of massdestruction. At the outset of World War II, it was President Roosevelt who appealed to all belligerents to avoid insensate attacks upon civilian populations. Yet within five years, the United States itself had taken the lead in "strategic" bombings of metropolitan areas on a scale which made earlier Nazi attacks upon Coventry, Plymouth, and London appear trivial. Many religious leaders, including the late Pope Pius XII, have sought to condemn the use of nuclear weapons except as instruments of retaliation. But military leaders both within the Soviet Union and the United States have made it clear that these weapons would be used in any major war. They have adapted their military strategies to include their prominent use, and no widespread sense of moral outrage has arisen against these developments. Quite probably one reason why this moral outrage has not been more widespread or vocal in the West has been the awareness of the West's heavy dependence upon unconventional weapons and its incapacity to compete successfully with the U.S.S.R. in conventional weapons without threatening the basis of a civilian way of life. Also, the political effectiveness of such expressions of moral outrage would probably make little impression upon the policies of totalitarian states, even though their effects upon the democracies might be very substantial. Advocates of unilateral nuclear disarmament, like Lord Russell, have stressed the need for biological survival of the species, but can only argue with difficulty that such a policy would notably improve chances for cultural survival.

A particularly curious novelty which nuclear weapons have

introduced into world politics arises from the increased vulnerability of the very states which possess nuclear weapons. Like all
earlier types of weapons, the atomic bomb is no respecter of nations or persons. Unlike more modest means of destruction, however, nuclear weapons, by virtue of the threat which they pose to
potential victims, confer upon their possessors risks of quick and
grave retaliation in kind. The presence within any nation-state of
nuclear weapons and of bases from which they are launched may
thus be seen as an invitation to nuclear attack by other states
which fear their use against themselves. To be sure, if today either
the Soviet Union or the United States did not possess nuclear
weapons and the other did, there would be no certainty that nuclear weapons would not be employed in war or that the very
presence of the bomb would not exert a profoundly disturbing
effect upon their relations at all times. But there can be no doubt
that, in the long run, the nations which today possess nuclear
weapons share with all others their dreadful dangers. In this sense,
the technological civilization required to produce such weapons is
far more open to destruction by nuclear weapons than less industrially advanced, agrarian, decentralized cultures. Significantly,
those nations least threatened by nuclear weapons lie, for the
most part, in the Southern Hemisphere, and they will probably
continue to be less vulnerable; for not only are the possessors of
nuclear weapons today those nations which are most industrially
advanced, but since they represent a highly developed state of the
technological arts, they therefore provide better targets.

We may say that world politics has arrived at a point where
a condition of nuclear egalitarianism is theoretically possible. The
possibility could become reality when nuclear weapons and adequate delivery systems are so widely diffused among nations that
each (regardless of striking differences in other kinds of domestic
power) is equal in its capacity to kill any other. This circumstance
is not only historically unprecedented and terrifying, but bewildering, since it throws many of our customary analyses of political
and military power awry. To be sure, widespread ownership of

mass-destruction weapons does not mean equality of power among states. It "merely" means equality of possession of the most dangerous form of power of all—the power to coerce by the threat to kill. In the history of political thought, this particular power has always been regarded as the supreme power, the power which political societies have left unregulated at their great peril.

THE DILEMMA OF POWER
IN A NUCLEAR AGE

This prophesied nightmare of nuclear egalitarianism should not lead us to think that if many or most states were someday in possession of nuclear weapons, they would then and therefore be equally powerful. True national power implies broad flexibility of behavior, broad choices among wide ranges of techniques by which states may seek to accomplish their purposes. Merely acquiring nuclear weapons or other mass destruction devices might seemingly enhance the prestige of their possessors (hence the scramble of states, now notably France and China, to enter the "nuclear club"), but power means far more than the capacity to kill—or "overkill." A state whose chief defense capability consisted of the possession of such weapons and the means of delivery might well discover itself utterly unable to act purposefully when faced with problems calling for far more limited, or more benign and constructive responses. A classic instance of the flexibility of American military power can be seen in the Berlin air-lift of 1948-9. The Soviet blockade of West Berlin threatened either to strangle the city and cause its surrender to the Communists or to precipitate a Central European land war had the United States not discovered its capacity to supply the city via the air-lift. One might conclude that a broad-gauged defense arm, coupled with many other resources of diplomacy and technology, may actually serve to circumvent situations which otherwise might lead to war. (At the outset of the blockade, General Clay and other military men had urged President Truman to send an armored train through to Berlin on the ground corridor, an act which certainly threatened to result in war.)

National power has taken on a new meaning for all states which possess or are on the threshold of possessing nuclear weapons. It may, in fact, be defined as the capacity to achieve foreign policy goals *without* recourse to nuclear weapons. For the use of nuclear weapons, by inviting retaliation in kind, may be regarded not only as supremely unethical, but an admission of utter failure and political bankruptcy since retaliation could easily mean the very obliteration of the society which first made use of them.

There is indeed an ironic aspect to the problem of national defense which all nuclear powers share. Since the advent of the airplane, airborne missiles, and the atomic bomb, the advantage in military strategy has shifted massively from defensive to offensive weapons systems; but at the same time, the self-protective features of the offensive weapons themselves are far more highly developed than the self-protection they afford the society possessing them. In the past ten years, far greater effort has been expended, by both America and Russia, in developing their offensive weapons and in finding methods of shielding these against so-called pre-emptive or preventive attack than has been expended in finding ways of protecting their respective societies against direct attack. The great vulnerability of metropolitan target areas within nation-states contrasts ironically with the considerable relative invulnerability of armed forces themselves. This peculiar circumstance is common to all nuclear powers, whose armed forces for over a decade have, by tactics and strategies of dispersion and protection, prepared themselves against nuclear attacks in a way that a complex civilization could not. Techniques of armed forces dispersal to avoid a "clustering" which might invite nuclear obliteration are not paralleled today by dispersal of the urban life of large industrialized states. Thus the shield itself, once the most vulnerable part of a nation, is far more adequately protected than the society which it is supposed to protect. The Polaris submarines, secreted in the vastnesses of the sea, capable on an instant's notice of dealing savage destruction to an enemy, are protected in a manner unparalleled within society itself.

As the vulnerability of society to demolition has increased, so has the invulnerability of mass destruction weapons. Let us go even further to recount this strange development. It is also the case that *governments* are actively seeking ways to become less vulnerable to mass destruction. To permit the continuation of governmental functioning after a nuclear exchange, the United States has already established a "shadow structure" of government: alternative loci of executive and even Congressional authority and a shadow bureaucracy which could spring into the breach if its "real" counterpart were to be obliterated. To be sure, we see the practical necessities for such measures. Civil anarchy would be sure to follow in the wake of nuclear exchanges if civil authority disappeared: that is, if only the "non-governmental" sector remained. But the irony remains: the most efficacious measures to shelter and protect the nation are those no society could adopt without a massive cultural transformation which few consider worthwhile. The liberal and humane tradition of the West, which has always considered government an artifact created by the people for the people, may thus have reached a philosophic impasse from which there is no real retreat unless there is some positive issue from the arms race.

A wholly new condition of politics might well have been reached when technology and the science of human management devise "systems" of defense, of governmental, administrative, and technological skills which, relatively immune to mass destruction could simply recreate society after massive nuclear exchanges. The post-war experience of West Germany testifies to the speed with which a highly technologized administrative and industrial system can be rebuilt on the massive ruins of an old physical plant and, within fifteen years, offer the *surviving* population standards of living far in excess of those enjoyed by its pre-war population. It has been said that it took Germany two centuries to recover economically from the Thirty Years' War, but only fifteen years to recover from World War II, which was physically far more destructive.

This is not to say that similar recuperative capabilities could await a society whose physical plant was subjected to nuclear holocaust, but rather that some of us may underestimate the recuperative powers of technological and managerial authorities, a point which Herman Kahn has raised in his *On Thermonuclear War*.[2] Some may be comforted by such skeptical reassurances, which suggest that much more might await a nuclearized state than mere reversion to barbarism. The comfort might seem colder when we reflect that possibly this technological and managerial vigor, given such ample opportunity to come into play when more organic parts of society were simply vulcanized, would represent the triumph of the same forces which already have so greatly contributed to our present dilemma of power.

THE PACE OF TECHNOLOGICAL CHANGE

The contemporary problem of national power cannot be adequately discussed without pointing to another of its peculiarly modern characteristics: the tempo of change in the material, scientific, and technological aspects of military power. Until the mid-nineteenth century, the pace at which new scientific or technological innovations were injected into the military forces of states was incredibly slow by contemporary standards. The pace at which such innovations affected basic military strategies was equally slow. Historians and students of military strategy invariably point to the radical effect which the introduction of gunpowder and firearms had upon the military and political order of West Eurpoean society. What is often overlooked, however, is the *gradual* manner in which these innovations came to be felt and appreciated.

Between the fourteenth and nineteenth centuries, the chief

---

[2] Herman Kahn, *On Thermonuclear War*. Princeton: Princeton University Press, 1960.

alterations in military power and effectiveness came from organizational and managerial changes rather than technological ones. Two such prominent historical alterations are: the famed *levée en masse* of the French Revolution—the radical military innovation which meant, in effect, the mobilization of the nation itself to fight wars; and second, the administrative nationalization of armed forces which accompanied the rise of the modern, dynastic, sovereign state (exemplified by the Prussian army reorganization in the eighteenth and early nineteenth centuries). Until quite recently, the chief impulses to military change have been managerial and sociological, but this is no longer true. Indeed over the past half century, new technological devices and weapons systems have been introduced into the armed forces of modern states at such a swift pace that a certain technological determinism seems to have come into play, forcing states to reevaluate constantly the character of their defense forces and often to revise them radically to meet, not merely new external threats, but the major threat of scientific and technical obsolescence.

This rapid pace of technological change must be appreciated in three general aspects: the enhanced tempo at which new weapons and new weapons systems are invented; the tempo by which strategic doctrines of nations accommodate themselves to such changes; and finally, the tempo at which the knowledge about such weapons and the ability to produce them is diffused among nations.

In the past fifteen years, certain political and cultural restraints have slowed down the actual rate of technological innovation in weapons and weapons systems, just as they have slowed the pace at which nations revise strategic doctrines to adjust to such weapons. One dramatic example of the former can be seen in the field of chemical and biological weapons development where, as Herman Kahn has pointed out, "progress" has been considerably "retarded" due to some American scientists' ethical repugnance toward biological warfare. There has also been powerful political pressure, both in the Soviet Union and the United

States, inside and outside their respective military establishments, which slows down the pace of innovation. (Witness, for instance, the powerful opposition within the Eisenhower Administration to the Gaither Report in 1957, which urged a massive acceleration of American efforts in developing its ICBM program and constructing radiation shelters.)[3]

The Smaller Powers

By and large such social and political restraints on the arms race should not cause us to lose an historical perspective on the total problem of innovation in the arms race. The massive budgets of the Soviet Union and the United States for weapons development are well enough known. Less familiar, however, are the research and development programs of smaller powers. Today 25 nations spend between a million and a billion dollars a year on national defense. This number is likely to grow rather than diminish. Underdeveloped nations may be hard-pressed to channel investment into peaceful areas of the economy and this restrains their participation in the arms race at a pace relatively commensurate with that of the U.S. and the U.S.S.R. It is still the case that many smaller powers, including those in underdeveloped areas, will share with the great powers the burden of nuclear weapons and other modern weapons systems. This is particularly true of totalitarian regimes within the less developed Soviet world which, like China, command the domestic power to shift resources forcibly to military purposes on a scale unimaginable in freer or less authoritarian systems like India.

In the arms race, we see that while the Soviet Union and the United States command striking leads over all other nations in weaponry, and seem because of their resources and pace of development to be increasing their qualitative leads, it is nevertheless only a matter of decades before a very large number of smaller

[3] Morton Halperin, "The Gaither Committee and the Policy Process," *World Politics*, April 1961, pp. 360-84.

nations can acquire very impressive and destructive strategic forces and acquire at the same time the political tensions and insecurities which possession of such weaponry entails. Herman Kahn has suggested the possibility that by the year 2000, at least fifty small nations might have developed "rather impressive" strategic forces, including means of delivery of nuclear weapons to remote targets.[4]

The pace at which nuclear weaponry is disseminated, barring international agreements, will accelerate with the passage of time. Yet what is equally important is the likelihood that if present rates of economic growth continue indefinitely in both the West and in the Communist bloc, the amount of gross national product available for military programs will most likely increase also. Some thoughtful commentators like Lord Russell[5] have suggested that an indefinite continuation of the arms race would lead inexorably (barring, of course, a nuclear holocaust) to mutual impoverishment, as states were forced to have recourse to ever more costly weapons systems. Recent experiences in both the United States and the Soviet Union do not bear this out. During thirteen years of cold war both the United States and its Western allies have seen a steady growth of living standards of spectacular proportions. What is more likely is that the search for abundance and for thermonuclear or other massive destructive capabilities are, unfortunately, quite compatible. Each feeds upon each. As war and technological progress are closely wedded to each other, so defense expenditures for war and general economic growth seem closely linked.

Undeniably, international tensions between the Communist and Western blocs since the mid-1950's have also heightened concern about the need for all forms of economic growth, both

[4] Herman Kahn, "The Arms Race and World Order," in *The Revolution in World Politics*, edited by Morton Kaplan. New York: John Wiley and Sons, 1962, pp. 335-336.
[5] See his *Common Sense and Nuclear Warfare*. New York: Simon and Schuster, 1959, p. 20: "Unless our disputes are brought within reasonable proportions, the populations of the most powerful nations and their followers will be willing to reduce themselves to starvation level in the search for means of injuring each other."

within the two committed camps and in the neutral zones of the world as well. What is now evident even in the Soviet Union is that *despite* heightened defense efforts, considerable progress in consumer industries is anticipated and probably inevitable. Even in the Soviet Union, given present rates of economic growth, very spectacular increases in future defense budgets can parallel dramatic increases in both investment and consumption; the same is true of the United States.[6]

THE PRESENT INSTABILITY OF POWER

Most thoughtful students of international affairs would agree that the present distribution of power, influence, and prestige in world politics—however difficult to measure—is highly unstable and certainly transitory. Power and influence may be measured with various gauges: the now-fashionable yardstick of gross national product (GNP), or the capabilities of military defense systems. The present distribution of power can also be measured by quite subjective standards: by the opinions which influential men have about power. Power may also be gauged by results, or the ability of states to accomplish what they set out to do. But whatever measure we use, of this we may be sure: that the present condition, that of the early 1960's, cannot long endure, even if there is no major war. And it is this general awareness of possible transiency which contributes so greatly to international insecurity and tensions. (In his interview with Khrushchev in 1959, Walter Lippman noted the wide gulf between his own idea of the "*status quo*" and that of the Soviet Premier. For Khrushchev, the *status quo* meant maintenance of the present pace of political change in world politics, not maintenance of the existing order, which could not be maintained anyway. The idea of an "existing" order makes no sense to a Bolshevik.)[7]

[6] See Charles Hitch and Roland McKean, *The Economics of Defense in the Nuclear Age*. Cambridge: Harvard University Press, 1960, Ch. 6, and particularly pp. 98 100.
[7] Walter Lippmann, *The Communist World and Ours*. Boston: Atlantic-Little, Brown, 1959, p. 13.

Since World War II, there have been profound changes, both quantitative and qualitative, in the distribution of power in the international community. Some of these changes, notably the spectacular economic recovery of Western Europe and the Chinese Communist revolution, were not anticipated, nor was the Cuban Castro revolution of 1958. Anticipated yet unappreciated in its dimensions was the pace with which the former colonies of European powers acquired their independence and began to act as new international entities. These changes remarkably diminished the preponderance enjoyed by both Russia and America in the first years after World War II. A particularly noticeable result was the shift of political influence within the United Nations away from the older states of the West to the new states of Asia and Africa.

Within the Communist orbit alone, equally momentous and unanticipated changes occurred. Commencing in 1948, the almost monolithic dominion enjoyed by the Soviet Union and the Bolshevik party during Stalin's time over Communist states and apparatuses abroad began to pass. Insofar as one might have spoken of a Communist international order in 1945, this was one dominated by the Kremlin and thus, in turn, dominated by the interests of the Socialist homeland, the U.S.S.R. Yet as the Chinese regime grew in power within the Communist world during the 1950's, it grew in doctrinal influence as well, exerting through its own diplomacy, its economic policies, and its pronouncements on Marxism and international affairs, a growing influence upon Communist policy, even in areas like Eastern Europe where, in Stalin's day, the Soviet Union was pre-eminent.

Many Westerners, observing these changes within the Soviet camp, discerned one feature of the new Communist polity which boded novelty for the future: since the dissolution of the Communist International in 1943, there was no supranational entity in the Communist world, no comprehensive, institutional framework to exert authority over an ever-broadening political system. A new Communist society of nations was emerging, containing seeds of discord and potential anarchy quite similar to those of the older bourgeois society of nations which Communism was supposed to supplant. The picture of a Soviet Union not master of its own house became one which Westerners might view with cynical pleasure and irony. What was not comfortable to contemplate was the possibility that this dwindling authority of the Soviet Union over the total affairs of international Communism might, in and of itself, create new problems for the West.

The mounting doctrinal dispute between the two giants of the Communist world, Russia and China, whatever else it might portend, began to accentuate a competition in Marxist orthodoxy. Each now sought to maintain authority and influence among Communist parties and ideologues elsewhere in the world through display of its own revolutionary élan. The dispute between Mao and Khrushchev ranged over such doctrinal matters as the inevitability of war, the revolutionary role of military aggression and subversion, and the manner of the allegedly inevitable transition of the non-Communist world to the Marxist cause. This dispute was no private matter. It was—and is—conducted under the watchful eyes of the whole world; and the outcome, like that of the Stalin-Trotsky struggle in the 1920's, might well shape decisively the emerging character of the Communist world. To be sure, during all of this time, the Soviet Union has waxed in strength and in influence in areas of the world where a more parochial, Stalinist Russia remained either impotent or essentially disinterested. Russia's mounting prestige in science and technology now supplements, if it does not supplant, the prestige which in its weaker, earlier days of the 1930's and 1920's, it had derived from being the sole territorial stronghold of Marxist revolution. The pace of its economic growth, particularly its visible accomplishments in heavy industry, have augmented its influence and prestige among many of the elite in underdeveloped countries, some of whom now see it as a more appropriate model to emulate than the American economy. Yet the position of unassailable supremacy in the Communist world has, for Russia, passed.

Lenin once said that the path to Paris lay through Peking. We can see in retrospect that *both* the shift of world politics away from Europe to Asia and the mounting successes of Communist China in Asia hastened the end of Russia's dominion and the Bolshevik Party's monopoly over Communist affairs. A Communist world composed solely of Russia and contiguous satellites, like those of Eastern Europe, was at least manageable. Even Tito really failed to challenge Stalin's monopoly of power in Eastern Europe successfully.

AMERICAN PRE-EMINENCE IN THE FIFTIES

If the Soviets' position in world affairs has altered markedly since World War II, so has that of the United States. On the eve of peace in 1945, the Soviet Union bestrode the greater part of the Eurasian subcontinent, and Soviet authority in the Communist world was absolutely unchallenged. Although the Soviet Union was physically shattered by the effects of Hitler's invasion, it was by no means organizationally demolished. On the other hand, the United States emerged from World War II militarily victorious. It was supreme among its Western allies, most of whom, like France, had been crushed in the war against Germany. Its physical plant and economic productivity were not only unscathed by war but had been enormously augmented by the experience of total war.

Between 1940 and 1950, the United States reigned supreme among the Western nations. Its economic power was used to reconstruct Europe and the world economy, and its military arsenal held a monopoly of nuclear power, thus surpassing the Soviet military force in destructive capacity. America's influence upon its European allies in defense matters was due to its preeminence in military technology and the inability of these allies to defend themselves against Soviet aggression individually or collectively, without America.

The giant-like proportions of the United States, as late as

1950, could be seen in the massive statistics of its annual industrial productivity, which in some activities (such as automobile production) exceeded the rest of the whole world combined. Because of its possession during much of this decade of a military capacity to destroy its major adversary in the cold war without fear of retaliation *in kind*, America's traditional hemispheric invulnerability remained pretty much a fact until well into the 1950's. There was little danger of a serious extra-hemispheric attack upon the continental United States. On the other hand, American retaliatory power, manifest in the Strategic Air Command, could deal devastating blows to any major enemy, notably, the U.S.S.R. There were, to be sure, supremely important ethical and political restraints upon the exercise of this power. These combined with prudent considerations such as America's relationship with its allies to prevent the use of these weapons at a time when, from a narrow technical point of view they might have been used with maximum effectiveness. Such restraints, however, did not inhibit the steady augmentation of nuclear weaponry. In the Western Hemisphere, despite its difficulties with Perón's Argentina, despite mounting anti-American sentiment particularly among intellectuals, and despite growing social and economic tensions to the south, the United States remained politically supreme, the uncontested leader of the Americas in world politics. Impoverished, culturally distant from the United States, and subject to constant cycles of revolution and dictatorship, most of Latin America, effectively excluded from the modern world of industrialization and economic growth, remained a back yard of American diplomacy, an object of pity and often derision, virtually forgotten in the great crises of Asia and Europe.

The U.S. in the U.N.

Above all, in the early days of the United Nations, until the Korean war, America's pre-eminence in international organizations was virtually uncontested in vital matters pertaining to the cold war. There were naturally limits to the degree of influence which the United States, before 1955, could exert upon the course of affairs in the United Nations. (The Soviet veto, for instance, was able to paralyze important functions of the Security Council.) Yet many Americans, perhaps rightly, viewed the U.N. and many of its subsidiary organizations as agencies through which American national purposes, whether economic, cultural, political, or military, could be channeled.

In 1949, for instance, when NATO was widely debated in the United States, many intelligent critics objected to the proposed alliance on the grounds that it would by-pass the U.N., that is, take upon itself international security functions which the U.N. supposedly was to perform. To be sure, this argument was even then sorely vitiated by the inability of the U.N. Security Council to function against one of its permanent members, the U.S.S.R. But the argument made one kind of sense: the composition of the U.N. membership in 1949 was still essentially European-Western. In 1950, following the Communist attack upon the Republic of Korea, the United States was able to muster a sizable majority in the Security Council *and* the General Assembly to legitimate its own defense of Korea in the name of the U.N. The subsequent enlargement of the U.N. to include large numbers of new Afro-Asian states makes it quite difficult to imagine any conceivable circumstances in the future in which the U.N. would legitimate or lend material assistance to any American military venture, defensive or otherwise, in the cold war. Thus the Security Council and General Assembly, whatever their other present roles in international affairs, could hardly be seen today as agencies through which Western collective security measures could be undertaken.

In matters of colonialism, of self-determination for new nations, and of economic development in the Afro-Asian area there were, to be sure, visible restraints upon American influence in the U.N. before 1950. Still the U.N. served as an effective agency through which measures to resist the spread of Communism could be undertaken and within which disputes among states in the non-Communist world could be subjected to negotiation and peaceful settlement. The U.N. likewise served the important purpose of diminishing international tensions within the non-Communist world (as for instance in the Pakistan-Indian Kashmir dispute).

With the passage of time, American influence diminished notably even in the U.N. The admission of new member states from the Afro-Asian world (which had been seriously underrepresented) markedly affected the kinds of issues with which the U.N. was confronted, as well as the tone of the organization in general. In 1945, the United States, together with Britain, the Commonwealth nations, the West European nations, and Latin American states, combined to form an overwhelming majority of the U.N. members. All of these were undeniably Western in their political outlook: most could recall generations, if not centuries, of self-government. All of them save some Latin American dictatorships manifested some degree of consistent adherence to constitutionalism, to parliamentary democracy, and to the values of Western open society. They were, in a sense, "old" to the society of nations. Among them, the United States could still pose as a relative newcomer and a revolutionary new state founded upon principles of liberalism, enjoying a far more abundant life and more democratic institutions and customs.

In the early days of the cold war, these states, notably the more highly industrialized states of the West Europe-North Atlantic area, formed the nucleus of the United Nations. To be sure, there were conflicts between them and the United States (as for instance over the matter of common policy towards the emerging states of Asia and Africa). Yet taken together they comprised a "cold war consensus." (They were the same cluster of Western communities which had formed the core of the struggle against Nazi totalitarianism in World War II.) While many of them, as we have noted, had come out of World War II seriously crippled, still their political centers of gravity lay in the middle, between the extreme Right and extreme Left. On the European continent, in Scandinavia and Western Europe, this "middle" comprised, immediately after the war, Socialists, Christian Democrats, and Liberals. Thus political stability within them sprang not from conservatism or authoritarianism but from moderate, welfare-state reformism.

Above all, we should bear in mind that the very institutional form of the U.N.—its legislative-parliamentary form, its broad schematic outlines of distribution of power, its provisions for membership, its provisions for parliamentary free speech—these characteristics were analogous to the political institutions which Europe itself, during the nineteenth and twentieth centuries, had developed and brought to maturity. They also reflected certain basic American ethical concerns about international politics as well. By inference, they stood in massive contradiction to the political behavior and principles of the totalitarian states which, by definition, could brook no public, open debate on public policy nor tolerate the open expression of divergent views on matters of any kind.

The Gradual Decline of American Political Influence

To summarize briefly, American political power seems to have been at its apex in 1945. It had then the largest military establishment in history—12,000,000 men under arms, a navy and air force greater than those of all other nations combined, and a monopoly on nuclear weapons. It had, too, an unscathed, gigantic economy, a position of unchallenged political-military supremacy in the entire Pacific and the Western Hemisphere, abundant food and material resources to assist the reconstruction of devastated areas, etc. Possibly in all history there was no precedent for such extraordinary influence and strength. Possibly too, there was no precedent either for the swift, *relative* reduction of political power in such a short time.

The swift demobilization of the American military establishment between 1945 and 1946 sharply diminished one crucial element of American strength. By 1948, American conventional land forces in Europe, the crucial center of tensions between America and Russia, were greatly outmatched by Soviet weapons and armies. The Anglo-American monopoly on nuclear weapons ended in 1949. Barely five years after the first nuclear explosions at Almagordo, the Soviet Union successfully tested its own nuclear device. And while America retained supremacy in air power during the 1950's, it, too, was gravely threatened by Soviet accomplishments with intercontinental ballistic missiles. Indeed the pace of Soviet progress in weapons development by the early 1960's brought Soviet military power to a state of near parity with America. Now only a delicate balance of terror—parity to deliver a devastating attack—could serve as a point of departure for debates on national defense. By the early 1960's, military competition between the West and the U.S.S.R. was proceeding along qualitative lines of weapons-system innovation and newer scientific advances. The Western nations remained in a relatively inferior position to the U.S.S.R. in conventional weapons. It was this inferior position in weapons of less than total war which created one serious defect in American military defense: the lack of adequate military power to deal with less than total crises with less than total means.

American power also altered markedly during the 1950's with respect to the shifting problems of international politics which came to the forefront in Asia and Africa. In the European crisis which followed World War II, American power had proved sufficient to help reestablish a constitutional, humane, and prosperous West European order. American economic aid under the Marshall Plan, coupled with American support of political forces of moderation and reform, managed to strengthen and revive Western Europe and weaken the powerful Communist movements in both Italy and France. Here, in the traditional center of European culture, society seemed to respond to such treatment. The existing structure of European society proved, at the same time, capable of pressing forward itself to new heights of productivity and prosperity. In retrospect, the American effort to restore a vigorous Europe and to facilitate its economic and political integration paid off. Even in Western Germany, after twelve years of Hitler's totalitarianism, a stable political order, dominated by a moderate two-party system, came into being and began in the 1950's to integrate itself into a new European economic order.

In Europe, the very success of American postwar policies diminished American political influence. The spectacular burst of European productivity and prosperity which began in the early 1950's ended Europe's dependence on the United States for economic support. Strong political leverage provided by American economic power, which had been at the disposal of American policy-makers at the time of the Marshall Plan, was correspondingly diminished. Indeed, such was the shift of relationships between Europe and America in the late 1950's that the seemingly perennial problem of the dollar gap (the persistent excess of European imports from America over its exports to America) was reversed. Thus in 1960, the United States found itself faced with exactly the opposite problem: the reversed dollar gap, and the surprisingly large outflow of American gold to Europe to rectify the new imbalance of payments.

Such was the price of success. In the halcyon days of the Marshall Plan, it had been the aim of American policy in Europe to free its allies from abject dependence on American aid, to restore their productivity and their sense of self-reliance. To this end, also, American policies in Europe had sought, notably in the early 1950's, to encourage Western Europe's economic integration through such institutions as the O.E.E.C., the European Coal and Steel Community, and the European Common Market. During the Marshall Plan period, American aid became an important lever to create in Europe a mass-market analogous to that in the United States, in which greater competition and vastly enlarged market opportunities could enhance Europe's economic strength and productivity. One chief consequence of this waxing European economic strength and self-reliance was a strengthening of the whole Western alliance and the enhancement of political stability throughout Western Europe. The worlds of Asia, Africa, and Latin America were in revolutionary turmoil, in many places threatened by Communist or totalitarian seizure through subversion. But Western Europe, stripped of its overseas colonies, carved out a new economic role in the world. It abandoned the once intense political rivalries which had torn it apart in the 1930's and seemed now to have decisively rejected the totalitarian alternative of political order.

In this new European order, some Americans saw, along with a confirmation of earlier American hopes, a decisive refutation of Marxist theory and doctrine. Here, in the most highly industrialized theater of international politics, industrialization and modern technology had not pushed European societies over the brink of revolution into Communism as Marx had predicted. Indeed, the new European welfare states proved to be strong bastions against Soviet totalitarianism. The temptation was great in the United States to enlarge and tighten American links with its European allies in a world where deepening political upheavals had elsewhere rendered illusory the hope that independence, national self-determination, and freedom from colonial rule were necessary first steps towards democracy. Elsewhere it was by no means certain that economic development and social reform could both be achieved by non-totalitarian methods and accomplished also without the estrangement of new states from the constitutional and humane traditions of the West.

American power had proved adequate to cope with the internal crises of Western Europe in the early postwar years but not with the crises between Europe and the non-Western societies now freeing themselves from Western tutelage and colonialism. After 1950, the active theaters of the cold war shifted from Europe, where the threat of Soviet invasion and Communist subversion had originally been greatest in the 1940's, to areas of revolution and political transition in the Middle East, Southeast Asia, and Africa. This tension was coextensive with the tension and conflict between the emerging nations and their former European masters. After the beginning of the Korean War, in those places where America accelerated its program of building containing walls of military power around the peripheries of the Soviet world, there arose also wholly unexpected tensions between the United States and many of these new nations. American insistence that they choose sides in the cold war was, for many of them, an annoying distraction from their own pressing internal problems of economic growth and political stability. To complicate matters further, the swift intrusion of American military power into areas such as the Middle East, North Africa, Pakistan, and Southeast Asia after 1950 provided new sources of tension between these countries and the United States.

The presence of foreign military power may be feared and respected, but it is rarely liked by its recipients, even when its purposes may seem benign. American power, when injected into these new nations as part of an American containment policy, came to be widely resented as confirming evidence of America's "imperialist" role in Asia. In Southeast Asia and also in the Middle East, the attempts of American policy-makers to build local defense systems against Soviet attack frequently had the ironic side-effect of disrupting power relationships among local non-Communist regimes and acutely exacerbating local political tensions. U.S. military aid to Pakistan, for instance, threatened to unbalance the delicate equipoise between India and Pakistan; military aid to certain Arab states in the Middle East, notably to Iraq before 1958, threatened the delicate equipoise between Israel and the surrounding Arab world and the uneasy balance among rival Arab states such as Egypt, Syria, Jordan, and Saudi Arabia.

America and the Emerging Nations

In areas of tumultuous social and political change which extended from Southeast Asia to the Atlantic coast of Africa, American policy came abreast of massive, complex, and often utterly insoluble problems. In the halcyon days of isolationism, Americans had often prided themselves upon their own revolutionary traditions; they held their own national heroes up to a watching world of colonial and subject peoples as prototypes for emulation. Washington, Lincoln, Jefferson, and Wilson had inspired Bolivars and Masaryks, Kossuths and Garibaldis and hosts of less eminent political figures to revolt against the dominant forces of the European great powers. But it is one thing to pose as liberators and free men without concern for the immediate political consequences of revolution (for what American seriously bothered, before 1914, about the political consequences of the disruption of the Austro-Hungarian Empire or the possible ramifications of the collapse of European authority in the non-Western world?). It is another to undermine imperial authority or to liberate subject peoples when much of the consequences of revolution would lie at one's own front door.

In the wake of World War II, American foreign policy first came up against this grave dilemma in the areas of Southeast Asia where European colonial authority and Japanese imperial control were suddenly being swept away. In Indochina and the Dutch East Indies, both liberated from Japanese occupation by American power, the sudden vacuum of power first posed this issue most dramatically. The United States might conceivably have solved this dilemma of power by assuming the imperial mantle; but it did not seek to do this. The problem it then faced was how to affect favorably the political destinies of the former colonial areas without alienating, on the one hand, America's European friends and allies and, on the other, the new forces of nationalism which had grown in strength during the war. In Indochina it vacillated, torn between its European ally, France, and the claims and demands of the nationalist forces of Indochina (still relatively independent of Soviet control). Thus much of Indochina was finally lost to Communist control. In Indonesia, America acted ultimately with greater resolution, putting the weight of American influence behind the Indonesian nationalists and deeply antagonizing the Dutch. This pattern of painful choice was often repeated elsewhere—in the Middle East, in North Africa, in sub-Saharan Africa.

In a cold war which compelled the Soviet Union to display its own support for colonial nationalist movements, the United States often found its own military and economic resources inadequate to the task of coping with a massive revolution in backward areas, whose object was to break the traditional political ties which had joined them to the West. Unquestionably, the pace of colonial revolt and independence, already at high momentum because of the disruptions of World War II, was further speeded up by certain unique features of the cold war. For, from an ideological point of view, both Marxism and American Liberalism rejected Western colonialism as ethically repugnant. Both had assumed its inevitable demise, if for quite different reasons. Inexorably, then, both had to taste the fruits of their own prophecies. The new elite of non-Western, non-Soviet worlds, aware of this new condition, in turn raised their own expectations and demands to new heights.

SELF-DETERMINATION Added to this particular dilemma of American power was the problem of the internal features of the new regimes. The rush of new regimes to statehood and membership in the international community after 1950 posed serious problems for American policy and for the West as a whole. The official American hope (and often expectation) was that these new states, in acquiring independence, might not only forge domestic institutions capable of administering social and economic reform and avoiding political chaos, but would do so with a minimum of demagoguery and xenophobia, and with the possibility of ultimately taking on the substance and form of Western democracy. But self-determination was not so simple.

Self-determination, so fond a piece of American liberal doctrine, may well have been a principle which had to be inexorably conceded to the aspirations of nationalist movements in the Afro-Asian world. But the principle, like the contents of Pandora's box, could not be controlled—at least not by American influence and power—once it was let loose. The fission of old empires into innumerable small states posed for much of the underdeveloped world the dismaying possibility of Balkanization: permanent fragmentation into small and vulnerable state entities which, like the succession states to the Ottoman Empire in Eastern Europe, might themselves become prey to other new imperialisms. In many parts of the underdeveloped world as, for instance, India, one major difficulty arose precisely because the self in self-determination was a matter of passionate, local disagreement. Liberation from Europe's imperial control merely liberated political violence about who was to succeed Europe.

India was the classic case. Indian independence in 1947 was followed by violent and traumatic civil war between India's two major cultural entities, the Moslems and Hindus. Elsewhere, as in the Middle East, it became all too clear that the "selves" which had achieved their independence of Europe were all too often mere artificial geographical entities which the colonial powers themselves had earlier arbitrarily carved out of the map, often in disregard of broader political and cultural movements and forces such as Pan-Arabism.

The Hashemite Kingdom of Jordan is one such instance, a kingdom carved out of the desert in World War I by Anglo-French agreements and governed before and after its independence in 1947 by a British puppet ruler, a British Brigadier, and British-trained Bedouins. Yet the arbitrary character of Jordan as a territorial entity is matched by most, if not all, of the new states of Africa. In the Middle East, as was common in all areas of Europe before the advent of the dynastic and national state, cultures and peoples were not arbitrarily boxed into firm, finite, territorial entities. Not surprisingly, when the Middle Eastern states acquired their independence from Europe after World War II, a mounting struggle began among them to see which would unite the cultural world of the Arabs.

In many of the new successor states, liberation and self-determination likewise posed (as they had earlier on the European continent) major problems concerning important ethnic or cultural groupings which now found themselves suddenly in a minority status within the new states. Under the old imperial orders of the European powers, many of these minorities once maintained their own cultural and political status as consequence of imperial protection. The advent of independence thus, for many of them, imperiled their own security in a new political order often indifferent to their rights and their claims for cultural survival.

Presumably one paramount American hope with respect to these new states was that such cultural and constitutional difficulties would prove to be transitional problems, not permanent political albatrosses. American foreign aid, growing in volume during the 1950's, became one form of leverage which American policy could use to mitigate these transitional crises. But the purposes of economic aid were too multifaceted to be tied to this single goal of local, constitutional pacification. In some instances (witness, for instance, Eric Johnson's abortive plan for a Middle Eastern T.V.A. to reconcile Israel and its hostile Arab neighbors in a joint program of land reclamation and water-power exploitation) American aid offers proved inadequate for calming troubled political waters. Economic aid had been quite effective in Western Europe in bringing about regional economic integration and lessening political rivalries. But all too frequently in underdeveloped areas it proved an absurdly inadequate device for reconciling local, political forces which disagreed about such fundamental constitutional issues as whether a political entity does, or does not, have a right to exist.

THE PRESSURE TO ALIGN These particular problems of transition were germane to broader American objectives in international politics, not so much because of particular American vested interests in the areas, but because the unrest and violence, overt or latent, affected the broader balance of power in world politics. (Several types of vested interests proved exceptions to this rule. In the Middle East, by 1948, the state of Israel and important American oil interests both severely attenuated America's "objectivity" in its dealings with the Arab states. Both had important domestic supporters in the United States which, at crucial times, exerted powerful influence over successive American administrations.) The future political orientation of these states in world politics was a critical matter. Their future political and economic relationships towards the Western and Soviet blocs could decisively affect the outcome of the cold war. Related to this problem, but not entirely identical, was the question of the character of their internal regimes: notably, whether they gave promise of remaining or becoming open societies in the Western sense of the term.

These overriding questions transcended purely military considerations in the cold war. They pertained not so much to immediate exigencies of military defense as to the longer range matter of the fashionableness and appeal of totalitarianism to men poorly exposed to any form of self-government. In much of the ex-colonial world, and in all parts of the underdeveloped world including Latin America, self-government was often a euphemism for local dictatorship and tyranny; the absolutist regimes of Ibn Saud and Trujillo were familiar vestiges of an older political order of paternalistic authoritarianism. Repugnant as they were to American liberals, they still posed no serious threat to American interests other than the threat of their own precarious weakness and vulnerability to other new political currents in the underdeveloped world. If the modern states of Western Europe were threatened by Soviet Communism, these were more so. For within them new forces of political unrest and new strata of political leadership, often blind to larger issues in the cold war, threatened to acquire political power and to mobilize mass support for purposes which, precisely because of their indeterminacy, were the more perplexing and dangerous.

Yet to these familiar absolutist regimes which had flourished during the nineteenth and early twentieth centuries in the stagnant eddies of international politics, there were added, in the postwar years, new states whose future internal political development and external orientation were equally conjectural. The new governments of Egypt, Indonesia, Korea, Ceylon, India, and Pakistan, in the incipient stages of self-government, all drew heavily upon Western political institutions, techniques, and constitutional lore, even as they were rejecting the principle and fact of Western political control. Within most of them, there emerged parliamentary or presidential regimes and political parties externally similar to their Western prototypes. Typically, their constitutional orders were closely modeled upon British, French, or other Western systems. Within many of these countries too there prevailed some regard for the niceties of the democratic process: free (or at least multi-party) elections; a free (or at least multiple, non-governmental) press; and constitutional processes which, while often violated in practice, remained ideal norms against which violations could be measured.

American resources often sought to sustain and enliven these political institutions, but there were serious limitations on their power to do so. For one thing, institutions which often appeared to Americans as comforting evidence of incipient democracy, as, for instance, parliamentary institutions in Iran, often obscured the real locus of political power which lay in essentially non-democratic forces. But much more important was the fact that such Western institutions in non-Western contexts were often utterly incomprehensible and, philosophically, too alien to the historical experiences of non-Western societies to excite much popular enthusiasm. Then, too, it soon became painfully apparent that the cumbersome, slow procedures of achieving political consent in a parliamentary democracy often compared unfavorably with the ruthless efficiency of the Communist totalitarian state, or even less ambitious authoritarian systems, in achieving economic development and social change. Hence, China and India, prototypes of totalitarian and democratic political orders, began a great symbolic contest to see which might most effectively win the battle of economic growth and political effectiveness. In such a contest, American foreign aid, together with that brought to India from other sources in the free world, might prove of decisive marginal significance in launching India's planned programs of economic growth. But economic aid in and of itself was essentially limited in its own creative power precisely because, in and of itself, it could not transmit political values not already present in abundance in the recipient country.

Perhaps what most seriously limited American effectiveness was the deep, cultural gulf which separated her from Asia and the intellectual gulf which separated American policy-makers from the new policy-makers in Asia, though many of the latter were frequently quite familiar with American culture. Beginning in the early 1950's, many Americans who were disturbed by the global spread of Communism and the growing power of the U.S.S.R. envisaged America as the center of a grand coalition of free nations, universal in scope, which could contain, surround, and perhaps ultimately stultify the Communist system. Many Americans, conservatives and liberals alike, believed that American political institutions and cultural values could serve as models for other nations. During World War II, many American writers (Henry Luce of *Life* and *Time*, for instance) had a somewhat blurred yet lyrical vision of an "American Century" looming ahead, a protracted period of time in which the United States would preside economically, politically, and culturally over the destiny of the whole world. But others, less optimistic or less confident, insisted that in the struggle between Western democracy and Communism there could be no "neutrals," indeed that neutralism was a kind of partisanship. If Soviet Marxism were launching a massive onslaught against the entire value-system of the Western world, then it was the moral obligation of all non-Communist nations to gather together under American leadership to survive and perhaps to triumph.

This optimistic expectation did violence to political realities in the non-Western world. Unlike the nations of Western Europe, the new Asian nations had no direct, unmediated experience with Communist aggression, Russian imperialism, or totalitarian rule.

Most of them (there were exceptions such as Korea), saw imperialism in terms of their own national experiences. Throughout most of Asia and Africa, the hand of imperialism had been a Western hand. Aside from Persia, North China, and Korea, Russian and Soviet expansion was quite remote, hard even to imagine. In the West, on the other hand, Russia had been looming over the political life of Europeans for more than a century. In Europe, from 1917 onwards, there was a constant dialogue among civilized Europeans about the merits and implications of the Bolshevik Revolution. The implications seemed sobering ones as Russia underwent a totalitarian transformation. When Europe, which Marx and Lenin had dogmatically assumed to be the prize that history would drop in the lap of Communism, learned by intimate experience what secular Marxism meant, it rejected it. No such vivid experience lay at hand for the Asian nationalist and intellectual. Indeed, although the greater number of them were *not* Marxist, the Communist parties and movements of Asia had joined with them for several decades in a common thrust against European imperialism. Even the mighty fall of China to Communism in 1949 had little effect on Asian intellectuals *outside* of China, for this, too, could be seen as a triumph against Western colonialism.

American Gradualism vs. Totalitarian Planning

Another American hope that was shattered in the fifties was the belief that the American example of a non-totalitarian democracy achieving great domestic prosperity without extinguishing individual liberties could exert an appeal to non-Westerners who now were on the threshold of self-rule. In fact the rationale of America's Point Four program of assistance to underdeveloped countries in its early days was this: that with American aid and self-help, non-Western nations could embark upon programs of development administratively compatible with democratic, non-totalitarian means. There was the further expectation that ultimately, if not immediately, the American image of a consumer-dominated economy—its ultimate *raison d'être* the satisfaction of basic human material needs—would stand in sharp contrast in the minds of non-Western economic planners with the monolithic, state-dominated economies of the Soviet world, whose primary objectives, at least in Stalin's time, were to augment military power and the power of those industrial sectors (notably, heavy industry) most immediately useful to the State.

Finally, Americans hoped to point out to the Asian new-comer to economic development that the American experience of economic gradualism, of development in stages, was far more humane than the Soviet style of economic growth. Not only was the Soviet style monolithically controlled and governed primarily by considerations of state power but also, in countless Five-Year Plans since the late 1920's, the Soviet state had ruthlessly wrenched Russian society out of its pre-industrial torpor at a cost of millions of human lives and often of cataclysmic suffering among the survivors. Stalin's collectivization program of the early 1930's was but the most dramatic instance of this dogmatic, callous, bureaucratic manipulation of men. The day when the average Soviet family might enjoy the material benefits of the giant system which, in theory, it owned, was perennially postponed. Worker were ceaselessly exhorted to higher production norms; slackers were brutally punished; trade-unions were reduced to servile instruments of state management.

Americans believed that these phenomena of totalitarian economic development, if contrasted with America's development and that of other free nations in the more advanced areas of the world, would make a great impression in America's favor on the still innocent Asian or African politician and intellectual. America's power was in its example and, so it was hoped, its generosity. For American liberals in particular, a stepped-up program of economic aid to these new nations would also prove that the only war America sought in Asia or elsewhere was the war against poverty and disease.

There were many variants on this American theme. As early as 1944, for instance, there were many American liberals (notably among the New Deal administrators) for whom America's entry into world politics seemed to offer the prospect of a vastly enlarged "New Deal" in underdeveloped countries. David Lilienthal, the Tennessee Valley Authority administrator, was the first prominent American liberal to propose the internationalization of the T.V.A. idea, harnessing great rivers such as the Yangtse to provide the energy base for regional economic development with American administrative and engineering assistance. This secularized humanitarianism, however, was anathema to many American conservatives who, with Clare Boothe Luce, referred to it as "Globaloney." Such conservatives as became interested in this problem of economic development stressed its *private* aspects. Though capitalism was anathema in many parts of the world, yet during the Eisenhower administration "capitalism" became a favorite exhortatory device of Republican statesmen and businessmen intent on selling America's way of life to Asians. None of these arguments meant much to impoverished Asians.

The economic crises of the 1950's in Asia, Latin America, and elsewhere had a pathetic urgency which was augmented by the waxing aspirations and expectations of nationalist leaders. In many underdeveloped countries the population explosion, a consequence of rapid introduction of Western medicine, not only further disrupted traditional societies, but also dragged down *per capita* income. The classic dependence of these non-Western economies on single-crop production and extractive industries to sustain themselves in the world economy was becoming increasingly intolerable. The primitive, pre-industrial state of most traditional societies, illiterate and disease-ridden, posed an urgent challenge to these new regimes. Frustrated by such difficulties, many Western-trained political leaders and intellectuals found little in the American pattern of gradual economic development other than its present skills, techniques, and resources to guide them through the morass of economic stagnation. The Soviet model of forced economic growth proved more attractive—by the pace of its accomplishments, not the brutality of its methods.

This matter of pace and timing was crucial, not only because a heightened regard among ex-colonial peoples for Soviet accomplishments might lead them into the Soviet camp, but because it was impossible to force the pace of domestic economic growth to match the Soviet example without using Soviet totalitarian methods. Soviet and Western aid competition in underdeveloped countries raised the unpleasant prospect of lifting local expectations to imprudent heights, thus deepening the social discontent and further weakening existing regimes. The very fact that American economic-aid programs, limited by the resources which Congress was willing to put into them, were not built upon a philosophy of radical economic change revealed their essential concern with the human values involved in the *present*. The American style in foreign aid was gradualist. It perceived desirable growth as occurring in stages, not in "great leaps forward." It sought to move by persuasion, education, and consent rather than by authoritarian order, indoctrination, and totalitarian mobilization. Above all, American foreign aid at its best was motivated by a deep desire to strengthen, and not destroy, whatever democratic impulses were present in the recipient country, and these essentially non-economic concerns themselves set limits upon their economic effectiveness. The "revolution of rising expectations," of which Chester Bowles had spoken in the early 1950's, required greater vigor and fewer illusions than any other previous foreign challenge which the country had faced.

SUMMARY

In summary then, the picture of America in world politics in the early 1960's had changed from that of the late 1940's. Instead of the tight bi-polar world which rose on the ruins of World War II, there existed in the 1960's a world in which American power and influence had noticeably diminished, not so much because of the spread of Communist totalitarianism, but because of the emergence of new centers of power, influence, and instability in both the free world and the Communist bloc. The Soviet Union, despite its pretensions economically to overtake the Western world and America in particular, actually had acquired great military might. It now posed a military threat to the Western world vastly more credible than any before. Yet what now was clear to any observer was the end of older fears and hopes: neither America nor Russia seemed to have in themselves the capacity to "organize the world," or even the more limited worlds around them which shared their own ideological views. With fearful swiftness, the unstable world was moving again toward a condition of multi-polarity, and its political instability was beyond the capacity of either bloc to control.

In the more confident days of World War II, Walter Lippmann commented in *U.S. Foreign Policy: Shield of the Republic* that "policy" only existed when there was a congruity, a balance between commitments (purposes explicitly undertaken) and power to fulfill them. In the years which followed, American power had grown extensively if one measured it objectively. So, too, had American commitments increased. The productivity of the American economy, despite a lagging economic growth rate which compared unfavorably with that of the U.S.S.R., had nevertheless kept the United States far in the lead of the other industrialized nations of the world. Its military power, while declining relative to the growth of the U.S.S.R.'s, had grown quantitatively and changed to incorporate new military devices. Yet by the 1960's, American power to accomplish certain minimal goals for its own people had markedly diminished. The United States, for the first time in history, was vulnerable to massive external attack and destruction; this condition, historically unknown to Americans, was now shared in common with all other men.

Until World War II, American foreign policy, precisely because of its limited objectives, had never pretended an ability to control world politics. Despite Woodrow Wilson's great aspirations, American power had never been employed to help organize international society. In the cold war, however, the United States suddenly became the powerful nucleus of a coalition of non-Communist states. Its political designs, once confined to narrower geographical areas and more modest political purposes, necessarily became "global" in scope. The grand design of containment of Soviet Communism seemingly transcended all other foreign policy purposes, though it certainly did not eliminate them. What American power could not accomplish itself had to be accomplished in concert with other states by diplomacy and concerted action. American insufficiency to initiate and carry out great organizational designs in the international society was as much a shock to liberal, internationalist Americans as was the earlier discovery of American nationalists that America could not survive *without* such great organizational designs. The fifteen-year cold war between America and Russia had moved into a new phase in which both America and Russia could no longer pose with much confidence as permanent or growing nuclei of strength within two camps. Henceforth, while American power might wax or wane, few could imagine that either it or Soviet power alone could suffice as central organizing instrumentalities in a future world. In the race to avoid thermonuclear destruction, international stability depended upon the initiatives and cooperation of men and nations which American diplomacy, alone or in concert with its Western allies, could not regulate or control.

SUGGESTED READING

Dulles, Allen W., "The Challenge of Soviet Power," in Jacobson, Harold K., *America's Foreign Policy*, New York, Random House, 1960, pp. 257-267.

de Jouvenel, Bertrand, *Power: The Natural History of its Growth*, British Book Centre, 1953, especially Book III.

Knorr, Klaus, and William J. Baumol, *What Price Economic Growth?* Englewood Cliffs, Prentice-Hall, 1961, especially chs. 1 and 2.

Marshall, Charles B., *The Limits of Foreign Policy*, New York, Henry Holt, 1954.

Nef, John U., *War and Human Progress: An Essay on the Rise of Industrial Civilization*, Cambridge, Harvard University Press, 1950.

Neumann, Franz L., "Approaches to the Study of Political Power," in his *Democratic and Authoritarian State*, Glencoe, The Free Press, 1954, pp. 3-21.

Spykman, Nicholas, *America's Strategy in World Politics*, New York, Harcourt, Brace, 1942.

CHAPTER
6

ETHICS AND POLICY

Both past and present show occasions when ethics and politics were so contradictory that only the misinformed or the liars could claim to reconcile them. Though many men today openly despair of morality in public life, none but the cynical or the disillusioned would deny that ethics is relevant to the international behavior of states. The fact that we speak of relevance rather than, say, necessity, shows the monumental difficulties of developing an ethical system to embrace a world of politics suddenly become global: a system which could account for the sudden coming together and into conflict of many cultures and political systems; and which, finally, could cope with the possibilities of national, cultural, or biological death involved in the struggle among political collectivities to survive or to prevail in a nuclear age.

Ethics is concerned with moral problems of human choice

and action; it is concerned with values, not just the choice between good and evil, but often with the choice between lesser good and lesser evil. Ethics presupposes both human rationality and the capacity to *be* or *become* moral, to be aware of both the fact of choosing and the nature of choices. It presupposes, also, the very idea of responsibility; one acts, one chooses, knowing that having done so, one would or should be held responsible for one's acts; that one is accountable for choice and deed; that, in fact, there could be standards against which such action or choice could be judged. Ethics also implies purposefulness: action or inaction, choice or refusal to choose are related to some goal. Thus ethics involves both the idea of freedom (to choose between right and wrong, better and worse) and the idea of necessity (to make choices within a given context, which provide them with meaning and rationality).

Political ethics must be distinguished from ethics in general. It assumes that there is a sphere of human action and choice which is specifically political; that the existence of political fabrics—nation-states, empires, and other communities—endows all human choices and actions affecting them with ethical connotations. It acknowledges the reality of political *power* in human relationships. It is thus uniquely concerned with the purposes for which power is exercised and the moral implications of the means used to achieve such purposes. Ethical convictions are meaningless or incomplete unless they take cognizance of their political context.

In this sense, we should perhaps first point to the perpetual tension in history between what might be called apolitical ethics, which are essentially indifferent to this political context and the political order, and political ethics, which take the political context or order for granted, at least as its starting point. We may, for instance, speak of the teachings of Jesus as being in a certain sense "apolitical"—essentially indifferent to the historical world, the contemporary, contextual world, but supremely concerned with the world to come. To Jesus, this difference did not mean the abandonment of ethics, but a lack of any serious concern for the political order of things. Such ethical indifference could be possible only if the real world of day-to-day events was regarded as essentially illusory, transitional, or irrelevant to the more perfect other world to come. Since Augustine, Christian thought has existed in a state of tension between this real world (i.e., the City of Man) and an ideal world (the City of God) and thus has endowed the former with deep political concern. Although certain sects, the Jehovah's Witnesses, for example, prove the exception to the rule, nearly all churches are explicitly involved in politics.

ETHICS IN SOCIETY

Political ethics may thus be said to begin at that moment when men begin to speculate purposefully about the characteristics and properties of "good" and "bad" societies, about men's rights in and obligations towards their community, and about such notions as justice and freedom. Common to most systems of political ethics are the notions (first formulated in the West by the Greek philosophers) of *polis*, state, community, the vessels within which such speculation should take place; for political ethics *begins* also by circumscribing the ethical universe within which the discourse is to take place, drawing a circumference about the community and, in the course of this, making a basic determination to *limit* this sphere: *this* is what we are talking about, this, and what it contains. Howsoever the political philosopher draws the circle, the circle must be drawn. It is essential to understand the limits within which political ethics is discussed.

(Of course, like the Social Contract theorists of the seventeenth and eighteenth centuries, it is quite possible to imagine a human condition where no society exists, i.e., a state of nature, without government or positive laws. Here such a circumscription was essentially meaningless: that is, a constitutional order simply did not exist, and individual men were the ultimate arbiters and justifiers of their actions. Naturally such a condition is historically fictitious except in rare circumstances of great crisis and chaos.

Civilization presupposes order; uncivilized man is no man at all.)

Within this *polis* or state-community have arisen the ethical questions which concern political philosophers. Political order is inseparable from man. All systems of political thought which claim to be ethical have in common the attempt to set criteria of justice and freedom for men within a system of law and authority.

THE NATIONAL INTEREST AS ETHICAL YARDSTICK

Classically and perennially the problem of man and society has been profoundly affected by the necessary, finite character of the society and state themselves. For example, in the Greek city-state of Aristotle's time, then, as now, problems of justice, goodness, and political morality were matters meaningful only within *the* state, *the* community, of which civil man was a corporeal member. The idea of the unfolding of human personality within a "rational" community first came into being with the Greeks. With it came the idea of an attainable, desired harmony between the community and men who, because they were citizens, were *therefore* able to become free and act morally under laws. Even those who would deny the possibility of such freedom within the state or society would take the idea of the state or society for granted.

The most serious perennial problem posed by this finite model of the state has been that the matter of ethics, too, was circumscribed by its domain. States had outsides as well as insides; a larger political world lay outside the state; even, now, the great globe itself. Was the domain of the state or the community co-extensive with the sphere of ethics? If the state could reach no further beyond its own finite limits than its own power would permit, then questions of political justice and freedom, the political questions which men were really concerned about, were also limited. If the good society were the *summum bonum* and the good society were finite, then ethics were finite too: that is, ethical matters in foreign relations and international politics could be decided upon in accordance with the needs of the good society itself. What is good for the good society was *the* good.

In modern terms, the national interest became the touchstone of ethics in the international arena. What other yardstick would there be? Within the good society, tranquillity, order, and justice might be said to prevail, and men might be expected to act, within its confines, in an ethical fashion. But things which the good society prohibited within its realm might be permitted to its men when they were abroad, when they acted outside such confines in the interest of the good society itself. Thus war, violence, and imperialism on occasion could be justified in the national interest.

Was there then no sphere of political ethics *above* that of the society? If there were none, then the only ethical limitations on the state's activity in its foreign policy would be the ethical restraints within the society itself: this is, that which is bad for the society itself is bad, but only for this reason. The ethical yardstick was the society's good. Those who held to this particular notion of finite, political ethics, could point to the outside—or international world—to the absence of overriding, constitutional order and cultural consensus about what was just and unjust; about what a good life was; and about which political form and authority were worth defending or establishing. For most politically conscious men, then, the sphere of possible political justice remained the polity. International politics was power politics and on that level, where states and societies met, power, influence, and naked force often were the arbiters.

(The steady development of international law, from the sixteenth century onwards, suggested that there was another level of political ethics: that states were to be *the* entities, the subjects of international law (just as individuals were subjects of municipal, i.e. domestic, law). There were several differences between municipal and international law, chief among which was the obvious, crucial one: there was no supranational sovereignty. The states themselves, while subject to law, were free both to interpret and enforce the law. It followed that they were free to determine their own ethical behavior. This development of international law during the modern period was of considerable importance, since it suggested the possibility that there were, or could be, standards of ethics by which states' actions could be judged. The state thus became, figuratively speaking, a moral entity, engaging as a corporate entity in deeds and relationships with *other* like entities which were objects of moral contemplation or condemnation. Still, to act ethically according to principles of international law continued to sound a hollow note, since the law itself continued to be interpreted by its subjects and thus was subjectified.)

Now, a logical difficulty enters this argument. If what was good for the good society was to determine its ethical actions within and without its domain, it was likewise possible that there could be more than one good society or, value judgments aside, more than one society could *claim* to be an "ethical repository of goodness," and to have "national interests" harmonious with its ethical aspirations. Then, in conflicts of interest between or among such states, which might also be conflicts between quite different concepts of political ethics (justice, freedom, and the like), what standards could be employed to decide who was right and who was wrong? (One might argue that a governing, ethical considera- tion in such a circumstance should be the preservation or achieve- ment of some kind of order *among* states: for instance, the bal- ance of power or the principles of international law. Yet few men regard "order" among states as an ethical concept. One may die or risk death for liberty, America, or Communism, not for the bal- ance of power or the Hague Tribunal. After Pearl Harbor, Ameri- cans fought Japan not because she had broken international law, but because she had attacked the United States.)

Here the objectivity of ethics in the good society gave way to subjectivity: conceptions of good and bad, right and wrong could easily be subjectified; the ethical nature of the state's behavior in world politics could be judged thus only in terms of its own standards. One could not pass moral judgment on the behavior of another state or culture from within one state or culture unless, by act of imagination, one got "within" that other entity and applied its own normative yardsticks to its own behavior. This made universal, ethical objectivity impossible in world politics. The vulgar formulation of this is *My country: right or wrong.*

The State as Agent for the Universe

As dismaying a condition as this limited ethics was historically, it was certainly no worse than one ethical alternative we have seen expressed at many points in Western history: regarding the society or state as the agent of some supranational or international *summum bonum.* It is one thing to declare that a society or a state has the right to decide what is good or bad for itself (self-determination), even for men to regard their own state and its welfare as the only locale within which justice can be realized. It is quite another matter when the society or state is deemed to be *the* agency through which higher, more universal principles of justice should be realized. As an organized system of political power, the state all too often in the nineteenth and twentieth centuries did just this. It arrogated to itself the task of seeing that universal principles were observed. If ethics did transcend the state, and, as the philosophers of the Enlightenment were to declare, arose out of *natural* rights of men and natural laws, why couldn't the state do this? This attempt was visible in the religious wars of the fifteenth and sixteenth centuries, when the specific, political motives and interests of states became inextricably confused with the deep, passionate, universalistic compulsions of Protestant and Catholic Christians.

But the attempts to ground a new *secular* polity upon principles declared to be universal became much more specific with the French, American, and Bolshevik Revolutions. In each instance we see something radically new and modern. For the new state, the "revolutionary" state stood qualitatively above others.

Its very open-endedness, the ever-present possibility of its enlargement raised the possibility of imbuing foreign policy with an ethical justification which transcended the traditional *Staatsraison* or *raison d'état* of older non-revolutionary states, whose only pretensions were to advance the state interests or the national interests of their own political systems. How quickly after the French Revolution and its Declaration of the Rights of Man did the armies of Napoleon carry these principles to the rest of Europe and impose them under the name of France! How often, also, were the liberal principles of the American Declaration of Independence, universal in their nature, carried in the baggage of American military and political expansion. Finally, and in far more tortured and painful a manner, how quickly after the October Revolution of 1917 did Marxism and its peculiar ethical doctrines become fused into the needs and power aspirations of the new Russian state, so that what had been universal now became particularized, an agency of its own "historical" agent.

It is a painful characteristic of successful, universal, ethical creeds to undergo or be constantly threatened by this process of ideological particularization. Even the partial realization of universal ideologies *within* one state may, as in the American experience, profoundly enlarge the ethical element in politics and even, as in this instance, greatly enlarge the horizons of human freedom. But the price is the same. What was universal, in becoming particularized, takes on the peculiar shape of its vessel. Thus the Declaration of Independence becomes not a universal statement for "mankind," but a classic "document in American liberalism," invested with peculiar *national* qualities and associations which severely limit its original limitlessness. To be sure, the original impulse to *enlarge* the political sphere within which these ethical principles might apply, may continue. Witness, for instance, the powerful attempts of American occupation authorities in Germany and Japan after World War II to democratize German and Japanese society. Such attempts, in fact, may meet with considerable success. But the universality becomes increasingly nationalized, and the charge of imperialism is heard on all sides.

It is easy to be cynical about this process; but on reflection, it seems inexorable and necessary. Whatever one's definition of human rights may be, and whatever their relation to political ethics, it is possible for them to be realized only within the *particular* context of *particular* states. In this sense, as Hannah Arendt puts it, human rights are nationalized. Human rights come from the state. Thus, in a profoundly tragic sense, statelessness in men is rightlessness: not to have citizenship, not to partake of the protection of the laws of the land is to have no rights at all. There is in this sense no tribunal for *individual men* higher than the tribunal of the nation. Even to be a subject of a totalitarian state confers upon individual men more rights than to have no tribunal at all. To live under the protection, or harassment, of unjust laws is, for most ordinary men, preferable to living under no laws at all.

On further reflection, there is an even more compelling reason for this process. Universal rights, universal laws, or whatever we may fancy them to be, have no real juridical substance. They are politically impotent unless imbedded in a real, political order where they may be constantly re-interpreted, refined, expressed, and enforced. Thus the American Constitution and its Bill of Rights, not the United Nations Declaration of Human Rights, is the constitutional sheet anchor for American citizens. The substantive and procedural guarantees it confers upon American citizens—free press, free assembly, freedom of speech—can be given concrete meaning only *within* an existing, powerful, political order. No such order exists on the international plane; and if it were to exist, one would wish to know a great deal about the specific, substantive guarantees it contained. And there is little reason to suppose that at this point in world history, guarantees of human rights under an international, constitutional order would be as firm as those which exist inside the constitutional order of the United States.

THE CRISIS IN ETHICS AND
WORLD POLITICS

The crisis of ethics and world politics today has four chief sources: the changing structure of political systems due to an organizational revolution in world politics; a technological revolution which vastly augments the means of destruction available to political communities in extending or defending their realm of authority and "justice"; the intermingling of systems of political ethics, some of which, like Soviet Marxism and American Liberalism, possess "universal" qualities; and, a condition not unrelated to all of these, a profound ethical resignation at being unable to do anything at all to arrest or limit any of these processes—a despair, incidentally, reflected not among merely passive and indifferent men, but even among thoughtful and active statesmen. All men today see the terrors of nuclear war as a prospect, but few thoughtful men know how policy, choice, or ethically imbued action can avoid what appears to be an unprecedented human cataclysm of such proportions that ethics itself disappears. (This may be seen in the genocide that was practiced by the Nazis against powerless European Jews at a time when unbelievably destructive air attacks upon German cities were wiping out hundreds of thousands of civilian lives.) Let us consider each of these.

The Organizational Revolution in World Politics

At certain periods throughout human history great philosophical or ideological struggles have caught up human societies, profoundly rearranging the whole fabric and significance of politics. These are great revolutionary epochs of international civil wars. These abnormal periods seem to have one thing in common: politics becomes a seamless web; international politics blends into domestic politics. The state, the "polis," this finite entity which in normal times is the political and ethical universe for most men, is broken into by transcendent political and ethical issues. Politics becomes "internationalized." The political choices of men and states about the way they shall govern and be governed, and about the scope and context of political issues become dramatically complicated, for the state is no longer *the* chief theater for the political dialogue, nor, for that matter, is it the theater in which political decisions can be made with any finality. In such times, many men find it difficult to discern where their loyalties, their political ties, their commitments lie. Out of bewilderment, expediency, moral anguish, and often from a sheer impulse to survive, they vacillate. The long, unhappy era of the religious wars in Europe was one such time. Ours is another.

In the nineteenth century, the German historian Ranke proclaimed the "primacy of foreign policy" and of international politics which meant, for states like his Germany, that foreign policy determined domestic politics. However appropriate this generalization was to the Bismarckian era, it is today at best a half-truth, obscuring the far more complex problem faced by all states, the immense difficulty of making such distinctions at all. The permeability of all states, even totalitarian ones, by so-called external developments makes us question whether the old distinction retains much meaning. Perhaps something like a Copernican revolution in thinking about politics is required when the units of politics are rapidly losing their integral qualities as closed political systems. This problem becomes acutely clear during revolutionary situations and was dramatically illustrated by the Congolese crisis in 1960.

This condition, intensified in Europe during World War I, deeply aggravated and complicated traditional problems of ethics and politics which commence, as we have seen, in discourse about a possibly manageable universe wherein justice, power, and order might be reconciled. Much of the traditional American optimism about world politics during the late nineteenth century sprang from genial deceptions concerning the realities of the American political universe itself: the unbroken constitutional traditions, the unique absence of serious constitutional contentions, the apparent political stability which was compatible with rapid economic growth and human freedom. The American Civil War was not about fundamental constitutional questions, as were the French and Bolshevik Revolutions. In fact, the seceding Southern states' constitution bore marked resemblance to the Federal Constitution; when solved, the issues of right of secession and slavery did *not* leave any unresolved constitutional issues. Therefore, Americans have never experienced what it is like to live in a nation where these basic issues are *not* solved.

Europeans have had just the opposite experience. The war of 1914-1918, and the Revolution which followed in Russia and in Eastern and Central Europe, seemed to strip Europeans of any delusions about the permanence of the *status quo*, without at the same time suggesting a different, enlarged context within which ethical questions could be made relevant to politics. If World War I momentarily "solved" the problem of Germany in Europe, no one was foolish enough to assume this was a just solution. It grew out of violent conflict and was supposed to be maintained by power and, if necessary, force.

It had once been possible in Europe to speak of the progressive development of a public international law, a public order of Europe compounded of treaties, conventions, and international understandings among states. These made up an international umbrella, protecting certain capacities of states to govern themselves and to regulate their internal politics with some degree of confidence about the permanence of the larger international context of things. This condition was most marked during the century between the Napoleonic War and World War I. It was a century of widespread optimism and complacency about human progress. After 1914, few men were so complacent again.

In the years between World War I and World War II, the fragile order of Versailles, with its attempt to subjugate Germany, was threatened both by the Germans themselves and by the enormously enlarged political and philosophical thrust of Communism and the Soviet Union. The rise of fascism in Central Europe, however variously it has been explained, meant that the *status quo* was now threatened by two movements, European in scope, if not indeed broader, and that the internal politics of European states came to *mirror* massive, supranational movements and ideologies. Purely national interests are difficult to formulate, advance, and defend when the nation itself is permeated by forces essentially transnational or supranational. This was so even with fascism (which eulogized the Nation and asserted the supremacy of Race and unique Culture). It, like Communism, knew no formal, national, territorial limitations. In Hitler's time, there was a pernicious link among Right-wing movements throughout the Western world. In Germany, during the 1930's, these reached their apex of power, but they operated in France, Spain, Belgium, Scandinavia, Italy, and Eastern Europe as well.

This historical digression could be amplified, but the point is clear: not since 1914 have men regarded the international arena and day-to-day postures of states as anything but transient; not since 1914 have thoughtful men really believed that politics *anywhere* could really be contained within the province of the nation-state; and finally, not since 1914 could anyone overlook the increasing tendency of ethical, normative issues of politics to burst the bounds of the individual state, blurring the formal dividing lines. Patriotism to be sure did not die. Indeed, during these years and notably among the fascist states of Europe and even in Soviet Russia it reached a pathological apogee after Hitler's invasion in 1941. Patriotism quickened the spirit of ordinary men in resisting the onslaught. The motherland, Russia, evoked far greater loyalties from average men than could Communism and Stalinism. Yet, and this was of crucial importance, the classical world of the eighteenth and nineteenth centuries, the political world inhabited by states with interests, states which could, with ceremony and ease, shift about in a world of alliances and alignments with little regard for moral and ideological affinities, this world ceased to exist.

Let us not delude ourselves. This massive, organizational crisis could not be explained by single things or by tangible, historical events as though, once explained, the condition could be remedied. What was involved here was a profound and rapid breakdown of form, the internal collapse of great institutions and empires, the external smashing of others. At the same time, fusing naturally into this were other forms, other integrative processes, some of which expended their energies quickly and disappeared. (The Pan American Union was one; there were countless others. Even today, when Communism and the Soviet Union seem, retrospectively, so massive an element of world politics, we forget how close both came to extinction in 1941-1942.)

The point could be exaggerated. Some elements of continuity and some political systems escaped this dismaying pattern of revolution, disruption, defeat, occupation, and civil war to find reprieve from the peculiarly modern difficulties described above. There were the small neutrals, small democracies such as Switzerland which survived because of domestic social stability, skillful diplomacy, and luck. Until the 1960's, there were the Latin American nations, still physically remote from the major theaters of conflict, still too culturally remote for their inhabitants yet to *sense* their own involvement in these things, and sheltered from world politics by an American, imperial hegemony. Then there were the English-speaking nations—Britain, America, Canada, Australia, and New Zealand—where constitutional continuity had proved compatible with social change; where war had not brought occupation or defeat; and where the swift growth of industrial processes had been combined with rapidly rising living standards. Here there was political and constitutional continuity, growth, and change, and political freedom remained. Above all, in these nations the inherent respect for the rule of law and for representative government withstood powerful impulses to revolution and the shattering of form. As a consequence, elements of order existed which seemed increasingly anomalous in the modern world but which proved to be touchstones of the emerging order of the

West, growing out of World War II. From them also came the political initiatives and the political theories, by virtue of which the League of Nations and the United Nations came into being.

The resulting ethical crisis of form and order cannot be oversimplified, but one simple dimension can be easily perceived: if men are greatly uncertain about the durability of the political context they live in, they will also be uncertain about the nature of their ethical universe. Being uncertain, they may also act quite unpredictably; for political ethics becomes absurd when the political context in which it could be meaningful dissolves.

Walter Lippman points this out in *The Public Philosophy*, where he defines the "public" as a Burkean "timeless" continuity of men which links together those of the community now dead with the living and the still unborn generations. Only this definition of the public, Lippmann says with some persuasiveness, will suffice to give representative government and public opinion philosophical significance. Yet how many "communities" of men exist in which this definition has any applicability? Who *are* those to come, and how are they to be linked to those who were before? What if such continuity simply does not exist? Does the public then not exist at all? And if so, who shall govern legitimately? The dispute in Algeria, after all, is really about who was *entitled* to come after. The massive resettlements of whole populations, the expulsions, etc., have made the problem even more difficult.

The Technological Revolution and the Means of Mass Destruction

A second source of this crisis of ethics and politics springs from the technological revolution which vastly augments the means of destruction available to states. So enormous is this problem that it often seems to dwarf its particulars; that is, we can be so stupefied about the larger issue of nuclear war that we fail to be much astonished or even interested in its less dramatic, yet fundamental details.

All of us are familiar with some characteristics of the technological crisis, but it might be useful to dwell on them. Most important is the macroscopic character of war which nuclear weapons now make possible. It dwarfs all previous conflicts in history and suggests apocalyptic consequences. Yet along with this, another quality rarely mentioned by those whose horror at nuclear weapons leads them to wish them away by some international act, is that as long as human knowledge and memory persist, so long also will nuclear weapons exist. The destruction of weapons stockpiles, difficult as this would be to accomplish, could not destroy knowledge. So long as knowledge existed, so long also would the Bomb figure prominently in men's thinking about politics. A third and necessary characteristic of this condition to acknowledge is the universal nature of this crisis. Much as men struggle to perfect means to intercept or destroy such missiles at their source, there is a tragic quality to this endeavor. No sure defense is known. Given the enormous power of the weapons, only virtual perfection of defensive systems would be enough. All nations share this novel vulnerability in common. None is exempt.

In the past, all wars have raised deep ethical concerns; first, because the state, calling upon its citizens or subjects to fight and die for it, was compelled to justify its call. Second, however, the state is rarely autonomous and rarely wholly irrational; even the most apparently nihilistic wars (let us say, for instance, Nazi Germany's onslaught upon European civilization) had their justifications. In a sense, international war is a conflict among organized systems of power, but this conflict is more than just that. Rational conflict in war is and has been a supremely important mode of effecting definitive solutions to problems insoluble by other means. It is worth pointing out the growing number of stalemated crises in world politics which, traditionally, war would have resolved: Korea, Germany, Laos, China, etc. Held in suspension, these unresolved issues seem to pile up on top of each other since neither side has thus far been willing to push any one of them to a final conclusion. It is obvious that each

of these is both a civil war and part of a larger, ideological conflict. In this sense, war has been a legislative enterprise, often an
order-building enterprise and, thus, invested with supremely moral
implications. (Note Lincoln's description of the significance of
the Civil War as testing "whether this Nation, or any nation so
conceived and so dedicated, can long endure.") Not the least of
these moral implications is the question of what kind of order was
being built.

(It is interesting to note how many pacifists within the
Western world during recent major wars redoubled their efforts
to plan for a post-war world, their speculations made possible and
profitable only because the outcome of the war could be sufficiently victorious to permit such speculation. In their concern for a
"just peace," they had to assume the very victory which would be
accomplished by the violence they rejected in principle.)

War has always been a supremely ethical problem for two
other reasons: its destructive and its coercive aspects. By its very
nature, war involves the performance of acts which, in context of
the civil society, are ethically repugnant and, in a sense, uncivilized: the killing and maiming of human beings; the devastation of
cities, towns, and countryside; the obliteration of great creations
of men—their homes, their temples, their works of art. In the
name of the good society, moral men could do things to the enemy
which would horrify them if done to their own. (It has been
pointed out that as war has become more destructive, it has become less "brutal." Modern instruments of destruction deperson-
alize the encounters; the wielders of instruments become increasingly remote from their victims. This process is epitomized in the
Polaris submarines, whose commanders could, theoretically, obliterate whole nations without even bothering to come up from
the bottom of the ocean for a breath of fresh air. Intimate brutality
may remain a feature of guerilla warfare but is obsolescent in
great engagements.)

War served the interests of the society and thus its ends
because, in other words, the destruction had larger meaning, a

positive significance which could warrant the suffering involved. Here the ethical problem was reduced to this: war as such was not necessarily moral or immoral; one sought, rather, to distinguish "just" from "unjust" wars. In modern times, war was perennially justified in terms of positive goals: the survival of the nation and the community; the defense or extension of human freedom.

MORAL PROBLEMS FOR DEMOCRACIES This was but one side of the coin, for if war were iniquitous from the viewpoint of the human, cultural, and physical damage it wrought, it was equally repugnant when viewed from the ethical premises upon which free societies were grounded. In all societies, the state, in a theoretical, juridical sense, had a monopoly on the instruments of violence. It could use force legitimately to maintain order. But both force and war seemed to make mockery of the standards of a democratic system or of any political philosophy other than absolutism and tyranny. This put the ethical problem in an extreme form: could a "free society," in the name of its own freedom, tyrannize others?

For centuries, Western political thought had struggled to legitimize political power, its exercise, and its purposes. Democratic theory, stressing the reciprocity of men's rights and obligations in civil society, stressed also the centrality of consent to law. Free men freely consented to the law-making procedures of a constitutional order. In democracies and representative governments, citizens should regard the laws and their execution as legitimate, obeying them willingly *because* their free consent had been implicitly or explicitly given.

Something was grievously wrong, with law, with society, or with the constitutional order if this were not so. Political order did not survive merely, or even chiefly, because there was a veiled threat of force behind the lawmaker. The executioner was not the hidden sovereign, the real guarantor of domestic political order and tranquillity (as DeMaistre, the French counterrevolutionary theorist, once alleged). Democracy and representative government were grounded on certain premises of human rationality and upon the premise that, however imperfect laws might be, consent was necessary. It followed that rational persuasion and the appeal to reason were necessary; free men were also supposed to be rational men. Other things necessary to make the system work were a free press and the freedom of men to assemble, to speak, to give expression to their ideas. Leaders were held accountable to the public for what they did or proposed to do. Their very acts were to be exposed to public scrutiny. Secrecy denied to the public the very kinds of knowledge required to pass rational judgment on things; it made democracy impossible. Without these essentials, consent was a mockery, both to democratic men's rights and to their intelligence.

War seemed to violate these principles in the international realm. As an executive device in foreign relations, war was force. If it were rational itself (if it were undertaken, that is, as a means of achieving certain ends for the state or society), if it were a continuation of politics with an admixture of other means, it was an act of force. It made free consent meaningless. When the Japanese government surrendered in 1945, it was not giving free consent to the objectives of American or Allied policy. It had simply been beaten, subjugated, and threatened with biological extinction. War was a compelling enterprise and the consent to peace was extracted from the defeated or weaker state by force. Power, force, violence, were the arbiters.

One could be highly sophisticated and say that even in war, reason was not abandoned. War could be seen as a game in which the players should act rationally. Surrender as an alternative to extinction was a *form* of free consent; but this was sophistry. If fundamental issues, touching upon the essential character and nature of political systems, were at stake, then the use of war to settle them was, apparently, in utter defiance of democratic principle. The terms of a "just peace" were decided upon by violence. In fact, war settled issues by denying free consent. To be sure, magnanimity and prudence on the part of a victor (as with the British at the end of the Boer War) might suggest that the victor believed there *should* be some consent from the vanquished for a durable peace. Lincoln's magnanimity in 1865 also took into account the need for fairness and justice. Not without reason did many Germans refer to the peace settlement after World War I, as a *Diktat*; for regardless of the substantive justice of the Versailles peace terms, the fact remained that peace was imposed upon the German government. It had the option of consent, or renewed war and possible utter defeat.

Another ethical problem affecting democratic values is that war and the preparation for it did domestic violence to democratic values. War meant emergency; it meant the tightening of reins of authority; it threatened to abandon many procedural niceties of a democratic order. Civil liberties, due process of law, prerogatives of parliaments and assemblies, freedom of speech, of assembly, of movement, all these could be gravely threatened within the most democratic society when it was struggling for victory or survival. To be sure, these freedoms might be restored when peace was re-established, but there were too many examples in history suggesting otherwise to overlook the dangers. Furthermore, in war, secrecy wrapped a mantle around fundamental decisions made by men in authority. For example, the grave decision made by the American government in 1940 to develop nuclear fission with all that this portended remained a deep secret from the American public and from Congress for nearly five years. Executive authority in time of crisis might itself be subject to arcane political constraints, but fateful decisions of war and peace could be made by a handful of men. Today, even more fateful ones can be taken by even fewer men.

Democratic governments called on men in times of war to sacrifice themselves, but it was often impossible to get their specific consent. Crises could come with swiftness (and the possibilities of swiftness increased as the means of delivering an attack "improved"). Often the more serious a crisis became, the less could the democratic niceties of open diplomacy and publicity be held to. (How, for instance, could one publicly debate the merits of alternative military strategies or diplomatic negotiations when an adversary's knowledge of them would better his own bargaining or military position?) Crisis augmented a sense of popular ignorance and powerlessness. In the democracies, of course, issues of foreign policy in times of crisis *were* publicly debated. Informed parts of the public still might know what was going on, what certain alternatives of decision were. But there remained the awesome centralization of authority and power in matters of peace and war.

Technological changes themselves accelerated this trend towards the centralization of decision-making. In thermonuclear crises, for instance, the American government might have only half an hour to decide whether to launch a preemptive strike against an attacker, simply to capitulate, or to make a retaliatory second strike. In December 1941, President Roosevelt, knowing the probability of Japanese aggression in the Pacific, could still afford to indulge America in the luxury of being attacked first and thus preserve its reputation as a non-aggressor, and a peace-loving state. So, for that matter, could the Russians in June 1941. This luxury is now no longer so pleasant to contemplate.

How then could the citizen, the democratic man, relate himself to these great events which, particularly in periods of crisis, appeared so overwhelming? In particular, how did he come to grips with the enormous difficulty of establishing a moral connection between himself and the things his government did in his name and in the name of his country? In totalitarian countries, the problem of individual moral choice and involvement was solved by the *extinction* of the individual himself. It was solved by the facts of totalitarian life: the explicit exclusion of the public from knowledge of and significant participation in the dialogue about politics generally and foreign policy in particular. It was solved by the sterile doctrine of Soviet Marxism that an inexorable history, abetted by appropriate elitist leadership, moved with certainty along the path to some distant victory and utopia. Even among the wholly impotent in the totalitarian world, there was the silent comfort of all powerless men that "things happened," that one was not really responsible and hence not really involved in an ethical dilemma. Political ethics become meaningful not just when men can *perceive* and distinguish bad from good but when there is the prospect of making a choice.

This is not to suggest that ethics was extinguished in the totalitarian states. Virtue could be privatized, made apparently meaningful in *small* contexts, within the confines of family or immediate, tangible situations. Honesty, decency, and truthfulness do not necessarily disappear in a totalitarian context. Indeed, under conditions of terror in public life, a private regard for such tangible amenities may be profoundly enhanced in its meaning for individual men. What totalitarianism could ruin in men was the individual sense of autonomous morality about *public* matters. Confronted by massive façades of power, the constant official reiterations of spontaneous solidarity, the overt or latent threats of excommunication, deportation, confinement, and even death, Soviet man could well be faced with the tragic choice of *accepting* fatalistically the things which "happened" or gambling that, just possibly, the doctrine might be right and individual moral choice itself really did not matter. (To play it safe, one might assume that *just possibly* a righteous God existed after all, even though chances were against it.)

A public dialogue in the totalitarian world about foreign policy or about politics in general is a contradiction in terms (unless it is a public dialogue among power factions unable or unwilling to screen from public view their doctrinal difficulties). But for the democratic citizen in the West, the ethical difficulty was compounded by the contrast between his world in which the political dialogue did take place and the totalitarian world where it was suppressed. It was one thing to live in the Western world where foreign policy, like all other questions pertaining to man's political life, was a matter of constant, and often well-informed, open discussion. In such a context, it was possible to conceive of a continuing dialogue of politics between governments *and* publics, among even the publics of the nations concerned. It was all too easy to diminish the importance of this openness of debate; to point out, for instance, that matters of foreign policy rarely interested people; that there were many people in even the most advanced Western countries who knew little, if anything, of what issues were at stake; and that public discourse itself among or between open societies did not in and of itself breed either natural understanding or amity. It often spawned serious tensions. But still, the very openness provided the possibility of mutual comprehension. One could, like Wilson (*and* Lenin) in Europe in 1919, appeal to people "over the heads of governments." Witness, for instance, the debate in Britain at the time of the American Revolution concerning the rights of the American colonists, a dialogue which was conducted through the war itself and in which even Americans could participate.

In a world where fundamental issues could not be discussed between the educated men of totalitarian and free societies, how could one hope for any future consensus between them? In the years of the cold war, the public moral dialogue about war, peace, nuclear weapons, the dangers of biological extinction, took place within the Western world, not between the Western world and the Soviet totalitarian one. The Communist world could not really permit the dialogue to move out of officially prescribed limits. A false dialogue was permitted between reliable, trained spokesmen of the Soviet leadership and Westerners, but this was a different matter. So, too, without question, some sort of private, confined dialogue continuously took place *within* the leadership of the Communist bloc and the Communist parties. The fact, however, remained: only in the Western world were the ethical dilemmas of the crisis openly and candidly discussed.

Significantly, the only genuine, conscientious, symbolic protests against nuclear weapons by individuals occurred in the West. Conscientious objectors in the West could picket, publicly demonstrate, sail vessels into nuclear test zones of the Pacific, and circle Polaris submarines in canoes to give vent to their deep concerns. The totalitarian world permitted such activities only when directed on its own behalf. To be sure, it could hire hooligans to smash embassy windows of Western states engaged in nuclear testing. It could organize mass demonstrations against what the capitalists were doing, but such criticism of the activities of the Soviet Union was not permitted.

But the moral issue could not be skirted in the West. It was a novel experience to live comfortably with nuclear weapons and the arms race, experiencing the continuous possibility not just of one's own possible death, but of the massacre of millions of others and the vicarious guilt which such an event would surely involve. The problem of ethics was further complicated by the utter futility of merely crying out against an insanity which, in reality, had its own monumental inner logic; the desperate international struggle to acquire power in order to escape the tyranny of power had made great nations the captives of these instruments and weapons systems.

ELIMINATING CONSENT Now the gravest ethical dilemma presents itself. Although in history war often involved *seemingly* limitless catastrophe (in reality quite limited, since the means of destruction were themselves limited), and often (as in the classic case of Carthage) the possible cultural extinction of a defeated state, empire, or community, it is more horrifying today that the techniques of war make it possible to obliterate life itself. This alone should have made nations refuse to develop such new weapons. On the contrary, however, this very fact made them even more desperate to acquire them, and for a simple reason: the sheer power of nuclear weapons *also* made theoretically possible a political dominion of terror, concealed or overt, which had never been possible before. Whoever had a monopoly of the weapon, or even a qualitatively superior striking force, had a political device which, theoretically, would virtually eliminate the need for consent in politics. *Who "deserved" this power?* In the attempt to survive as cultural entities or to triumph (as in the Communist states), nations race to lead in weapons, and thus risk biological death. This theoretical problem, which appears to be permanent (unless human civilization is destroyed), was largely overlooked in the first years of the nuclear age since it was a Western power (notably, a "liberal" United States) which first developed the weapon, and, aside from its first use at Hiroshima to "break" a belligerent state, restrained itself from similar acts of total threat in the years of its nuclear monopoly. In 1940, no one who knew about the possibilities of nuclear fission, including Albert Einstein, doubted, however, that such a monopoly in the hands of a totalitarian state like Nazi Germany would be used to establish global nuclear hegemony. A dominion of nuclear terror is now theoretically possible only if one state or one unified, political force could compel all other states to give up their own nuclear stockpiles. As an escape from this dilemma, some Westerners (notably, Lord Russell) have suggested the need to admit the logic of circumstance and surrender to Soviet nuclear tyranny in order to survive biologically; but the implications of this have been too formidable and radical to contemplate. Thus far, men have not been compelled to make the choice between biological survival and cultural capitulation on the one hand, and cultural resistance and biological death on the other.

THE NEED FOR SACRIFICE Throughout history, all political ethics, whether or not ideologically encumbered by association with political power, were profoundly concerned with the problem of goals. Paramount among such goals was the survival or creation of a political entity in itself deemed to be good. Thus the necessity of sacrifice, even of physical death, was always implicit, if not explicit. City-states, nations, empires, religious and mass secular movements habitually extolled the men and women who gave up their own lives for the transcendent purpose of achieving some goal which lay beyond their particular mortality. The parks of all great cities are filled with memorials to them; their names figure most prominently in the earliest civic instruction of children. Sacrificial death in war and other political affairs could be endowed with significance in the minds of those who risked it since, after all, one would not be wholly extinguished. One's life (and significance) would continue in the memory of those who survived.

This could even be possible for him who, engaged in sacrifice, was aware of the immediate futility of the particular act which would certainly result in death: thus, succeeding generations might, knowing of it, acknowledge the absurdity and profit. As one young *Kamikaze* officer, a young Japanese university student, wrote on the eve of the mission which he knew necessarily would involve his own death, "My ambition to make my beloved country become a great empire like Great Britain is already in vain. . . . Japanese who could walk anywhere in the world, freely —that was the ideal I dreamt. . . . We as individuals have no right to say anything; but sincerely I would like to plead to the Japanese people to make Japan a truly great nation some day. . . . Tomorrow there will be one less liberal in the world. He may look lonely in the past, but he may at least himself have full satisfaction in his heart. Goodbye." [1]

To put it more bluntly, the idea of sacrifice was central to political ethics. Much as civilized and responsible men might try to avoid the need for such grave decisions, much as a peaceful order, like that of Victorian Europe, might obscure the issue, underneath all there lay this premise of political order and justice: the willingness to sacrifice when the time came. To be sure, this matter of sacrifice could cause profound disagreement. When was it necessary? What was one sacrificing for? In broad terms, however, few men who thought about it long enough could disagree; just communities of men could not ensure their permanence if their members forsook such an obligation. Even the pacifist, forswearing the use of force and the sacrifice which that conceivably might entail, still acknowledged the need for personal sacrifice as means to his own conception of a community where force itself would be outlawed, or made unnecessary.

Today sacrifice has become most dangerous among the

---

[1] Quoted in Edmund Stillman and William Pfaff, *The New Politics.* New York: Coward, 1961, p. 108.

strongest. Small, relatively weak nations may fight among themselves in the classical manner. Here the brandishments of force, demagoguery, ultimata, appeals for sacrifice may still have some transitory meaning. It may still seem to them that their own concepts of freedom and justice can be attained (if not right now, then at some future time) by these means. F.L.N. and O.A.S. terrorists in Algeria for instance thought this way; they exhorted men to total sacrifice and even set the example themselves, but only because they knew that the sacrifice would *not* be really total. No one in such a context of conflicts could plausibly threaten total extinction and its obvious concomitant, the extinction of the meaning of sacrifice. Throughout much of the underdeveloped world, it is by a strange quirk that relative powerlessness thus enhances power. One has little to lose; since "everything" does not really seem to be at stake in revolution and revolutionary war, one *can* afford to act like an irresponsible utopian, pretending that it is so. La Pasionaria, the Communist heroine of the Spanish Civil War, said, "It is better to die on one's feet than live on one's knees." This has meaning though only if others of one's own kind survive to make the choice themselves. It is meaningless when applied to whole cultures and civilizations.

This enhanced power of the powerless is dangerous from almost any point of view. If the self-styled revolutionary confrères of major powers, acting within their local contexts (Korea, Algeria, the Congo, Cuba, etc.) exploit apparent weakness to press for the impossible, they do so either with indifference or ignorance of the massive, cumulative dangers of their own activities. If the voices of real extremism have been stifled in Europe today among civilized Europeans, it is largely because most civilized Europeans know that political extremism risks biological suicide. Ethical extremism risks cultural extinction.

Such is the dilemma of power in the affairs of political societies. It would be ironic indeed if mutual terror brought men everywhere to temper immoderate claims and demands. But the crucial question is who judges moderacy and immoderacy? How does one sift among the policies, the desires, the aspirations of human beings organized in communities to decide which are moderate and which are not? What tests do we use? And what happens when the one community's necessities are a threat to other communities? What makes an aspiration legitimate? For even if an overriding awareness of the nuclear threat made men sober, fear does not make community. Hobbes was wrong.

The Intermingling of Political Ethics

Let us turn to the third contemporary source of this crisis of ethics and world politics mentioned above: the intermingling of systems of political ethics, some of which, like Marxism and Western liberalism, possess universal qualities. This particular source of crisis is the greatest challenge to America's particular pretensions and aspirations in world affairs.

During World War I, before America's entry, Woodrow Wilson frequently described America's position toward the conflict as "disinterested" and set forth the benign possibilities of her mediation with the phrase "organized opinions of mankind." By the first, Wilson meant not apathetic but concerned in a particular way. To him and many others of that era, "disinterestedness" meant detached objectivity, a condition of watching and judging something which did not involve personal interest. By the second, Wilson had in mind the supposed existence of a consensus of political judgment among men against which the activities and policies of nations could be judged. Both phrases presupposed the possibility of objectivity; the latter presupposed the possibility of consensus in large bodies of detached and informed men. Both asserted the possibility of viewing events and actions in world politics not only dispassionately but justly.

Wilson spoke for a detached America, one which saw few interests of its own in the conflict to prejudice America's objectivity in viewing the merits of either side's claims. Or so he thought. Such detachment was impossible. Would a predominantly Germanic America, for instance, have shown as much willingness to associate itself with the Allies in 1917 as did a predominantly Anglo-Saxon America? Could a Wilson who numbered Gladstone and Coke among his private heroes, whose Scotch-Irish forebears had been composed of Presbyterian clergymen, so distance himself from England that these things made no difference? Perhaps America had no interests in the particulars of a Balkan territorial settlement then; did this also mean that it had no interests in the survival capacity of the West European democracies?

Today we say Wilson was either obtuse, hypocritical, or not sufficiently aware of the subjective character of his judgments. In any event, he was wrong. Interest and subjectivity are universal human attributes of mind and action. Opinions may be organized, but the idea of international objectivity is absurd. Furthermore, the fact that opinions are organized does not mean they are right or unchanging.

THE NATIONAL COMMUNITY AS ETHICALLY SUPREME Let us go back a step. The classical assumption was that while such detachment was impossible, a common body of shared ethical premises affecting political behavior within a system of law was possible only within a community where there *was* a common set of values, a common understanding about the nature of the community itself. Objectivity in judging events and in assessing their implications was needed above all. A moral touchstone was required to determine what was politically good or bad. In modern times and for practical purposes, one principal point of departure was the *national* community. To be sure, this assertion of the ethical supremacy of the national community did not go unchallenged. Set against it in the European experience during the eighteenth and nineteenth centuries were all of the lesser parochialisms: sub-regional ties to communities other than the nation; ties to the larger cultural and religious institutions which pre-dated the nation-state, notably the Roman Catholic Church and the Holy Roman Empire. Some men of intellect and some of faith found this ethical supremacy of the nation subversive of larger or transnational communities. Finally, in the nineteenth century and after, the national community and its ethical supremacy was challenged by the Marxists who regarded it as a device by which *one class* of society might tyrannize the rest. For the Marxist, ethical solidarity was based on class, and the triumph of class over nation-state was not only inevitable, but historically justified.

This was part of a continuing debate in Europe during the centuries of its political supremacy in world politics. Transplanted to America, the dialogue was modified significantly. The possibility of religious freedom *within* a secular national community served to muffle the ancient antagonism between church and state. Also, the triumph of the principle of territoriality as basis of nationality and citizenship muffled the ethnic-national tensions which had so exacerbated the European struggles for nationality and nationalism, for American nationalism lauded the country's multi-ethnic character. As much as it insisted upon the linguistic supremacy of the original Anglo-Saxon culture, the new national entity succeeded in incorporating many races into a new, non-racial nation. Blood and soil, the conventional foundation of European nationalism, proved absurd in a democracy which eulogized the democratic man and in which mobility—of class, occupation, and geography—was the rule. Overcoming race, America also overcame class. Of course, these American triumphs were incomplete, and for the American Negro, tragically insufficient. But the goal remained.

Even so, America did not solve the problem of ethics; it merely raised the dialogue to a higher level. Transcending European particularities, American nationalism created a "more perfect union," of course incomplete, larger and more embracing, but still finite. To the older, more confined European world, the American community had transcended the ethical limitations of the more fragmented cultures from which almost all Americans had come. When European nationalism reached the heights of xenophobia and internal bitterness in the 1930's, this example of the New World finally helped to mitigate the excesses of European nationalism. But in the broader, global context which followed in the wake of World War II, Americans discovered to their profound dismay and disillusionment that in large parts of the underdeveloped, non-European world, their achievement of a multi-ethnic, non-racial, political universe was deprecated and misunderstood. Indeed to many non-European nationalists, America exemplified the very thing colonial Europe had stood for: "white" culture in a predominantly non-white world. United States immigration laws, domestic racial discrimination against non-Europeans, segregation in housing, education, and occupations all seemed to confirm that America was now a dominant element of a European Old World confronting a New World of revolutionary, new, non-European men. Its ethical pretensions were weighed against its historic intimacy and involvement in Western culture and civilization. (In a General Assembly meeting in the late 1940's, when the United States delegation pressed upon Arab and Israeli representatives the need for a peaceful settlement of their war, an American Senator arose to urge that the two sides come to a "genuinely Christian settlement" of their grievances.)

PROBLEMS OF THE MELTING POT   We could dwell at length on this sobering American experience, but it should be seen in a much larger context. Censured by the non-European world and feeling guilty because of it, many American liberals stressed America's responsibility to set a moral example of good inter-racial relations. Many "realists," arguing from less inspiring moral grounds, reached the same conclusion. In a predominantly non-European and non-Caucasian world, America's universalistic pretensions (so plausible in a European context) looked shabby and were endangering its prestige. But was America *more* guilty than others? One could point out America's shortcomings when the yardstick was its own philosophical standards, but there were few external standards and examples which matched these. In post-war Europe, anti-American sentiment among left-wing intellectuals, particularly in England, was nurtured on American racial difficulties, notably "lynching" and segregation, but there was something pernicious in the moral outrage. British naturalization and immigration laws had historically been sufficiently tight to virtually exclude from British national experience the massive difficulties presented in the American "melting pot." In a nation which had virtually no Negro population, there was no "Negro problem"; and the bitter race riots of the late 1950's and early 1960's in British industrial cities, a consequence of rising Jamaican immigration, served ironic notice on British intellectuals that Americans had no monopoly on imperfection.

It would be misleading to stress the most obvious aspect of this condition: the sudden crushing together of many different political cultures into proximity as a consequence of the shrinking spatial dimensions of world politics. In and of itself, this experience was historically unprecedented and posed serious problems. Until the end of the nineteenth century, political co-existence among major political entities was the more feasible simply because many of them were unaware of each other's existence. Whole civilizations could flourish simultaneously in almost total ignorance of each other. This mutual inaccessibility kept politics within finite limits. What accounted, in large measure, for the inaccessibility were the limitations on human knowledge, on man's ability to move physically, to transmit messages, and to transmit culture.

Such contacts could always be limited by state policy. Witness, for instance, the many efforts of authoritarian states to regulate the flow of information and people across borders by political means. The point here is that historically such political measures were but marginal supplements to more powerful, natural restraints on human contact. The latter were the ones which technology undermined.

The intimate confrontation of previously isolated cultures posed explosive possibilities for which no one was prepared. It was not only the possibility of mutual permeability and the reciprocal shattering of traditional modes of thinking and behavior, as expressed in "East" met "West," or "America" met "Asia," etc. Unfortunately the multifarious encounters were invariably regarded as meetings between "weaker" and "stronger." Even in the earlier confrontation of Europe and non-Europe in Africa and Asia, it spelled centuries of colonial subjugation for those cultures which, unlike the Japanese, proved incapable of setting limits on the encounter. For all who succumbed, it meant the radical disruption of traditional ways of life. For some, like Mehamet Ali in Egypt and Kemal Ataturk in Turkey, it was a challenge to *transform* the internal political, administrative, and cultural modes simply in order to survive as political entities. These encounters were relatively few and far between until the mid-twentieth century, however. Another important factor was the seeming obduracy of apparently resilient cultures to the changes which the encounters made possible. This relative slowness is now a thing of the past. Technological and political change can be encompassed within a decade and whole societies can be transformed, as it were, in the twinkling of an eye. Above all, Europe's own historic role as initiator of contact, change, and cultural dominion has come to an end.

Now this crushing-together posed perplexing ethical problems of which we are all too dimly aware. There was, for one, the supreme question posed by encounters between cultures in different stages of development: did vulnerability mean inferiority; did inferiority mean unworthiness? In an age when whole cultures could be bulldozed, where traditional modes of life, long undisturbed, could be wiped out along with their artifacts, was there no test of their capacity to survive save sheer force? It was all well and good to sympathize with the victims and preserve some artifacts. But the real problem was that victims of cultural change were essentially directionless. They simply ceased to have any ethical yardsticks or even pointers to tell them: *This is the way we should go.* The process of encounters, when closely observed, became indeterminate as well as amoral.

THE EUROPEAN MODEL   On the level of world politics, however, this problem posed *particular* kinds of ethical questions. The society of nations, as a visible community of sovereign states, had developed within a European context. As such, despite its own grievous shortcomings as a political system, it had observable characteristics best understood within a specific Western, European context of time and history. The antagonisms among states and national entities within this older European system are too familiar to be recapitulated here, but above them, transcending them, there had been historical continuities of action and form. Furthermore, the concept of the society of nations was one which the "best" Europeans had hoped would some day be extended to cover the entire globe, thus infusing a coming world order with the amenities of the initial European one. But the coming into being of global political interrelatedness threatened the supremacy and the superior vitality of even the European core of that society. That society of nations had common roots within a Christian-Judaic-Roman tradition; it had worked out its operating procedures slowly over the course of centuries. (For example, basic criteria of diplomatic procedures and relationships had been first worked out in the modern Western context in the Treaty of Westphalia in 1648; the conceptions of diplomacy by conference, of the balance of power, of the concert of power, of multilateral international organizations, of a supranational parliament of nations all arose in time and historical fashion out of Europe, which gave them juridical and philosophical form.) Crude, even primitive, as such procedures and institutions may have been, they comprised a distinct corpus of European juridical and constitutional principles and practices. In these conventions, the non-Europeans had played no particular role for, until the twentieth century, they had been the subjects of world politics.

The prospect of the spatial extension of the forms of the European society of nations had been one which many Western liberals, notably Americans, associated with a particular kind of historic goal, a world of free and independent states, associated under some larger framework of international order, loose or tight, federal or confederal, which could in itself develop ultimately into a world community of nations. Here, in this dream, the prospect of both freedom and order was displayed.

The conception was teleological, but the purpose itself was firmly imbedded in the historic traditions of Western political thought. (In the medieval era, for instance, it had been the "remembered unity" of the West under Roman dominion and the spiritual assertion of a transcendent Christian community of men, which at least had made plausible the concept of a future *civitas dei*, which in turn made it intellectually possible to conceive of a transcendent community of nations.) It is impossible to extricate the programmatic expectations and hopes of secular, European liberals (and Americans) from this remembrance of an historic unity (however finite it really was in a global sense), and from this religious proclamation of human kinship, Biblical in its ultimate source.

The rudimentary international organizations, such as the League of Nations and the United Nations, bore a heavy impress of these European legacies, and much of the spirit of such emergent institutions could only be accounted for by Western thought. However impotent one might think "mere debate" in the assemblies, or whatever flaws one might see in their constitutional structures, it still was true that here, in Geneva, in the United Nations in New York, the amenities were Western. The notion that in a free assembly, nations could speak freely, that parliamentary procedures, legacies of Western legislative experiences, could guarantee adherence to constitutional principles of due process, that no nation should be "shocked into silence," these things bespoke a Western tradition of civility. Many men hoped and expected that out of such experiences of international legislation and administration, however rudimentary, might come something more encompassing and more effective. The new nations of the non-European world, so it was thought, could be co-opted into this system; the experience of it would, or could, train them in the amenities of a civil international order. These were the expectations and it was said that the race was not only between organization and catastrophe, but between enlarged civility and annihilation.

Now the crushing together of many differing political cultures posed singular difficulties for this older, Western conception of progression in time toward an international civil community. In the Western liberal tradition, it had been assumed that a precondition for such a future order would be not merely universality of state-membership in it but that a dominant grouping within the international order itself would consist of states which had a domestic respect for these civilities, juridical and legislative procedures, and other amenities of a constitutional order. Weak as the League of Nations was, it still had manifested these qualities. They had been infused into it by the pre-eminence not only of its chief Western supporters, the British, the French, and the parliamentary democracies of Western Europe, but also by the hovering presence outside of it of the United States. The very effectiveness of the League and its successor, the United Nations, among Western liberals was further based upon the adherence to the civilities of discourse, free debate, and due process of procedures, which were conditions also of a free society. In a sense, the strength of these traditions did depend upon the continued preeminence of the free nations with stable regimes in the multinational organizations.

Yet the new nations, so rapidly infused into both the society of nations and the international organizations which existed as superstructure over it, gravely imperilled this condition. They themselves were malleable. Some were wholly alien to Western political concepts. Others displayed little capacity for civil amenities in their own domestic politics. For many, the confrontation with international politics in the wake of their own national independence brought into question their own stability as separate state entities. For many, also, sudden independence merely made possible their deterioration into political forms which, however appropriate to their immediate difficulties, bore little resemblance to the Western systems from which they had been liberated. In the throes of social change themselves, they introduced a new element of instability into both the society of nations and international organizations. If the League of Nations had been killed by aggressor states from the outside, the United Nations now found itself gravely endangered from within because of the dwindling influence and authority of the more stable, older states which had shaped its original form. The hope remained, of course, that these traditions could be ultimately infused into the new nations, but there was nothing inexorable about this. The process might be a two-way street, and the very difficulties of these states themselves, injected into the organization, could severely tax the latter's own capacity to maintain itself.

It would be easy to see in this commingling of states and political systems a kind of massive anthropological encounter of cultures long separated from each other and suddenly brought into proximity. If this had been the case, the ethical problem would at least have been comprehensible, for then the crisis of world politics could be diagnosed as the confrontation of traditional entities, imbued with traditional national aspirations, with peculiar and unique national values. This kind of a world, composed of the most heterogeneous political systems and the most variegated religious backgrounds, would provide difficulties enough in determining what standards should be applied to their encounters. Such encounters could breed serious international tensions but there were ways of dealing philosophically and politically with such matters.

Cultural co-existence among differing linguistic or ethnic entities was not impossible. Political scientists, social scientists, and students of jurisprudence had long struggled with formulae to permit such co-existence, even within existing state entities. In Switzerland, the very ethnic-linguistic groups which had engaged in fierce nationalist struggles outside Switzerland during the nineteenth and twentieth centuries, had composed their own difficulties and managed to live within a tripartite culture of Germans,

Italians, and French. In Canada, French-Canadians and English-Scots-Irish Canadians had managed to compose their differences in a federal system.

What was generally conceded to be necessary in modulating such encounters was a common acceptance of the cultural plurality of the world. Men raised and educated in a cosmopolitan, urbane tradition did not find this impossible, and other men could be taught these civilities. Racial and religious prejudice could be seen as vestigial parochialisms in a world which, nearly every "civilized man" would agree, could no longer tolerate them. Social scientists could demonstrate that intolerance was closely associated with other parochial qualities of mind, environment, and physical estate: with poverty, ignorance, pessimism, rigid authoritarian personality structure; in short, with all the features of human behavior which, so it was said, humanity could no longer afford. And in the mid-twentieth century, after the subjugation of Nazism, few men talked much about reducing politics to racial or cultural politics, the politics, that is, of state entities waging war upon each other in defense of unique features of traditional cultures.

This was true even among the Communist states after Stalin's time and in many respects during his reign. For Soviet Communism, unlike National Socialism, did not seek to exterminate cultures but rather to capture them and, in the interests of the Socialist ideal, put them to the service of totalitarian ends. The notorious treatment of both Jewish and German minorities in the Soviet Union during the Stalin period (which were significant exceptions to this more general rule) did not disprove the rule.

Indeed this appeared particularly true in the newly liberated states in Africa and Asia. The nationalist leadership in these areas was chiefly preoccupied not with the atavistic concerns of their own cultures but with the achievement of their independence from their Western colonial masters, and with the transformation of their societies into modern entities. The leaders were themselves in large measure educated in the very Western cultures against which they turned in revolt and often far closer to the amenities of Western life than to the primitive cultures they came to rule over. Concerned with political change, they embraced change, embracing also many economic and cultural alterations which would undermine the traditions of their societies.

The real problem was not the meeting of cultures but the meeting of unequals. It made possible sharp and poignant contrasts between impoverished and rich men, a confrontation of well-established, relatively stable political entities, like the Anglo-Saxon countries, with exceedingly fluid and problematical ones. It was a political confrontation (if we speak now of the West and the underdeveloped nations) of the residuary legatees of stable Western democratic institutions with nations with virtually no experience of managing the complex affairs of large political orders, democratic or otherwise. And finally, it was a confrontation between nations and cultures which were unequal in one major respect: their respective abilities to manage social transition without major domestic social upheaval. Their great resources of technique and capital seemed to compound the dilemma, for much, perhaps the survival of Western freedom, hinged upon the extent to which the new nations *would* continue to emulate Western values. Unfortunately there seemed no necessity for them to do so.

Among the various interests which the overdeveloped countries retained in the underdeveloped world were many which grievously hindered their own larger purposes: a certain obtuseness, disregard, or residual nonchalance of large Western corporations with heavy investments in these countries toward essential political problems. They were nonchalant, too, toward urgent problems of domestic economic reform and often indifferent towards the nature of local government, so long as these were avowedly anti-Communist, apparently stable, and friendly to local American interest, governmental or private.

But even omitting the Western corporations' inhospitableness to guided revolution and the depth of Western self-interest, the problem of imperialism would have remained. One wished these new states to move, gradually or otherwise, along the political paths trod earlier by the Western open societies. One wished that their difficulties in meeting economic crises, in diversifying their industries, in moving upward on the ladder of development could be met without recourse to totalitarian means and the possibility of an irrevocable shift to totalitarianism. Force seemed out of the question. The American demand for a people to choose freedom by orderly, constitutional means could not always stand up against the Soviet glorification of violence against established local governments. Beginning in the early 1950's the United States, through vast programs of military assistance, sought to make some of these new states viable—able to withstand outside attack and military invasion. But this was a different matter from the use by the United States of military force against regimes or the participation of American troops and other personnel in warfare within disrupted states. For such actions raised not only the ethical problem of intervention but prudential questions as well: what did one do when other men were unwilling to defend themselves? What did one do when democracy and other fundamental Western values simply did not take?

THE BOLSHEVIK REVOLUTION Spatial proximity and the meeting of formerly distant cultures and polities became more the confrontation of the novel than of the traditional. After World War II, the colliding cultures may have been old, but the political forms in which they expressed themselves were new. There were not only new states like Mali, Ghana, Ceylon, Indonesia, Jordan, etc., but new regimes so markedly different from their predecessors as to be virtually unrecognizable. To make things even worse, it soon became obvious that the old, liberal dream of a unilateral progression of nations towards a more perfect international union had been smashed. Throughout the twentieth century, many writers, philosophers, and statesmen doubted its possibility for what might be called classical reasons: they doubted that such supranational integration could take place at all. The classic realists saw a world of states with interests. They pursued relationships among themselves by diplomacy and war. There seemed to be such a classic, cyclic quality to these continuous dynamics of international politics that one could develop laws of politics about them. Not only did war and peace succeed each other but also shifts in the balance of power did not mean an end to the balance. It seemed, furthermore, that these conditions would always exist. Thus a tidy optimism could be perceived in the realists' own pessimism: the confidence that the essential condition was immutable; anarchy had its own order, conventions, and traditions, just as hell hath its own laws.

But the Bolshevik Revolution seemed to prove that both the realist and the progressive utopian were wrong. Aside from its many other grievous implications, this historic event, as we now look back upon it, had a simply extraordinary effect upon the ethical issues in international politics. It was not only that Marxism-Leninism introduced into men's concept of politics certain universal theories about political change and about human actions in effecting this change. It was not merely Marxism-Leninism's insistence that revolution and class war were both real and ethically legitimate nor, for that matter, the Marxist doctrine that human society as a whole would be ultimately transformed according to predictable laws. It was in the realm of world politics that Marxism-Leninism simply denied the very real world of states and nations in which the new Soviet state existed; it rejected, as well, the very minimal premises upon which the nascent, fragile, supranational organizations were built. And finally, with the passage of time, as the Soviet Union and other Communist states came to manifest some permanence, there developed in the Communist world a political system, a nucleus of constantly waxing power which denied any permanence or legitimacy whatsoever to any political institutions which lay outside it.

In contrast to both the pragmatic conceptions of politics in the Western Anglo-Saxon world and the conventional realism of conservative Continental thought, what Marxism stressed was a profoundly new utopianism. At the same time that it relegated the existing political orders of the non-Socialist world to the rubbish heap of history, it also radically disposed of the very problems which Western political thought had so long grappled with when dealing with world politics and the politics of the finite polity. However much Marxist-Leninist conceptions of world politics altered with the passage of time, after the birth of the Soviet State in 1917, they consistently denied any but a transitional reality to the world of politics as it appeared.

It was, of course, nothing new to proclaim that appearances often deceptively obscure hidden processes of change. But Marxism added something radically new to this: a philosophical attack upon all existing political forms. In Marxist thought, everything political was provisional. The process of transition itself was one of successive, inevitable apocalypses abetted by conscious human will. The shape of present things, including the shape of world politics, would crumble into ruin and would make possible not only a wholly new era of relations among peoples, but a radical transformation of human nature itself. The dim and vague predictions of a new world order in which all political entities would disappear into a final, stateless, coercionless world of material abundance, held out the ultimate promise: political power itself would ultimately be abolished and thus, in a sense, political theory would cease to have any meaning at all.

The tensions between this apocalyptic promise of Marxist thought and the emerging realities of Soviet politics and foreign policy became obvious from the moment the Revolution triumphed in Russia. For the Soviet state itself, from 1917 onwards, became involved as an entity in the real world which its own doctrine denied. Its survival as a Socialist nucleus within a particular traditional state, Russia, not only enormously enhanced its power, but also involved the intermixing of traditional aspirations of the Russian state with the new doctrines and motives of

Communism with which its leadership was imbued. Involved in the day-to-day struggle to survive within a hostile world, the new Soviet state took on itself the responsibilities of statehood. As an entity among other entities, it developed apparatuses of power both to defend itself (as the Socialist motherland) and to extend itself further into the surrounding, capitalist world.

Whether the doctrinal and ethical compromises entailed in this accommodation were, as Trotsky early alleged, a betrayal of revolution, or whether they were necessary adjustments to a particular historical situation, is beside the point. The point was that the new Soviet state, experiencing the confrontation with reality, did not abandon its doctrine. And the doctrine remained, a fundamental attack upon traditional conceptions of reality and of political thought in general; rooted now in a substantial segment of the globe and continuing to attract revolutionary adherents elsewhere in the non-Communist world, it proclaimed the imminent demise of all systems of order still outside its reach. Its involvement in the affairs of the transitional world thus made all arrangements, all treaties, conventions, and other commitments provisional. Its membership in international organizations, such as the United Nations, was likewise provisional.

It was all well and good for some Westerners to point to the various ways in which the Soviet Union had become, like the rest, a state with interests, a state subject to constant accommodation of pressures from within and without. It was hopeful to see, occasionally, signs within Soviet leadership that its perception of external political realities had improved, even to the point of contradicting certain doctrines. But the intellectual-philosophical problem was that through the decades, the essential point of Marxism remained: a recalcitrant world of political reality could be, as it were, overwhelmed. Philosophy thus could work its way *into* political and social reality and transform it. Communism was thus not merely a faith, it was something more profound than either faith or reason. Its very power sprang from the knowledge that seemingly obtuse and recalcitrant "facts" of human nature were essentially malleable and "provisional." The supreme irony, unnoticed by many Westerners profoundly shocked by this presumptuousness, was that any number could, in theory, play this game; even, for that matter, Westerners themselves.

In the realm of world politics, the advent of the Soviet Union raised certain particular difficulties. The most obvious, of course, was the unique character of the political order which Soviet Communism introduced into the world of once normal international relations. For the Soviet Union was a constant contradiction in the day-to-day world of things. It was a movement and it was an order. It was nationally and ethnically unique and finite: Russia; and it was philosophically universal: Communism. It was, or came to be, a totalitarian state, capable of great ruthlessness, deceit, and manipulative flexibility, and it was also a philosophy which seemed fundamentally to proclaim the abolition of political power. Finally, even though Soviet Marxism sought by force, revolution, and subversion to extend the scope of its totalitarian influence more broadly, it was also intrinsically incapable of giving concrete philosophical substance to the supposed future order which was to be brought into being. Using power and abusing it also, it denied the ultimate need of power in the utopia it proclaimed inevitable. Thus skirting the ultimate problem of power, it was utterly incapable of designing the ideal world it supposedly longed for.

In a very fundamental sense, Marxism, as manifested in the Soviet Union, had less to say about problems of ultimate order than its major antagonist, Western liberalism. For much as the latter mistrusted power and sought to establish checks upon it, it did not reject power. Nor did it reject the idea of order. The Western liberal ideal of a world confederal or federal system as an ultimate political goal of thought was, if unrealistic, at least tangible. Gradualist liberals could place some hope in emerging supranational organizations, such as the United Nations and its ancillary apparatuses, seeing in them emerging manifestations of ultimately necessary forms. Against such tangible forms and proposed constitutional orders, Marxist philosophy had nothing whatsoever to propose which was not in itself provisional.

This essential emptiness of Soviet political thought about ultimate constitutional forms posed extraordinary difficulties for Marxism everywhere—notably after the Soviet Union in the 1950's began to lose its place of unchallenged doctrinal and political supremacy in the world of Communist states. Inexorably, the Communist world of states began to take on sinister resemblances to the so-called bourgeois system of states, but with this difference: no one in the Soviet world could, without overtly refuting Marxist doctrine, construct tangible proposals for ultimate international institutions. The dissolution of the Comintern in 1943 had left the Communist world thus bereft of even a rudimentary constitutional system for procedurally regulating the affairs of Communist states among each other. The philosophical difficulty here was obvious. Any concrete politico-constitutional order for the Communist world, once it had triumphed, would refute the very premise upon which Communism was built: that political power would disappear. Little is made of this profound difficulty of Soviet thought, the simple point being that no Marxist could formulate a coherent constitutional doctrine for utopia nor contemplate the gradual nascence of ultimately permanent political forms without betraying himself.

Objectively speaking, absolutist Soviet utopianism was required, in and of itself, to be wholly provisional, unless a condition of absolute totalitarianism, far more massive than Stalin's had ever been, could be imposed upon the real world of politics, including the politics of the existing Communist states. Thus, finally, the interesting prospect (in a wholly theoretical sense) was of a "final apocalypse" fought out among Communist states themselves for totalitarian supremacy to finally dominate and remake the world.

SUGGESTED READING

Acheson, Dean, "Morality, Moralism and Diplomacy," *Yale Review*, June, 1958, pp. 481-493.

Butterfield, Herbert, *Christianity, Diplomacy, and War*, New York, Abingdon-Cokesbury Press, n.d.

Butterfield, H., "The Tragic Element in Modern International Conflict," *Review of Politics*, April, 1950, pp. 147-164.

Camus, Albert, "Letters to a German Friend," in his *Resistance, Rebellion, and Death*, New York, Knopf, 1961, pp. 1-32.

Jaspers, Karl, *The Future of Man*, Chicago, University of Chicago Press, 1961.

Lefever, Ernest, *Ethics and the United States Foreign Policy*, New York, Meridian Books, 1957.

Morgenthau, Hans, "Western Values and Atomic War," *Commentary*, October, 1961, pp. 277-304.

Niebuhr, Reinhold, *Moral Man and Immoral Society*, New York, Scribner's, 1932, esp. pp. 83-112.

Niebuhr, Reinhold, *The Children of Light and the Children of Darkness*, New York, Scribner's, 1944.

Wolfers, Arnold, "Statesmanship and Moral Choice," in Jacobson, Harold K., *American Foreign Policy*, New York, Random House, 1960, pp. 67-84.

THE CONSTITUTIONAL

SETTING OF POLICY

Order is the first desideratum for the simple reason that chaos means non-existence.

REINHOLD NIEBUHR

IN THE PAST TWENTY YEARS, organizational innovations to cope with international crisis have profoundly affected all spheres of American government and policies. The kinds of public transactions occurring between the United States and other nations have grown. Traditional American diplomatic and military establishments have been enlarged beyond belief, and their tasks both diversified and intensified. Secret intelligence and propaganda have been added to them. The overseas activities of once domestic governmental agencies like the Departments of Labor, Agriculture, and Treasury have become global in scope. Requirements of speed, flexibility, and adaptability have greatly strained traditional modes of administration. New international organizations add a further multilateral dimension to the encounters and transactions of states. Everything is related to everything else. This organizational revolution is hardly unique to the United States. But due to the central position of the United States in the non-Communist world, the making of American foreign policy, never an easy task, has been altered beyond belief.

The management of foreign affairs seems to many people an arcane and obscure affair. Not secrecy alone (a perpetual problem of democracies in foreign affairs), but also complexity, have made it virtually incomprehensible to the man in the street, and deeply puzzling at times even to many men who work within the labyrinthine corridors of government itself. American social scientists and journalists today attempt to light up these corridors by crystallizing or photographing the complex processes of decision-making. But they constantly run up against the extraordinary difficulty that the processes appear so ephemeral, and so contingent upon changing global political problems. The processes seemingly depend too upon constant shifts in locale and intensity of human power, vigor, lethargy, purpose, and resources. Representative government and democracy are based in theory upon the principle of consent of the governed and the accountability of government to society; but consent, accountability, and responsibility are often hard come by, in such times.

THE UMBRELLA OF
CONSTITUTIONAL ORDER

We might first ask whether these processes take place under the larger umbrella of some established constitutional order. Today many states in the society of nations are, in a certain sense, only processes, so new, provisional, and transitory do their political institutions appear. Nearly a third of the total United Nations membership today consists of nation-states which did not exist ten years ago. But even many "older" state entities today appear equally provisional as far as their basic constitutional order and their claim to statehood is concerned. A governmental process which we see today may, like that of the United Arab Republic, simply not exist tomorrow. The legitimacy of a particular existing constitutional order may be widely challenged, both at home or abroad. In some states, there is not even a rudimentary popular consciousness of nationality, much less a popular acceptance of the existing constitutional order of things.[1] Such conditions provoke instability and indeterminancy in foreign affairs. Harold Lasswell's generally insufficient description of the State as a "manifold of events" [2] is quite appropriate for many of these valuable and volatile nations, notably those of the new Afro-Asian bloc, where tradition, custom, and a domestic political consensus are too rudimentary to amount to much.

A state or political community must have a stable constitutional order if it is to survive in the sea of events around it. Yet such an order, essential elements of which are popular consent and understanding, is present in the world today only among a few of the more highly integrated and historically deep-rooted political communities of the Western world. Clearly it exists in Great Britain and the United States. Their political orders are regarded as much more than ephemeral processes. They are widely comprehended, authoritative arrangements of political

---

[1] An extreme instance of this political condition may be seen today in the relationship of the West German *Bundesrepublik* and the Soviet *Deutsche Demokratische Republik* of East Germany. No one would deny the existence, in Germany as a whole, of something known as consciousness of nationality, but there is hardly any popular consensus about the desirable territorial or constitutional order of things. West German Foreign Minister von Brentano, when asked whether the *Bundesrepublik* would be willing to negotiate about the relationship of these two regimes, replied, "Yes, but not with the prison guards" (namely, the East German authorities). Washington *Post*, October 15, 1961.

[2] See his *Psychopathology and Politics*, rev. ed. New York: Viking, 1960, Ch. XIII. "The time-space abstraction of the 'group,' " Lasswell writes, "is just as 'real' or 'unreal' as the time-space abstraction called the 'individual.' They are both equally real or unreal, and they stand and fall together." This definition would be equally adequate and puzzling to both Queen Elizabeth and Mr. Moise Tshombe as descriptive of their respective states.

power. The state itself is subordinate to this constitutional order, which, so it is said, both legitimizes the exercise of political power and sets limits upon it. While one might point to some states in the Soviet or Communist world as also possessing rudimentary elements of popular consent and political continuity, it should be pointed out that force and violence play an essential role in their constitutional stability. Marxist theory about the state explicitly proclaims its provisional character: i.e., the state is an historically contingent entity which shall pass away when certain objective transformations have taken place in society. Marxist doctrine thus provisionalizes even the institutions of the Soviet world itself. (*See* Chapter 6.)

A supreme constitutional problem of all national political entities is that of arranging both authority and political power so that the state may legitimately, purposively, and effectively act in the realm of world politics, a realm occupied by many other states similarly claiming their sovereign rights. In relatively stable political entities, the foreign policy processes thus possess a certain orderliness and stability. These foreign policy processes are products of a perpetual tension between constitutional forms and unique political contingencies of the moment.

A constitution is not merely a description of transitory allocations of political influence and power in a state; it is also something less than a description of the totality of form and order in the whole society. In Western political thought, a constitutional order signifies a government of laws, not of men. Ultimate authority theoretically resides in supreme law, with which lesser laws, enacted by men, supposedly should harmonize. A constitutional order is ideally an order in which political power is legitimized, allocated, limited, and synchronized. A constitutional order not merely legitimizes the exercise of political power but also serves to ensure its orderly, civil transfer so that there may be continuity of government among men. Two general types of politics might be distinguished here for our purposes: the political system which is constitutional by the above definition and the one which is not.

For while all regimes and governments exercise political power by nature and customarily seek to perpetuate themselves, some are essentially formless or even limitless both in the power they seek, and the objects over which they would employ it.

A nonconstitutional political system could be defined as one in which the actual distribution of power differs radically from the proclaimed or specified distribution of power which a written document, basic law, or customary usage may speak of. (Of course a written constitution may actually serve to obscure the essential order of things.) But in the modern totalitarian state, a nonconstitutional order may have a certain formlessness of a political system which defies conceptualization because it contemptuously rejects restraints and forms. This quality has frequently been pointed out in Nazi totalitarianism. Not only did Hitler smash the Weimar Constitution without even bothering to replace it with another "paper document" (something which the Bolsheviks, with their greater reverence for the State, did do quickly after seizing power); the very absence of any constitutional specification of rights and obligations, of distribution of powers, of any enduring perquisites and duties, or functional authorities meant that both in theory and fact the whole system was subject to change at any time. Thus, in a sense, there was no limit to power, since no form persisted. The concentration camps of Auschwitz, Belsen, and elsewhere are memorials to this condition. Attempts by Nazi constitutional apologists to legitimate the regime by proclaiming a direct, unmediated relationship between the Führer and the German Volk, whose will he supposedly expressed (just as Castro embodies the Cuban "will"), veiled a fatal constitutional flaw in the system which Hitler's defeat in war only further obscured: the system specified no legitimate procedure by which the charismatic leader's power and authority could be transmitted in orderly constitutional fashion to a successor. H. R. Trevor-Roper describes the Nazi political system as a court, but it was the court of a king, who, like the donkey, had neither pride of parentage nor hope of progeny.

A Juridical Contradiction

A curious juridical contradiction inheres in many Western constitutions, including that of the United States. While the domestic power of the state over its subjects is typically limited by the constitution (which specifies checks upon executive and lawmaking power) still, the power of the state in the larger context of the society of nations is invariably regarded as sovereign and plenary. Seen from the outside, the state is a juridical entity in international law, to be held accountable for its actions in the international society. It is also an entity which, charged with promoting the security and general welfare of its people, should act in a unitary fashion, even though its domestic, constitutional attributes of power may be juridically separated and divided. John Locke, one of the foremost political theorists of the English speaking world, sought to account for this necessary contradiction between the plenary sovereign power of the state and its executive in foreign affairs and the limited power of the constitutional state and executive power *within* the society. According to Locke:

There is . . . [a] power in every commonwealth which one may call natural, because it is that which answers to the power every man naturally had before he entered into society. For though in a commonwealth, the members of it are distinct persons, still in reference to one another, and as such are governed by the laws of the society; yet in reference to the rest of mankind, they make one body, which is, as every member of it before was, still in the state of nature with the rest of mankind, hence it is, that the controversies that happen between any man of the society with those that are out of it, are managed by the public; and an injury done to a member of their body engages the whole in the reparation of it. So that, under this consideration, the whole community is one body in the state of Nature, in respect of all other states or persons out of its community.

This therefore contains the power of war and peace, leagues and alliances, and all the transactions, with all persons and communities without the commonwealth; and may be called federative, if any one pleases. So the thing be understood, I am indifferent as to the name.

These two powers, executive and federative, though they be really distinct in themselves, yet one comprehending the execution of the municipal laws of the society within itself, upon all that are parts of it; the other the management of the security and interest of the public without, with all those that it may receive benefit or damage from; yet they are always almost united. And though this federative power in the well or ill management of it be of great moment to the commonwealth, yet it is much less capable to be directed by antecedent, standing, positive laws than the executive; and so must necessarily be left to the prudence and wisdom of those whose hands it is in, to be managed for the public good. For the laws that concern subjects one amongst another, being to direct their actions, may well enough precede them. But what is to be done in reference to foreigners, depending much upon . . . them, to be managed by the best of their skill, for the advantage of the commonwealth.[3]

Thus the domestic, executive authority of a constitutional commonwealth might be required to obey and to execute the laws made by a legislature and be subject to many constitutional restraints on his power. But in the realm of foreign affairs these legislative-executive functions became, in a sense, fused. To act swiftly, purposively in world politics to protect or advance the interests of the society itself, the federative power was thus liberated in significant ways from constitutional constraints. Locke sees an executive as a Janus: one head looking inward upon the constitutional society, benign and limited in its power and authority; the other, looking outward to the world, authoritative and powerful, speaking, acting, and legislating with the authority of the whole society itself. This Lockean distinction between federative and executive power is embodied in the United States Constitution.

The American Constitution and the Problem of Power

The Constitution and foreign policy can hardly be discussed without first pointing to the remarkable durability and adaptive-

---

[3] John Locke, *Of Civil Government*. New York: E. P. Dutton and Company, 1924, pp. 191-192.

ness of the American political framework. The Constitution is more than 170 years old, older than the written constitution of any other modern state. The unwritten British constitution may, of course, be regarded as a far older, though a far more elusive juridical order—an amalgam of customs, uses, prerogatives, statutes, and Acts of Parliament. In contrast, the constitution of the French Fifth Republic today is only four years old; and France, since 1789, has had more than seven written constitutions. But equally remarkable, the constitutional entities which the Constitution originally prescribed have persisted vigorously despite the massive changes in American society and culture since the eighteenth century. Most Americans take it for granted as the juridical framework within which political life occurs. All major movements in American political life, even those which have stood on the radical fringes of the political spectrum, have accepted the Constitution as a desirable, enduring framework of political power and discourse. Since the eighteenth century there has been no significant American political movement which explicitly rejected it or posed any constitutional alternative.

By way of contrast, in nineteenth and twentieth century European politics, all of the major continental states have had profound disputes about what constitutional order was preferable. Thus, Professor Duverger, in writing of French politics, has made the interesting distinction between the "parties of order" and the "parties of movement," between those for whom a constitutional order was a paramount concern and those for whom political transformation was deemed superior to order itself. No such distinction could possibly be made in American politics, unless the American Communist Party were included in the argument. But even American Communists have recently been pressed into doctrinal conformity by denying un-Constitutional purposes! The great debate during the New Deal in the 1930's about the legitimacy of Roosevelt's social reforms was between those who denied their constitutionality and those who defended it. The great debate between North and South, preceding and during the Civil

War, was couched also in constitutional terms, both sides stressing the correctness of their own constitutional interpretations. What was originally designed for thirteen states and four million people, chiefly farmers and craftsmen, now applies to a nation of fifty states and 180,000,000 people, living in a highly complex industrial society. Perhaps in no earlier period in history has a constitutional system ever shown such vigorous adaptability and staying power.

The Constitution has been a framework within which a political dialogue about domestic and foreign policy has taken place, but it also has been a powerful agent to "legitimately" organize, diffuse, and separate political power and rights. During international crises, when alternative American courses of action have been subjects of domestic political debate, the meaning of the Constitution has invariably been re-explored, particularly, as we shall see, with respect to the extent of interrelationships and limits of federal, Presidential, and Congressional powers. The chief purpose of the Constitution was to "establish a more perfect Union," but an ancillary purpose was to subject political power and to distribute it among disparate functional elements of the American body politic. In the *Federalist* papers, Madison justified this latter purpose: "We must not shut our eyes to the nature of man . . . All power in human hands is liable to be abused. No form of government can be a perfect guard against the abuse of power. The recommendation of the republican (form of government) is that the danger of abuse is less than in any other."

Skepticism about human nature and concern for human liberties and political order and prosperity thus established a continuing tension between the domestic constitutional order of a republican polity (with power distributed and separated) and the international needs of a sovereign state, which require a separate and more trenchant kind of authority. This tension has been enduring and necessary. As a consequence, the federative power necessary to the survival of a state has constantly endangered the organizational principles of a free society at all times.

Fear of possible abuse of centralized power runs like a thread through the history of American political thought. The dangers it poses to contemporary American freedoms were recently stressed by President Eisenhower in his Farewell Address to the American people in January 1961:

> In the councils of Government, we must guard against the acquisition of unwarranted influence, whether sought or unsought by the military–industrial complex. The potential for the disastrous rise of misplaced power exists and will persist.
>
> We must never let the weight of this combination endanger our liberties or democratic processes. We should take nothing for granted. Only an alert and knowledgeable citizenry can compel the proper meshing of the high industrial and military machinery of defense with our peaceful methods and goals, so that security and liberty may prosper together.[4]

This remarkable caveat against possible abuses of military power obscured from public attention at the time a warning by Eisenhower against another possible threat to individual liberties from quite another source: "In holding scientific research and discovery in respect, we must also be alert to the equal and opposite danger that public policy could itself become the captive of a scientific-technological elite." [5]

This fear was anticipated by the framers of the constitution. Constitutional power was spatially and functionally dispersed: spatially, between a federal government and the governments of individual states; functionally, between executive, legislative, and judicial branches of government. The first ten amendments to the Constitution specify civil rights enjoyed by citizens against both federal and state authority. Within the overarching federal government, power was given in classic, Montesquieu fashion, to the President, the Congress, and the Supreme Court. The Bill of Rights, added to the Constitution as its first major amendment, specifies restraints upon the exercise of power by the state. It

---

[4] *The New York Times*, January 18, 1961.
[5] Ibid.

denies to authority, to government as a whole, certain powers which could conceivably make it limitless in power over the public and over individuals. Certain specified human rights of thought, expression, and action were juxtaposed to political authority, and the state, in theory, should not erode them. Freedom of speech, due process, free assembly, a free press—these provisions of the first ten amendments made explicit certain implicit characteristics of constitutions in general, i.e., the limitations upon state power *vis-à-vis* the public. Thus the authority of the American constitution came in part to consist of its own self-restraint and the restraints which it supposedly should instill in those who were to exercise legitimate authority in its name.

A tension developed between these doctrines of separation and limitation of powers and the exigencies of world politics. Domestic constitutionalism restrained power and established checks upon the modes and objects of its employment. A concern for national political and military security could often recommend exactly the opposite. In foreign affairs, protection of national interests and extension of American power abroad often seemed to require secrecy, authority, and almost authoritarian power. In conflicts of interest, ideology, or purpose among sovereign state entities, any state which was enfeebled by internal constitutional arrangements might be unable to act decisively. Such a state could not long endure and would inevitably fall victim, perhaps to its own domestic political virtues. Not without good reason did Tocqueville, in the early nineteenth century, write that democracies such as the United States seemed institutionally deficient in the realm of foreign affairs, incapable of pursuing any fixed design and perpetually inhibited by domestic political processes and whimsical wills of the public. What in a domestic context was virtue was in an international context a vice. Democracy, incapable of the purposefulness of authoritarian states, could be destroyed (or transformed into authoritarian form) by engaging in the necessary acts in which it was by nature least skillful.

Logic, wisdom, and reason cannot dissipate insoluble political problems. The *Realpolitik* tendency was toward sharp centralization of state power for foreign policy purposes. The Constitutional tendency was to restore balance in politics and to assert the *separateness* of powers. During grave crises, the matter recurrently rose to the surface of American political discourse.

Some Constitutional lawyers thought this tension originated in deficiencies of the Constitution as a written document. Professor E. L. Corwin has described the Constitution as a "standing invitation to struggle for the privilege of directing American foreign policy." But the essential difficulty was not only what the Constitution (as written document) said, but what it did not or could not say, and finally, what the particular problems were which the founding fathers* probably preferred to evade by silence. The Constitution clearly specified basic, organizational forms and principles of the domestic polity, but its prescriptions for foreign affairs powers were brief, insufficient, and ambiguous. The difficulty was unavoidable: how to preserve the theory of separation and limitation of powers yet at the same time construct effective agencies of power, and authority, in dealing with other states.

We should not detract too much from the Constitution. It confirmed the supremacy of federal agencies and authorities over individual states in the management of foreign affairs; it vested the supreme and exclusive powers of treaty-making, war-making, and diplomacy in the federal government. Treaties were exclusively to be negotiated by the federal government. When ratified, they were to become the "supreme law of the land," thus, presumably, prevailing over both state laws and prior Congressional legislation. States were enjoined from concluding treaties with other powers.

---

* Eisenhower, during his benign reign, sometimes spoke of the Constitution and the Declaration of Independence as the "founding documents," an awkward yet intriguing remark which few Americans noted. It seemed to suggest that the "documents" had simply ordered the "founding fathers" to write them. The innocence of the remark reflects a widespread popular reverence, if not a mystique, which Americans have for these documents: if the Constitution did not exist, God would have had to invent it. On such strange, unfathomable premises do some stable constitutional orders persist.

Command over national armed forces was vested in the President as Commander-in-Chief. He could dispose of them as he saw fit. The power to declare a state of war was vested in the Congress, which itself was a creature of the federal government. By inference, so too did Congress come to possess the power to declare a state of war ended. The President, "by and with the advice and consent of the Senate," was empowered to negotiate and to conclude treaties. Finally, the President was empowered to "send and receive Ambassadors," a power subsequently interpreted to imply that he could also "not send," and "not receive," the essential power of recognition and non-recognition of foreign states.

Here ends the catalogue of "enumerated" powers over foreign affairs. Yet even when these scanty specifications were set alongside other constitutional provisions, potential institutional conflicts were obvious. Meager as the specifications were, they bore seeds of dissension. What was not said also proved ultimately more important than what was.

The enduring constitutional issue rested in a single problem. The United States was a sovereign state in a system of sovereign states. If such sovereign power were supreme, how much of it could constitutionally be reposed in a sovereign executive without endangering the limitations, checks, and balances upon which the constitutional system was grounded? Or, to put the question in another way: how much and what kinds of constitutional powers did the executive require to make possible the rational, purposeful, and powerful conduct of foreign affairs? A deep-felt suspicion of power in the American democratic tradition gave rise to another question: how could a democratic political order, reposing upon the "consent of the governed," be reconciled with intrinsic authoritarian necessities of foreign affairs?

The Problem of Inherent Power

An early constitutional question was whether, in fact, the authority and power to conduct foreign relations derived from the

Constitution alone. Was the source of authority, as some suggested, possibly meta-constitutional? If so, then what possible restraints, other than political ones, could be imposed upon the exercise of powers derived from some law or authority beyond or above the Constitution itself?

The possibility was that both the power to conduct foreign relations and the supreme attribute of sovereignty itself arose because of the United States' sovereignty in the society of nations. This attribute and authority was inherited from its former possessor, the British Crown. Whether power had passed directly from the British Crown to the federal authorities of the new Republic or whether it came indirectly to those authorities via the individual states themselves (which, in the Constitution, supposedly had bequeathed them to the federal government), was somewhat beside the point. All states in the society of nations had such plenary powers. James Wilson first asserted the theory during the Constitutional Convention of 1787: "When the United States declared their independence, they were bound to receive the Law of Nations in its modern state of purity and refinement." [6]

This notion of inherent power, arising from the fact that the United States of America was a sovereign entity at international law, was elaborated by later American statesmen and jurists. In the hands of statesmen and Supreme Court Justices, the doctrine grew. America's entrance as a sovereign entity under international law implied the existence of a single government with unified and adequate power. Ironically it was Justice Sutherland, one of the willful "old men" of the Court of the 1930's (whose narrow conceptions of Presidential and federal power over domestic matters during the New Deal marked him as somewhat of a juridical troglodyte), who carried this meta-constitutional doctrine to its furthest extent. In the now-famous case of Curtiss-Wright in 1936 (a constitutional test of the extent of congressional and

---

[6] Quoted in Edwin S. Corwin, *The Presidency: Office and Powers.* New York: New York University Press, 1957, p. 172.

executive authority over foreign commerce), Justice Sutherland wrote:

> A political society cannot endure without a supreme will some-where. Sovereignty is never held in suspense. When, therefore, the external sovereignty of Great Britain in respect of the colonies ceased, it immediately passed to the union.[7]

This possibility suggested extreme constitutional difficulties. It suggested that sovereign executive authority in foreign affairs, juridically speaking, drew strength from traditional laws of the universe of the society of nations. Yet in this universe of states at the time of the founding of the Republic, the conception of state sovereignty was all too tightly associated with Continental European conceptions of *Staatsraison* and *Machtpolitik*. In the eighteenth century society of nations, the dynastic states derived legitimacy from the "grace of God," not the "will of the people"; in practice these states assumed that state interests were fundamental and that their pursuit was the exclusive task of the sovereign statesman or ruler. The national or dynastic interest could thus be established by the ruler himself, his ministers, and his bureaucratic associates and translated into policy and action. Acts and declarations of war, treaties, alliances, peace itself, and the military and diplomatic maneuvering which all these involved were matters of *Grosse Politik*. Normally they were shrouded from public view by the majestic machinery of the state. They were subject to few constitutional restraints or limitations of the people and their elected representatives. The Continental European tradition thus stressed the unitary and authoritarian character of sovereign power in foreign relations. The people and their elected representatives, if any, had no legitimate role to play in the control and conduct of foreign policy. But then, they had no significant role to play in domestic policy either. The constitutional dilemma posed for the American Republic was, at the time, unique.

[7] 299 U.S. 304, 1936, pp. 316-17.

In the famous pseudonymic debate concerning Presidential foreign policy powers in 1793 between Hamilton and Madison, Madison (replying as *Helvidius* to Hamilton's *Pacificus*) accused Hamilton of seeking surreptitiously to invest the Presidency with the prerogatives of the British Crown:

> . . . By whatever standard we try this doctrine, it must be condemned as no less vicious in theory than it would be dangerous in practice. It is countenanced neither by the writers on law; nor by the nature of the powers themselves; nor by any general arrangements . . . to be found in the constitution.
>
> Whence then can the writer have borrowed it? There is but one answer to this question. The power of making treaties and the power of declaring war, are royal prerogatives in the British government, and are accordingly treated as executive prerogatives by British commentators. . . .[8]

The particular issue then at stake concerned the constitutional justification of the President's power to proclaim neutrality in the war between France and England.

This constitutional novelty arose not just from the intrinsic tension between the Constitution as written document and the prevailing laws of the society of nations but from a qualitative difference between the American constitutional order and the traditional political orders of Europe out of which the laws of nations themselves had arisen. The American experiment, as its founders readily acknowledged, was unique. Democracy was to come into play. Such fundamental attributes of democracy as participation in law-making and popular consent to laws could not fail to flow over into the field of foreign affairs from the domestic realm wherein they were to play. Conversely, constitutional understandings pertaining to powers of the Presidency and the federal government in foreign relations could not help but profoundly influence and affect both democracy and republican practice.

No matter what the Hamiltonians, including Sutherland, wrote, there still were severe juridical limitations on federal and

---

[8] Quoted in Corwin, *op. cit.*, p. 180.

Presidential authority in foreign affairs which the Constitution made explicit. The society of nations to the contrary, Congress, not the President, had the constitutional power to declare a state of war. President and Senate were *jointly* empowered to use the treaty power for national purposes and objects, and in addition, the Constitution reserved certain powers and rights to the states and to the people. Could the President, perhaps, acting as the "federative power," or acting as Commander-in-Chief, or acting under the authority of the treaty-making power, then accomplish things which the Constitution otherwise forbade? The boundaries and frontiers of the individual states, for instance, could not be changed without the consent of the states concerned. Did this mean then that the Presidency and the "sovereign" federal authority by treaty could *not* do constitutionally what all other sovereigns, under the law of nations could: agree to international treaties and conventions affecting internal conditions within them? If a treaty, as the Constitution itself so stated, were to be regarded as the "supreme law of the land," could such law perhaps legitimately do things which ordinary Congressional law was constitutionally enjoined from doing? The Supreme Court case of *Missouri vs. Holland* in 1920 posed the issue: could a Congressional law implementing an Anglo-American conservation treaty vest in federal authorities regulatory powers within states for protection of game? Admittedly they had invaded a heretofore sacrosanct province of states' police powers which the Constitution until then protected. But the Court, through Holmes' decision, sustained the treaty, and revealed the possibility that:

> Acts of Congress are the supreme law of the land only when made in pursuance of the Constitution, while treaties are declared to be so when made under the authority of the United States. It is open to question whether the authority of the United States means more than the formal acts prescribed to make the convention. *We do not mean to imply that there are no qualifications to the treaty-making power; but they must be ascertained in a different way* . . . It is not lightly to be assumed that, in matters requiring national action, "a power which must belong

to and somewhere reside in every civilized government" is not to be found . . . The treaty in question does not contravene any prohibitory words to be found in the Constitution. The only question is whether it is forbidden by some invisible radiation from the general terms of the Tenth Amendment . . . Here a national interest of very nearly the first magnitude is involved. It can be protected only by national action in concert with that of another power. . . .[9]

Justice Frankfurter once referred to some lawyers' habit in argumentation of displaying a "parade of the horribles." By this he meant that any power or law can be made to appear intolerable if one dwells long enough upon its intrinsic possibility of abuse. A parade of horribles could also be assembled from the motley possibilities of constitutional abuse, stalemate, and paralysis, which this whole matter of constitutional authority raised. Holmes might well have been right: when a national interest of the first magnitude was involved, the neat and tidy restraints of the Constitution seemed to give way to overriding necessity. But this did not eradicate the problem. It is always philosophically important to consider even constitutional problems *in extremis*.

As the Holmes decision points out, the exercise of the treaty power could conceivably be a constitutional battering-ram, possibly demolishing customary constitutional rights of states. But if, as *Missouri vs. Holland* seemed to suggest, the treaty power was a theoretical skeleton key to doors which even Congress was constitutionally forbidden to unlock, it could do even more. It might (as right-wing Brickerites loudly proclaimed in the 1950's) threaten even individual liberties of American citizens. Treaties might erode guaranteed rights of the due process of law, among others.

It was not only the treaty power itself (and the attendant power which the Presidency had long exercised in international relations, that of the executive agreement) which might do this.

[9] 252 U.S. 1920, p. 416. Quoted in *The Constitution of the United States of America, Analysis and Interpretation*, Washington, D.C.: U.S. Government Printing Office, 1953, pp. 428-429. (Italics mine.)

The executive agreement, a less pretentious but more prolific kind of international agreement than the treaty, is a creature of many forms, yet generally regarded as indispensable to the orderly conduct of foreign policy. One form of executive agreement is the international agreement between the U.S. government acting in executive capacity and some foreign state or international organization, binding upon the United States but not subjected to Senatorial consent. There are three particular subspecies: those which, as drafted, require and obtain Congressional legislative approval and implementation; those which are made, like many American commercial agreements, upon the basis of prior statutory authorization of Congress; and those which, like the Yalta agreement of 1945, are subject neither to prior Congressional "authorization," nor approval, nor subsequent consent. In practice as well as in theory, most really substantive international agreements entered into by the United States Government are both negotiated and designated by the Executive branch as treaties, but the Executive has wide, theoretical latitude in deciding what to call them. A cynic would define an executive agreement as any agreement not called a treaty by the President. But even exaggerating the iniquities of the White House, which might be tempted to dodge the difficulties of a Senatorial two-thirds by dressing an agreement in shabby clothing and slipping it in through the servants' entrance, there are good reasons why no Administration would, except in dire straits, play such tricks. For one thing, Senators are notoriously sensitive about prerogatives (including their treaty prerogative). For another, the act of Senatorial approval of international agreements endows the latter with more majesty than mere enactment by the President or mere approval by Congress as a whole, as with ordinary legislation. Thus Senatorial consent gives the substance of the act more authority by giving it greater repute in the international arena as well as in the minds of the American public. Brickerites and McCarthyites in the 1950's, who sought to curtail use of the executive agreement and the objects which treaties might properly deal with, ignored the administrative chaos which elimination of the executive agreement would bring about. They ignored, too, the real political restraints upon Presidential power in international agreements which required no constitutional amendment to come into being. They were amply there already.

The exercise of any one right or power by any branch of the federal government in foreign affairs could conceivably work mischief. Senator Henry Cabot Lodge and his colleagues proved this in 1919 when they killed Wilson's League and the Paris Peace Treaty. Willful, shrewd assassins in the Senate could use their treaty power like a stiletto, to dispose of a hated Chief Executive, even if the ensuing cost to the nation as a whole might be considerable. Conversely, any tyrant might envy the great powers of the President as Commander-in-Chief (see below). Their proper constitutional use depended in large measure on the character and purposes of those who possessed them. If there were possibilities of conflict and abuse of power among governmental institutions and such potential abuses were obvious, then conflict must be anticipated by responsible men, constantly aware of the dangers of national paralysis and disunity entailed in sustained partisan struggle.

But no Constitution could avert what Madison once called the "dangers of factionalism." Factionalism was inherent in political life. While its force and passion sometimes arose from petty interests and ambitions, factionalism might also be a reflection of deep substantive issues at stake in political choices. Political debates over institutional powers, the Constitution, and foreign policy, paralleled profound debates about national policy and purpose. Even honest political men could employ the Constitution to block some political purpose from its realization. What was unique in the American experience was that these passionate debates about constitutionalism and foreign affairs were arguments about what the existing Constitution was, what it said, or what it implied. The argument was not about *alternative* constitutional orders. The American Constitution was thus both the regulating mechanism of debate and conflict and a framework of dialogue which reasonable men welcomed.

Conflict over substantive foreign policy issues might thus appear as conflict or deadlock among constitutional entities. When this was so, substantive conflicts could masquerade as constitutional ones. When the will of one entity (the Presidency, for instance) threatened to carry the day on behalf of a particular policy or purpose, one way to inhibit the purpose was to challenge the constitutionality of that entity's behavior. Another was simply to exercise, to the fullest possible extent, the constitutional powers of other entities to block action. The frequency with which constitutional issues arose in periods of foreign policy crisis suggests that the debate over forms was one aspect of a debate over essentially non-constitutional matters (whether, as in 1793, to intervene against England in the Anglo-French war; whether, as in 1940, to intervene on behalf of England in the war between Hitler and the West). This suggested that the Constitution itself might at any time become the hapless prey of the institutions which it prescribed, or even worse, that the institutions themselves were prey of larger forces in the nation which the Constitution neither prescribed nor foresaw.

But before we turn to particular instances where this difficulty of interpretation was most dramatically revealed, we might point out a mitigating fact: the unity of the framework around which dispute took place—the Constitution itself. At no time in American history, not even during the Civil War, was the Constitutional framework itself attacked. In foreign affairs, particularly when great issues of the moment are at stake, the vigor of the constitutional debate over powers as such cannot be attributed to the substantive policy debate alone. Much more, it points to the desperate need in crisis to legitimize action and to link action and purpose to enduring forms and public values. The matter of constitutional legitimacy itself is no idle thing. Without it, power itself could easily dissolve in the hands of those who wield it. Worse still, the power might be wholly severed from constitutional authority and become despotic. Thus, in a sense, we can say that such recurrent constitutional debates were, in fact, *supremely* constitutional.

THE PRESIDENT VERSUS CONGRESS The primary zones of constitutional dispute over foreign affairs lay in those powers which the President and the Congress shared jointly; and in the realm between the President's authority and the gamut of other constitutional and institutional authorities which the Constitution delineated. The conflict invariably centered upon the Presidency. Here, even in the earliest days of the Republic, when the enormous range of domestic Presidential authority and influence were scarcely imagined, the contemporary issue of Presidential authority in foreign affairs was first delineated. From accumulated precedents, constitutional understandings gradually arose. Explicit constitutional grants of power were enlarged by extrapolating their inherent logic. Like inverted pyramids, great Presidential prerogatives were based upon apparently trivial explicit grants of power. The power to "send and receive Ambassadors," for instance, grew by custom and usage into the mighty Presidential prerogative of determining the government's right to establish diplomatic relations and to negotiate with other governments. As John Marshall, the great juridical architect of federal powers declared in 1799, the President was the "sole organ of the nation in its external relations, and its sole representative with foreign nations."

But this *dictum* left a major problem unresolved. The President could conceivably exercise his monopoly of these powers of communication, yet confine it to the transmittal of others' ideas, something like a mailman. The unresolved issue was whether the Presidential monopoly of communication was also the monopoly of initiative and planning. As time passed, this executive power to communicate and negotiate proved susceptible to enlargement. The flourishing bureaucratic apparatus in the Office of the President, the Department of State and its Foreign Service, the ancillary military agencies, all of these in time became subject to the will of the Presidency in their day-to-day operations. Congress had no comparable capacities to act continuously as an initiating agency in foreign affairs. The emergence of parties and factions in the legislative body (a possibility which Washington had feared, but which Federalist theory anticipated) denied to it that centrality of purpose and direction which the Presidency, as an institution of unified executive authority, possessed.

Essential to effective foreign policy action are secrecy and dispatch, attributes which a legislative body could hardly possess. Nor could it long command the capacity of seeing foreign affairs as a whole. The steady numerical enlargement of both its branches decided the matter. The Congress, as representative body, naturally oscillated between two constant, antagonistic purposes: framing national legislation with regard to larger national purposes and representing many local, parochial, and special interests. Logrolling might sometimes suffice as legislative custom in framing domestic policies and laws, but log-rolling in foreign affairs invited disaster in international politics. As long as the United States faced the united purposes of other states, its own policies could not be the hapless products of special interests, pressure groups, and conflicting constituency interests. Congressmen and Senators were caught up in the contradictory roles of lawmakers and representatives of lesser interests. But the President was responsible to the nation as a whole, and if he was articulate, he could speak and act for the nation as a whole.

THE PRESIDENT AS COMMANDER-IN-CHIEF From the constitutional understanding about the Presidency as "sole organ" came both procedural and substantive powers over diplomacy. From the President's powers as Commander-in-Chief of the armed forces came equally great authority. The Constitution here was far more explicit:

> The President shall be Commander in Chief of the Army and Navy of the United States, and of the Militia of the several States, when called into the actual service of the United States. . . .[10]

[10] Article II, Section 3.

Here monopoly of authority and power was unambiguously assigned. Command was to be constant and except for the militia operative in both war and peace. Command over military forces entailed, presumably, the power to disperse and dispose of these forces, to command them to engage in actions (even in "peacetime") having as their object the protection of the United States and of both its broad, strategic, and its more particular interests. Constancy of command, also, gave the President the power to discipline and coordinate all lesser military authorities of the nation. The Navy and War Departments and later the Defense Department, under nominal civilian control, enhanced Presidential and political supremacy of military force. In theory if not always in practice, Presidential authority subordinated American military power to tight political control and surveillance.[11]

The Commander-in-Chief power, much more than the treaty power or the Executive power over diplomacy came to pose the most serious difficulty for a constitutional system of checks and balances. The Constitution gave Congress the power to declare war, yet this power had obvious limits. It was unrealistic to assume that Congress could monopolize the initiation of war. The theory of Congressional initiative and monopoly of decision skirted the fact that many wars could "initiate themselves," could be forced upon the nation and upon Congress by factors over which Congress had no control at all. They might, for instance, be due to the interaction of Executive policy and the responses and acts of other states. Congress often found itself in the position of the lady who informed Thomas Carlyle that she had decided to accept the universe, and was told, "Madame, you had damned well better." The power to declare frequently amounted to the power to recognize a pre-existing reality.

Such pre-existing reality in world politics could, to some degree, be shaped or affected by Presidential action, by diplomacy,

[11] Interestingly enough, while generals have served as President and, in the case of George C. Marshall, as Secretary of State, no military man has served as Secretary of Defense, War, or Navy.

by military action, by broad outlines of policy and specific actions. On hundreds of occasions during the nineteenth and twentieth centuries, American Presidents or military forces operating under Presidential authority, engaged in combat operations abroad with no specific sanction from Congress. During America's neutrality in World War I, President Wilson in 1917 armed American merchant vessels by virtue of his executive authority, setting the stage for conflict with German naval vessels and thus for war. In 1940 and 1941, President Roosevelt, acting as Commander-in-Chief, showed how a vigorous Chief Executive, by disposing American military and naval forces, could involve them in an ambiguous status of non-belligerency, even limited war, with no declarative act of Congress authorizing this. And so it went.

Was the distinction between war and military actions short of war merely semantic? The problem became more and more difficult, as the world around America worsened in the mid-twentieth century. There were more American military casualties in Korea (1950-1953) than in World War I, yet diplomatic and constitutional amenities of the 1950's seemed to dictate that Korea was a mere "police action." To be sure, Congress could have subsequently declared the Korean incident a war, but the U.S. decision to defend the Republic of Korea by force had been taken by the President with no prior sanction from Congress. As such, it was linked by contemporary Administration spokesmen at the time to precedent-setting sorties of American troops and Marines in Latin America, China, and elsewhere, which also had not been dignified by prior Congressional act. Many Americans, directly or vicariously participating in the Korean "affair," which was a bloody and frustrating one, sensed a qualitative distinction; and were not the more sure of their purposes because the distinction was never made clear to them.

No Executive power has been more written about or widely discussed than this power which the President wields over the military. No constitutional checks upon it other than the Congress' power to impeach, to investigate, and to appropriate funds, could really come into play here. But such powers were at best negative and always hard to focus upon specific Presidential acts, intentions, and policies. Congress, by revolting, could conceivably withhold requested defense appropriations. In theory, it could strip any Administration of power adequate to wage a particular war, in fact, all war, including those Congress itself might think desirable. Such latent threats hardly sufficed as an instrument of policy control. In fact, when Congress in 1901 threatened, by withholding naval appropriations, to restrain Theodore Roosevelt's truculent and exhibitionist adventures, the President responded with his own counter-threat: to send the fleet half way around the world using existing appropriated moneys and then have Congress pay the return fare. The game was one in which a shrewd or adventurous President could always hold the upper hand. The Congressional investigatory power was also inadequate. One does not toy with military power nor demand that the Executive divulge military secrets by threat or order of subpoena. Congress might pass resolutions to restrain Executive power over the disposition of military and naval forces as, in fact, the Senate Republicans had sought to do. Yet what restraints could be enforced?

DECLINE OF THE CONGRESSIONAL ROLE IN FOREIGN POLICY Congress' cold-war role in national security and foreign policy severely tested legislative prestige. It also tested the adequacy of institutional mechanisms which the Constitution prescribed for foreign affairs. During the American Revolution, the Continental Congress had acted for a time as a self-styled war council and national "strategy board." But the Congress of the United States never made a tradition of this. Its size and heterogeneity made it incapable of choosing among alternative foreign or military policies. In the twentieth century in time of crisis, Congress was in fact cast in the ignoble role of the parsimonious father to an irrepressible, insatiable adolescent. The irritable object of constant flattery, solicitation, and demands but rarely the initiator of plans, Congress was nevertheless expected to facilitate the plans of others. Legislative business and distractions made it impossible for individual Congressmen, much less Congress as an institution, to devise or initiate adequate alternatives to those plans which Administrations periodically presented to it as virtual *faits accomplis*. What was true of domestic policy was far more true of foreign policy, for here the Executive was the storehouse of information and intelligence *par excellence*. He could be the ceaseless thinker and the swift actor. During foreign policy emergencies, the range of national options and choices in foreign affairs were widened or narrowed by Executive actions which Congressmen often learned of through the newspapers.

Congress might remain the object of Administration solicitation and courtesy. Battalions of Executive agents periodically visited the Capitol to defend or lobby for particular policies or legislation. But Congress itself was incapable of making its own grand designs. It did, on occasion, take the initiative. But when it did, its actions appeared more like spastic forays, undertaken in exasperation or pique rather than in reasoned anticipation of the consequences.

One device of Congressional pique was the restraining "resolution," such as that which expressed the "sense" of either house that such and such an executive action should not be taken. (For instance, the Senate and House periodically pass resolutions opposing Communist Chinese admission to the U.N. or American recognition of the regime.) In a Constitutional sense, Congressional resolutions could not prevent recognition from taking place, if and when an Executive decided upon it. But behind such resolutions lay greater powers which could be called into play if the wish were disregarded. In the summer of 1961, for instance, attempts were made in both the Senate and House to stipulate that no U.S. funds could be expended for international organizations of which Communist China was a member. Thus conceivably Red China's admission to the United Nations would have meant the end of U.S. financial support of the U.N. which might then have collapsed in bankruptcy.

As the international crises continued, it seemed that Congress' positive role diminished (like that of Bagehot's Queen Victoria) but without its rights, its *amour propre*, or its great negative powers being correspondingly diminished. It should be consulted; it could warn and advise; its more influential legislative members were objects of great solicitation (as Bagehot's was of Bagehot's Disraeli). Frequently, in fact, they were "co-opted" into decision-making circles of the Administration so that implementing legislation might be facilitated. But unlike the Queen's, the very real negative powers and rights of Congress never disappeared, notably the power of the purse and the power to refuse assent to legislative implementation of Executive wishes and policies. The appropriations power meant the power to invigorate or enfeeble national purposes; assent or denial to treaties and international agreements could decisively affect the maneuverability of even the most vigorous executive. International undertakings, such as sustained and strategically phased foreign aid programs, might require long-term commitments of the United States, including commitment of capital which required long-range appropriations from the Congress. Not parsimony as much as the impulse to retain control of a traditional legislative function created difficulties here. The power of the purse remained the power of continuous review of purpose.

In the days of the Marshall Plan, when Congress was asked for appropriations for major relief and recovery plans for war-devastated Europe, the Administration skirted the time problem with the argument that European aid was self-liquidating and that it could, in time, be terminated if adequate funds were made available by Congress. This closed-endedness of a major foreign policy problem became one of the most attractive features of the program, since Congressional outlays could be made to appear ultimately unnecessary. Appropriations hitched to a plan proposed by the Europeans themselves were gauged as "recovery measures."

As it turned out, the argument was correct. Between 1948 and 1952, Europe (including England) had recovered its economic posture, and by the mid-1950's, aside from military assistance, stood on its own feet. Present foreign aid programs for under-developed countries, however, have an over-all limitless character to them. Thus ascertaining the necessary amounts of appropriations and the objective ends of the program become political matters precisely because one knows neither what the desirable economic goals should be, who should develop them, nor how long they would take. European recovery goals in 1948 were hitched to a comprehensible parity base of pre-war years, and could thus be grounded in "reality." No such parity base could command much agreement for the underdeveloped countries. One wishes to get their development programs underway, but this is much more difficult than Europe's where the program could aim at restoring things which once existed.

These matters posed serious problems for the enduring vitality of democratic institutions. The possibility of Congress' ultimate degeneration into a clamoring, irresponsible group of Samsons, blind yet strong, capable of vengefully pulling down the pillars of the temple, was no worse than its becoming a docile, servile institution, like Bismarck's *Reichstag*, ignorant of executive purposes in foreign policy and resigned to the condition. Congress, for all its shortcomings, served essential democratic purposes in foreign policy. It remained a public forum where popular representatives could concur or disagree with Executive purpose. It was a seismograph of public moods which no government could ignore. As frustrating as such Congressional activities might seem to some busy, distraught policy-makers, Congress could make them and the public more aware of what was really going on around them and conceivably remind them of alternative possibilities. Congress could also be an arena in which contentious Administration agencies could dispute in quasi-public or even open manner about policies on which there was no Administration consensus.[12] One might complain about the pernicious influences of certain

[12] See, incidentally, the subtle and trenchant article of Roger Hilsman, "Congressional-Executive Relations and the Foreign Policy Consensus," *American Political Science Review*, September 1958, pp. 725-44.

blocs within Congress, which, like the Southern Democratic-Midwest Republican isolationist coalition, often appeared seriously estranged from the real international world and greatly over-represented in strategic positions of Congressional committee influence. But the possibilities of obstruction in this open process were surely less than the peril entailed in Congress' decline. This was a supremely important constitutional consideration, for the open society required the Congressional open forum as well as Congressional agencies of consent in which men of power could be called to account in public for their actions. Secret foreign policy as in authoritarian or totalitarian regimes risked "privatizing" power itself, repressing conflict which could not be permanently repressed without the use of force. At worst, "privatization" of foreign policy meant the closing of the open society. The manifold inconveniences of Congressional action in foreign policy, often of considerable damage to America's reputation abroad, could not be compared to the more numerous risks entailed in an America which might suppress the very agencies by which, traditionally at least, the consent of the public and its sense of participation in matters of state had been elicited. (Congressional access to executive information about foreign policy does not necessarily mean that the information becomes public. Nearly two thirds of the meetings of the House Foreign Affairs Committee during the Eighty-sixth Congress' first session were held as closed sessions; over 60 per cent of the meetings of the Senate Foreign Relations Committee were closed, a far higher score than for any other committees of Congress.[13])

The Power of War and Peace

The problem of Presidential-Congressional power over war and peace seemed to grow in complexity, as the nation's vulnerability and its closeness to international conflicts increased. In bygone years there were times, like those before the Spanish-Ameri-

---

[13] Washington *Post*, November 20, 1961.

can War, when Congress did take initiatives for war, deliberately pressing its views on a reluctant Executive. The Spanish, like Heywood Broun's fifty-first dragon, awaited impotently and in gloom the outcome of this Congressional debate. War began when Congress finally decided to strike. To a lesser extent, this was also true of America's entry into World War I. For Americans, war began when Congress commanded it. America's geographic remoteness from major powers and the nature of the weapons systems at the time enhanced this Congressional power which, in war and peace, was the power to assent or decline. Thus traditionally the eves of great American wars were occasions of grand debates, which were by no means confined to the halls of Congress itself. The debate took place across the land.

These rituals of debate about war were repeated on the eve of Pearl Harbor. Certainly they helped clarify in the public mind the issues at stake. At no time until Pearl Harbor did the Roosevelt administration contemplate asking Congress for a declaration of war. Whether the President actually wished war with Nazi Germany is still not clear, but it surely was clear that he had decided as early as the spring of 1941 to wage "limited naval war" against Hitler (not Japan), and to wage it on the basis of commander-in-chief powers requiring no explicit Congressional sanction.

So long as circumstances warranted such Congressional debates about war and peace, more often than not they gave popular sanction and consent to warlike undertakings. They inhibited warlike measures which might not stand broad public scrutiny; they helped clarify national purposes; they also legitimized the use of force by government in a way that no authoritarian state could. Tocqueville said, "There are two things which a democratic people will always find very difficult—to begin a war, and to end it." But beginning was the most crucial matter. Democratic theory always exalted this crucial matter of consent. The strict accountability of military to civilian authority and ultimately to popular control, had been a major issue at stake in the grievances of the original colonists in their dispute with England. Recall Jefferson's eloquent indictment of George III in 1776: "He has kept among us, in times of Peace, Standing Armies without the consent of our legislatures . . . He has affected to render the Military independent of and superior to the Civil power . . . He has combined with others to subject us to a jurisdiction foreign to our constitution," etc. Colonial grievances against the crown consisted also of deep irritation that the wars it instigated bore no relationship to the popular wishes of the colonists themselves.

And thus, while little in the Constitution actually sustained it, there was a deep Populist spirit in the nation which kept alive the notion that democracy should come into play in crucial matters pertaining to war and peace. If there were to be no taxation without representation, then there should be no war without consultation.

Populism in foreign policy manifested itself in many complex ways in American diplomatic history, but the purpose of establishing formal, constitutional checks upon the President's war-making, and Congress' war-declaring power on behalf of the people was to turn, in the 1930's, into a curious, abortive crusade against war itself. In the midst of the early Roosevelt New Deal, attempts were made in Congress to establish tight legislative checks upon the war-making power. The Ludlow war referendum, the proposal of an Indiana Congressman, was the most notable of them. By constitutional amendment, it would have drastically altered the foreign-policy process. Except in instances of direct enemy attack upon the United States and its territorial and insular possessions, the United States could not legally go to war without a popular plebiscite, a "war referendum" adopted by majority vote. It was widely felt that such a referendum might check the designs of a militant President bent upon war.

The success of this innocent anti-war power crusade would have impaired the maneuverability of American defense forces in crises where the possible enemy was encumbered by no such restraints. Had the referendum become part of American constitutional processes, it is interesting to speculate, for instance, about its pertinence and applicability to the two wars which the United

States soon engaged in, World War II and the Korean War. In the former, the plebiscite would have proved useless and superfluous, since the first overt aggression was committed by the Japanese at Pearl Harbor, and American authorities, deliberately intent upon avoiding the stigma of a pre-emptive strike against an enemy whose hostile intentions were well known, chose to await such an act. In Korea on the other hand, had American forces (which were not themselves objects of the initial North Korean thrust) been compelled to await a popular referendum before engaging in action, Korea would probably have been overrun. Thus the Ludlow purpose, noble as it may have seemed, would either have paralyzed American military power or compelled Executive authorities to avoid the consequences of the law by engaging in "bootleg" wars thus (as in the case of the Eighteenth Amendment) weakening the authority of law and executive power.

But there was a further innocence in the assumption that the people were invariably less bellicose than their rulers and that the people could not be manipulated in such balloting to force war upon a nation when war itself was imprudent. If the Ludlow Amendment proposal, which had considerable Congressional support in the mid-1930's, failed to be enacted, it still reflected a widespread mood of optimism and voluntarism in America that the ethic of choice was still far ahead of the ethic of necessity in all realms of public policy, that war and peace were matters which America itself had the privilege of deciding for itself.

The Ludlow proposal failed, finally, in 1937. Everything militated against it. No heterogeneous people could be expected to become an ultimate court on the day of judgment about war and peace. The democratic process could be fatally time-consuming in an open world where a secretive enemy could watch and listen in on the councils. The totalitarian capacities for secrecy and dispatch seemed, even in the 1930's, decidedly superior to cumbersome democratic processes. Why make them more cumbersome? As a practical matter, no constitutional gimmick could surmount this awesome problem of democracy and war nor solve the problem of consent without creating even worse difficulties. In the simpler days of the Athenians, an assembly of citizens was the arena for consent and consensus on war and peace. In the public square, orators had argued the pros and cons of war, speaking amidst the very men who might ultimately have to fight it. If the decision was for war, the assembly would elect its war leaders. Then, those very men who had voted would go out to battle.

The New England Minuteman was, briefly, the Athenian's American counterpart. In 1775 and 1776 on the eve of Revolution, "free Americans" had met in assemblies and conventions to decide the issue of reconciliation or war with Britain. Then they went home for their squirrel guns. The memory of original democracy deeply affected Americans' later attitudes towards war, thanks to history books and national folktales. Virtuous as this popular method might seem, it now appears both primitive and incongruous. Bertrand de Jouvenel has pointed out that the modern analogy to the Athenian procedure is the wildcat strike in industry. For there, the workers of the plant, disregarding their union, get together and decide to go on strike, which they then do. But judged by modern standards, this is disorderly conduct.[14]

In time of crisis, the sovereign state would not even be sovereign, it would forfeit its responsibility to protect its citizens if stripped of its capacity to protect the nation against attack when vigilance and speed were essential and popular consent a luxury. Past geographic insulation and remoteness from international politics, coupled with great latter day power, endowed America with more than a century's respite from a problem common to all polities: in times of great crisis, one is compelled to trust Leviathan. William Seward, Lincoln's Secretary of State, anticipated the modern problem of democracy and consent in foreign affairs.

[14] *Democracy in the New States: Rhodes Seminar Press.* New Delhi: Congress for Cultural Freedom, 1959, p. 32. The contrast between Athenian democracy and present day American procedures for instigating massive military action in the face of a grave nuclear threat is a sharp one indeed. Only the President's "little golden phone" may order aloft the terrible, swift agents of thermonuclear holocaust. In a crisis, his decision might have to be made within a matter of minutes.

"We elect a king for four years, and give him absolute power within certain limits, which after all he can interpret for himself."

The Constitution provided for competition in foreign policy-making power. It offered a temptation to abuse delegated powers and a prospect of stalemate among antagonistic institutions. Perhaps because of this, it was also an incentive to cooperate prudently. The separateness of executive and legislative entities could generate a sensitivity to institutional prerogatives which time and tradition enlarged. However, as the Presidency, the Senate and the Congress developed their own traditions and asserted their rights and privileges against each other, other institutions evolved which gave these Constitutional entities power from the "outside."

New bureaucracies, created by Congress, came to have an influence comparable with that of institutions prescribed by the Constitution. In the realm of foreign affairs, this organizational growth around the Office of the President resulted in the rise of mammoth bureaucracies. Once created by Congressional act, they became, nominally and legally, "children" of the Executive. Their activities, while often elaborately prescribed in Congressional statute, were juridically subject to the direction of the President himself. The Department of State and the Foreign Service, once minuscule appendages to the Presidency, proliferated into giant organizational systems, with networks and agencies spread across the face of the globe. Congress retained the ultimate power to disestablish such institutions, just as it possessed power to prescribe by legislation their internal order, management and resources, but these were purely theoretical powers. In practice, as the agencies grew, so did their power until they seemed to have as much status and influence as Congress, if not more.

If congressional control and oversight of foreign affairs became increasingly difficult, it grew equally difficult for the President himself to seize and maintain control of this cumbersome apparatus. To a certain extent, executive style was crucial. Some Presidents, like Wilson and the two Roosevelts, tried to exert their own authority to its fullest Constitutional limits in foreign affairs. They sought to arrange the system so that its widespread operations could be informed by a unitary strategy and an internal logic. Other Presidents, like Eisenhower, defined their calling more modestly. They delegated policy-initiation to subordinates, while retaining merely an umpire role in the most crucial decisions.

Harold Laski once said that the efficiency of administration depended on the "creative use of officials by elected persons." But even strong executives know the limits of control. Foreign policy in the twentieth century could be made "on the cables," in the flow of dispatches, which is one way of saying that things could happen without anyone responsible really knowing what was going on. The left hand could do something which even the head, much less the right hand, didn't know of. Administrative reforms and vigorous Presidents might seek to check such anarchic tendencies. A strong executive might seek constantly to inject his own purposes into the reluctant flesh of bureaucracy, but the Constitution itself provided few answers for the problem. In the era of big government, power could diffuse as it grew; to take on new international responsibilities was also to take on new agencies with their own capacities for irresponsibility. The danger, perceived most clearly in American foreign policy after the cold war began, was that the governmental process, increasingly cumbersome and fluid, might become a substitute for the constitutional system itself.

The Party System

It was not only the executive agencies, like the Department of State, the Pentagon, etc., which created the trouble. The extra- or quasi-governmental institution, not beholden to Executive or even Congressional control, also waxed in strength and influence. The party system, which the Constitution had not anticipated, was the first of these major non-constitutional entities to come upon the scene. In the early nineteenth century, it quickly penetrated the formal institutions of government, linking and dividing them in complex and subtle ways. George Washington had feared the coming of a spirit of faction, believing parties to be a threat to the institutions of government themselves. But he could not have foreseen some of the merits which partisanship had for a constitutional system of separated powers. Like the Boss system in municipal governments, it could informally link otherwise separate agencies and institutions and make them work purposively together. The party system permeated the formal Constitutional entities. While it caused new opportunities for discord, it also created possibilities of collaboration between Executive and Congress. A strong President, exerting influence and control over his own party in Congress, might to that extent ameliorate the difficulties of purely institutional antagonism between the White House and Capitol Hill.

But conversely, partisanship could at times worsen pre-existing institutional tensions. In Woodrow Wilson's time, the Treaty of Versailles and the League of Nations fell victim to formal institutional jealousies between Congress and the Executive, specifically, between a Republican Senate and a Democratic President. Much depended upon the same party controlling both institutions, for the Constitution had not anticipated the problems which a President of one party and a Congress of another would create. Some European parliamentary systems worked more smoothly, many observers felt. When executive authority rested upon a parliamentary majority, the opportunities for purely institutional impasses were diminished. But the American system could freeze incompatible partners in marriage as long as both of them lasted their prescribed elective terms. In the twentieth century, impasse occurred in Wilson's Administration, in Truman's, and in Eisenhower's. The problems in each instance were similar: how to construct common, institutional purposes in foreign affairs at a time when the domestic purposes of parties included each other's political defeat.

The party system, however, posed problems for foreign policy completely outside these formal constitutional entities. As the American two-party system came into being, it was composed of congeries of state and local parties which were not easily subject to discipline and control from the top. The internal government of American parties was loose, diffuse, and greatly decentralized. The parties were, in fact, clusters of autonomous parties. The Democratic Party in the twentieth century was perhaps the better instance of this. Its two centers were in the local organizations within the large northern industrial cities and the liberal-boss machine alliances and struggles which took place within them and, on the other hand, in the one-party South, where the Democratic party predominantly represented a conservative-rural interest wholly out of tune with the problems of modern, industrialized America. To further complicate matters, the Democratic Party of the North, which exerted a far greater appeal than the Republican Party to lower income and new ethnic groups in America, was itself further divided among interest and factions which had peculiar concerns about foreign affairs.

The Republican party, equally decentralized, also suffered from this tendency to polarization between the more economically powerful interests of eastern and western big business, with its own extensive concerns for American overseas financial and commercial interests, and the more parochial mid western and rural elements of the party which tended to ignore or reject foreign-policy problems.

Two constitutional processes seemed to make of each Party two overlapping systems: the Presidential election system and the Congressional election system. Every four years, the party found it necessary to reconcile intra-party feuds and disagreements to elect a Presidential candidate. Whether elected or not, the party candidate himself could command influence over the apparatuses of party power and thus could force some consensus within the Party to frame a platform reasonably in congruence with his own policies. In Presidential election years, the need of each party to appeal to uncommitted or independent voters forced perennial reconsideration of party policies on a national level. If elected, the President could hope to exercise some considerable command over the diffuse elements in his own party by patronage, by lending or withholding his support to party candidates in their constituencies, and by appeals to the broader public.

The Congressional system, however, worked differently. Few Presidents, even in Presidential years, dared openly intervene in the political processes of local parties to select and build up their own candidates to create their own party. Some influence was always possible, but Presidential leadership was always subject to massive constraints and inhibitions within a political system composed of jealous and ambitious men. Direct Presidential intervention in party primaries to support candidates committed to a President's policies could always backfire. To be sure, a President's power over his party could be subtly exercised, but even such power could not overcome the centrifugal forces which were constantly at work to parochialize the parties. In point of fact, neither party permanently possessed a centralized policy-making organ at the top which could constantly exert discipline and unity upon Senators and Congressmen. National conventions and national committees of both parties might occasionally claim to speak for the party, but when discipline was added to speech, the attempt usually failed.

If discipline could rarely be imposed upon the Congressional parties in the Senate and House, both bred their own partisan agencies of power and discipline. But these could by no means speak with final authority about the purposes of parties as such. Powerful Congressmen, rising through seniority in Congressional committees to leadership, might hold views diametrically opposed to the announced policies of their parties and even of the Administration of their own party. The Presidential party, strongest in election years, could recurrently infuse order and discipline over individual congressmen. But the Congressional party had powerful limits set upon concerted party discipline and leadership.

These political facts of life could not but affect the conduct of foreign policy and set limits upon the formal Constitutional separation and allocation of foreign policy power. In normal times, Congressmen were beholden to particular constituencies for whom foreign policy problems were too remote, too intangible, or too complex to make any particular political difference. But there were particular areas of American political life in which foreign policy issues could always arouse popular passion. Congressmen who came from such districts could not help being deeply affected by them.

One such type of Congressional district might have large numbers of constituents whose homelands had been overrun by Soviet Communism. During the 1950's, Congressmen from such districts found themselves under constant pressure to reproach the Administration for the "laxity" in its liberation policies towards Soviet satellite states. Here Hungarian, Polish, Czech, Serbo-Croat, and other Americans of East European descent took a passionate interest in foreign policy matters which was not shared so intensely by other Americans.

In times of war or threat of war, constituency interest could become deeply aroused by the imminence of sacrifice and death, not to mention taxes. Yet as a rule, while powerful constituencies existed and influenced Congressmen's attitudes towards many issues of domestic policy, there could, by definition, be no foreign policy constituency save that of widely scattered, public affairs pressure groups and an informed public who saw foreign affairs as a whole and, in sustained fashion, lent support to legislators who took the broad view in their voting on Congressional measures dealing with foreign affairs.

BI-PARTISANSHIP IN FOREIGN POLICY The problem of party, Congressional, and presidential power should make us see the difficulties of legislating the national interest in foreign affairs. In crisis periods, when national unity seemed most urgent, the political processes seemed extraordinarily cumbersome. In practice, of course, there came to exist within the formal and informal political institutions something resembling a nonpartisan, political consensus about foreign affairs, which could create powerful support for broad foreign policies an Administration might use to strengthen itself abroad. From the late 1930's until the present time, such a broad foreign policy coalition came into being, cutting across party lines and through both the Executive and the Congress. Powerful leaders in both the Republican and Democratic parties, influential opinion-makers, were skillfully drawn together by successive Administrations to lessen the worst evils of Congressional parochialism and partisanship. "Bi-partisanship" became the by-word. Its principal objective in Franklin D. Roosevelt's time was to knit together an enduring political coalition of Republicans and Democrats on matters of foreign policy and national defense so that world politics would not remain an arena for party conflict. On the eve of World War II, Roosevelt, breaking with political precedent, brought into his Cabinet two prominent, opposition Republicans, Henry L. Stimson and Frank Knox as Secretaries respectively, of Army and Navy. In 1940, with Administration encouragement, a powerful, bi-partisan, public pressure group called the Committee to Defend America by Aiding the Allies was formed to strengthen Administration policies towards Europe and Hitler. During and after the war, other Republican leaders like Senator Vandenberg, Senator Warren Austin, and Wendell Wilkie were brought into or close to Administration counsels. On occasion they served as Presidential emissaries in diplomatic negotiations. They were appointed as Administration delegates to international conferences. They sat as U.S. representatives at meetings of United Nations bodies. They lent political support to emerging foreign policies in the post-war period.

During the cold war, the Truman Administration continued the practice, making use of such prominent Republicans as John Foster Dulles as advisers and diplomatic negotiators on major issues. In Congress as a whole, this cooperation of opposition figures in executive activities not only blurred traditional dividing lines between Congress and Executive, but the lines between parties as well. In consequence, much vital foreign policy legislation was successfully enacted in Congress; the sharp, cutting edge of partisanship was blunted. Democratic Presidents used bi-partisanship more extensively in major foreign affairs appointments than did Eisenhower. But the device was not abandoned. In the present Kennedy Administration, key positions like Secretary of the Treasury, Director of the Central Intelligence Agency, and Secretary of Defense were filled with Republicans.

Bi-partisanship thus became an informal constitutional understanding to evade the dangers which both the Constitution and the party-system constantly posed. Yet like most constitutional understandings, it was never put in writing. To describe it might undermine its frail foundations. Bi-partisanship was an ephemeral concept resting upon a pragmatic premise that the Constitution and the party system simply could not work unless much of the traditional conflict and animosity about foreign policy could be reduced.

During the 1930's and 1940's, before this constitutional understanding had come to be a fairly fixed element in the American political order, there were many serious proposals to revamp the American Constitution to avoid the worst pitfalls of partisanship. One such proposal which commanded wide support was that the treaty-making power be constitutionally revised so that the two-thirds approval of the Senate be removed as an obstacle to ratification of treaties. Another proposal, considered earlier by Woodrow Wilson, was that the President and Vice-President both resign their offices in the event that the Congress came under control of the opposition party, so that the Speaker of the House or some leader of the opposition could lead and control an otherwise leaderless majority. Presidential government then would give way to Parliamentary government. Neither of these proposals are given serious consideration today. Both President Truman and President Eisenhower found ways of living with a Congress which was of the other political complexion, although in the last year of Truman's Administration, this cohabitation was often exceedingly unpleasant.

Thanks in part to bi-partisanship, after 1945 no major treaty was rejected by the Senate and no major piece of administration legislation setting up new institutions of foreign policy was rejected by Congress. By the mid-1950's, a Congressional consensus about foreign policy embraced such major, substantive, American policies as support for the U.N., the North Atlantic Treaty Organization, the foreign aid program for underdeveloped areas, and the new institutional ties which bound the United States in formal or informal alliance with many nations in Europe and Africa. This Congressional consensus was apparent in the continuing willingness of Congress to commit astronomical sums of money to national defense, the most costly element in the whole panoply of American foreign policy instruments. The Constitutional impasse, once widely feared, had apparently been avoided. Regardless of the merits of particular policies or programs (which was an entirely different matter), the Congress had apparently refuted Tocqueville's dictum about the inconstancy of democracies in their foreign affairs and their incapacity to persist long in any significant, international endeavor.

Senate and House consensus bi-partisanship commanded the support of most Senators and Congressmen from the more populous, industrialized states and Congressional districts, but a shadow opposition has existed during the cold war, a kind of negative bi-partisanship concentrated chiefly among Senators and Congressmen from more rural, underdeveloped parts of the country. This negative consensus, waxing and waning as issues of foreign policy changed, linked Republicans and Democrats. In practice, the negative coalition sprang chiefly from Southern Democrats and from Midwestern Republicans. In philosophy, this coalition proclaimed a patriotic commitment to older styles of American behavior in world affairs. Its chief spokesmen called continuously for unilateral American action in the cold war (as opposed to coalition diplomacy and containment). Its bellicose nationalism often combined with a political skepticism about American overseas commitments and the use of American power. It rarely could tolerate subtle distinctions among the many political problems which faced the United States abroad. In matters of national defense, negative bi-partisanship called for emphasis upon massive development of American striking forces, based chiefly in the Western hemisphere, notably upon a large nuclear retaliatory force. It constantly evinced suspicion of many of the heterogeneous allies which the United States had assembled in its effort to contain the spread of Communism. Fearful of Socialism as well as Communism, it tended to oppose American aid and assistance to many states abroad which, though anti-Communist, had welfare programs and programs of state ownership. Above all, this negative bi-partisan coalition was hemispherically oriented and concerned that cold war exigencies not alter substantially the shape of the American economy and the appearance of American life. Conservative in domestic, fiscal policies, it constantly sought to diminish the amount of material assistance sent abroad. Suspicious of cosmopolitan influences in American life as well, the coalition contained within it many who confused modernity with Communism, who sought to blur essential lines between necessary social reform at home and abroad and what it called Communist subversion.

At its best, this negative bi-partisanship was exemplified by the late Senator Robert A. Taft, whose own philosophy about foreign affairs derived from his extraordinary confidence in America's abilities to survive unimpaired a world left largely to its own devices. At its worst, it was exemplified by the late Senator Joseph McCarthy, whose philosophy was to shake the very foundations of the nation that he conceived to be corrupted by an internal, omnipresent, Communist threat. Ethnocentric and suspicious of all movements in world politics, this shadow bi-partisanship, though it commanded many followers in urban America, found public support in the states and districts where older ways of

American life in its more backward form persisted: in the under-developed South and in the rural Midwest, which, culturally in particular, had been least directly affected by anything new in American life.

This persistent negative coalition, never a majority in either house of Congress, still set limits upon American maneuverability in diplomacy. It opposed negotiation with Russia or with such Communist states as Yugoslavia or Poland which, to greater or lesser extent, had broken with Soviet dominion. Above all, the coalition set limits upon resources which the United States could use in dealing with the underdeveloped nations and in strengthen-ing the feeble political orders present in these states. Its national-istic philosophy stressed the need to maintain a vigorous American economy under a system of "free enterprise," minimally involved in a world economy. Yet it also betrayed a surprising lack of con-fidence in the nation's ability to shape the course of political economic events abroad.

The alliance between Southern conservatism and Midwestern Republican conservatism in the 1950's complicated American dealings with the new Afro-Asian States. These new nations had come into being at precisely the same time that the struggle for Negro emancipation in the American South resumed after a cen-tury. Southern conservative Congressmen, resisting social change at home, could hardly have been sympathetic to U.S. assistance to the new African republics abroad or any nations composed of men and women they would not admit in their own schools, restau-rants, stores, or churches. Segregation in the South thus became iniquitously linked with segregation in world politics.

In sum, bi-partisanship had two faces. The one created by Roosevelt, Vandenberg, Truman, Eisenhower, and Dulles looked out to the world and saw the world problems. The other faced inward, fearfully rejecting the world. The strength of bi-partisan-ship depended upon the amount of fear latent within the Ameri-can body politic. War crisis could liberate such fear. McCarthy-ism flourished during the Korean War and Birchism, its counterpart of the 1960's, flourished upon Communist victories and setbacks for Western policies.

So bi-partisanship again displayed the perpetual tension between the domestic requirements of a civilized polity and the international power requirements of a major state whose national purposes demanded constancy at home and flexibility abroad. Unlike the Constitutional provisions which bi-partisanship was designed to soften, it amounted to a new, informal device whereby both popular and legislative consent to foreign policy might be more easily obtained if not in substance, then in form. But there were always two seemingly contradictory dangers in bi-partisanship. If the opposition party leadership were swallowed up in the very executive activities from which Administration policy sprang, there was the danger of no significant debate on national purposes occurring within the framework of the party systems. Thus an essential check on Presidential power might be lost. A broad consensus between the major party leaderships might obscure two essential elements of a democratic system, a locus of responsible, executive leadership and a locus of responsible opposition. Against this was the opposite peril that, in its search for opposition consent, the Executive might be swallowed up in the objections, the reluctances, and the partisan motives of the opposition party. Thus the necessary thrust of executive leadership might be blunted.

This was clear when America first started drafting proposals for a new international organization, the United Nations, during World War II. Senator Vandenberg, brought around from an earlier, nationalist-isolationist philosophy, had exerted an important influence on the Democratic Administration in incorporating in the draft Charter the so-called veto power which was to be so effectively used by the Soviet Union in blocking United Nations actions in major crises. A considerably softer veto power, permitting extensive Security Council action in cases requiring peaceful settlement of disputes, would have proved beneficial to American postwar purposes. But Vandenberg's nationalist stance, on behalf of the more nationalistic elements in the Republican Party,

230]   POWER, FREEDOM, AND DIPLOMACY

was ironically incorporated into the Charter with the pleased connivance of the Soviet Union. If the United Nations Charter thereby obtained Senatorial approval more easily, the compromise made by a Democratic administration avoided the pitfalls Wilson had encountered with his League in 1919 in the Senate. It is quite likely, however, that a Charter with considerably more efficacious voting provisions would still have gained far more than the necessary two-thirds approval.

One particular peril lay in the very temptations which were always present in the convenience of the bi-partisan formula: that an Executive, convinced that opposition party consent to *slight* innovations in foreign policy might easily be obtained, might out of expediency abandon necessary, basic changes in policy direction (achieved by direct Presidential appeals to the public which, if successful, might considerably reduce opposition obstructionism.) In 1940, President Roosevelt, facing Republican opposition to his foreign policy, finally constructed his own bi-partisan coalition. He simply took prominent Republicans into his Administration and into his designs, men already sympathetic with his interventionist policies in the European war. This was activist bi-partisanship; the adding of Stimson and Knox to his Cabinet enlarged the thrust of Roosevelt's leadership. In 1940-1941, the public battle for aid to Britain and France was led by a Kansas Republican newspaper-man, William Allen White, and other quite "respectable" Republicans, long known to be sympathetic to the President's foreign program, though they were hostile to some of his previous domestic reforms. In this manner, the public was educated to the national peril and awakened to the need to change Congress' obstructionism.[15] In the 1944 elections toward the end of the war, the Roosevelt administration had turned its major artillery savagely upon Congressional die-hard isolationists with substantial success, and the first post-war Congress, the Seventy-ninth, thus became

[15] For an account of the public battle against Republican isolationists in 1939-41, see Walter Johnson, *Battle Against Isolation*. Chicago: University of Chicago Press, 1944. Here, Johnson discusses the William Allen White Committee.

at least capable of giving consent to a broad range of necessary post-war international institutions.

A different and dangerous kind of bi-partisanship cited above, was the taking for granted by an Executive of the existing distribution of power in Congress and the existing consensus of leadership, and the consequent narrowing of Administration initiatives in foreign affairs to ones which, other things being equal, might prove acceptable. Thus the politics of bi-partisan consensus might well postpone major change and initiative in foreign affairs. The caution exhibited by the Kennedy Administration in its dealings with the Eighty-seventh Congress on matters of foreign policy was widely remarked. In the first months of the Kennedy Administration it was surprisingly deferential to powerful possible opponents of national policy. In the wake of the Cuban debacle in May 1961, the new President's first impulse was to fly to New York City to consult with General Douglas MacArthur, at the General's convenience! Arthur Schlesinger, Jr., wrote early in the new Administration that the close election of 1960 had required that Kennedy "create his own mandate," one which clearly was not shown in the November results.

It has often been said that a constitution is a living entity, but its essential nature often escapes the comprehension of men who study it merely through judicial interpretations or through readily perceptible innovations of usage and custom. This chapter has sought to indicate that the American Constitution contains within itself a perpetual and possibly necessary antagonism between two polar constitutional demands: an authoritarian one, dictated by exigencies of the external environment; and democratic ones, dictated by the requirements of a democratic society. The authoritarian pole suggests the constant need for centralized strength, purposefulness, constancy, and flexibility in foreign affairs. In moments of international crisis, when these needs often seemed too paramount, there is always a debate about the adequacy of democratic institutions in a crisis and about the inherent threats of abuse of emergency power. The democratic pole suggests not only the need for popular consent both to legislation and national foreign policies but also the procedural conditions within government and society to make such consent appear and be rational, to make public policy in the international realm in some fashion subject to popular control. In the twentieth century, there have been too many instances which Americans could observe in other nations' experiences where both democracy and representative government foundered in crisis, where parliamentary deadlock or democratic lethargy preceded and contributed to national disasters, or where democratic institutions were simply discarded in favor of totalitarian political orders when they could not meet the requirements of international crisis.

SUGGESTED READING

Beloff, Max, *Foreign Policy and the Democratic Process*, Baltimore, The Johns Hopkins Press, 1955.

Burns, James MacGregor, "Bi-partisanship and the Weakness of the Party System," in Jacobson, Harold K., *America's Foreign Policy*, New York, Random House, 1960, pp. 58-63.

Corwin, Edwin S., *The President, Office and Powers, 1787-1957*, New York, New York University Press, 1937, pp. 170-226 and pp. 227-262.

Dahl, Robert, *Congress and Foreign Policy*, New York, Harcourt Brace, 1950.

Dillard, H. C., "Treaty Making Controversy: Substance and Shadow," *Virginia Quarterly Review*, XXX(2), pp. 178-191, 1954.

Huntington, Samuel P., "Civilian Control and the Constitution," *American Political Science Review*, September 1956, pp. 676-699.

Koenig, Louis W., *The Invisible Presidency*, New York, Rinehart, 1960.

Oliver, Covey T., "Treaties, the Senate and the Constitution," *American Journal of International Law*, July 1957, pp. 606-611.

"Constitutional Issues Raised by the Position of the United States in World Affairs," *American Society of International Law Proceedings*, 1951.

CHAPTER

8

POLICY AND PUBLIC

For some forty years, the vital and once expansive civil institutions of Western democracy have been on the defensive everywhere. At first glance, the assault upon them appears to have come chiefly from two Marxist sources, both of which have an investment in a very powerful political order of the Communist world. The one most clearly perceived by Americans is the ideological assault of Marxist-Leninist ideas upon the philosophical foundations of Western liberalism and representative government, an assault, incidentally, joined by many non-Marxists also with the purpose of undermining the very basis of liberal democracy. This assault was made not only upon the legitimacy of the liberal state (in Lenin's words, the instrument of the ruling classes), but also upon its capacities. It was said that liberal and representative government could not govern and could not cope with the mounting tensions, pressures, and contradictions of a modern industrial society. Furthermore, as it became increasingly estranged from the masses, it sought by force to retain an authority which had already disappeared.

The assault, of course, was far more general and fundamental. It was upon the state in general and upon political power as such, and the appeals of the doctrine to powerless men everywhere must be understood in this light. But the chief target was the most dynamic political order of the late nineteenth century and in the early twentieth, the Western institutions of representative government.

THE BOLSHEVIK REVOLUTION AND THE ASSAULT ON THE WEST

The threat also came from the political institutions in which Marxism-Leninism was embodied after the Bolshevik Revolution of 1917. In the Soviet Union, the state in Communist hands became something much more than an agency of the ruling classes. It became a powerful instrument to remould, reshape, and transform society into something qualitatively new. The authority of this Socialist state in an ideological sense lay in its revolutionary and managerial capacities and their alleged appropriateness to the historical context in which they were used. In the hands of Soviet administrators, agencies of political power became agents of revolution. The Soviet state became the agency through which revolution itself was to be expressed. This was its supreme justification. Many Westerners and disillusioned Communists pointed to the betrayal of original revolutionary purposes and the fact that the Soviet state, far from "withering away" as Marxist orthodoxy prophesied, constantly augmented its strength. Others recoiled at the ruthless, despotic abuses of power in the hands of administrative revolutionaries like Stalin. In the collectivization program of the early 1930's, in Soviet treason trials and purges, and in the techniques of totalitarian police power, the new Soviet system seemed not just a horrible caricature of Lenin's own caricature of the bourgeois state, but even worse—a massive, totalitarian order in which all the civilities of political life were swept away. But such dismay could not mask the fact that the system was extraordinarily powerful. Judged by any conventional index of political power, the Soviet system continued to grow in prestige and might. The brutality of Soviet power in Eastern Europe after World War II, which planted Soviet imperial rule in all the states east of the Elbe by military force, displayed the most iniquitous features of Russian Communism. All Europeans experienced or saw close by the tanks, "people's police," administrative murders, and brutal defiance of popular will by Party cadres and their hand-picked supporters.

But this glimpse of Soviet power, occasionally heightened by Soviet police power or military force was only a fragment of a much larger picture. Within the U.S.S.R., particularly after Stalin's death in 1953, all could see that the Soviet state did not rely merely upon force and brutality. Much as one looked for signs of popular discontent, there was no locus of *political* opposition, no obscure or visible signs of alternative political choice either in institutions or in informal resistance groups within the U.S.S.R. Tensions within Russian society were tensions *among* agencies, institutions, and men who had either accepted or resigned themselves to the reality and ideological premises of the new Socialist society. Soviet Communism triumphed in a far more fundamental fashion than Nazi totalitarianism had in the 1940's.

In Nazi Germany, political liquidation, while an efficient device and a barbarous crime against humanity, had been limited by the style of Nazism itself. Aside from a few real radicals (notably those within the Himmler S.S.), the Nazi leadership at no time proposed to demolish wholly and then reconstruct German society. What measures it took forcefully to remould a recalcitrant Germany into a New Order did not alter the social structure of German society, so that, after the re-emergence of non-totalitarian institutions in the rubble of post-war Germany, there was a surprising resumption of pre-Nazi political life (of non-totalitarian, non-monarchist parties) and of voting behavior which strikingly resembled the parties of the 1920's. For all its unspeakable iniquities, the Nazi political system seems to have put German society in a sociological deep freeze. Of course, much more can be accomplished by a totalitarian society in forty years than in thirteen, but also—and this is essential to understand—Soviet totalitarianism proposed something which Nazism never pretended: i.e., to restructure radically the whole social order around a monumental administrative technology which, in essence, was terribly modern. Nazism, nihilistically infatuated with its romantic vision of a Wagnerian past, never had this unswerving, systematic commitment to innovation.

The waxing might of the U.S.S.R., constantly and tediously proclaimed by all of the entities of the Soviet state and the Communist Party, sometimes seemed ludicrous to observant Westerners who could observe the gap not only between Soviet goals and their fulfillment, but between their fulfillment and the prosperity so commonplace in Europe and America. Former Vice-President Nixon could try to humiliate Premier Khrushchev in a modern American miracle kitchen, but the West seemed to miss the point. The Soviet Union did not count its achievements in the comforts of civilized life but in the organs of technological, scientific, and military power into which it had forcibly diverted the energies of a whole people. The chief thrust of Soviet economic, scientific, and managerial power was directed far beyond the normal, Western goals of a more abundant life for ordinary people; they aimed above this. And only after the first spectacular Soviet achievements in space science in 1958 did it become apparent to all that the Soviet system was capable of great feats in science and technology. America's reputation as the unrivalled technological innovator had been challenged, and with it, the idea that only a "free society" could provide sufficient intellectual conditions for prolonged scientific progress and inquiry.

The New States

An equally disturbing assault upon Western traditions of civility and representative government came from the areas of the world which lay outside the cluster of Western states and outside the orbit of Soviet totalitarianism. In the new states which began to enter the society of nations in ever growing numbers after World War II, there arose an institutional vacuum to be filled with new political and constitutional orders. The compass of these new states extended from West Africa to North Asia. They came into being as a consequence of revolt against foreign and chiefly Western rule: through internal revolt against long-established, Western-supported oligarchies; through secession from other non-Western states (as in the case of Pakistan); and through peaceful, gradual transfers of power and authority from former colonial powers.

In the morning after independence, the new states faced the classic problems of infant polities: the need to establish new authority, internal order, constitutional permanence, and at least elementary standards of justice. To these classic problems, others were added, for the new states often lacked any rudimentary cohesiveness in their social structure, the kind of cultural or linguistic homogeneity which, for instance, had already been present in the new United States of 1787. Indeed the traditional bases of society, which might have become the cultural foundations of a new independent order, were rapidly being torn asunder by social and technological change and by the acculturation of new elites to the managerial and technological opportunities which they saw in the older, industrialized societies. Political infants, they were thrust with extreme suddenness from colonial backwardness into the sea of world politics.

The nineteenth-century liberal confidence in the spread of democratic, representative government gave way in mid-twentieth century to growing doubts about its political capacities and its relevance to the political problems of these new states. The steady progress of nations to independence and self-government under representative institutions had once been widely anticipated by many American liberals. What now complicated matters was that the revolutionary doctrine of Marxism had extraordinary appeal in the colonial areas of the world where the older empires were breaking up. For many of these new nations, the experiences and accomplishments of the Soviet Union in economic transformation from primitive to highly complex industrial conditions seemed far more relevant than the experiences of the bourgeois, Western world in its own earlier political and economic development.

By the mid-twentieth century, Western parliamentary democracy and the concomitant principles of the open society seemed durably rooted only in the United States and in a surrounding cluster of other Western nations which had possessed these institutions long before World War I. The momentum of representative government, with its constitutional order permitting and requiring public participation in the shaping of national policy, had seemingly been spent. One should neither exaggerate nor minimize the nature of this condition. The cluster of free societies which were also stable polities encompassed most of the North Atlantic region. Taken together, they comprised well over four hundred million people. Among them, both productivity and economic prosperity far out-matched the performance of the entire Communist world. The intellectual vitality of this core of Western civilization was far from broken by World War II and quickly rose to new heights. But aside from the United States, which had never shared in any significant extent their role as imperial governors of the underdeveloped world, the political authority of the Western states in the outside world had been irrevocably broken and their tutorial capacities in self-government were rarely solicited by the new societies which had now gained political independence from them. Technicians, yes; philosophers and teachers, no.

What Goals for a Pluralistic Society?

One feature which sharply distinguished the public order of these Western open societies from the totalitarian orders of the new Communist states was the seeming monolithic political purpose which informed the Marxist states and the plurality of purposes within the open societies. In the case of the Soviet Union, it was not just that the formal machinery of Party and State made possible an extraordinary centralization of power. (When Premier Khrushchev, in October 1961, presented to the Twenty-second Party Congress the draft of his new party program, aimed at creating "a utopian community society within the next twenty years," he remarked that the Congress "had the honor" to receive it.) It was also that the monolithic structure was informed by overriding doctrinal and programmatic purpose. In the Western democracies on the other hand, no such monolithic structures or purposes existed to permit of coherent, overriding, national goals. When President Eisenhower, disturbed by the seeming absence of American goals and purposes, appointed a committee on national goals, fearful that this executive act might smack of authoritarianism, his impulse was to finance it through private foundations rather than to assess the taxpayer and Congress. Whether a committee was sufficient to clarify such ends is as peculiar a question as whether a foundation was the proper agency to endow it.

The free society, so it was widely believed, cherished most of all the competition and conflict among its many, pluralistic components. Pushed to an extreme, the idea of the free society was that of a process, a set of interrelationships amongst free men, directed by no guiding hand of history, gently regulated by a Constitutional order which all were supposed to accept. The ultimate test of this process was what the people wanted, not what State, Party, or Revolution demanded. In America in particular, politics was governed by a seeming pragmatic sanction. Politics and economics presented a never ending continuum of problems which practical men were supposed to solve. Public conflict was the essence of this process. Cumbersome in time of peace, the process itself offered no guidelines of overriding public interest or national interest.[1] Yet in time of great crisis, the process seemed capable of powerful and dynamic enterprise. Once the problem had been defined, the democratic system often proved able to generate great public energy and ingenuity. Above all, it had its humane rationale which even some sensitive Marxist philosophers in the Communist world perceived. As Professor Adam Schaff, Poland's senior Marxist philosopher remarked, "The strongest propaganda trump card against Communism and Marxism today in the capitalist world is the problem of the rights to freedom of the individual . . . , the problem of democracy."[2]

The picture of the processes at work, however correct it might be to some, could have a dismaying effect upon men who supposed that there was more to America than that. Mr. Arthur Goodfriend, an American writer and government official, saw with dismay the effects of an American scholar's lecture before a highly intelligent Indian audience on the political processes and American foreign policy. He wrote:

> We took pains to arrange a full dress meeting of Delhi's Foreign Policy Association, an august and influential group which, despite the best efforts of USIS, remained skeptical about America's position in almost every area of world international affairs. Over a hundred Indians came, eager to hear an expert present the American side of the story. Historically, the speaker emphatically declared, the United States had no foreign policy. Now, as in the past, it was improvised on a day-to-day basis. Headlines, political pressures, personal proclivities in the White House, State Department and Congress were the major formative influences. Unsure of where our own self-interests lay, and heedless of the self-interests of others, we fumbled over more precariously our awful material and military power. Where it all would end, he didn't know. The Indian chairman, rising to thank him for his

[1] See Chapter 4, p. 84.
[2] Quoted in *The New York Times*, October 17, 1961.

contribution, was almost mute with embarrassment. He happened
to be a journalist who, time and again, had risked his reputation
defending, in public print, the inner logic of the American position.[3]

During the nineteenth and early twentieth century, the
United States grew to maturity as a free society within a larger
context of political isolation, military security, and a world in
which the institutions of political democracy seemed inevitably
on the march. We can in no way understand the extraordinary,
enthusiastic response in America and abroad to Woodrow Wilson's Fourteen Points unless we sense the profound appeal it had
for men still confident of the universal applicability of national
self-determination, democracy, free elections, and the open society. For strangely enough, the high-water mark of liberal, representative government's popularity was reached in the midst of
World War I. At a time when the military-political struggle in
Europe was between two camps of traditional, European states,
the ideological struggle was between their value systems and the
ideological principles of Wilsonian liberalism and quite soon
thereafter, between Wilson and Lenin.

Ideologically, Wilson might have later been regarded as an
impractical idealist, far too heady and universalistic to speak for
American national interests. Yet the brief, powerful enthusiasm
with which Wilson's message of democracy was received in Europe attested to its appeal not only as an alternative to Bolshevism and the older authoritarian political orders of continental
Europe; it attested also to the surprising vitality of America as a
political example.

But the high-water mark of 1917 has not been reached again.
The survival of American democracy in a world in which democratic
institutions elsewhere had perished or been discarded would be
very much open to question. Conversely, the strength of American democracy could be said to depend in very large measure
upon the flourishing of vigorous open societies elsewhere in the

[3] Arthur Goodfriend, *To Drag a Lion*, unpublished manuscript.

world. To be sure, there are severe limits upon the influence of democracy, not the least of which arises from the need to deal "realistically" and live with nations which have either repudiated or never experienced any measure of democracy in their public life.

Since the cold war began, some doctrinaire, American liberals have insisted that no American support, economic or other, be given to states which explicitly reject democracy on ideological grounds or which in practice flout the procedural values of democracy. These people have characteristically displayed greater animus against authoritarian traditionalist regimes like Franco's and overtly Communist states closely linked to the Soviet Union than they did to apostate regimes like Yugoslavia and Poland, or despotic regimes like Nasser's or Nkrumah's which clothed tyranny in the rhetoric of revolution. Doctrinaire American conservatives, on the other hand, often opposed U.S. aid to any state democratic or other, which rejected principles of free enterprise and capitalism in favor of state planning or socialism. Needless to say, had the demands and advice of *both* groups been accepted by the American government, the only eligible recipients of American aid would have been countries like Switzerland, Canada, and Australia, which had little or no need for it anyway; and foreign-aid, a major fulcrum of American influence in world politics, would have been either non-existent or unnecessary.

WHO IS THE PUBLIC?

What does "the public" mean? (Students would be ill-advised to look up this essential political concept in the usual source, *The Encyclopedia of The Social Sciences,* which in its eight volumes does not once list it.) Etymologically we could define it as the nation, the state, the commonwealth—all-embracing definitions of the political community as a whole and the things which pertain to it. Yet more commonly we conceive of the public as an aggregate of the individual members of a communal

entity. We distinguish the public from agencies of the state which
govern it or which exert political authority and power to carry out
its commands or to act in its name. Finally we also distinguish
the public from those things which are, or should be, considered
private. For while the public is regarded as the aggregate of men
in society who collectively share, or are said to share, common
purposes through time, in all of Western thought, there has been
a perpetual tension between the three components of organized
political life: the state, the public, and the private. Western men
have been aware of this tension since the time of Socrates and
Jesus. For individuals may have ideas which, if left uncontrolled,
could subvert the existing public's integrity; and the "other-affect-
ing" actions of individual men may set them at odds with the
prevailing temper of their community. On the other hand, there
has always been the claim on behalf of men as individuals that
there should be a private sphere of conscience which neither the
public nor the state may trespass against except for the most
grave reasons. Totalitarian states today claim to have resolved the
tension, but to the extent that they have, they have done so by
violently fusing all three components at the price of individual
freedom and liberties, of conscience and action. The closed society
brooks no privacy.

But what is the public if it is an "aggregate of the individual
members of a community"? If it is an entity, how might its wishes
and its interests be ascertained? The very idea of the public seems
to be something quite particular, set off, for instance, from *other*
publics in other national or political communities. Hence the
term is not all-embracing. We speak of the American public, in
whose interests American foreign policy is conducted and we also
speak of a British public, even of an Egyptian one. The particu-
larness of the idea reveals its spatial limitations, its "exclusive-
ness."

The difficulty of ascertaining its meaning does not stop here
however, for the aggregate, like the Sphinx, is never articulate.
Try as we may to "capture" it, to discover what it thinks, it is

elusive. Its spatial, temporal characteristics constantly change. As of 7 a.m. on a July morning in 1960, the population of the United States for an infinitesmal slice of time was estimated by the Census Bureau as 180,000,000. This then was the Public, until the next birth and the next death altered the statistics. Births, deaths, immigration, and emigration alter its substance from hour to hour each day of the week.

Edmund Burke once described the public as a metaphysical entity, a partnership "not only between those who are living," but also with "those who are dead, and those who are to be born." But could such a definition suffice for a nation like the United States which augmented its own population incessantly until recent years, with immigrants from other communities who had left to come here? As a nation of immigrants, America's ancestors lay scattered in graves from the Urals to the banks of the Yangtse and the Congo. Where were its children yet to be born to come from? The convenient image of the public as a link in a great continuous chain of ancestors and descendants made little sense to the majority of Americans in a democratic society, most of whom habitually rejected ancestor worship and who rarely even knew the full names of all their great-grandparents or, indeed, where they had once lived. (There was a notable increase of interest in genealogy in America among the older Anglo-Saxon stock, during the enormous influx of immigrants in the late nineteenth century from other parts of Europe.) Burke's conception of the public, metaphorically akin to the water in a bathtub with plug open and spigot running, does not hold up when there is more than one spigot.

(A grisly suggestion was made recently by Mr. Herman Kahn, who divides the American public into two communities which he calls Country A and Country B. The former is that part of the American public likely to survive a nuclear exchange; the latter, that which likely would not. Conceivably a major nuclear exchange directed at metropolitan areas but sparing rural ones would not only reduce the aggregate population considerably but leave, as remainder, a highly "atypical" cross-section of the public, with quite different attributes than those of the total community before the calamity.)

Supposedly it is in the interests of the public that foreign policy is conducted. The metaphysical speculation is essential and the point well-taken when we note the core of Burke's definition: that the Public can not be conceived of in a momentary sense. By what "right" for instance, should one generation of Americans arrogate to themselves privileges or pleasures the indulgence of which would rob future generations of any enjoyment? Does sovereign authority lie then in the "will of all," expressed at one moment in time by one generation of Americans?

Tom Paine thought so. In his reply to Burke's assertion that a living generation could not free itself from obligations to past ones, Paine remarked:

> There never did, there never will, and there never can exist a Parliament, or any description of men, or any generation of men, in any country, possessed of the right or the power of binding and controlling posterity to the "end of time," or of commanding forever how the world shall be governed, or who shall govern it; and therefore, all such clauses, acts or declarations, by which the makers of them attempt to do what they have neither the right nor the power to do, nor the power to execute, are in themselves null and void. Every age and generation must be free to act for itself, *in all cases*, as the ages and generations which preceded it. . . . Man has no property in man, neither has any generation a property in the generations which are to follow. . . . That which a whole nation chooses to do, it has a right to do.[4]

Elsewhere, in Paine's *Common Sense*, written on the eve of the American Revolution, he swiftly dismissed as an argument against independence the ethnic and cultural ties which bound the colonies to the mother country:

> But admitting that we are all of English descent, what does it amount to? Nothing. . . . The first king of England, of the

[4] "The Rights of Man," in *The Complete Political Works of Tom Paine*. New York: Peter Ecklet, 1922, pp. 13-14.

present line (William the Conqueror) was a Frenchman, and half the peers of England are descendants from the same country; wherefore, by the same method of reasoning, England ought to be governed by France.[5]

Yet of the two, Burke possibly came closer to a profound political need for a metaphysical concept of a continuing community of men linked together as a continuing public. This communal conception did not necessarily imprison a living generation of men in a strait jacket of obligation to those who had gone before, but it did compel living men to have some sense of perspective on the needs of a national community as a whole. The very fact that this profound quarrel between two men now dead is relevant to our discussion testifies to the very continuity of things which Paine himself so disliked.

Americans often dismiss such philosophical questions about the public, preferring instead to see the public in procedural, juridical, or merely common sense terms. For all practical purposes, the American public could be politically defined as the electorate, those entitled periodically to vote their leaders in or out of office; or as all persons enjoying American citizenship and nationality; or simply as the "man in the street," whose homespun wisdom about current events could be extracted from him by newsmen. With the development of opinion-polling devices the public could also be defined, in a shadowy sort of way, as "opinionated" responses to questions, as a running commentary on events which could be quantitatively, statistically, and attitudinally broken down into categories by social scientists and IBM machines. Finally, when dissected by sociologists, the public could be seen as a highly complex system of interrelated groups, subpublics of an ethnic, religious, occupational, regional, or educational nature of enormously varying influence on political decisions, perceiving events through lenses ground and polished by their own unique experience, their own cultural and psychological traits.

[5] "Common Sense," *ibid.*, p. 23.

Whichever way one looks at the public, the constitutional definition seems supreme: the public was the aggregate of men in society juxtaposed to the state, to political power in the whole people, proceeding through time, altering in character, engaged, consciously or unconsciously, in a great collective national endeavor; suffering, dying, or benefitting from consequences of policies undertaken in its behalf by the leaders who were responsible to it.

The public was also victim or beneficiary of the virtues, vices, and errors or truths of judgment of "itself" and its rulers. The sociological public, or the public as process, could severely affect public policy, setting limits to political enterprises of government by establishing collectively an intellectual or ethical milieu out of which absurd policies might spring or by demanding things of government. The open society, permitting and encouraging the expression of dissent, facilitating the organized expression and the open dissemination of political ideas, took the calculated democratic risk of public dissent. Yet in the name of the nation as a whole, and for its security in international affairs, national purposes and goals in world politics had somewhere to be defined and actions taken. These things the sociological public, the public as collective opinion, could not itself provide. Traditionally suspicious of both great power and centralized authority, Americans required in the mid twentieth century a Leviathan, an executive authority capable of acting with swiftness, secrecy, dispatch, and purposefulness in foreign affairs. What mattered was how this Leviathan functionally related itself to the Public.

The Public's Role in Foreign Policy

In his contribution to Gordon Craig's *The Diplomats*, Dexter Perkins, an American scholar of foreign affairs, has written:

> In a sense that is true in no such degree in other nations, American diplomatic action has been determined by the people. There were ardent debates on foreign policy in the first days of our na-

tional history. There have been debates ever since. Uninstructed though the average citizen may be in the facts of international life, he still has an opinion with regard to them. If he does not know, he thinks he knows. And this conviction on his part is one that cannot be disregarded. Nor do those who conduct our affairs in the main desire to disregard it. The democratic tradition is deeply rooted in our history. The men who stand at the levers of control are almost always men with substantial political experience. Their habits, their prepossessions, their convictions all lead them to pay heed to the voice of the great body of citizens, to shape their decisions with that voice in mind.[6]

The American public in the Western context of the late modern era was the first for whom democratic spokesmen insisted that no qualitative distinction be made between the democratic processes of domestic policy and foreign policy-making, that both processes be essentially public, *open* ones, and that the acknowledged leadership always be held publicly accountable. To some extent, the Constitution itself required this publicity, by assigning to Congress and the Senate, both representative bodies, crucial powers which could be continuously exercised only in public. (It was the original intent of the framers of the Constitution that the Senate's treaty-making role be "conciliar" and an adjunct to the President's executive role. In practice this never was the case. Congress' war-making powers and its related powers of the purse, etc., were *always* public.)

The popular American temper transcended the Constitutional claims. It constantly pressed for adherence to certain procedural and substantive practices in foreign policy, such as publicity of governmental aims, open diplomacy, and unrestrained *public* debate about major foreign policy issues. Insofar as the real example of American diplomacy proved in some measure harmonious with these ideal requirements, American diplomacy itself could set an example to other nations to do likewise. When

[6] "The Department of State and American Public Opinion," in Gordon Craig, ed., *The Diplomats*. Princeton: Princeton University Press, 1953, pp. 282-283.

Wilson, in 1917, called on the European powers to abandon traditional practices of the old diplomacy, and to take up the practice of "open covenants, openly arrived at," he was not just expressing an idiosyncratic utopian belief but a widespread conviction which many Americans had had for a long time.

There are, of course, weaknesses in such a "populist" point of view and a certain naïveté in the excessive faith in public rationality and the doctrinaire, simplistic belief that openness in debate, negotiation, and policy making would facilitate international agreement. It is true that, ideologically and historically, the flowering of this political belief in America occurred under unique and favorable circumstances. For surely a strong case could be made for democratic controls on foreign policy processes in a relaxed international atmosphere where urgency and secrecy were rarely called for, when foreign affairs did not rank particularly high among the policy activities of the nation, and when, in fact, a very wide range of choices was available to the nation in its dealings with other quite remote states.

The American populist attitude towards foreign affairs seems to originate in America's eighteenth- and early nineteenth-century experiences with the European state system. It was particularly related to a widespread American revulsion *both* to the internal constitutional orders of the traditional European societies and to their behavior in a European system of power politics. Until well into the twentieth century, the international diplomatic practices of European states, including secret diplomacy and secret alliances, were widely regarded in America as antithetical to popular aspirations. The fact that America long appeared able to remain outside of this system by its own voluntary choice thus enhanced the virtues of the American democratic ideals. American non-involvement in the European balance system supposedly enlarged her range of choice in world politics and also assured the American public of a wider influence upon foreign policy.

A kind of residual colonial mentality led to an anti-authoritarian bias, much like that which now pervades many of the new

African states. Until well after the American revolution, the western hemisphere remained a theater within which the traditional European balance system played itself out. Until the end of the Napoleonic Wars, North America also remained a theater in which European wars took place. As most Americans saw it, the *ultima ratio* of such wars was decided upon in distant European chanceries. Until the American Revolution, the American colonists paid the taxes and suffered their farms and settlements to be laid waste for reasons they could poorly comprehend and over which they had no control. The fact, also, that all really important wars continued to originate within a European geographic context further reinforced an American belief that war was somehow caused by peculiarly European conditions. If these conditions could somehow be remedied by an infusion of democratic practices, the dangers of war would be correspondingly lessened.

Acrimonious foreign policy debates have had a significant role in American political history. In the twentieth century alone, three such debates, linked in complex fashion to domestic power struggles within the nation, nearly rent the fabric of our political life. They occurred during World War I, on the eve of World War II, and during the Korean war. But even in peacetime, public disagreement about the American national interest has often made it difficult to steer a constant course in international diplomacy or to attain sufficient forcefulness and clarity of purpose to achieve objectives abroad. The populist tradition combined with constitutional arrangements to keep these disagreements and debates on the surface of American life. A free press, Congressional debate, and the popular demand for open diplomacy all contributed to the acrimony of these public debates.

Public cleavages about foreign policy are often very closely related to public disagreements about domestic issues as well. Often, they are aspects of much broader intellectual and cultural cleavages. This is an unpleasant fact of politics. Some of us would wish that the national interest of the United States should be wholly rational, a balance between clearly defined undertakings and clearly discerned problems in the external milieu. Yet even the most rational decision-maker often finds that the domestic political context provides him with certain definite aspirations and goals. Often it severely constrains his own free judgment about what course of action to take.

To be sure, the decision-maker possesses wide discretionary power when public checks upon his freedom to act are quite weak. This is especially true in moments of international crises, when the government's monopoly on military power and the instruments of violence provides a vigorous executive with considerable freedom to act. There are many areas of foreign policy where both Congressional and public influence on day-to-day decisions are extremely slight and where a wide ranging executive power (in overseas diplomatic and military establishments) can decisively influence crisis policy. Yet on no occasion is the policy-maker, the President, the Secretary of State, or their agencies, wholly free from the domestic political milieu.

A classic example is Roosevelt's "quarantine" speech. Faced in 1937 by German and Japanese aggression in Europe and Asia, aware of the dangers which these developments posed to the United States, President Roosevelt, in his famous Chicago speech, urged that peace-loving nations join together to check them. The immediate public reaction in America was highly unfavorable. Sensitive to public responses and aware of the difficulties which adverse public opinion might have on his domestic program, Roosevelt quickly backtracked and abandoned his idea. Not until 1940, when Axis aggression reached flood proportions, did Roosevelt return to this theme.

However deep such political conflicts have been, they have usually taken place among forces which have accepted the constitutional, territorial, and *national* basis of an American national interest. To be sure, conflicts between American corporate institutions and other pressure groups, and between the two major political parties over particular foreign policies have existed throughout American history. Yet by and large, the social forces which comprise American politics have taken for granted certain fundamental premises about the political order within which they live, and this has, in turn, delimited the sphere of popular conflict about goals. As we have noted before, the American political system, unlike those of many European, Asian, and African nations, is not deeply torn by fundamental philosophical disagreements about first principles. In Europe in the nineteenth and twentieth centuries, such disagreements enlarged already deep fissures within the social structure of nearly every European power, and as a result, any talk about a popular consensus concerning foreign affairs or other national purposes became almost absurd.

In Germany and France, two extreme examples, ideological cleavages which found expression in powerful political movements were profoundly at odds with each other concerning the constitutional order of the nation and the direction of the nation's foreign policies. The parties of the Left, largely excluded from political power until the mid-twentieth century, held a near monopoly upon utopian theories of international politics. They were strongly opposed to imperialist expansion and to military power. Important segments of the population found themselves thus for long periods of time wholly alienated from the national interests of their own countries. In France, until the era of Fascist totalitarianism, the parties of the Right, fearful of both domestic revolution and of external threats to the existing regimes, sought to formulate national interests which would simultaneously diminish the threat of both. In the twilight years of the French Third Republic before it was crushed by Nazi Germany, the ideological cleavage between Left and Right was so great that the idea of a national interest virtually disappeared. A common saying among French conservatives was "better Hitler than Stalin." The French Left thought just the opposite.

The basic theories about American politics surrounding the constitutional system have grown out of the eighteenth-century Enlightenment. Constitutional struggles in American politics have commonly been concerned with what one constitution means rather than with *which* constitutional order was most desirable. In this respect, American constitutional history resembles that of most other English-speaking nations.

In addition, and by way of comparison with many other great powers in world politics, there has been a surprising public consensus in the United States since the Civil War about the territorial basis of the nation.

Before 1860, the character and swiftness of America's Westward expansion was a source of deep antagonism between the South and the North. Territorial expansion threatened constantly to dislocate the delicate balance between the free and the slaveholding states. The war with Mexico, for instance, was strongly opposed throughout much of the American North, since an American victory, with its territorial prizes, would extend the influence of the Southern plantation and slave system. These sectional disagreements about the territorial character of the United States have not entirely subsided. Expansion of the federal union by admission of new states still affects the balance of political forces in the whole national community. Quite recently, strong yet covert opposition to the admission of Hawaii and Alaska to the Union was expressed among Southern legislators in Washington, since conferral of statehood on them would further weaken the influence of conservative Southerners in Washington.

There is no "terra irredenta" which extreme American nationalists wish to recover (for territorial America has never suffered significant territorial amputations or frustrations). By and large, continental America, its insular possessions, and its two new states, Hawaii and Alaska, are regarded by Americans as the permanent territorial domain of the United States, neither more nor less. This seeming fixity of the American territorial realm sharply contrasts with the territorial realms of almost all other major powers, most notably, the Soviet Union, the frontiers of which are today swollen by reason of its post World War II expansion in Eastern Europe and the Far East. To be sure, some Mexicans still recall American seizure of their territory over a century ago, but there is no significant irredentist movement directed by any major power or neighboring state against the American heartland. The continental realm of the United States is taken for granted as the geographic form of the federal union. It is this realm which, for example, American defense policies seek ultimately to protect and defend. Extreme nationalists in the United States may and have pressed for the enlargement of the present sphere of American military-political control in areas outside of this realm, but unlike earlier nationalists in American history, they have rarely pressed for political annexation. Theoretically, of course, the United States Constitution specifies the federal union as an open-ended political system, providing as it does for the incorporation of new states by act of Congress. But today there are no significant pressures within America for extending this system beyond its present limits.

This widespread public sense of the legitimacy of America's territorial realm has lent stability to America's present foreign relations. But there is also, significantly, a public consensus in the United States about the *territorial* basis of American nationality. This, too, contrasts sharply with the experiences of many other nation-states in international politics. The North American continent was settled in relatively modern times. But the indigenous races of Europe, Africa, and Asia existed before the arbitrary division of these great land masses into territorial nation-states. The American nation-state, in its territorial form, existed *prior to* both the settlement of America by new immigrants and the development of a firm cultural basis for American nationalism.

This difference between the American experience with nationalism and that of most older cultures is crucial for our understanding of the social basis of an American national interest. For it has meant that as the spirit of nationalism emerged in America, it assumed a territorial rather than a tribal nature. (At the time of the American Revolution, the original colonies were pre-eminently English in their cultural characteristics, preponderantly Protestant in religion, and already possessed of a high degree of cultural homogeneity, despite considerable differences between the Southern plantation colonies, Puritan New England, and the more heterogeneous Middle Atlantic States. The later waves of immigration from the European continent after the 1840's did not alter the linguistic and cultural pre-eminence of the older Anglo-Saxon, Scots-Irish stock, which dominated American politics and culture until well into the twentieth century. The price for what the sociologists have called upward social mobility was a heavy one, for such groups as the Germans and Scandinavians which did adapt to the dominant American culture, involving repudiation of their cultural background. Yet as a general rule, they paid the price. The American territorial state helped ease the cultural transition since it provided for an unusually high degree of social, occupational, and geographic mobility.) In America, cultural nationalism represented a fusion of many ethnic groups into a non-ethnic nationalism. In much of Europe, Asia, and contemporary Africa, the imposition of territorial, political states upon old, overlapping, indigenous cultures resulted in deep tensions and antagonisms among nationality groups which, throughout the course of centuries, acquired their unique indentities from common experiences, habitual association, and consanguinity. In Central and Eastern Europe as well as many parts of Asia, when frontiers were drawn across the political map to separate new national states, it proved impossible to create culturally pure nations, co-extensive with territorial states.

On the European continent and elsewhere, the term "minority" has had connotations quite different from those in the United States. There "minorities," separated from their ethnic brothers in neighboring states by seemingly arbitrary cartographic decisions, sought protection from the dominant majority in the state for their language, their customs and their religion. Often, joining with their brothers elsewhere in Europe, these minorities struggled for political autonomy, independence, or *Anschluss* with foreign states.

In Germany and most of Eastern Europe before World War

II, dominant nationality groups within new states sought forcibly to assimilate minority groups into the dominant order, or even, as was the case in Hitler's Third Reich, to wipe them off the map entirely. Within the nation-states of Europe and Asia then, inter-ethnic tensions produced deep antagonisms in their international politics. In any event, it often made impossible the development of a stable domestic social basis for the foreign policies of states.

To be sure, various ethnic groups in America have often differed sharply amongst themselves about the appropriate foreign policies which the United States should adopt—yet characteristically, American minority groups, whether Irish, German, Negro, or other, have sought or demanded access to the cultural values and privileges of the dominant community. While European minority groups "wanted out," American minorities, typically, have "wanted in."

A pertinent example of this may be found today, in the politics of American Negro groups. Since the 1920's, the growing political articulateness of American Negroes found two types of expression: on the one hand, groups such as the N.A.A.C.P. fought for cultural and political assimilation into American society—following the classic patterns of other minority ethnic groups before them. Others, like Marcus Garvey's Negro movement of the 1920's, and the Muslim movement of the 1960's, rejected "assimilationism" and exalted the superiority of the Negro "race." Garvey's movement went so far as to seek the establishment of an African "homeland." Charges that Garveyites collaborated with the Ku Klux Klan—both in agreement that the Negro community was a "nation"—contributed to Garvey's collapse.

Domestic Order and International Disorder

But there is today an absurd incongruity between the apocalyptic possibilities of world politics and the normal facts of everyday public life in America. Judged by its performance to date, the American political system has achieved political and social progress at no sacrifice of the need for political order and constitutional continuity. Its political institutions never have collapsed under the strain of problems they confronted. Congressional democracy and presidential leadership have contested in dubious battle with each other for more than a century and a half and both have successfully withstood the onslaughts of different or new ideologies. Sectionalism and regionalism, great centrifugal influences in American life, capitulated after the Civil War to the powerful centripetal and culturally homogeneous forces of urbanization and industrialization. The nationality struggle between disparate ethnic groups on which many nation-states foundered proved not to be an insurmountable obstacle to national unity, while the class struggle, so prominent in European political experience, never rooted itself deeply in the American public consciousness.

It is notable that the symbolic architectural features of Washington, the national capital, display this essential simplicity. The white, classical mode of public buildings, interrupted only by Victorian extravagances, exhibit an extraordinary consistency of style; while the public monuments to presidents, generals, and senators are interesting in that without exception, *all* of those who are there commemorated are honored for their commitment to legitimate values of the constitutional order.

This firm institutional setting of American society has parallels and analogies elsewhere, particularly among other English speaking peoples and the Scandinavian states. What is unique is that the geographic dimensions of the American system have also remained relatively fixed. In a world where frontiers and constitutional forms of most great powers today are widely regarded as tentative, illegitimate, or abnormal, those of the United States seem remarkably stable. The frontiers of the Soviet Union today, even including those which border upon Communist China, are by no means generally taken for granted.

The political innocence about world politics which accompanies this stability has, on occasion, prompted Americans to mis-judge greatly the depth of political complexities and passions in other parts of the world and to take offense when American motives in international affairs are viewed with distrust. But the same stability has frequently been a source of powerful, latent energies in the conduct of United States foreign policy. The confidence in a supposed harmony between American purposes and humanitarian objectives elsewhere in the world has frequently provided a popular enthusiasm of purpose and zeal for order-building enterprises in the international community which a more self-interested *Realpolitik* alone could scarcely have encouraged.

But the incongruity between domestic order and international disorder has also been a source of intellectual and spiritual weakness, for it has clouded over certain essential problems which all political communities face. Prevailing political attitudes in all political communities at all times are affected by the fact that their domain is finite. No political order of things has ever been co-extensive with human civilization; all states have had, as it were, their outsides and their insides. Perhaps the closest that the Western world came to achieving an identity between civilization and political order was during the time of the Roman Empire. At its height, the imperial order managed nearly to approximate the extent of the then known civilized world. We may thus say that, for the empire, the problem of foreign relations was solved. What lay "outside" posed few threats to the Empire itself. But finally, the Imperial system proved unable to control the Asiatic sources from which the agents of its downfall came.

The democratic state faces certain elemental, unchanging problems. It must provide a shell of constitutional order within which social life can proceed in a regular, predictable way; a political system which, in Harold Lasswell's phrase, can determine "who gets what, where, when, why, and how" without breaking down in the process; and a defense system which can shelter the inside community from external military threat, or in other words, can regulate the relationship between the internal order and its curity, these state functions may be obscured, but in moments of outside political environment. In times of great stability and se-political crisis, they come to the surface. For the democratic state in particular, the search for a balance between political order and individual freedom can be exceptionally difficult in times of crisis. In wartime, individual freedoms are often sacrificed, limited, or even extinguished in the collective effort of the community to survive. Perhaps after the crisis has passed, the constitutional order may reassert itself and normalcy may be re-established.

Contrary to predictions of many liberals, the United States engaged in total war with the Axis powers without permanent impairment of individual freedoms or of the essential institutions of American democracy. Before Pearl Harbor, some isolationists who opposed our intervention, predicted that war would end the processes of free elections (not to mention free enterprise). Yet the institutions of democracy were not grossly abused even during the most critical parts of the war. The callous, administrative relocation of Japanese-Americans on the west coast is a striking exception. In contrast to the time of World War I, there was remarkably little xenophobic hysteria, even against German-Americans, and far fewer infringements of civil liberties.

Indeed the November 1946 elections, which ushered in the peacetime, Eightieth Congress, too prematurely reasserted "normalcy" and Congressional libertarianism against the executive power which had conducted the war to victory. The Laborite victory in Britain in 1945, showed the same swing against the executive authority which had conducted war. The Soviet Union was the only victor which never once weakened its military or state power. Stalinist terror continued until Stalin's death eight years after the war; but then, the Soviet Union had been totalitarian long before the war broke out. There is no evidence that total war *necessarily* precedes or produces totalitarian states. Both Germany and Japan emerged in defeat as constitutional democracies. To be sure, the end of World War II saw a greatly enlarged camp of Communist totalitarianism, notably in Eastern Europe.

But this had more to do with the geographic distribution of Soviet military forces than with indigenous developments in the states which succumbed to Soviet rule. Had Soviet power been pushed much further back into Asia by Nazi forces, and had the Western Allies still triumphed, the sphere of democratic, constitutional states unquestionably would have been larger. But this is a military rather than a sociological matter. Considered from a purely domestic point of view, American democracy probably emerged from World War II in a sounder condition than it had been in during the late 1930's.

America's traditional isolation and its relative economic self-sufficiency have blurred public perception of these difficulties. The apparent ease with which all major, outside threats to American security were solved until recently has made the public regard them as essentially abnormal. Foreign policies designed to deal with them proved politically acceptable to the American public if they could be tagged as capable of solving, rather than just meliorating them. To be sure, this attitude toward problems bespeaks a pragmatic, optimistic temper. But optimism tested against refractory, unyielding reality can give way to great impatience and even irrationality. Tocqueville's chief criticism of American democracy was its inconstancy and its inability to persevere through complex enterprises to their end.

The last of these incongruities between America's public milieu and that of most of the remaining world is the one between an American private opulence and economic egalitarianism, on the one hand, and the widespread poverty and inequality in so many other societies. While this condition is generally admitted by Americans, the dimensions of the problem are too often avoided. The American population numbers about 6% of the whole world's, but the American nation today produces 33% of the world's total energy each year, and consumes about 36% of it.[7] This energy base, derived in part from abroad, makes possible the high living standards which Americans enjoy. This in-

[7] See *United Nations Statistical Yearbook*, 1961, pp. 274-275.

equality is unlikely to be erased in the near future; in the past decade America's percentage, both of production and consumption of energy, has in fact slightly increased, rather than diminished. Major war might radically change these equations; but without this intervention of calamity, it is likely to be the case that trends of economic change will continue to favor the mightily-developed nations at the expense of the late-comers. Even the Soviet Union, which incessantly proclaims its goal of surpassing America in productivity, lags far behind in the production and consumption of basic consumer goods which Americans take for granted. In the industrializing non-Western, non-Soviet worlds, the population explosion perpetuates the dismal lag of real per capita income growth behind the growth of gross national product. While per capita income growth in America is taken for granted by most Americans, per capita income *diminution* is a fact of life to most people in underdeveloped countries, where the economy must run faster just to remain in the same place as before.

At the beginning of the cold war, part of the Stalinist offensive against the United States consisted of its portrayal of America, under "monopoly capitalism," as a nation of impoverished and unemployed people. Many Americans took amused offense at this false picture and tried to correct it through a variety of mass media directed toward the Soviet world. But was it better, or worse, to be depicted as poor and exploited rather than opulent? The real picture of America's economic condition could ironically do as much damage to America's prestige as could this caricature. In his book about the Castro revolution in Cuba, C. Wright Mills put these plausible words into a Cuban revolutionist's mouth:

> That power and wealth, Yankee, that's why it seems so crazy to us when your Government says to us what it has been saying, that our Cuban government was following . . . a pattern of relentless economic aggression . . . against the United States. . . . Now, please do think about that a moment. Isn't it slightly

ridiculous? We are about 6 million people, you are 180 million. Your economy . . . is approximately 200 times the size and wealth of ours. We don't even yet grow our own food, much less make the tractors we need to help us grow it. You spend more in a year for lipstick and things like that than all of us down here earn for a full year's work. . . .[8]

Relatively equal among themselves in per capita income, Americans tower over all other nations in a massive display of abundance which could certainly be envied, but not conceivably imitated, by most other people. Even if the existing population of the world outside America aspired only to attain the present per capita income of Americans, the fulfillment of this aspiration would require an astronomical increase in total world energy consumption—from an estimated annual world consumption of energy of 4236 million (measured in millions of metric tons) in 1960, to something in the neighborhood of 25,000 million. No statesman could anywhere promise this—the more so since population growth rates in underdeveloped countries promise to double existing populations within forty years, and erase whatever benefits increased gross national product might have for the per capita real income. In America, leisure, abundance, and educational opportunities might have overfulfilled the norms of nineteenth-century reformers; but in most of the rest of the world, such aspirations seem absurd even as dreams.

Few Americans are conscious of the radically-changed relation between their own national abundance and world politics, and of the explosive possibilities in this dysfunctional relationship. During the nineteenth century and well into the twentieth, the American economy seemed to be an *accessible* economy of abundance. Emma Lazarus's poem, which is inscribed on the Statue of Liberty as a welcome to a stream of immigrants now cut off, ironically still calls out: "Give me your tired, your poor, your huddled masses yearning to be free." Between 1820 and 1920,

---

[8] C. Wright Mills, *Listen, Yankee: The Revolution in Cuba*, New York: Ballantine, 1960, p. 32.

more than 33 million immigrants—mostly from Europe—came to the United States. But since 1950, a total of only two and one-half million immigrants have entered the United States; only eight million have come since 1920. For most people, the American economy now is an inaccessible economy of abundance. The one supreme, ethical justification of abundance, that it was available to those who might freely come to partake of it, is gone. Its continued ethical justification, on a small planet, now would seem to depend upon the degree to which American productivity and expertise are spent to help others who can no longer possibly come. But the magnitude and complexity of the problem today make it seem nearly insoluble.

THE AMERICAN CHARACTER AND CRISIS

Equality, abundance, privacy, enjoyment of leisure and consumption, and social mobility are both the ideals and the conditions of American life. The American national character which they helped produce has long been acclaimed for its optimism, ebullience, and expansiveness. With these qualities was a tradition of humanitarianism which could be tapped for political support of American foreign policies designed to assist other nations in their economic development. Tocqueville and later observers saw in this composite American character certain public vices which were counterparts of private virtues. The public temper about politics was highly privatized. American individualism, insofar as it persisted in an age of mass society and adaptiveness, was absorbed in the individual enjoyment of things. But could such virtues as excellence and public-spiritedness, which some European aristocracies allegedly claimed to possess, be fused into an egalitarian democracy?

An indictment of democracy runs like a thread through American cultural history. Could a people of plenty be continuously concerned with the public good? The democratic American public habitually underpaid and underestimated its teachers, its civil servants, and its political leaders. Americans prized and enjoyed a beauty of sorts and comfort in the privacy of their homes but tolerated gross ugliness in their surrounding countryside and in their cities.

Automobiles were the quintessence of American individualism. They clogged the streets and highways and their external form undulated in sympathetic response to ever changing consumer preferences. Their gaseous fumes, emitted in discharge of private errands, covered whole metropolitan regions. The roads built to carry individuals on their errands cut wide and ugly swaths through cities and the landscape. Refuse littered highways; alongside all major routes in America were monstrous graveyards of rusting, discarded steeds. The lavish amounts of money spent in America for highways and autos reflected astonishing geographic mobility. At all levels of society, Americans were constantly in motion.

Although this is not the proper place to deal with American national character, it may be noted that many of our contemporaries who have tried to relate it to the idea of the public and the latter to the processes of foreign policy-making could not fail to note the bizarre incongruity between these American traits and the international crisis the nation faced. Critics of democracy have frequently pointed to the apparent irrelevance of American private life with its creature comforts as against the international crises. Others noted the dysfunctional role so often played by this privatized public in major international crises where calm and persistence were called for. Still others thought that this private abundance and the good life of the barbecue pit masked the people's loss of control over public affairs, and the cartelization of control into massive instruments of economic, military, and political power.

Dexter Perkins to the contrary, few Americans paid any continuous attention to foreign policy, though it would be hard to find many other societies where a higher percentage did, or to prove that continuous attention *necessarily* improved it. The

American public fell far short of the civic ideals praised by traditional liberal political thought and by social studies textbooks. Here, as in other highly industrialized nations, intense functional specialization of personal work seemed to make the larger world remote. The intricacies of world politics reached the great public via newspapers, television, and radio. In times of very great crisis when something unexpected happened, popular opinion might suddenly crystallize. But the crystallization was after the fact; often punitive, and once opinion was set, it was often difficult for it to catch up with rapidly changed circumstance. In normal times as well, opinion might be too unstructured to form a solid foundation for policies which required strong public support in order to be effective. Elected public officials, always dependent upon periodic reaffirmations of support, could rarely afford to ignore the mercurial responses when the barometers of world politics suddenly dropped. And the opposite, rigid inflexibility, was just as bad.[9]

In his study of the shapelessness and vacillation of American public opinion towards Japan in the 1940's and 1950's, Bernard Cohen has written:

> There are few signs of a consistent and enduring involvement in the affairs of that country which could produce a set of abiding images, a catalogue of signs and symbols, to give the mythical American a continuity of judgment. Without these images there is no steadfast perspective on Japanese policy; events are transient and unidentified phenomena, much of the meaning of which is lost because there is no context. These characteristics of American public opinion are not uniquely operative toward Japan; in some respects they describe the views of the general public toward a wide range of foreign policy problems.[10]

Scholarly and popular tracts about American public opinion during the cold war could be classified under three general points

---

[9] Walter Lippmann, *Essays in the Public Philosophy*. Boston: Little, Brown and Co., 1955.

[10] Bernard Cohen, *The Political Process and Foreign Policy*. Princeton: Princeton University Press, 1957, p. 55.

of view: one, deeply pessimistic about the value of the populist tradition itself and the alleged pernicious effect it exerted upon rational and purposeful foreign policies; another which simply denied this populist tradition any visible relevance to the way things really were done in a mass society; and a third which described the way in which the public participated in the foreign policy process. Walter Lippmann, in his *Public Philosophy*, saw the day-to-day public as a tyrant reigning over its executive servants, limiting or destroying the rationality of national foreign policies, assailing its elected representatives when things went wrong, tying its leaders to impossible programmatic demands, and all this producing a "functional derangement of power" in government which he said had progressively enfeebled the constitutional democracies. George Kennan joined Lippmann in this critique of the democratic public. He saw it as an immense dinosaur-like creature, in normal times happy in its torpor but when belatedly aroused, a destructive, idealistic giant which could thrash through the jungle, its anger and impatient irrationality a force which troubled foreign policy-makers could appease, and perhaps ultimately calm, yet rarely if ever synchronistically harness to rational designs.[11]

Others like sociologist C. Wright Mills denied the relevance of the public to the very real system of power which dominated and manipulated it. In his *Power Elite* and *The Causes of World War III*, two polemical tracts, Mills stated his thesis that public and foreign policy in America were made by powerful and irresponsible elites composed of the very rich, the warlords, the corporate rich, and a bureaucratic political directorate. The classic public of democratic theory had been swallowed up. If the images of classic democracy were still used as working justifications of power, said Mills, they now were images out of a fairy tale, "not adequate even as an approximate model of how the American system of power works." The "public" had been transformed into

[11] George Kennan, *American Diplomacy*, 1900-1950. New York: Mentor, 1952, p. 66. "I sometimes wonder," Kennan wrote, "whether in this respect a democracy is not uncomfortably similar to one of those prehistoric monsters with a body as long as a room and a brain the size of a pin."

"mass society." According to Mills, "the higher immorality is a systematic feature of the American elite; its general acceptance is an essential feature of the mass society."[12]

This was the two-pronged offensive against the existing foreign policy process, the one, contemptuous and disillusioned with the public's "arrogated" role; the other, denying its relevance altogether. Lippmann made the classic appeal for a return to "traditions of civility," in which the "people," acknowledging both the limitations of its right to speak for the Burkeian public of living, dead, and yet-to-be-born, would also confess the limits of its own wisdom, information, and executive capacity. It should, rather, permit its rulers to act and define, to deal with the complexities as they best saw fit. If this were not done, representative government would surely die. "While the right but hard decisions are not likely to be popular when they are taken, the wrong and soft decisions will, if they are frequent and big enough, bring on a disorder in which freedom and democracy are destroyed."[13] Unless the Western democracies could recover some of the lost principles of the public order, with its necessary broad public purposes, they would perish. Traditions of civility, overthrown by modern philosophers, should now be restored to rescue men from the pit of despair which the demise of a meaningful conception of the public had hastened.

One could escape Lippmann's gloomy metaphysics and Mills' mass-society thesis by making use of new and sophisticated empirical studies of political behavior and foreign policy. Empiricism, in fact, helped to restore a sense of perspective to a seemingly hopeless situation. Lippmann, for instance, indicted the modern democratic state for its failures: its harsh demands in 1919 for a punitive peace with Germany, its tardy recognition in the 1930's of the perils of Nazism, and its insistence, during World War II, upon "unconditional surrender." These imposed

[12] C. Wright Mills, *The Power Elite*. New York: Oxford University Press, 1956, p. 343.
[13] Walter Lippmann, *op. cit.*, p. 162.

such severe constraints upon policy-makers that they often did things they should not have and did not do things they should have. McCarthyism was a prime example. And Lippmann wrote at a time when McCarthyite cries of treason echoed throughout the country, when public servants were harassed, impugned, subjected to kangaroo courts, and even dismissed from public service for trivial and often false reasons. Something seemed to be wrong with the mood of the American public at such times.

What Lippmann did not do, was to place the modern democratic state in a context that would demonstrate its relative capacities for stability, rationality, inventiveness, and adaptiveness. In the context of twentieth-century politics, the Western democracies *as* political orders had done considerably better in regulating their internal affairs than had authoritarian survivors of the past, like Franco's Spain and Salazar's Portugal. In fact, authoritarian states now were nearly all defunct, at least in Europe. Could the totalitarian states really do much better? Hitler's Germany, for all its vaunted efficiency, had not only permitted its rulers to make the *worst* errors of policy, but in some respects had been an efficient chaos. Even its wartime military mobilization programs had failed to tap the productive capacities of Germany to anywhere near the depth which the democracies had managed to reach in total war. This particular totalitarian order met its ultimate rebuke in total failure.

In the worst days of McCarthyism, the nadir of American democratic experience, when loyalty purges and fanatical charges of treason rocked the American government, some rationality had remained in the Eisenhower Administration. To be sure there was appeasement, but never capitulation to the extreme demands of McCarthyism, which were American disengagement from the U.N., from N.A.T.O., and from any negotiations whatsoever with the Soviet Union and with other Communist states. Peace, no matter how temporarily, had been negotiated in Korea, in Indo-China, and the state treaty with Austria in 1955 had been achieved in peaceful accommodation with the U.S.S.R. All of

these things and many more had been accomplished without passionate eruptions of public nationalist sentiment. The demands
of ultra-nationalists and minority ethnic organizations that the
United States liberate Eastern European satellites from Russian
rule, even at great risk of thermonuclear global war, diminished
steadily during the 1950's. Right-wing Congressional efforts, widely
supported and financed throughout the country, to amend the
Constitution via the so-called Bricker amendment were crushed.
The Administration and federal government thus combined to
retain the necessary constitutional authority in foreign affairs
which Brickerites and the radical right wished to strip them of.
Above all, global war was averted by diplomacy in concert with
power, and America stood by its chief foreign policy commitments, in refutation of Tocqueville's predictions of democratic incapacity for sustained designs.

Above all, America remained an open society in the cold war.
Its public institutions did not become shadows of the garrison
state. The infirmities and shortcomings of mass media did not
preclude their reform. Those who wished to take advantage of the
openness of publicity and criticism, continued to do so without
automatically encountering the reprisals of the State.

The public was neither the shapeless, manipulated mass
which Mills portrayed, a victim of manipulative mass media, and
of tyrannical, irresponsible oligarchs. It was not the petulant, impatient, normally lethargic tyrant which Lippmann and Kennan
saw. American public opinion, whether or not it was a "great
Hamiltonian beast," was not homogeneous. It was a composite
of cultural and ethnic components, Protestants, Catholics, Jews,
Anglo-Saxon Americans, German-Americans, Italian-Americans,
and many others. America was rural and urban, educated and ignorant, male and female, hateful and loving, active and passive,
articulate and inarticulate, psychiatrically normal and psychiatrically aberrant. It was an occupational complex of professionals,
skilled and unskilled workers, of Republicans, Democrats, and
others. These were the individuals tied by loyalties and by func-

tional involvement in multifarious organizational systems of power; in corporations, trade unions, universities, religious bodies, voluntary associations. For the most part, they were linguistically homogeneous. They were closely knit in American society in a way that few other people were. Scattered through American society were the elite leaderships, decision makers, opinion makers, intellectuals—the influential whose voices in public or private places were listened to and who themselves "listened to voices" and were not "by nature" irresponsibly cut off from the social and ethical problems of their times, and who, presumably, commonly shared some willingness that the nation survive and prosper.

To follow the strands of these social tissues, to search out additudinal postures and intellectual commitments among all of them, has been impossible except in a highly impressionistic fashion until recently. Before Dr. Gallup, American "public opinion" had been the discernible attitudes of newspapers, men of public affairs, politicians. Gallup's first public of the 1930's, the object of yes-no questionnaires, had been a "yes-no" public (or a "don't know" public) with the questions which were prearranged by pollsters allowing one-syllable answers to enormous philosophic questions as well as immediate, trifling ones.

Gallup's poll and others like it became more sophisticated through time. Sociological, attitudinal research facilitated deep inquiries into public attitudes and moods. It became possible on a hitherto unimaginable scale to probe into the consciousness of the American public, not as a vague collective entity, but as a heterogeneous plural society. It was no longer possible for demagogues or anyone else to claim, with no fear of contradiction, that the public wanted this or that.

In the mid-1930's, Father Coughlin, a radical right-wing Catholic reformer, whipped up substantial opposition to American entry into the World Court. At his behest in a radio appeal in 1935, hundreds of wires and letters were rained upon Congress and the President to protest Senate ratification of the treaty and succeeded in deluding both the Administration and members of

Congress about the state of public attitudes towards the treaty. Today, highly sophisticated opinion polls can offset such raids on the public policy till.

WHO'S ON THE RADICAL RIGHT? Public foreign-policy attitudes differed sharply along such lines, as did a rational perception of the state of world politics. Ethnocentrism, the nationalism of the radical right, found its chief response among lower-income, poorly educated Americans and among rural and displaced rural fundamentalists, disturbed by the spiritual and social derangements in their immediate lives. Among psychic aberrants, this temper or mood was closely linked, as well, with xenophobia, social and political intolerance, and a tendency to see political processes as essentially conspiratorial. It was often linked to anti-Semitism in the mind of the "authoritarian personality" (an unfortunate misnomer for those actually in cultural and philosophic revolt against authority, large-scale organization, and the forces they believe to be in control).

These crisis strata of the public constituted a seed bed for public eruptions of protest in time of specific foreign policy crises. The loose structure of American politics permitted such open dissent and the barometric sensitiveness of newspapers and other mass-media to their activities enhanced the influence of the radical right, as did the income which those organizations tapped to sustain their enterprises. In an older era, these crisis strata of American politics had taken an apparently isolationist position as far as foreign policy was concerned. In the 1930's and the early 1940's, they had opposed "Roosevelt's war" in Europe, linking Administration foreign policy purpose to malignant designs to "sell America out" to the British, to Soviet Communism, to cosmopolitan and reformist elements in America which they widely envied, feared, and despised. Fearful of crisis, they were swift to find its roots in domestic conspiracy and "alien infiltration"; eager to assert their own fundamentalist commitment to "traditional" American ideals, they were quick to deny the loyalty of other Americans.

Isolationism was an inaccurate description of their shifting philosophies; these were fundamentalist nationalists. Their bellicosity in time of great crisis demanded the terrible, swift sword of American retaliation against enemies. They asserted America's capacity to act unilaterally against all comers in world politics. They abhorred all foreign allies not wholly subservient to American power and their own fundamentalist ideals. In the crises of the 1930's and the 1950's, they preferred a "hemispherist" defense posture to complex alliances with "foreign" nations which they congenitally distrusted. With the advent of American strategic airpower in the 1950's, they seemed to have acquired a superb strategic rationale for their parochial *Weltanschauung*. Nuclear retaliation against enemy attack, anywhere in the world, would make it theoretically unnecessary for their pure, uncontaminated America to be sullied by protracted cultural involvement in the complex affairs of other countries, notably ones whose political and cultural influence they greatly feared.

These foreign policy attitudes could erupt with startling swiftness, as McCarthyism bore witness. Their chief political targets were the "power elites" within American life, a concept they understood poorly but frequently associated with an all-embracing Communist conspiracy. Fundamentalist nationalism knew no particular cultural home, but its recruits seemed chiefly to come from disparate sub-cultures in American life: from fundamentalist Protestant sects; from Irish Catholics; from small-town small businessmen chiefly lodged in the Midwest; from some ex-Communists who had moved from the gloom of one conspiracy into the gloom of another. At all times, the plausibility of their beliefs and doctrines seemed to depend upon "events." Flourishing upon catastrophe, the radical right had no genuine "policy alternative" to existing ones other than periodic purges of American leadership, preventive war, and grass-roots movements having as their purpose the limiting of resources (other than military power) to the foreign policy instruments of government.

American culture has no monopoly upon such things. This philosophy of the radical right, if we could call it that, was certainly never elevated into a doctrine adopted by the state, as Marxist doctrine had been. That it was widely regarded as "alienated from reality" testified to its essential powerlessness and its inability to do more than protest, indict, and demand what rationality itself forbade.

Reality confronted could be a sober antidote to their demands. During the Korean War, the radical right found powerful expression in Congressional moods of frustration, impatience, and bellicosity. Many Congressmen demanded a "final solution" to the Korean War by widening it into Manchuria, the Chinese mainland, and even into the territory of the U.S.S.R. When President Syngman Rhee of the Republic of Korea, in an address to the U.S. Congress in 1954, urged precisely this, displaying the fearful price of such an endeavor, Congress was stunned. As the left-wing journalist I. F. Stone reported in Washington, Congress in joint session listened to Rhee's plea for preventive war in "shocked silence." "The silence which so pained Rhee indicated eloquently that behind the febrile rhetoric are sober men, prepared in fact to reconcile themselves to the co-existence whose possibility they deny. The danger in the rhetoric is that they dare not admit publicly, indeed hardly avow to themselves, the saner calculations of their actual policy."[14]

It was, however, disturbing that its influence upon public moods depended upon events in world politics which, to a very large degree, were themselves shaped by American policies and actions abroad. Denis Brogan, the English historian, tried to explain the passionate appeal of the radical right in terms of widespread public belief in American omnipotence. If one believed that America always "won" in world politics, that America had "never lost a war," that American strength was essentially invincible, then all setbacks and defeats could be attributed either to

[14] *I. F. Stone's Weekly,* August 9, 1954.

bungling and incompetence or to treason and deliberate sabotage.[15] An oversensitivity to the changing fortunes of the American radical right could paralyze governmental action. Fear of it among sensible policy-makers could clothe rational action in bellicose, deceptive, and self-defeating rhetoric, or chain policy to purposes designed to appease the mood while not solving the external problem itself.

But at all times, the mood of the radical right was not a dominant trait of American public opinion. It was a condition *within* American public opinion. Studies of public attitudes toward foreign policy matters showed far greater rationality, sobriety, and consistency as well as a greater comprehension of unexpected and novel events. Dominant American elites, opinion-leaders, professional activists, businessmen, better educated and successful people, seemed far more capable of perceiving events and policies rationally than their polar opposites. It is disturbing to democratic theory that this was so and continues to be so. The powerless, the poor, the Americans who were most unfavorably affected by the great cultural changes of their own times, seemed far more congenial to ethnocentric nationalism, bellicosity, and political pessimism about world politics. Within this middle range of American public life, enlarged by improved material conditions and opportunities and by greater access to higher education, lay the new public of America. Increased leisure offered them new opportunities to contemplate the formerly alien, outside world which the radical right feared and withdrew from.

Leisure and abundance, as Tocqueville had predicted, could

[15] Denis Brogan, "The Illusion of American Omnipotence," *Harpers*, December 1952, pp. 21-28. Brogan's thesis suggests that the radical right has no monopoly on conspiracy theories about foreign policy. After Castro's seizure of Cuba, Senator Thomas Dodd of Connecticut, a right-wing critic of the State Department, and Professor C. Wright Mills, a pro-Castro liberal, both agreed that Cuba's drift toward Communism had been abetted by official American policies and intentions. They only disagreed about the nature and purposes of the conspiracy. That the Cuban revolution lends itself to neither simplistic theory may be seen in Theodore Draper's two articles, "Castro's Cuba" and "Cubans and Americans," in *Encounter*, March and July 1961.

"privatize" personal concerns, withdrawing the American individual's attention from the public arena into a self-limiting enjoyment of the mass circulation magazines, TV, automobile-polishing, and conspicuous consumption. But it could also liberate attention and interest in politics. Both philosophy and politics require much leisure for most men, and at least some relief from the problems of survival and anxieties about personal problems. Tolerance, optimism, sensitivity to reality, all seem related in American culture to the conditions and the opportunities of the abundant life, within reach of more and more people. The fluctuating fortunes of an American internationalist temper thus seem closely tied to the material promises of the American system itself. Both "realistic" and "idealistic" support for the United Nations, for American foreign aid, for temperate, prudent, and sophisticated American diplomacy, might be found within this important stratum of public life.

Even within upper middle-class America, there were still differences in the disposition of various cultural-ethnic groups to share this stable internationalist consensus. American Catholics and certain fundamentalists of Protestant sects were far less prominent within this consensus of rationality than were Jews, Episcopalians, Presbyterians, Quakers, Congregationalists, and Unitarians. This suggests, among other things, that neither education or affluence alone account for predispositions of the sort described above. The socio-cultural and theological characteristics of American religious sects and denominations are reflected in their secular educational systems and in their cultural attitudes towards politics. Recent studies of American foreign policy associations and world affairs councils (exceedingly influential opinion-makers) show that typically, Jews, non-fundamentalist Protestants, and secular Americans are heavily represented, while Catholics and fundamentalist Protestants are barely represented.

Interestingly, it also appears that Unitarians, Congregationalists, Quakers, and Reform Jews share far more enthusiastic attitudes toward the United Nations than people from other denominations. This is related, I am sure, to their universalistic and monotheistic creeds, which were heavily influenced by philosophical doctrines of the Enlightenment. Universalistic monotheism transcends national cultures, as does secular internationalism.

Jansenist Irish Catholicism, on the other hand, was a quasi-heretical, religious movement, closely associated with a nationalist revolt of Irishmen against "British cosmopolitanism" and imperialism. Transferred by immigrants from Ireland to America, during the mid-nineteenth century it successfully fused itself into traditional American Anglophobia, and cultural insularity. Native American prejudice against Irish Catholicism, expressed as late as the 1920's in the Ku Klux Klan, was matched by equally fervid proclamations of Irish-American loyalty. Thus while there have been perpetual tensions between fundamentalist Protestant nationalists and Irish Catholics, they share a pervasive hostility to cosmopolitan forces in American life, to secular academic intellectualism, and to cultivated elites in American life which sprang from unegalitarian milieus of American culture. That the radical right relies so heavily upon these sources detracts from purposive political movement. The radical right has also been perennially split on other grounds. While occasional organized militancies, such as the John Birch Society, have sought to infuse it with paramilitary, quasi-fascistic principles and style, many of the radical right view this with alarm, since paramilitarism and authoritarian organization violate their own strong anti-authoritarian biases, highly tainted with traditional individualism.

It is an anomaly of the American public temper that a stable public consensus behind "reasonable" foreign policies, attuned to the real world of world politics, required a constantly widening sphere of economic security, abundance and affluence, education, and leisure. The disenfranchised and disinherited of America had to be co-opted into the sensitive and attentive public by increasing their material and spiritual involvement in the contemporary benefits of American life. In the 1960's, the classic instance of this was the American Negro, profoundly shocked by his own exclu-

sion from such benefits at a time when non-white men abroad
already had achieved their own independence from white dominion. Yet to a lesser extent, the same problem existed for the white
American deprived of the better things of life. Abundance is relative. (What yardstick of abundance or access to better things of
life could be used? In 1960, there were more American Negroes
studying in institutions of higher education than there were Englishmen studying in British colleges and universities! Yet British
intellectuals indicted America for its racial inequality.) Abundance may narrow the gap between lower- and higher-income
Americans via growth-rate policies and social-welfare legislation,
but it may also widen the gap between America as a whole and
impoverished underdeveloped nations. If American popularity
abroad had reached its greatest heights in the New Deal era, it
was in part because misery likes company. The attempts of pragmatic American reformers to set the tone of conscience were
sympathetically received by similarly inclined reformers elsewhere.
Would a poverty-less America be better liked or its prestige more
enhanced abroad?

In another respect, a stable popular temper, nurtured in the
security of an affluent economy, was itself the more dependent
upon that security. Whatever measure existed of American constancy in pursuit of world order, international organization, and
free societies, sprang from the favorable conditions of American life which had been spared the political traumas of so many
other countries. The nagging irritations of an unresolved cold
war, the continuing encroachments of Communism and the Soviet states upon both the free world and the underdeveloped
countries, the growing fear of thermonuclear war—these novel,
"objective" conditions of world politics could surely affect deeply
the public temper of a nation which was unaccustomed to continuous threat of war with its accompanying dangers of social
disruption and extinction.

MAKING AMERICAN OPINION There is a complex web of
American organizations, economic, political, and cultural, which

together with mass media and the government itself serve as milieus for molding public opinion. The American party system is perhaps the most visible part of this organizational web. The American parties should ideally be concerned with politics and public issues. Periodically, inter-party conflict on all levels of American political life could serve as occasion and focus for public attitudes about foreign policy. Discerning politicians would scan the election returns for clues to shifts in public mood. Significant clues about changed philosophical positions within the parties could be obtained from national party platforms. The periodicity of free elections also contributes to recurrent intra-party self-questioning on important political issues. Foreign policy could significantly be affected by the outcome of these democratic rituals, notably, the Presidential and Congressional elections. A President with a strong mandate could be the stronger for it. Groundswells of the popular mood manifested themselves in such times. In 1946, a Republican Congress, committed to normalcy and conservatism, ushered in the American postwar atomic age, imposing harsh limitations on executive action in world affairs. At election time, the free society *publicly* reassessed national policies and purpose. Politicians, knowing this, transmitted such concerns to statesmen who "made" policy. By such devices, a democratic public collectively influenced the course of national action. Often it could paralyze or negate action, circumscribing the area of movement and maneuverability of an Administration, setting limits upon national resources for foreign policy, subtly influencing the rhetoric of candidates seeking election, and in turn subtly affecting the posture and reputation of America abroad.

The party organizations themselves comprised only a small fraction of the "elites" which helped to make opinions. That part of the American public which played so crucial a role in shaping attitudes and opinion, was composed of intellectuals, mass media commentators, educators, leaders and opinion-makers of voluntary organizations, businessmen, churchmen, and purveyors of popular culture. American public life was thickly infused with these men and women, and popular conceptions of political reality could be conveyed through them. As in the 1930's, a Will Rogers or a William Allen White could exert an influence far beyond his supposed professional powers. In the 1960's, public attitudes on foreign affairs could be expressed through eloquent men in all walks of life. In local communities, which national political issues continued to invade, such opinion leaders were even more numerous. In a rapidly changing international context, the meaning which opinion leaders assign to events becomes a crucial matter.

He who could most eloquently or with greatest clarity define, in public, the nature of crisis and the motives of action, who could most clearly delineate conflict in world politics, could thereby profoundly influence public opinion. The President, through the authority of office if nothing else, could do this par excellence. Via mass media he could instruct the public about the meaning of new things and about appropriate responses to them. Yet in the free society, he did not have a monopoly of public interpretation. Indeed, the nature of American party affiliation meant that, at all times, a considerable minority of the public was inclined for partisan reasons to be at least skeptical about his interpretation of things and prone to draw the opposite inferences about events and challenges to the nation.

Mass media were themselves neutral, but they made it possible for the public to discover "what happened" with extraordinary swiftness. The public could be brought into almost sickening confrontation with great disasters, such as the Budapest uprisings of 1956, as well as with more pleasant things. In the open society, this was the condition. In the closed, tribal societies of the totalitarian world, things were considerably different.

Premier Khrushchev's denunciation of Stalin and the cult of personality was common knowledge in the Western world at the very time it occurred in 1956, but not until *five years later* did Soviet mass media permit the people of Russia to share with top Communist leaders a knowledge of Stalin's excesses.

Nor, for that matter, did the Soviet public see a photograph of a nuclear explosion until ten years after it had taken place. For all of the deficiencies of American Kremlinology, the educated American public is far more aware of the nature of Soviet politics and Russian history than is the mass of Soviet citizenry. It is extraordinary that a people five thousand miles removed from the scene can know more about the general characteristics of a polity than those immediately involved in it.

To fashion rational perceptions, the open society then depended heavily upon the processes by which information about events was diffused. There was no particular party line. "New occasions teach new duties," Lowell once wrote. When the occasion happened, there were no party cadres to go out and to "indoctrinate" the masses about appropriate, dutiful responses. Assent, as it were, had to be engineered within a public milieu which permitted dissent and in which the engineering was no one's particular monopoly. Spectacular events like Pearl Harbor could galvanize public sentiment and establish national unity, but less spectacular, secular movements and trends in world affairs and more ambiguous, international happenings did not necessarily elicit rational or immediate responses. Newspapers, radio, television, and opinion leaders convey interpretations of events and suggest responses to them, although the amount of *information* in most mass media is pitifully small and forced to compete with automobiles, detergents, cigarettes, washing-machines, and popular violence for the listening audience. Aside from national party conventions, and prominent disasters, few major events of international importance are covered systematically by American television, encumbered as it is by its own commercial necessities and manipulative compulsions. The disgraceful Army-McCarthy hearings in Congress were extensively covered by mass media as a public service, but this was an exception to the rule.

It was at all times essential to reach the attentive, active publics in America with a coherent display of a multi-dimensioned reality of world politics. Great social catastrophes cry out for public speculation. The capacity of the American public to respond rationally to international events requires this essential, continuous communication of fact and multiple interpretation. The unexpected fall of China to the Communists in 1949 gave rise in the American public arena to false and simplified accounts of betrayal and treason. So, too, did the Korean War and the Communist coup in Cuba. An uninformed public is an unprepared public. In America at least, an unprepared public is also one prone to accept facile and demagogical representations of reality, whether from the Right or the Left. Yet what is so essential, within this mass public of a mass society, is the *quality* of the intermediate layers of opinion leadership, located in all occupational, cultural, and religious layers of the American society. This is the crucial zone of the American public, the educated elites of America, free and informed, capable of action and voluntary activity in time of crisis.

In the early 1950's, they proved most inarticulate and passive to the onslaught of McCarthyism and its conspiracy theories of politics which sprang with such vigor from the radical Right. The personal, political, and organizational insufficiencies of McCarthy and McCarthyism, not sustained public reaction to them, set limits on McCarthy's effectiveness. But the future of American democracy in international crisis depends upon a perceptiveness and vigor which, if it does not exist, has to be reinvented. We need the faith Pericles voiced in the popular conscience long ago in ancient Athens: "Although only a few may originate a policy, we are all able to judge it." The American public has been put to this test in a cold war which, perhaps, policy alone can not end, but which public opinion in all nations could comprehend and learn to live with, without mutual destruction.

SUGGESTED READING

Almond, Gabriel, *The American People and Foreign Policy*, New York, Harcourt, Brace, 1950.

POWER, FREEDOM, AND DIPLOMACY

Hero, Alfred, *Americans in World Affairs*, Boston, World Peace Foundation, 1959.

Kennan, George, *American Diplomacy: 1900-1950*, Chicago, University of Chicago Press, 1951.

Levinson, Daniel J., "Authoritarian Personality and Foreign Policy," *Journ. Conflict Resolution*, I, 1957, pp. 37-38.

Lippmann, Walter, *Essays in the Public Philosophy*, Boston, Little, Brown, 1955.

McAllan, David S., and C. E. Woodhouse, "Businessmen in Foreign Policy," *Southwest Social Science Quarterly*, March, 1959, pp. 283-290.

Millis, Walter, S. J. Murray, and John Courtney, *Foreign Policy and the Free Society*, New York, Oceans Publications, 1958.

Mills, C. Wright, *The Power Elite*, New York, Oxford University Press, 1956, esp. ch. I, pp. 8-13.

Pearson, Lester B., "Democracy and the Power of Decision," Jacobson, Harold K., *America's Foreign Policy*, New York, Random House, 1960, pp. 20-33.

Potter, David M., *People of Plenty: Economic Abundance and the American Economy*, Chicago: University of Chicago Press, 1954, esp. chs. III and VI.

de Tocqueville, Alexis, *Democracy in America*, Oxford University Press, World's Classics Series, chs. XII, XXXII, and XXXIII.

INSTITUTIONS, PROCESSES AND MEN

*The last word on how we may live
or die
Rests today with such quiet
Men, working too hard in rooms
that are too big
Reducing to figures
What is the matter, what is to be
done*

W. H. AUDEN

T HE BAROQUE VICTORIAN, mansard-roofed edifice which stands alongside the White House in Washington now houses the Executive Offices of the President. Built during the 1870's, the State War-Navy Building, as it was originally called, was praised by Ulysses S. Grant as one of the mightiest triumphs of Western architecture. Visitors may still appreciate its elegant, spacious corridors and offices. This building was the focus of American foreign policy-making for half the span of American history. Its nearness to the White House, its spaciousness, and its seeming monumental permanence made it a fitting background for American statesmanship. Here, in one city block directly across from the Executive Mansion, American foreign policy was made.

All this has changed now. Aside from the White House, such symbols of the centralized authority over foreign policy have been diffused throughout Washington and the entire world. Since the middle of World War II, military authorities have had their headquarters in the Pentagon, across the Potomac River in Virginia. In 1948 the State Department, greatly swollen in size, was moved to new offices in Foggy Bottom, a rehabilitated swamp in southwest Washington. In its functional, antiseptic corridors and offices, thousands of diplomats and civil servants work. New foreign policy entities have sprung into being since World War II: the Central Intelligence Agency, the United States Information Agency, the Arms Control and Disarmament Agency, the Peace Corps, the National Security Council, and many others. These are scattered across Washington, nearby Virginia, and Maryland. All bespeak the enlarged scope of American diplomatic and foreign policy concerns.

This growth can be appreciated in numbers, costs, and communications. Scarcely two decades ago, the State Department in Washington employed less than a thousand foreign service officers and civil servants. That number has now increased five-fold. By the mid-1950's, the State Department and Foreign Service employed more than forty thousand men and women at home and abroad including a large number of foreigners, and this does not include the civil servants of the other foreign policy agencies. In its Washington office, the Central Intelligence Agency alone probably has more personnel than does the State Department. In the early 1960's, annual American expenditures for defense and foreign policy approached in value the annual total U.S. output of goods in the early 1930's. The daily communications and internal transactions of these agencies have grown in complexity and depth. The number of incoming and outgoing messages of these agencies exceeds, in one hour, the total number sent and received in the first decade of U.S. history.

THE COLLAPSE OF CATEGORIES

This bureaucratic growth barely suggests an administrative revolution which has taken place during the cold war. Don Price, a veteran administrator, has called this revolution the "collapse of categories," a fusion of executive departments, agencies, committees, and councils into a process of foreign policy-making and a further fusion of these agencies into the private, nongovernmental world of business, industry, agriculture, labor, the arts, sciences, and education. Traditional distinctions between foreign and domestic affairs have been crumbling for quite some time. Very few things except cats on beaches stop at the water's edge. A political scientist estimated in 1948 that nineteen agencies of the federal government were concerned with "*all* aspects of foreign relations because they operated only within the limits and directions set by our dealing with the other nations." Another twenty-three agencies "enforced laws usually designed to regulate the activities of individuals who were acting in foreign relations." Another forty-six agencies were concerned in whole or in part with foreign economic policy.[1]

All dynamic sectors of American society, culture, and government now shade off into a surrounding sea of world politics and economics. Likewise, foreign policy concerns shade off into American private life, giving rise to almost unheard-of problems. For instance, traditionally the Department of State was the federal government's negotiative agency with foreign governments. But during the summer and fall of 1961, State Department officials found themselves engaged in negotiations with Maryland officials and restaurateurs to enable non-white foreigners to eat in public restaurants denying similar privileges to non-white U.S. citizens.

The consequences of this collapse of categories were not anticipated by Americans in the first half of the twentieth century. Until the Second World War, it seemed that foreign and domestic affairs were fused because domestic influences were simply bursting the seams of continental America. Until 1939, America's politics were isolationist. But long before that, many private and governmental interests had burst the confines of territorial Amer-

---

[1] James L. McCamy, *The Administration of American Foreign Affairs.* New York: Alfred A. Knopf, 1950, pp. 107-120.

ica, spreading into a vast, evidently benign, vacuum of opportunity in the outside world. Foreign affairs was a nonpolitical area of contention among private commercial and industrial interests. Foreign policy making before 1933 consisted in large measure of governmental agencies' efforts to satisfy the aspirations and needs of various sectors of American society which were marginally involved in the economic and political universe lying outside a militarily secure American continent. Until 1939, the American universe of foreign affairs was a Ptolemaic one. The moon, stars, and sun of world politics moved around the United States.

Until the mid-1930's, U.S. tariffs and commercial policies were engineered by Senators and Congressmen to strike a political balance among competing domestic business and industrial interests. Their log-rolling created economic policies which, by and large, reflected the interests of various American firms and industries. After World War I, when American agriculture faced the problem of chronic overproduction, the outside world became a dumping ground for our agricultural surpluses. The New York Stock Exchange and private banks and corporations, which were governed by the behavior of the American market and the predilections of private investors, governed, in turn and haphazardly, the spastic and irregular outflows of American capital into Europe and the underdeveloped world. In the mid-1920's, Herbert Hoover, then Secretary of Commerce, described his Department and its Bureau of Foreign and Domestic Commerce as the "advance agent" of American businessmen. Indeed they were, with their agents abroad, drumming up trade for American exports in every conceivable part of the world. Their various successes further disturbed America's balance of trade and payments, helping to undermine the precarious balance of the post-war world economy. Other American products like tourists, movies, teachers, missionaries, and educators, joined this laissez-faire game of uncoordinated cross-cultural transactions. Potentially influential as America was then, it left the political regulation of world politics to others and benefited but briefly from the flimsy peace which the crumbling European order provided, while publicly lecturing Europe on its deficiencies.

In *Idea of National Interest,* written in the early 1930's, Charles Beard describes the laissez-faire processes by which American foreign policies were made during the Harding-Coolidge-Hoover era, when agencies of government were all too often agencies of private economic interest. Beard argued the need for centralized coordination of political and economic foreign policies, so that a national interest could prevail over, or at least harmonize, particular interests. However, remembering what he wrote about, he could never free himself from the conviction that the stated national interests of the U.S. government were merely cover-ups for private or selfish motives. Later, during World War II, Beard interpreted Roosevelt's interventionist policies in the European war as a conspiracy to keep the New Deal in power, and American business interests viable by means of fabricated crisis.[2]

Such were the joys; so long as the old order of world politics held together, it was America's oyster; the collapse of categories between foreign and domestic affairs meant that the latter had triumphed over the former. But when the old economic order finally collapsed in the period from 1929 to 1931, the political order quickly followed suit and was finally destroyed in war. In 1947, when some of the dust had settled, the United States found that it was the only remaining Western nation with sufficient power and influence left to pick up the pieces. This is ironic because America's political irresponsibility in the interwar years had largely contributed to the collapse of the old order.

Between 1940 and 1950, the agencies of American foreign policy which were traditionally the arms of national, private, and domestic interests were enlarged and reshaped to perform political functions infinitely more complicated and urgent than their old responsibilities of appeasing domestic interest groups. The

[2] See Beard's *President Roosevelt and the Coming of World War II.* New Haven: Yale University Press, 1948.

Departments of Agriculture, Commerce, Labor, Treasury, and Interior, the traditional agencies of domestic power and policy, were also called upon to perform political functions abroad. From 1940 until today, the history of American foreign policy, in large measure, has been that of a vast organizational revolution, one which has by no means ended. The remaining traditional forms of American diplomacy are interlaced with the new in complex webs of regional and universal international organizations. In this complex network, American policy is formulated and acted upon.

In this process of political transition and administrative revolution, there were two interrelated developments, each novel to the American political tradition. The first of these was the attempt, within the federal government itself, to interweave and bring into focus a broad range of once-separate activities: defense, foreign political and economic policies, informational, intelligence, and cultural activities. The second development was the fusion of American defense, political, and economic policies with those of other states and supranational organizations in common international enterprises. The first had to do with the coordination of "national security policies" within the federal government. The second sought to integrate America's policy machinery into a complex network of postwar alliances and alignments. The first tendency, the synchronization of political, economic, and military policies, was a familiar one in older European states, long immersed in international *Realpolitik*. But it was not familiar to many Americans who saw in it the ominous threat of a highly centralized garrison-state. The second was even more unfamiliar, since it seemed to imply the end of traditional American conceptions of national sovereignty.

Treaties, conventions, and executive agreements established new international and decision-making authority over foreign policies. America was drifting away from its once sharply defined constitutional processes. But since no powerful super-sovereign existed in world politics, this drift and diffusion of political responsibility seemed to blur traditional constitutional loci of authority and responsibility. Both of these policy-making tendencies, the one federal, the other supranational, encountered opposition from many forces in American society which were as suspicious of centralized political power as they were of the delegating of decision-making authority to supranational institutions. Both tendencies raised the question of what "policy" actually was and was supposed to do.

WHAT IS POLICY?

The *Oxford Dictionary*'s old-fashioned definition suggests the difficulty. It defines policy as "political sagacity, statecraft; diplomacy; in a bad sense, political cunning. . . . In ref. to conduct or action generally, prudent, expedient, or advantageous procedure; prudent or politic course of action; . . . a course of action adopted or pursued by a government, party, ruler, statesman, etc."

These definitions barely suffice. Like all "policy," foreign policy can be unsagacious, imprudent, inexpedient, disadvantageous, and still be policy. It may be a course of action unwittingly or unconsciously followed or accepted by policy-makers. To be sure, policy can be a "settled course of action," a concert of judgment among statesmen. It can also be the bitter fruit of deadlocked judgments and paralyzed wills. In fact, policy may be no policy when a choice among alternatives is not made, but postponed. It can be capitulation to necessity in times when choices narrow fatally to one single choice and the decision-makers simply bow to the inevitable. On occasion, policy may betray a politician's surrender to domestic pressures, to irrational national moods, to influences of other nations, or political influences. Ideally, policy compasses creative designs, a rational perception of reality, bold leadership, and administration. Often it does not.

An example of paralysis of national will, and therefore policy, may be found in Henry Stimson's autobiography, where he discusses the shattering impact of Europe's financial disasters in 1931 upon President Hoover's morale. Stimson, who was then Hoover's Secretary of State, described the President's gloom, pessimism, and seeming paralysis of will as he searched for some device which might rescue what still remained of the international monetary order. He described the President, at a meeting with him and the Secretary of the Treasury, as "tired, and . . . he went through all the blackest surmises. . . . It was like sitting in a bath of ink to sit in his room."[3] Gloom and indecision gave way the next morning to vigorous action. Hoover's proposed "moratorium" on loans and war debts became American policy, though it came too late to be of much use. In this instance, as in too many others, policy followed crisis.

THE MAKING AND IMPLEMENTING OF POLICY

At any point in time, American foreign policies appear as a cluster of pragmatic statements and political and economic commitments of action and resources to wide-ranging ends and specific undertakings deemed consonant with them. These commitments relate ideally to the welfare of the American community in whose name they have been made. As we saw in Chapter 4, they express a supposed national interest. Yet redefinition of ends and the selection of means to attain them entail the daily application of large designs to specific events. Statesmen also need to estimate, mobilize, and allocate the resources with which to mould these designs.

Policy-making entails the imaginative anticipation of events, drawing inferences about the ways in which American decisions may affect the world of reality with which they seek to deal purposively. Policy-makers cannot anticipate consequences if they are blind, deaf, or simply indifferent to crucial conditions or happenings abroad. In a certain sense then, the analysis of realities pre-

[3] Henry L. Stimson and McGeorge Bundy, *On Active Service in Peace and War*. New York: Harper, 1948, pp. 204-205.

cedes policy-planning; empirical study precedes the construction of "grand designs." Between 1945 and 1947, for instance, the evidence of Stalin's expansionist activities in East Central Europe and the Middle East persuaded American policy-makers of a Soviet threat to the free nations there. Between March 1947, when Truman declared America's opposition to Communist subversion of independent states, and 1948, when Communists seized Czechoslovakia by internal coup d'état, U.S. policy gradually moved into the stance of "containment." The grand design was to try to check Soviet expansion by military, economic, and political means.

This massive shift of purpose and resources from wartime alliance to post-war opposition stimulated a grand debate in America among bi-partisan supporters of this new policy, Republican isolationists, and pro-Communist Wallaceite Progressives who espoused close U.S.-Soviet collaboration. In this redirection of policy, we see how intellectual formulations can affect action catalytically. Faced with two unacceptable alternatives, American withdrawal from Europe and Asia or preventive war against the Soviet Union, U.S. policy-makers during these years accepted instead the Kennan formulation of the conflict: war could be avoided and the freedom of the West preserved by American perseverance not to liberate captive nations from Soviet rule, but to build "situations of strength" on Russia's peripheries in order to prevent its further expansion. This formulation became the grand design. From it derived all of the military and political institutions and commitments America was later to make to ensure that the design worked. In this instance, as in others, high policy resulted from a fusing of innumerable actions and judgments into a pattern which someone, a Kennan for instance, might name. Then a persuasive word or slogan, "containment," for instance, can focus action and give established actions new meanings. (George Kennan's famous tract, "The Sources of Soviet Conduct," was first published in the July 1947, *Foreign Affairs*. It may be found as appendix to his book, *American Diplomacy: 1900-1950*.)

Succeeding American policies *vis-à-vis* the U.S.S.R. conformed to Kennan's theoretical construct. But grandiose formulations may obscure or deliberately masquerade as policy. In 1952, during the Eisenhower-Stevenson campaign, Republican party leaders (particularly John Foster Dulles) denounced the containment policy as immoral, proposing instead that a new administration "liberate" oppressed peoples from Soviet imperialism. "Liberationism" became a theme of the early Dulles' foreign policy. Nevertheless, U.S. policy in Europe remained one of containment. Even Dulles stopped short of carrying out his own promises, being too intelligent a man not to see that the consequences would be war.

Establishing policy is also a matter of choosing among alternative courses of action to attain certain ends. It is giving life to a design. In the late 1940's, when Western Europe was gravely threatened by Communist subversion and Soviet military forces far outmatched U.S. forces in Europe, U.S. policy-makers chose to implement containment in Western Europe chiefly by economic means. In this instance, when translated into action, the grand design became an effort to revive the war-shattered European economies and strengthen them internally against subversion. Between 1948 and 1950, U.S. containment in Europe consisted principally of economic assistance to Britain, France, Italy, and the smaller European democracies. To be sure, American nuclear power was a deterrent to overt Soviet military aggression (if military attack was ever seriously contemplated by the Russians). Not until 1950 did U.S. aid to Europe shift from economic aid to military aid.

In this manner, policy designs programs, allocates resources, makes commitments to foreign governments, and mobilizes Congressional and public consent. Grand designs such as the North Atlantic Treaty Organization in 1949, which committed the U.S. to protect European states against Soviet aggression, became investments of men, natural resources, and intentions. In time, the designs themselves become more than policy. They become in-

stitutional manifestations of national or even supranational interests. Crucial decision-making authority may be delegated to
such institutions. Common multi-national strategies may be developed by them. Some measure of real control may then pass
out of the hands of individual states and their constitutional
authorities into the hands of delegates. During the cold war,
American foreign policy has constructed new organizational enterprises and encouraged others to do so also. The institutional
entities uniting Europe today, the Common Market, the Coal
and Steel Community, even the parliamentary institutions of
Strasbourg are in considerable measure creatures of American
policy and encouragement. In such instances, policy creates new
political and economic entities which then take on a life of their
own. Then they in turn feed influences back into the very governments which originally gave them life.

Flexibility or Vacillation

Thus persistence toward some major foreign policy goal entails long range commitments to programs, institutions, and systems. It involves not just the designing of bold new programs but
the staging of them. Policy involves promises. Thus in the case
of the best of designs, consistency of aim and long-term commitment lead to a certain kind of inertia. For, once having made a
choice at the crossroads, it is not easy to retrace the steps and
try a different path. Often it is impossible. Once a particular
policy wins its own powerful supporters these inescapable characteristics of on-going policy limit and restrain policy-makers. Choice
of action is narrowed so that action can occur. The choice, for
instance, of one new military weapons system among many; of
one foreign aid design among many; of one alliance system
among several, such choices entail the rejection of others.

Because consistency of commitment is an essential ingredient
of policy and vacillation weakens the credibility of promises, there
is a latent difficulty in the need to reassess policy constantly. If

unexamined, policies may outlive their usefulness. But statesmen with a reputation for redesigning policies may be accused of inconstancy. In some instances, this reputation may mean the difference between survival and extinction.

For example, flexibility of policy, the willingness to negotiate with the U.S.S.R. over Berlin and Germany, may be deemed essential if risks of thermonuclear war are to be diminished there. Yet a policy so flexible that it created doubts about the credibility of America's long-standing commitment to the freedom of West Berlin, to the long-range goal of German self-determination and unity, and to NATO's strategic defense policies might weaken America's negotiating position and conceivably disrupt the Western alliance.

In international politics commitments and promises are not only made to friends or allies. They also play a crucial part between antagonists and even enemies. For instance, agreements between the United States and the U.S.S.R. are essential in maintaining what order there is today in international affairs. Such agreements need not necessarily be written into treaties or international conventions. They may be due to a kind of "common law" relationship, tacitly observed on both sides because of known penalties for infringement or known benefits of compliance. In Berlin today, despite Soviet threats to abridge unilaterally the four-power agreements in the city, there is a complex and even ritualistic understanding which has grown out of long practice of co-existence. Such understanding controls the behavior of both sides. Mutually fearful of escalated conflict growing out of local disorder, both sides, even during the tense summer months of 1961, have cautiously observed most of the other's intricate rights or privileges. When Soviet and East German authorities feared the unabated drain of refugees from East Germany, they built the wall along the sector boundary between East and West Berlin. In so doing, they violated one element of a complex set of agreements. Yet all the while, they scrupulously observed other Western rights and privileges in the city. Thus they gave notice of their own intent to delimit the local conflict. In 1956, during the Budapest uprisings, when there was a possibility of revolt among other Soviet satellites, American and Soviet authorities tacitly cooperated with local German authorities to prevent mobs of West Berliners from moving into the Eastern part of the city, an action which would have certainly resulted in great violence. In the Korean War, complex understandings developed between the belligerents concerning the limits of the conflict, geographic, technological, and purposive, and because they were strictly observed on both sides, Korea became a classic instance of limited war, one in which each belligerent independently agreed to accept constraints in the employment of power and violence. Today the survival of most Americans and Russians, not to mention most other peoples in the Northern hemisphere, depends upon just such complex, tacit, yet essential understandings. Ambiguity of purpose or ambiguity in response to hostile acts could have disastrous results.

A classic instance of Communist miscalculation of enemy response occurred in Korea in June 1950, when North Korean Communists launched their ill-starred aggression against the Republic of Korea. Two grievous American actions during the winter of 1949-50 had prompted the Communist error of attacking on the assumption of no direct U.S. military retaliation. During the winter of 1949-50, the Eighty-first Congress (thanks to a coalition of isolationist Republicans and a few Democrats) defeated the Truman Administration's Korean Aid bill by the narrow vote of 192 (132 Republicans, 49 Democrats, 1 American Labor Party) to 191 (170 Democrats and 21 Republicans). Congress thus put the Communist world on notice that Korea was not high on American priority lists.

Shortly after this, in January 1950, Secretary Acheson publicly indicated that Korea lay outside the U.S. perimeter of strategic defenses and that its security guarantees lay not in bilateral agreements with the U.S., but in the United Nations Charter. The following June, North Korean forces attacked South Korea, grossly miscalculating American military responses, which were speedy and violent, though limited in their scope. Dulles, Acheson's successor in the State Department, perhaps learned too well from this one ambiguous commitment. He strung a series of unambiguous security pacts like a line of frozen laundry all around the periphery of the Communist world.

To sum up, flexibility in the context of negotiations may contribute to the settlement of disputes, but flexibility of response may also lead an adversary to miscalculate. If flexibility passes for lack of clarity it may invite unacceptable encroachments and demands. So, too, it might convey unreliability and inconsistency. When Dean Acheson was Secretary of State in 1950, he came under heavy fire from isolationist Congressmen who pressed for reduction of U.S. military commitments in Western Europe. In a public speech at the time, he commented on the need for display of American firmness and continuity of purpose:

> A new species has come on the horizon. This new species I call the re-examinist, because the re-examinist says, "I want to re-examine all our policies and all our programs."
>
> . . . Now it's possible that a re-examinist might be a farmer that goes out every morning and pulls up all his crops to see how they have done during the night. . . . Or it might be that this kind of a re-examinist is someone who comes down to breakfast in the morning and looks at his wife or at her husband and says, "Do I really love that man or woman? How did I ever turn up here with her or him?" Or he can put on his hat and go down to the office and look around and say, "Am I really in this business? Are these my partners? How did I get mixed up with these people? I wonder if I shouldn't have been an atomic scientist after all?"
>
> . . . No nation and no group of people who wish to lead a nation in this day and age in which we live are worthy of leadership, if at every moment they wish to tear up and examine the very roots of the policies upon which the whole future of the free world depends.[4]

[4] Quoted in McGeorge Bundy, *The Pattern of Responsibility.* Boston: Houghton Mifflin, 1952, pp. 85-87.

The Role of the State Department

Let us assume the ideal, that foreign policy is singular and unitary, synchronized, coordinated commitments and goals, harmonious promises and programs. In everyday affairs, this ideal does considerable violence to political reality. Inconsistency lurks in incongruous deeds, between statements and actions, between sequential contradictory gestures and actions. Nevertheless most statesmen aspire to the ideal. McGeorge Bundy spoke of it this way in his assessment of Acheson:

> Diplomacy, some have thought, is the sum of the functions of the State Department, but the clear tradition is greater than diplomacy; it is a tradition of high policy, and those Secretaries who have tried to duck the duty are not the ones who are remembered. In high policy, diplomacy is one instrument—a great and determining means to an end. . . . But policy has, necessarily, other means; . . . economic . . . , information . . . ; military strength. . . . These elements of action are so many and so closely entwined that in the end the decisions go back to the nation as a whole, and to its elected leaders. . . . But the highest official who is called to give his whole mind and effort to these matters, the man whose very title is a mark of this concern and duty, is the Secretary of State.[5]

Some Secretaries of State have achieved a symmetry in their actions. Of John Foster Dulles, Eisenhower's Secretary of State between 1953 and 1959, a highly critical foreign diplomat once said, "Dulles was architectonic in his foreign policy. It had a structure like a cathedral. He had the most magnificent and detailed position on every issue. . . . When all was said and done, it was practically a Gothic cathedral." [6]

Unity of direction and leadership in American foreign policy arises from the constitutional primacy of the President and the

[5] *Ibid.*, p. 3.
[6] *Ibid.*

derived authority of his Secretary of State. The relationship between these two men, the degree of personal intimacy and intellectual compatibility, their capacity for close collaboration, the congruence of their judgement, these qualities set the style of what Bundy calls "high policy." Presidential supremacy provides the Secretary of State with his authority. He stands above all other Cabinet officials in authority over foreign affairs and in other perquisites of office. (For example, he sits at the right hand of the President in Cabinet meetings, he normally has priority over all other Cabinet members in access to the President, he is designated by law as keeper of the Great Seal of the United States. Until 1947, the Presidential Succession Act provided that, in case of disqualification of both the President and Vice President, he should act as President if otherwise meeting Constitutional qualifications.)

In theory, the Secretary's pre-eminence over other Cabinet officers in foreign affairs extends to the State Department. The Department is supposedly the right hand of the President, the chief instrument of planning, synchronizing and negotiating policy. In practice, this is not always the case. Other governmental institutions, the National Security Council for one, today perform many of the State Department's traditional tasks. Since 1947, when it was established by act of Congress, the Council became a permanent institution, directly under the President, in which defense policy, economic policies and diplomacy could be brought into proper focus with each other. Representation on this Council consists of the Secretaries of Defense, Treasury, the Army, Navy, and Air Force, the Joint Chiefs of Staff, and the Director of the C.I.A. By means of this institutional device, major policies in the cold war could be developed, scrutinized, and reviewed by all the agencies responsible for them. The gulf between political, economic, and military affairs and resources could be narrowed.

The search for harmony of purpose in committee raises its own difficulties. It is no substitute for initiative and leadership.

The Council has been a milieu for seeking an inter-agency policy consensus. But frequently that consensus has been the lowest common denominator of agency views. Reconciling such views is a poor substitute for executive confrontation of hard choices. A strong President or Secretary of State, like John Foster Dulles, could ride herd over such institutions by the power of his intellect and persuasiveness. The Council's statutory power is that of recommending policies to the President. The President himself can ignore or by-pass it. But the Council, as symptom of the administrative need to clear policies among agencies and fuse judgments arising from various areas of government, reflected the decline of the State Department itself.

The State Department's decline as the central agency of policy formulation began on the eve of World War II, when the President, conscious of internal deficiencies in the Department, seized the initiative over policy, and pushed the Department aside in order to get things done. During the war, it shrank into obscurity. Major decisions of foreign policy were made by the President and his personal advisers, often with no prior advice from or consultation with the Department. At the Cairo Conference in 1942, when Roosevelt and Chiang Kai-shek met to discuss postwar goals in the Far East, not a single State Department representative was in attendance. James Byrnes, Roosevelt's close adviser in the late war years, tells that when Roosevelt was en route to the Yalta Conference in 1945, aboard a naval vessel, neither the President nor any of his chief advisers knew until they had nearly arrived at their destination of the fact that State Department position papers and background papers for the conference had been prepared and were actually aboard. "When I saw some of these splendid studies," Byrnes wrote, "I greatly regretted that they had not been considered aboard ship."[7]

Due to the nature of his office, the President may select aspects of high policy for his own special attention. But the fusion of political and constitutional roles in the office itself prohibits

[7] James F. Byrnes, *Speaking Frankly*. New York: Harper, 1947, p. 23.

much more than that. Unlike his counterparts in almost all other countries, he is simultaneously chief of state, chief executive, the leader of his political party, the chief advocate and expounder of the totality of domestic and foreign policies, the supreme teacher (if he chooses to be) about political problems, the final co-ordinator of a wide variety of commingled pressures and policies. The demands which each of these roles puts upon him make it impossible for him to act at all times as the nation's chief negotiator in diplomacy or even as the ever attentive designer of policy. Together these roles obviously give him a theoretical power and influence far outweighing those of any other individual statesman in the world. Their demands, however, wear down his energies and time.

By way of contrast, the Secretary of State, in recent American history at least, has virtually no political authority other than that derived from his office and its special relationship to the Presidency. Rarely in recent years has he been a political leader or figure in his own right. Like Marshall, Acheson, Dulles, and Rusk, he typically commands no political constituency at home. He has not been elected to public office. Rather, he has risen into prominence via administrative channels within the federal government. Since the turn of the century, only Bryan, Charles Evans Hughes, Frank Kellogg, and Hull were influential politicians before taking this office. Save in Jefferson's time the office has never been a stepping stone to the Presidency. In fact, no Secretary of State today could realistically conceive that his reputation in national politics could be much enhanced by his record in office. As a maker of compromises, a bringer of bad tidings, as the agency through which dangerous and unpleasant realities in world politics are conveyed to the American public, the Secretary may emerge exhausted from his tenure of office to enjoy the respect of men who knew his difficulties, but not as a popular figure.

What this means is that the Secretary of State, irrespective of his personal persuasiveness and influence, derives much of his power from a close attachment to the President himself. A Dulles biographer has described his relationship with Eisenhower this way:

> Dulles kept his pipeline to the White House open and clear at all times. He never permitted it to become clogged by misunderstandings that could sap his influence. He devoted hours upon hours of his time to keeping Eisenhower informed and making sure that he had his approval. . . . Of all the members of the Cabinet . . . he alone had freedom of the President's office.[8]

This was also Dean Acheson's style. "There never was a day," Truman wrote later in his *Memoirs*, "during the four years of Dean Acheson's secretaryship that anyone could have said that he and I differed on policy. He was meticulous in keeping me posted on every development within the wide range of his responsibility. He had a deep understanding of the President's position in our constitutional scheme and realized to the fullest that, while I leaned on him for constant advice, the policy had to be mine— it was."[9]

This ideal relationship, while constitutional, is by no means natural. It did not exist between Truman and James Byrnes nor between Roosevelt and Hull or among other pairs of the foreign policy team. A President with a wide-ranging mind and an active personality like Wilson and both Roosevelts, activates and enlarges the White House's powers and may thus run rough-shod over a Secretary. The President may at his discretion assemble in the White House a band of personal advisers who may not only influence him more than his Secretary but may also be used by him to formulate and negotiate high policy. Colonel House and Harry Hopkins had a vast personal influence with Wilson and F.D.R., respectively, despite their lack of any formal authorization to act. As with F.D.R., the President may in fact come to despair of the usefulness of the State Department or even to suspect it of lacking enthusiasm or commitment to his own policies.

---

[8] Gaston Coblentz and Roscoe Drummond, *Duel at the Brink*, Garden City: Doubleday, 1960, p. 26.

[9] Harry S. Truman, *Memoirs*, Vol. II. New York: Doubleday, 1958, p. 430.

In such instances Presidents may openly or covertly by-pass the formal bureaucracy in order to get things done.

Sometimes the President, sensing in his Secretary an obduracy, an unwillingness to mesh, or even a rivalry of policy, may simply dismiss or ignore him. In World War I, Bryan's pacifism made him incompatible with Wilson. His resignation followed. During the New Deal, Cordell Hull's political conservatism made him suspicious and hostile to Roosevelt's more leftish advisers. His intense infatuation with certain problem areas of policy, such as Reciprocal Trade and international organizations, was offset by often quite doctrinaire attitudes about the broad range of policy. Roosevelt adroitly avoided an open break with his Secretary, using Hull where necessary, using others where Hull was insufficient, keeping Hull on because of his immense prestige among American conservatives and his dedicated commitment to the principles of internationalism, which both men shared. But throughout the war years, "high policy" was Roosevelt's monopoly, though he had a wide range of advisers.[10] The White House "made" wartime policy. Hull and the State Department administered those parts of it which were given them.

The Roosevelt-Hull formula (like that of Wilson and his second Secretary, Lansing) of a weak Secretary and a strong President acting as his own Secretary of State, even as diplomatic negotiator, chains and abuses the Presidency. Even as doughty a President as Truman has called the burdens of the Presidency "crushing." In Roosevelt's and Wilson's time, they were just that. The Office of the Presidency cannot incorporate the wide range of functions which the Secretary himself performs, if only because the holder of the office is a human being with limited strength and durability.

But there are other reasons why the President should not also

[10] See Robert Sherwood, *Roosevelt and Hopkins*, rev. ed. New York: Harper & Brothers, 1950, pp. 134-135. Another thing which held Hull to Roosevelt was his wishful belief that the President had chosen him as his successor.

be the Secretary of State. Techniques of international diplomacy and negotiation have been profoundly influenced by jet planes and ease of movement. Popular feelings, in the cold war, place great strain upon political leaders to negotiate, to go to the Summit, to solve outstanding differences. A strong Secretary, whose thinking is closely synchronized with the President's, can spare him most of the travel and the political difficulties which arise if the President is absent from Washington for long periods of time. Dean Rusk has written, "The President is as mobile as a jet aircraft, but it is not clear that the Presidency is equally so." A President on home base is always close to essential elements of power and decision-making. Abroad, or on a Georgia golf course, he is not.

But another risk inheres in a Presidency deeply immersed in personal diplomacy and negotiation. As with Roosevelt at Yalta and Wilson in Paris, summit diplomacy means the personal confrontation of powerful men, the ultimate deciders. Summitry, theoretically, can expedite agreement. Thus far logic takes us. It can also expedite careless agreements or agreements which by their nature in no way reflect a deeper consensus or fusion of purpose back home. Powerful as Roosevelt was and as necessary as the Yalta Conference of 1945 might have been in laying a basis for post-war U.S.-Soviet relations, still Presidential carelessness in negotiation in that instance left an abiding rancor in American public opinion about what had been "negotiated away" there. As in the Kennedy-Khrushchev meeting in Vienna in June 1961, a Summit meeting can also be a sparring match closely watched by millions. Such circumstances may easily make serious negotiation impossible or arouse such deep personal animosity that future negotiation about important things is more difficult.

There is always an important distinction to be made between policy-making and diplomacy. When they are fused in meetings between chiefs of state, personal irrelevancies, undue concerns about prestige, *amour propre*, and jealousies can inhibit negotiation in a way that they would not when diplomacy is conducted by agents. A President can say, "Let me talk to a better, or more friendly Ambassador." He can never say, "Send me a better Prime Minister next time." Animosity can run very deep in the relationships between foreign secretaries, as Eden's hatred for Dulles has shown.[11] But this is far preferable to hatred among chiefs of state.

POLICY AS REACTION

In the best sense, policy is not diplomacy but design. But it is, secondarily, execution and action. The world of policy is awash with events, often wholly unanticipated and disconnected ones. During the summer and early fall of 1961, a series of separate yet interreactive events took place around the world. A Soviet-built wall and Khrushchev's nuclear ultimatum to the West about a separate peace treaty in Germany threatened a thermonuclear crisis for the whole world. In the Middle East, Nasser's United Arab Republic suddenly split into its original components, Syria and Egypt. Soviet thermonuclear tests, begun on a large scale, frightened the whole world. The Secretary-General of the United Nations was killed on the eve of the General Assembly meeting in New York, when the Russians were about to stage an onslaught against his policies and his authority. In Russia, Stalin was post-humously overthrown and his body dropped in the ashcan of history. Several Latin American republics hovered on the brink of civil war (as usual).

In theory, high policy anticipates events, heading off some, welcoming others. It seeks to establish some rational congruence between a new or newly perceived problem and the pre-existing world of reality around it. It thus lives upon words and abstractions like documents, cables, memoranda, action-papers, telephone messages. In short, it lives upon ideas and perceptions.

For these reasons, even when design exists policy is often "reactive." It responds tactically to events and problems. A new

[11] See Anthony Eden's memoirs, *Full Circle*. Boston: Houghton Mifflin, 1960.

event calls for swift and broad consultation, cooperation, and understandings among divergent governmental viewpoints and philosophies. Finally, it needs both private and public justification, to Congress, to foreign governments, to entire countries.

Within the sea of events through which policy moves, there are long-range problems which statesmen may always keep in mind. Yet often, because of their occupational immersion in the world of immediate things, the "inevitable" is neglected and the probable ignored. In a sense, the world's population problem is a policy problem to be anticipated and dealt rationally with. Early in the next century, *pari passu,* the world's population will be three times its present size. The world hovers on the threshold of a much more monumental, demographic revolution than we have thus far experienced, with cataclysmic consequences. *Pari passu,* within two decades a very large number of states will have their own nuclear arsenals. (Perhaps nuclear weapons can become a new form of birth control.) Changes in agricultural sciences and medicine are recasting the whole problem of food scarcity in the world. Medical discoveries are radically altering life expectations. Innovations in energy resources shift and redistribute power among nations. Finally, deep undercurrents of human ethical predispositions, mores, and cultural needs lie hidden under the surface of these things, preceding major social changes and deeply affecting them. Long term political changes may cast shadows before them before some great symbolic event, like the twenty-second Party Congress in Moscow in 1961, registers them.

Unfortunately policy-makers live in a world of yesterday, tomorrow, and next year. They must adapt themselves to each arrogant event in the present. Each fragment of change must be pieced together into some kind of revised picture of reality. Policy bereft of some large architectural design may degenerate into a series of patchwork responses to happenings, which themselves may acquire the reputation of policy even though no policy may have been intended.

U.S. policies and actions in Latin America during the 1950's are examples. Until the Castro revolt in 1958, Latin America had been a neglected backwater of American policies and attention. Few Americans attached much importance to the fact that U.S. policies in Latin America had helped keep many contemptible tyrants, like Batista, in power. The fact that U.S. policies long ignored the mounting pressures for domestic economic reform was also widely overlooked. Few Americans noted either that since the turn of the century, U.S. private economic interests and investments, notably in northern Latin America and the Caribbean, had helped to exacerbate intolerable economic inequality by concentrating on a few extractive industries, ignoring the need for balanced economic growth and reform. In the eyes of many Latin Americans, this inattention, exploitation and support of dictatorships were U.S. policies. That these so-called policies were essentially compounded of neglect was rarely recognized.

This kind of risk is run by any great policy-making enterprise. George Kennan once remarked that the United States was like a "giant in a small room." A slight motion, no matter what for, had its effect on the others in the room even when it was purposeless. For this reason, the American policy process contains complex networks, "radar screens," intelligence, and reporting systems designed as sentinels to scan the horizon of world politics for clues of impending changes. Perhaps no other nation except the Soviet Union relies so extensively upon such voluminous data as does the United States. Without this stream of intelligence, policy may become *weltfremd*, alien to the world of reality or the world may be misinterpreted.

Several interesting problems arise in this information and intelligence process. Relevant information about problems must get to the right place at the right time. On Pearl Harbor Sunday for instance, an alert warning to U.S. defense installations in Hawaii was mistakenly sent from Washington by commercial Western Union, an oversight of some unknown Washington functionary. As the messenger boy cycled towards the naval base with the warning, he could see the smoke and fire of the Japanese attack.

In early 1947, State Department foreknowledge of British plans to withdraw their military forces from Greece, curtailing their overseas commitments, never reached high policy levels in Washington until the eleventh hour, despite the fact that this withdrawal made Communist overrunning of the Eastern Mediterranean area a very likely possibility. The electric, almost spastic response of the White House to this crisis in the form of the Truman Doctrine came almost too late to save Greece from going under. Not until late February had the British Government notified the Secretary of State of its intention to withdraw from Greece no later than April 1, five weeks hence. In his *Memoirs*, Truman described the context in which this fearful news belatedly broke in on his attention:

> At the time I was weighing the problem of aid to Greece and Turkey, Ernest Bevin [then British Foreign Secretary] had just made a public statement about our Palestine policy that cast a dark shadow over our relations with Britain; the economy bloc in the new Eightieth Congress was threatening to cut some vital government programs out of the budget, including overseas information services; Secretary Marshall was getting ready to attend his first Foreign Ministers' Conference; there were events in Argentina, in Indonesia, in China that called for decisions; Senator McKellar was blocking the atomic energy program by his stubborn opposition to the confirmation of David Lilienthal as chairman of the Atomic Energy Commission; the bill for the unification of the services was at last ready for Congress; the press wanted me to announce my plans for 1948. . . .[12]

A few weeks later the Greek-Turkish Aid Program and the Truman Doctrine happily emerged, a program which was described this way by Truman:

> I believe that it must be the policy of the United States to support free peoples who are resisting attempted subjugation by armed minorities or by outside pressures. . . . The seeds of totalitarian regimes are nurtured by misery and want. They spread and grow in the evil soil of poverty and strife. They reach their

[12]Truman, *op. cit.*, p. 102.

full growth when the hope of a people for a better life has died.
We must keep that hope alive." [13]

But other distractions nearly made the resistance too late.

A more complex problem about information and intelligence
might be called the "frame-of-reference problem." What is the
proper context for information or intelligence about a problem?
This is often one of the most difficult and perplexing issues of
policy-making. Immediately after World War II, when Japan
had surrendered, U.S. defense authorities pressed strongly for U.S.
retention and annexation of the former Japanese Mandate islands
in the Pacific. Retention of these, it was argued, was necessary to
a strong U.S. strategic position in the Pacific. In Japanese hands,
the Carolinas and Marianas had become powerful naval bastions;
even though nominally the League of Nations had given them to
Japan to hold in trust before the war.

This military insistence upon outright U.S. annexation in
1945 was opposed by the State Department. Annexation would
have meant betrayal of America's declaration in the Atlantic
Charter that it sought "no aggrandizement, territorial or other."
Infringement of this commitment, which even the Soviet Union
in 1942 had accepted in principle as a basic war aim, would not
only have violated an open and dramatic statement of principle
but would have weakened the moral grounds on which the United
States might oppose Soviet violations of the Charter and other
wartime agreements. In this instance, military authority won out.
The United States designated the trust islands as Strategic Trust
Territories and retained control of the islands under the ambiguous formula of Strategic Trust Territories nominally under U.N.
Security Council protection and supervision. In fact the islands
were subject to no international control. In this instance, military
considerations prevailed over political-diplomatic ones, and the
United States unilaterally violated its most basic political undertaking in the war. (Interestingly enough, the Soviet Union, crav-

[13] *Ibid.*, p. 106.

ing its own strategic trust territories, approved the solution in the Security Council.)

Grand Design and Local Reality

This frame-of-reference difficulty can also be seen in the conflict between local or regional and global conceptions of policy. Immersion in the particulars of a local problem may blur policy-makers' eyes to the larger picture. During the Korean War for instance, after American and U.N. forces had thrown North Korean troops back across the 38th parallel, extremely powerful pressure came from General MacArthur's command for authorization to extend the theater of hostilities to Manchuria, enabling them to smash local Communist power in Korea. In Washington, even after Chinese Communist forces disguised as "volunteers" had intervened in the fall of 1950, this pressure from MacArthur to break into the "privileged sanctuary" from which the Communists received their supplies was strongly resisted. What was feared was the impact of widening a local war upon America's total military resources; upon American and NATO strength in Europe, which might be seriously weakened by diversion of forces to the Far East; upon America's relations with its European allies which, like Britain and France, feared also that a widened war might provoke Soviet retaliation in Europe. Finally, there was the supreme concern and uncertainty about Soviet responses. If American forces were to strike into Manchuria, close to Soviet Siberia, might Russia also abandon its own self-imposed limitations in the war and widen the scope of conflict in ways quite unfavorable to the West?

This was a classic instance of the problem. In Tokyo, before his dismissal by the President, General MacArthur saw the free world's fate pinned to the fate of the Korean peninsula; in Washington, President Truman and all of his chief advisers—Marshall, Acheson, Bradley—saw Korea as part of a complex of interconnected problems. From that vantage point, weighing the Korean

War against all other aspects of American interests and policy, they decided to impose limits and restraints upon local purposes. In effect, they decided that Korea was a war which could not be won, because the risks of enlargement of conflict far outweighed the advantages of local victory. In consequence, global war possibly was averted. America's North Atlantic alliances remained unimpaired, but the Korean war ended in frustrating, negotiated compromise and stalemate. For the first time in nearly a century and a half, America had fought a major war and had not won it.

Infatuation with particulars is no worse than its opposite vice. Abstract global strategies may blur perception of unique, local circumstances. To say that American foreign policies are "global" in scope does not mean that there is harmony among them. A policy developed to deal with problems in Africa may negatively affect U.S. relations with its European allies and friends, and vice versa. American policies directed toward closer U.S. integration with the European economy may clash with policies seeking closer rapport with nations in the underdeveloped world.

An instance of a global design blurring a local circumstance occurred in the early years of the Eisenhower administration. In the Truman years, American containment policies had sought by means of a series of regional alliances to align American power and purpose with that of other "free nations." In 1947, the Rio de Janeiro Pact set up such a regional alliance in the Western Hemisphere between the United States and the Latin republics. In 1949, NATO extended America's commitment to the defense of Western Europe against Communist aggression. Still other pacts were negotiated, like the ANZUS pact which tied America to Australia and New Zealand in a defensive alliance. By these means, American policy after the war linked American purposes with three groupings of states: its traditional Western Hemispheric neighbors; the West European democracies which it had joined in the war against Hitler; and the two English-speaking Commonwealths in the South Pacific.

During the Eisenhower administration, however, this design

of regional alliances was artifically extended to cover a whole range of states—façade republics, tottering Middle Eastern oligarchies, Fascist Spain—a cordon of feeble allies stretching around the remaining perimeter of the Soviet Union. In the Far East, the United States organized the Southeast Asia Treaty Organization, linking together an incongruous patchwork of small and problematic regimes—Pakistan, the Philippines, Thailand—and the United States. In the Middle East, the U.S. and Britain encouraged the development of the Baghdad Pact, a "Northern Tier" of Moslem states which were close to the U.S.S.R.: Iran, Iraq, Jordan, and Pakistan. In the Far East also, a U.S.-Nationalist China security pact guaranteed Chiang Kai-shek's regime against attack from the Chinese mainland.

By 1956, John Foster Dulles thus had constructed a global security system, a representation of global strategy and purpose pleasing to abstract minds and to doctrinaire military men. Yet the more symmetrical it came to be on paper, the more this global design did violence to local realities. Its newer agreements, like SEATO and the Baghdad Pact, rested upon sand. NATO was different. The major component of the American alliance system, it rested on strong regional foundations, strong, free, constitutional nations, most of whom traditionally had ties of deep friendship and common purpose with America.

Aside from Portugal, all of the original NATO members were constitutional democracies, committed to welfare state economies, enjoying high standards of living. Their common industrial strength and promise were great. Among them was spread a leadership which shared common awareness of their solidarity in the war against Nazism and their common opposition to Communism. There were strong political parties of moderation in all of them. But the new Southeast Asian and Middle Eastern pieces of this grand alliance system were all imposed upon radically different local political realities. The Middle East was in the throes of a violent animosity between the Arab states and Israel. There was an intense rivalry among the leaderships of the more influential

Arab states themselves and there were surging revolutionary pressures such as those which had led to the Colonels' revolt in Egypt and, ultimately, to Kassim's insurrection in Iraq in 1958.

Under these conditions, regional military alliances and military assistance programs intensified local tensions among non-Communist states. SEATO and U.S. military assistance to Pakistan worsened antagonisms between India and the United States, and India and Pakistan. The Baghdad Pact intensified hostilities between Egypt and its neighbors, Jordan and Iraq, by upsetting the power balance among them. The Baghdad Pact, like SEATO, was directed to the same global purpose that NATO had been, containment of Soviet expansionist drives. The Baghdad Pact, as a mutual alliance, was the classic instance. The absence of any consensus among non-Communist states in the Eastern Mediterranean about the *local* political order made the concept of Middle Eastern defense absurd and meaningless. Who was defending whom against whom? Iraq and Jordan against Egypt? The Arab world against Israel? Local regimes against street mobs? Or against competent and able reformers? The attempt of American policy to force local political reality into congruence with a grand global design ran afoul of these particulars and finally collapsed. In 1958, the Baghdad Pact was abandoned by Baghdad itself when the once-reliable, conservative Nuri-es-Said regime in Iraq was overthrown and its leaders murdered by street mobs, nationalists, Nasserite agents, and happy indigenous Communists.

This continuous tension between large designs and the empirical world is inescapable. No amount of administrative perfectability in the policy process can escape it. Policy-making involves hard choices. In the Middle Eastern Suez Crisis of 1956, which vacillating American policy had in some measure helped provoke, the hard choice was then between America's support of its NATO allies, Britain and France, or support of the principles of the United Nations Charter. The choice was also between supporting the aggression of allies and risking an enlarged war with the Soviet Union which this ill-starred aggression might provoke. American support of Algerian nationalists' demands for independence in the 1960's risked further alienation of France from NATO. Support of France against the Algerian FLN risked accelerating Algeria's drift toward Communism. In instances where harsh choices must be made, the administrative machinery of policy-making can do little more than identify and clarify choices. Unfortunately it cannot foresee the consequences of each alternative. The large issues which events provoke must be decided by the President himself. As Truman said, "a President either is constantly on top of events or, if he hesitates, events soon will be on top of him." [14] And, as a French statesman, Pierre Mendes-France once said, "to govern is to choose."

POLICY AS PROCESS

Even when it is the fruit of collaboration among a few men of power, foreign policy rests ideally upon a concert of purpose among a wide range of men and agencies. Teamwork, to use a homely Eisenhower designation, links information, advice, and resources to Executive choice and orders. It is a search for concert of judgment and action. Great decisions are sometimes made by lonely men at the top of a pyramid, but most decisions and policies are not. Their origins can be traced to countless streams of thought and action.

Because Presidential style and authority are, in the last resort, paramount, so is the composition of the President's team. The ways in which he uses it, and it, him, determine the processes of high policy-making. A Chief Executive depends on his team for information, advice, and delineation of choices. Overly dependent on it for all of these, he may become prisoner of advisers and staff. Like Eisenhower, he may content himself with *its* definitions of choice and priorities. Like Kennedy, he may try to ride herd on policies and advisers both, reaching down into agencies of power to staff them with men congenial to his thoughts, purposes, and

[14] *Ibid.*, p. 1.

temperament. But in either case, as Dean Acheson has written, "when the whole function of determining what is what, and what to do about it, is gathered into one hand, or into a small group at the top, the resulting action may or may not be strong, but it is likely to be ill-adapted to reality and self-defeating." [15]

Policy-making teamwork may be determined in some measure by the available institutional structure, but when we scan the history of institutions, noting the radical changes, we see that policy teamwork is deeply affected also by the unique nature of policy problems themselves and the way in which these problems are defined and seen. If existing administrative resources seem compatible with the defined problem, then the team can be moulded to meet the unique characteristics of the problem at hand. High policy should then be seen as a kaleidoscopic process, a shifting of agencies, personalities, and influence about one central point, the Presidency. Executive style, the appropriateness and relative influence of existing agencies and advisers, the unique features of the delineated problem, these, together with inertia and habit, combine to determine process. Often, the very intellectual definition of a foreign policy problem can bare the inadequacy of existing institutional mechanisms to cope with it. Conversely, it can confirm their strength.

Definition suggests new devices. To cite but one recent instance, when the European political-economic crisis of 1946-1948 had been defined, it was possible to construct a wholly new design of American and multi-national institutions to deal rationally with it. Had the crisis been differently perceived and differently defined, quite different policy-making entities might have been created. As it was, the Economic Cooperation Administration, the multi-national Organization for European Economic Cooperation, etc., became the policy entities of the Marshall Plan and remained so until its purposes had been accomplished in the early 1950's.

Thus the act of defining problems can also be the act of re-

---

[15] Dean Acheson, "Thoughts About Thought in High Places," *New York Times* Magazine, October 11, 1959, pp. 20ff.

defining old or inventing new agencies and instruments. Foreign policy processes in the cold war are plastic, since definitions of problems ceaselessly undergo change.

A recent instance of this redefinition was the establishment of the U.S. Disarmament Agency by Congress in the summer of 1961. This agency, designed to engage in research on both technical and political aspects of disarmament was also to provide a locus of continuity in the planning of disarmament policies for the American government, a task which had heretofore been the neglected stepchild of too many agencies.

We may see this when we look at one major change in foreign policy making during the past twenty years, the institutional fusion of political, military, economic, and intelligence agencies together into one large process. The steady decline in authority of the Department of State (as distinguished from its Secretary) since 1940 was due not only to its bureaucratic mediocrity but to inherent limitations of traditional style and purpose. Traditionally, even today, the State Department has been the chief agency of U.S. diplomatic negotiations with foreign states; traditionally, but no longer, the State Department was also the supreme agency for providing high policy makers with political intelligence from abroad and speaking authoritatively to foreign governments about American policy and purposes. So long as they dealt primarily with governments, not peoples; so long as they were not essentially operational; so long as they stayed remote from the tissues of other nations and cultures; so long as American military power was normally held in abeyance for wartime use and was not an ubiquitous element in everyday foreign affairs, while these conditions held, diplomacy was paramount among the agencies of foreign policy and the State Department was supreme.

Supplementing Diplomacy

The decline of diplomacy as the central agency of foreign policy was relative, not absolute. Since 1947, the nature of foreign policy problems has been radically redefined and diplomacy has been surrounded by supplementary operational apparatuses, not to displace it, but to enhance, strengthen, supplement, and carry out its essential objectives.

Supplementation was threefold. It meant widening the scope of consultation within high levels of government to bring together diplomatic, military, and economic advice on common problems. It meant devising operational entities to carry foreign policies out once policies such as foreign aid programs reached the point of implementation and administration. Finally, it meant widening the scope of American activities in intelligence and covert work which, even when at one with diplomatic purposes, could not be carried out by diplomatic agencies which normally observed the amenities of international behavior of states and the rules of international law.

Each of these supplementations of diplomacy raised special problems for the policy-making process and each seemed to admit that diplomacy and the Department of State were insufficient foundations for policy. Policy-making grounded exclusively on a President and Department of State which radiated directives to other agencies might fail in its essential objective of rationally harmonizing purposes. It could blind policy administrators to the multifarious political implications of their own work.

This was especially true of the military, for while the doctrine of civil supremacy of the military was in the sound tradition of a democratic society, to exclude the military from participation in high political matters was to deny to that process essential advice about military resources and capabilities. It also denied military men any sophisticated perspective on the relationship of force to politics. Ill-advised about this relationship, military power might stumble awkwardly ahead in implementing directives, unconcerned or unaware of the political effects of its own actions.

In an ideological and revolutionary age, narrow preoccupation with specialties of power could be disastrous to high policy. Trained in classic traditions of Western strategic lore, the military viewed its role as the nation's antagonist against formal military entities of other states. In the European theater of war between 1941 and 1945, this limited conception of themselves blinded many military officers to the ideological issues at stake in war. If winning the war were defined only in terms of destroying the formal military enemy, then the enemy was Germany and German military power, not Fascism and Nazism. Ironically, in this instance, implementation of total war in the classical sense of war between state entities led to the doctrine of unconditional surrender on the one hand—which hardened popular German support of the Third Reich and blunted the opposition to Hitler within the German military itself—and, on the other hand, to U.S. military collaboration with Fascism's collaborators in other European states like Petain and Weygand in France and Badoglio in Italy.

Preoccupied with winning the war against Germany, American military power also overlooked the emergency postwar constellation of power on the European Continent between the U.S.S.R. and the Western democracies. The military, many of whom, like General Eisenhower, viewed their task narrowly as "carrying out directives," needed broader instruction in politics and needed, in turn, to have their voices heard in the staging of political policy.

New, formal entities could ease the reconciliation of technical viewpoints with high policy and inform high policy about resources and tactics. In 1947, when the American defense establishment had been reorganized, the President's National Security Council reflected the changed definition of the policy process. Here, creative tensions among diplomatic, military, economic, and psychological policy agencies could, in theory, be brought into the open with resulting wider perspectives for policy-makers. Closer synchronization of functional policies could be made possible. Diplomacy could benefit from continuous advice and consultation with the Joint Chiefs of Staff. Both might benefit from awareness of the relationship between economic policy and their own concerns. All could act more rationally when informed by the intelligence services of C.I.A.

Yet supplementing diplomacy in the policy process raised more problems. Was diplomacy itself, i.e., the State Department and Foreign Service, to be wholly divested of operational activities (overseas foreign aid for one)? And if so, if stripped of supervisory control, how could such activities be kept congruent with high policy? What role was an American ambassador to play in shaping and coordinating all the local activities of U.S. agencies which were surrogate to other Washington centers of power? If American mission chiefs in foreign countries had no such authority there was the danger in microcosm, of mutually contradictory activities.

And there was another more important problem. The increasing number of operational agencies overseas, coupled with the intrusion of these agencies into high policy making, might cripple the primacy of high policy, making it the slave of its technical agents. The relative influence of governmental institutions cannot be measured solely in terms of their mass, but mass could hardly be ignored. In the cold war, when the military were most generously endowed by Congress with money and power and when circles of military power could attract the support of such new agencies as the Atomic Energy Commission, the danger was in the pre-eminence of military response to political problems. An otherwise parsimonious Congress which favored and paid for military strength while it deprecated the effectiveness of diplomacy, allowed the Pentagon to tower over traditional agencies, some of whose functions were crippled by Congressional stinginess.

Intelligence and Espionage

The supplementing tasks were apparent in new operational and advisory agencies assigned tasks which the State Department and its foreign service were never designed for. Espionage, for instance, had never been regarded as a proper activity of peacetime

American diplomacy. Before World War II, most Americans regarded such practices with abhorrence. Espionage, intelligence, and official, covert violence were deemed antithetical both to democratic government, with its respect for open politics, and to nations which respected the rights of others in managing their own affairs.

Since World War II, such former iniquities have become an independent arm of normal American foreign policy. The Office of Strategic Services, set up in 1942 as a temporary wartime cloak-and-dagger agency, became the Central Intelligence Agency after the war. Its worldwide apparatus, managed in secret with virtually no Congressional oversight, today numbers nearly thirty thousand men and women, more than the State Department and Foreign Service combined. The budget has been estimated at three to four times that of the State Department. Since the late 1940's when it was an operational and intelligence arm of American policy, it has deposed or fought unfriendly regimes; it has covertly helped defend other free societies from subversion; it has financed opposition groups in unfriendly states, and it has strengthened groups deemed hospitable to American interests. The C.I.A. routinely gathers and analyses information and intelligence from all parts of the world. It has gathered, sometimes by unorthodox means (such as the ill-famed U-2 flights of 1960), information pertinent to American security problems. In one instance, the equally ill-starred Cuban invasion of May 1961, the C.I.A. directed and assumed operational charge of the invasion of a foreign country.

While these covert enterprises, concealed from normal diplomatic activities, are usually necessary to cold war crisis, they raise the problem of how to superintend them and how to keep their activities and policy judgments more easily observed by the public and more in harmony with high policy. Inside such a far flung, covert apparatus, the C.I.A. agents' informational judgments were to be an essential part of the ultimate judgment which preceded action. For this reason errors of analysis might conceivably cripple broad American aims.

The C.I.A.'s disastrous mishandling of the Cuban "invasion," its most publicized failure, certainly obscured its quiet triumphs (who could tell about all of them in fact?). Once the press had investigated and publicized a disaster which no official secrecy could really conceal, it was easy to see what caused the failure. The C.I.A., given operational control of an enterprise composed chiefly of Cuban exiles from Castro, grossly misconceived the degree of popular resentment against Castro within Cuba. They placed responsibility for the enterprise in the hands of an ignorant and tactless man and staffed its leadership with discredited followers of ex-dictator Batista, men who opposed all the social reforms which the Cubans so desperately demanded. Moreover, the clandestine operation, hastily drawn up in secrecy by an agency which did not itself make high policy, had notably failed to assess the profound political disagreements among Cuban exiles. It could not make clear, to Cubans in exile or in the island itself, what higher purposes, other than the overthrow of a very popular pro-Communist demagogue, informed the enterprise as a whole. Finally, the enterprise was mishandled as a military expedition due to the prudent refusal of high policy makers to employ the kind of American military power which would certainly have brought military success, but would have meant the direct and bloody conflict of Americans with the very Cubans they were supposedly "liberating." It would have been a Western Hemisphere Budapest and would have made all America's inter-American policies, including the Alliance for Progress, a shambles.

Such activities were alien to American diplomacy. They were unpopular with many Americans who found clandestine intelligence and clandestine use of power repugnant. The very scale of their operations meant that a quasi-totalitarian enterprise was fastened upon a political democracy with the purpose of informing its leadership and enabling it to act more rationally. But how could one discover if the Agency's agents and methods clashed with the policies of a free society? Confidence was called for, much more, in fact, than that which Americans reposed in agencies whose activities were subjects of constant public scrutiny.

A humane, sophisticated director like Allen Dulles, the product of a lifetime of diplomatic service, could comprehend ethical and political problems raised by his novel enterprise. The C.I.A.'s director, as one scholar wrote, "must be a rare combination of administrative expert, imaginative scholar, courageous master spy, and a person of keen political sensitivity to the political ideals of the American Republic . . . a master judge and politician, but not a political partisan, and should be possessed of an inner integrity and common law sense." [16]

As the *New Republic* wrote of Allen Dulles' successor, John McCone,

> Where self-effacement, balanced judgment, fine discrimination are prime requisites, Mr. McCone brings an impulsive temperament, an arrogant manner toward subordinates, a dogmatic rather than skeptical cast of mind [the lack of] a rudimentary sense of the ambiguities, the causes, of upheavals that are rocking every continent and with which C.I.A. must contend. . . . The Administration may find it has surrendered one of the prime weapons we have to counter the Communist conspiracy—*intelligence*.[17]

The qualities enumerated by the scholar quoted above were deemed essential not only to a director, but to all policy leaders within the subterranean depths of the organization. The clandestine world of intelligence evaluation, cloak-and-dagger politics, conspiracy, and counter-espionage, could corrupt the intellect or distort the perspective of even honest and brilliant men.

Not that the jungle of secret intelligence was unreal. Like all climates of intrigue and deception, it was one which free societies wished, ultimately, to liquidate. However, a society which utilized such work could be corrupted if it did not impose effective limits

---

[16] Harry Howe Ransom, *Central Intelligence and National Security.* Cambridge: Harvard University Press, 1958, p. 92.

[17] *The New Republic*, October 9, 1961, p. 4.

upon its own agents so that politics could remain fundamentally open and above-board. To keep the realities of that clandestine world, so congenial to Communists, at one with the realities of the open world required sensitive political leadership within the C.I.A., to freshen its perspectives by immersion in the activities of the open society. For in secret intelligence were the same clamors for action, decision, and evaluation that one found everywhere else. Roger Hilsman has described the self-doubts and torments of a high intelligence official.

> He said, waving his hand around his office, that here he sat, a typical bureaucrat. Here was a box containing the output of all the intelligence agencies—dailies, weeklies, monthlies, and special studies and reports. This was his "reflection" box. But over here was an in-box—look at it! Piled high. And here was a squawk box from the big boss' office, and in the room outside, he said, I had seen the line of people to see him. What was his job? His job was to get those cables from that in-box to the out-box, to get answers out, to get some action—to get something done. He had not time for the reflection box. And so he must do things off the cuff, right off the top of his head. His job was to put out fires. And it frightened him sometimes how much of putting-out fires there was and how little of thought and reflection.[18]

Perhaps the Central Intelligence Agency found itself in the same dilemma that other decision-makers were in. The predictive and anticipative roles of intelligence had the same disease of today and tomorrow as did the men it was supposed to educate and advise. One scholar, writing of the C.I.A., suggested that this deficiency might, in fact, be more severe than the threats posed by the clandestine character of the information and the intelligence process: "The substantive problem [in strategic intelligence] may emerge as a result of the reflections of a man employed to do nothing but anticipate problems. In actual fact, the intelligence business employs all too few such men." [19]

[18] Roger Hilsman, *Strategic Intelligence and National Decisions*. Glencoe, Ill.: Free Press, 1956, p. 80.
[19] Sherman Kent, *Strategic Intelligence*. Princeton: Princeton University Press, 1949, p. 159.

Information—Propaganda

To these covert enterprises, deemed essential to policy making, were added others which were overt, but which posed equally troublesome problems for a democratic society. Information and cultural programs, a euphemism for propaganda, became the long arm of America's official prestige, just as the C.I.A. had become the long arm of America's guile. Like the C.I.A., the prototypes of the United States Information Agency were visible in earlier creations of totalitarian states. As massive agencies of intelligence and subversion had first been bred by the closed societies and their state and party apparatuses so, too, had centralized propaganda in the twentieth century first been developed on a large scale by Fascist and Communist parties and states.

In a sense, both the C.I.A. and the U.S.I.A. represented democracy's tribute to the power of totalitarianism: the compliment of imitation. Propaganda was not unknown in American diplomatic history, as Benjamin Franklin's effective role in "selling" the Revolution to eighteenth-century Frenchmen had shown. But the totalitarian states had been first to make continuous use of "total espionage" and "total propaganda" as modes of subverting free societies and their other enemies. Neither the Fascist nor Communist parties and states drew any distinction between foreign governments and foreign peoples. Just as there were few restraints upon their power of mass indoctrination at home in the eras of Stalin and Hitler, so there were fewer ethical restraints upon their employment abroad. To the totalitarian regimes, "total diplomacy" meant the concerted, simultaneous employment of all forms of power, striking into the tissues of foreign societies to persuade, cajole, terrorize, and disrupt them. The neat distinctions which both democratic and traditional authoritarian regimes had drawn between diplomacy and force, peace and war, suasion by reason and suasion by deception, made no sense to revolutionaries, whose views of the political process were dynamic and violent.

Liberal democracies had traditionally shied away from the use of total power in foreign policy for much the same reason that they had shied away from the use of total power and total terror over their own peoples.

Traditional diplomacy dealt with governments. The U.S.I.A. was symptomatic of a new diplomacy, where governments reached over the heads of governments to speak to whole peoples. A cynic has defined propaganda as the "art of deceiving your friends without actually convincing your enemies," but it had to be much more than that. It sought to establish rapport, to win friends, to persuade others of common purposes when such existed, to heighten American prestige, to break through barriers of ignorance, to commune with men whose opinions of America might make the essential difference. As one U.S.I.A. Director has remarked, its task was a

> new dimension in the conduct of foreign relations. It is no longer a matter of governments dealing with governments. Ever since Woodrow Wilson's plea for open covenants openly arrived at, the trend has been to contact the people directly, to take the world's masses into our confidence, to penetrate the living space of the common man, reaching as many as we can. . . . People everywhere are becoming more literate, more awakened, more concerned with their fate. The Agency's task is to respond to this hunger for knowledge.

Traditional diplomacy suspected these new devices or held them in contempt. If they were not deemed hucksterish, they were deemed ephemeral activities of no lasting consequence. Traditional diplomacy dealt with official elites and their opinions. The new diplomacy of propaganda and mass suasion dealt with societal aggregates, non-governmental elites, working with novel instrumentalities: mass media, libraries, exchange of persons, art exhibits, magazines, books, exhibitions, pamphlets, person-to-person contacts. All of them were supposedly part of some larger purpose.

In the case of America after World War II, the new diplomacy of suasion and people-to-people contact proved an interesting but painful experiment in world politics. In his draft of the Declaration of Independence, Jefferson spoke of the "decent respect to the opinions of mankind," as being one touchstone of America's resolve to justify publicly the reasons for its Revolution. American cold war propaganda, also sensitive to such opinions, sought to inform men but also to remould them into more sympathetic rapport with American purposes and American society.

The agonies of American ventures in this new field of politics arose chiefly from two vexing problems. First, how could the open society, composed of many different voices, possibly speak with one authoritative governmental voice abroad? Who had the power to give words to that voice? To what extent should that voice consider foreign policy in telling America's story? Concerned with American prestige and reputation, should it conceal the defective and portray only the good? How should it speak about the many deficiencies of American democracy when the very perpetrators of these deficiencies had their own representatives in Congress alert to messages of this sort and ready to combat them? Totalitarian governments, able to crush domestic opposition, labored under few of these democratic liabilities. American and Western traditions of free press and free speech meant, moreover, that even when the official voice spoke with authority, voices of dissent could cut it down to size, or speak even more loudly.

There was a danger, therefore, that the voice of democracy would sound from a Tower of Babel, confusing the outside world about the nature and purposes of America. An alternative was to search for the lowest American common denominator of agreement about policy and purpose, but that voice would be innocuous. Offending no American, it might interest no one else. It could concentrate on the iniquities of its totalitarian opponents, refuting their lies and their propaganda, thus becoming a querulous, negative truth train, taking its direction from its enemies' track.

A second vexing source of trouble for American propaganda came from another quarter. Information programs were designed to inform and persuade, to establish synapses between Americans and peoples of other cultures. But their *raison d'être* in the cold war was to nurture a climate of receptivity to America's deeds and purposes. There was no disagreement on the necessity of influencing foreign opinion if one sought some abiding consensus between Americans and other peoples about purpose and values.

Caught between the wish to "sell America" and its policies abroad and to establish a deep, humane rapport with influential (or potentially influential) foreigners, U.S. strategies of information and propaganda faltered, but urged their case. These opinions *were* crucial. How did one go about establishing equations between necessary but unpalatable policies, deemed consonant with American national interests, and the repercussions of such unpopular policies upon foreign elites and opinion-makers? How much and what kind of guidance was to be sought from the "opinions of mankind," in furtherance of America's basic aims? The Scylla of *this* waterway was a policy deaf to foreign opinion, inner-directed and self-confident, sure of its correctness, and contemptuous of the feelings of others. The Charybdis was policy so sensitive to breezes from afar that it lost sight of national interests in the desire to give no offense to America's friends and allies.

And there were problems concerning the relation of propagandistic diplomacy to foreign policy. The science of communication was in its infancy when the cold war started. Purposive, intercultural encounters had always been problematical. When one sought to use them for political ends, the following questions arose. Regardless of the message's particular content, to whom was it going? How was it received? How did particular messages, sent under governmental imprimatur, fit into the broader scope of messages and communications which less inhibited, non-governmental America was also sending abroad? Congress, suspicious and in part hostile to the implications of government propaganda, set harsh financial limitations upon the resources which U.S. propaganda had at its disposal. But these fixed limitations only dramatized the limited resources of America's informational activities in a world of nearly three billion people of all shapes, sizes, colors, and influence.

THE UGLIEST AMERICANS   The cold war brought with it certain cold facts. It was difficult to be both liked and respected, admired and feared. There were no reasons why America, as a superpower, should be any more loved than any other super-power in history had been. It was true that Soviet propaganda about America seized upon its vices and distorted its successes. But anti-Americanism in non-Communist countries was not due only to Soviet strategies or American shortcomings.

There was little in Americans' reading of their own history that prepared them for the eventuality of being disliked or misunderstood and less for being criticized for their shortcomings. A "nation of nations," as Americans thought themselves to be, did not like to be thought of by foreigners as Simon Legrees. An egalitarian culture did not like to be regarded as a materialist, capitalist country. A nation embarking on a long, costly, and problematical career of world leadership resented being called imperialist. An open society did not appreciate being portrayed, as not only Soviet but many other propaganda organs were to portray it—as a McCarthyite police state. Americans did not like the fact that many intellectuals were convinced of their much touted imperfections and even invented others. Above all, what was offensive to many Americans was the contempt in which their own culture was held by many sophisticated Europeans as a culture-less culture. Soviet propaganda could nurture such ideas, but it did not give birth to them.

America's image could not be separated from its strength or its deeds. Its mounting power and influence in the world after 1947 generated anti-American sentiments, even among those who benefitted from American support. Charity and foreign aid do not in themselves make friends; power and riches are rarely loved. Ironically, America often seemed most popular as a culture among the peoples of the world most cut off from it. Among the enslaved nations of Eastern Europe, American popularity was often dizzy-ingly high; while in Western Europe, irritableness, born of envy and often of powerlessness, bred resentment even where American charity and the American tourist were most in evidence. In non-Western areas, men who knew virtually nothing else of the United States, knew of its imperfections. American tourists might be "ambassadors of good will" and try to change some of these opinions, but often their demeanor only confirmed prior prejudices and their irritated responses to irritable encounters made an impossible situation worse.

Moreover, it was impossible to separate national reputation from national policies and actions. No amount of people-to-people contact could spare the U.S.I.A. from the wrath of Near Eastern street mobs when American policies turned against them. Familiarity with America's more benign, cultural attributes did not make acceptance of American foreign policies any easier. A successful and generous operation like the Marshall Plan spoke with greater suasion than any propaganda alone could. The gradual warming of Indian-American relations during the 1950's was possibly due more to a growing, common enmity to Communist China than to feeble signals from the Voice of America or exhibits of North American folk art.

Still the preeminence of America made sensitive foreigners listen carefully for American slips of tongue. With instantaneous communication, an event in the United States or an action of the American government often seemed to erase years of careful programming. As a Chinese once remarked, "A whisper in Washington is a shout all over Asia."

With its limited resources, the U.S.I.A. was tempted to focus informational strategies upon narrow strata of elites, to try to influence the influentials. Notably in Asia, with its teeming multitudes, it seemed impossible to do much more. This approach to the elite rankled the populist sensibilities of some Americans. It worried others, particularly those for whom Communism was an ubiquitous giant, present at one and the same time in rice paddies and salons, in steel mills and in peasant hovels, delivering its propaganda in fluent patois. They feared that in dealing with today's influentials, we might overlook tomorrow's. The U.S.I.A. personnel who stayed in the cities might not, thereby, contract dysentery, malaria, and a hundred other diseases, but they might fail to establish essential cultural lines with elusive men of future power and possibly great faith.

The Americans' fondness for Tom Dooley and for the heroic, mythical *Ugly American* illustrated their search for essential human contact and friendship with other peoples. It showed a desire to share, albeit vicariously, their poverty, misfortunes, hopes and aspirations, and to make men who never had heard of America sympathetic to American ideals. To lose sight of these forgotten men was to lose sight of a central issue which many Americans believed was at stake in the cold war. Free societies needed rational men. Ignorant men could not constitute the mass of free societies. For lack of information about America and its purposes in world politics, a future world of free men might be lost.

No other instrument of American foreign policy showed the limitations of American influence in the ideological struggle for men's minds so publicly and so consistently. Exposed to incessant attack from American nationalists at home for insufficient militancy and parochialism, U.S. information programs could become the spokesmen of militant nationalism abroad as well. Expecting either too little or too much from such a limited weapon, many Americans were tempted to write it off as hopeless, or to impose upon it further impossible tasks.

The vicissitudes of American propaganda could be best explained by the contradictory and multiple virtues of the American people. How could the open society, whose government was no man's master, engage in foreign messianism on behalf of *American* values when its own appeal lay in its pluralism? Attempts to sell America and American foreign policy, moreover, were often resented by audiences who recoiled from such indoctrination. To cite one instance, the Eisenhower Administration's attempts to sell "people's capitalism" miscarried among those who regarded capitalism as anathema or as irrelevant to their own economic problems.

In short, was America too plural to speak with one certain voice? Was it too multi-faceted to be portrayed artistically as an ideal monolith of perfection, as Soviet propaganda portrayed Russia? As one American historian wrote,

> If the Lincolnian view [doubt about one's capacity to make a perfect world] involves us in the seeming contradiction of defending our institutions without insisting on propagating them, this is nothing but the contradiction within the idea of freedom itself, which affirms value but asserts it only to allow a competition among values. We must refuse to become crusaders for liberalism, in order to remain liberals. . . .[20]

An overly sensitive consciousness of the liberal tradition spoke poorly of the essential toughness of liberalism itself and its capacity to fight for its own principles. An excess of pessimism or realism, which depreciated America's capacities for rational suasion and watered down the essential message of the open society, could wreak havoc in a cold war where totalitarianism fought with ideological certainties. A callous or an overly sensitive parochialism, which relativized America's role in world politics and despaired of ever finding the essential messages of a free society could become the great conversation stopper, ending the dialogue about the meaning of freedom.

Because Americans had no overriding doctrine to inform the world of their message, it did not mean that totalitarians would triumph because they did. It frustrated those who, revering their country, tried to picture it as good, or better than, their own illusions about it. But diversity and freedom could, perhaps, prove as infectious as a national capacity to admit imperfection. When Adlai Stevenson, traveling abroad in 1953, was asked whether Senator McCarthy's voice was an "authentic voice of America," he replied that it was an authentic American problem. America's

[20] Daniel J. Boorstin, *The Genius of American Politics*. Chicago: University of Chicago Press, 1953, pp. 188-189.

authenticity lay in its problems and its accomplishments, both of
which a free society could afford to admit freely and display.

SUGGESTED READING

Barghoorn, Frederick, *The Soviet Image of the United States*, New York,
Harcourt Brace and Co., 1950.

Bundy, McGeorge, *The Pattern of Responsibility*, Boston, Houghton Mifflin
Co., 1951.

Graebner, Norman, *New Isolationism: A Study in Politics and Foreign Policy
Since 1950*, New York, Ronald Press, 1956.

Hilsman, Roger, *Strategic Intelligence and National Decisions*, Glencoe, Ill.:
Free Press, 1956.

Langer, William and Gleason, S. F., *The Challenge to Isolation 1937-1940*,
New York, Harper, 1952.

McCamy, James, *The Administration of American Foreign Affairs*, New
York, Alfred A. Knopf, 1950.

McLean, Joseph E., ed., *The Public Service and University Education*, Princeton, Princeton University Press, 1949. Especially George Kennan, "The
Needs of the Foreign Service," pp. 97-103, and Frederick Dunn, "Education and Foreign Affairs," pp. 121-143.

Stein, Harold, "Foreign Policy and the Dispersion of Power," *Public Administration Review*, XIII(3), pp. 196-201, 1953.

Eighty-sixth Congress, Second Session, Senate Foreign Relations Committee,
The Formulation and Administration of United States Foreign Policy.
A study prepared by the Brookings Institution, Washington, D.C.:
Government Printing Office, 1960.

THE FACES
OF DIPLOMACY

Dᴉᴘʟᴏᴍᴀᴄʏ ɪs ᴀ mode of tactful, civilized conduct gracefully smoothing the rough edges of competitive, sensitive societies and men. Chiefly, however, it is an instrument and procedure by which nation-states conduct their political affairs and other business among themselves while at peace. It is thus the legislative process of world politics. Power and force can establish or change equations of strength among nations, thus limiting diplomacy's influence. Power may enable a state to deal unilaterally with adversaries and neighbors at gun point, but diplomacy's object is to attain political agreement. Diplomacy maintains, repairs, or weaves patterns of orderly relationships and understandings among states. It communicates the nature of its national intent to others, and, conversely, discerns and comprehends theirs.

Through the myriad forms which diplomacy assumes today (secret and open; bilateral and multilateral; professional and amateur, etc.), it is the supreme legislative process in world politics. Today it transcends in importance the political activities of domestic legislative bodies in most states. It is impossible to point to any piece of U.S. Congressional legislation passed since the mid-1930's which matches in political significance certain major acts consummated by American diplomacy since then. The legislative process of international diplomacy laid out the designs for the Marshall Plan, N.A.T.O., and more recently, the Alliance for Progress. In these and other designs, Congress legislated implementing laws, giving flesh and energy to them; but the form arose from a diplomatic, not a legislative, context.

States may each claim sovereign authority over themselves. They may recognize no law higher than their own municipal law. But it is only through diplomacy that new systems of international order come peaceably into being and old ones remain viable. What legislature and legislator are to the internal processes of the nation-state, diplomacy and the diplomat are to the political processes *among* states. There is, however, this difference. The domestic lawmaker of the nation-state is the legal creator of law, while the diplomat (at least among constitutional polities) is agent of those who make policy and law. The diplomat is an instrument of policy, the honest (or sometimes dishonest) broker of international affairs.

THE INTER-GOVERNMENTAL WEB

Since the early seventeenth century, a complex mode of formal relationships has existed among territorial states. This has increased in complexity, but not in essential form. Intricate webs of criss-crossing diplomatic relationships among states remind us again that the most important agents of international politics are territorially based states.

For instance, if American domestic politics resembled this international system of politics, we would see, perhaps, a confederal system of territorial states, each paramount in sovereign authority, each maintaining formal relations with every other. Each state capital, were it Sacramento, Harrisburg, or Albany, would house forty-nine embassies and legations of other states, a total of 2,450 in all. Each state would possess its own foreign affairs ministry to deal with the others. All would seek, at least in peacetime, to conduct their political relations with each other by processes of political negotiation, treaty, and executive agreement. To be sure, some states, like New York and California, as populous and great industrialized powers, would dominate the scene. Others, like Mississippi, would be like small, underdeveloped countries with unstable regimes and a revolutionary potential. The swift rise of Texas to political importance might, however, threaten the equipoise of power within the system.

This analogy might be pursued indefinitely. It is used here merely to show, by exaggeration, the role diplomacy must play in the gestation of public policy in an international community of territorial states. To repeat, diplomacy conducts relations among discrete territorial entities which commonly acknowledge no higher legislative theater than that which governs their own territorial community. The loyalty of men, as well as their habitual obedience under law, is to this territorial community. For that reason, politics among states is cumbersome and ambiguous, less constrained by generally accepted customs, procedures, and law. The processes of politics function within a state through lawmakers in constitutionally designated political bodies. Externally, they are carried on through regularized channels of communication and negotiation, peaceably, through bilateral channels of diplomacy between individual states, and in a wider sense, through multilateral bodies and conferences which closely resemble the legislative bodies within the national state itself. War and diplomacy, treaties and executive agreements, custom and habit are international equivalents of domestic constitutional laws, legislative processes, and constitutional understandings.

In time of peace or no war, diplomacy dominates these international techniques; in time of war, instruments of violence are supreme. However, as military power has its role in the peacetime relations among states, so diplomacy does in war time. Diplomacy and war are not necessarily antithetical. Rather, there appears to be a functional division of labor between them. Both serve the policies of national communities. One serves them with the negotiatory skills and craftsmanlike intelligence of lawyer, reporter, and bargainer; the other, with strategic and tactical employment of force and the threat or use of physical violence. Both skilled diplomacy and war can achieve or avert political change. But neither can achieve the supreme end of all states without the other: to survive and flourish as entities of political order in a world where no higher political order exists. Diplomacy without power is powerless but force without diplomacy may be blind, inarticulate, and destructive.

Some political systems, like that of the Nazi state, exhibited a contempt for traditional diplomacy. It reduced diplomatic agencies to mere appendages of military power, and viewed all modes of international intercourse via established organizations such as the League of Nations as degenerate. Nazi diplomacy became the handmaiden of a savage military nihilism seeking to destroy the fabric of traditional European civilization and culture.[1]

The Historical Diplomat

Because of its unique political role, diplomacy has acquired professional status in the Western world and is regarded as surrogate for a non-existent system of world order. Even before the development of modern diplomacy, the diplomat was the messenger of one ruler to another. He received and transmitted information. As emissary, he was also imbued with the authority to bargain, negotiate, speak, and to represent. Although subject to the sovereign power of his own government, when abroad, he was

---

[1] This diplomatic transformation is described in my study of the German foreign office, *The Wilhelmstrasse*, Berkeley, University of California Press, 1954.

nonetheless its embodiment. His actions were endowed with special political significance. The rank and privileges accorded to him in his post also betokened the esteem in which his own government was held. As a symbolic presence of government, the diplomat's personal idiosyncracies might take on a representative character. Nothing he said or did publicly could be divorced from political significance.

Although the ambassador's duty to deal as agent of government to government set obvious limits upon his role *within* the political life of the country, the successful diplomat could move without friction in the circles where high policy was formulated. Doing this, he could exert influence, and elicit information for his government. If small groups of influential men governed the politics in the host country, then that diplomat was the more successful who could move with ease in such circles.

For such reasons, governments habitually made representatives of men possessing certain political skills which were not necessarily esteemed in the political processes of their homeland. In his assigned post abroad, a governmental agent was beholden to the sufferance of the regime to which he was accredited. Tact, subtlety, politeness, circumlocution, an even temper, the supposed qualities of the successful guest, were at a premium. Though an alien in a strange land, he must not be contemptuous of his surroundings; as stranger, he must not be too strange; as representative of his own nation, he must not demean or misrepresent it by eccentric behavior.

Moreover, as representative, he had also to represent the unique characteristics of his own culture. He could not, so to speak, fade into the cultural scenery of his post. As messenger and negotiator, he could never disavow his own government's high policy, even when it was displeasing to him. But as observer, he must be aware of the unique political problems of his locale, even when these contradicted the picture of reality in his own government's policies. These are the difficulties and challenges of the diplomatic profession.

And there were other problems. The professional diplomat lived between societies. He was caught in the vicissitudes of national rivalries and crises. He was committed to a lifetime of remoteness from the wellsprings of his own nation. Shifted periodically by the whim or administrative judgment of superiors from one mission to another, he was still obligated never to become alienated from the national purposes necessitating this curious life. If the psychic rewards could be considerable—the chance of involvement in high policy; the chance to observe a culture in a unique way; to act, observe, and report for his nation in the most implausible conditions—so, too, were the irritations and hazards.

Above all, there were constitutional and political constraints upon the diplomat. In its precise meaning, diplomacy was not statesmanship. Statesmanship was the art of managing the total affairs of state. Diplomacy served statesmanship and was subservient to it. It was an agency, not a creator. High policy was made by politically responsible executives. They had the ultimate authority, not those who were their eyes, ears, and hands.

Western diplomacy fitted into the structure of the modern state. At home, foreign affairs were the supreme responsibility of the sovereign or executive. Among the ministries of government, foreign offices ranked high. Among states which recognized each other, ambassadors and ministers were exchanged routinely. Embassies and missions became permanent pieces of furniture. In the nineteenth century and after, Western states commonly tended to professionalize their diplomatic services, which had once been haphazard arrangements according to momentary needs of state. Like other departments of government, foreign offices were hierarchically and functionally established to permit the orderly conduct of the intergovernmental transactions. Expertise in negotiation and representation called for special talents and training. Thus the foreign service became a specially trained and selected cadre of functionaries. Qualities such as truth, accuracy, calm, patience, good temper, modesty, and loyalty might be highly esteemed, but other quite specialized knowledge and skills were also required. These were the powers of perception and analysis; repertorial ability; a knowledge of international law, foreign languages, geography, history, and economics. If the main strategic object of diplomacy was normally to obtain something without recourse to violence, it was still the case that method and style were its paramount tactical strengths. Diplomacy was bureaucratized.

SECRET DIPLOMACY   The practitioners of diplomacy were regarded as normal elements of the international, political process. Within the European state system of the eighteenth and nineteenth centuries, politicians normally spent much of their lives as diplomats. The geographical closeness of the European states and the supreme importance of foreign policy, alliances, and political friendship to the normal affairs of politics, meant also that diplomacy assumed a natural and enduring place in the ordinary affairs of state. In such circumstances, affairs of state were normally enveloped in political secrecy. Even in the late nineteenth century, alliances among states were often known only to a narrow circle of officials.

Hidden from public view, and in many respects shielded by custom and constitutional understandings from parliamentary or popular control, traditional diplomacy troubled those men who were concerned about a popular consensus in foreign affairs and about the responsibility of diplomacy to elected, representative bodies. They were also worried by the making of such critical political decisions without normal public or parliamentary discussion.

But diplomatic secrecy also had strengths. It could often cool international animosities and insulate delicate transactions among states from the passions and misunderstandings which open, public debate invariably risked. To the extent, however, that diplomacy was hidden from public view there was a dilemma which democratic states were the first to recognize: namely, secret negotiation might possibly facilitate international accord and thus the presumed interests of the states involved, but if diplomacy were secret, how could such acts of state become legitimate without undermining the foundation of responsible government? If democratic governments were based upon a doctrine of popular consent to law, could popular consent be excluded from the realm of foreign affairs, which is responsible for war and peace? (See Chapters 7 and 8.) With Locke, one might assume that foreign affairs were qualitatively different from ordinary public affairs, that the special dangers of international politics, the risks of war, the need for swift response to new conditions, the universal climate of secrecy, all made democratic processes unwieldy. An open policy debate might serve the enemy by revealing in advance the intentions which secret diplomacy could often conceal profitably until the proper time. For such reasons, even representative government might justify concealing certain of its international activities and even purposes. (The Lockean executive of law in the international arena becomes the maker of law in world politics.) But the antagonism between diplomacy and democracy was, and remained, intrinsic and constant.

AMERICAN DIPLOMACY

Into this established condition of diplomacy the American republic intruded as the practitioner and advocate of a new diplomacy which jarred traditional modes of conduct. In the eighteenth and nineteenth centuries, its new diplomacy was juxtaposed to the diplomatic habits of the older, Western states. At the same time, there arose in the context of American political thought an enduring tension among three quite distinct, yet interrelated conceptions of what diplomacy was, or should ideally be. These three images of diplomacy were simultaneously to play upon American foreign policy in practice throughout the history of the American Republic. The tension engendered among them was recurrently aggravated by crisis and by the increasingly dangerous environment in which they each played a powerful part.

Until the mid-twentieth century, as we have seen, America's remoteness from the European seat of world politics and the strength it gained in isolation, had minimized the importance of diplomacy in the totality of American governmental processes (see Chapter 3). For European nation-states, diplomacy might spell the difference between life and death, defeat and survival. But aside from certain instances in American history (during the Revolutionary War and the early years of the Civil War), diplomacy seemed to have no comparable importance for the United States. So long as America's vital interests were confined to the Western Hemisphere and were paramount and unchallenged there, the principle of non-involvement in power politics elsewhere in the world diminished the importance of diplomacy to foreign policy as a whole. Diplomacy was confined chiefly to peripheral problems of territorial enlargement and mundane problems of economic expansion and trade. (See Chapters 2 and 3.)

Not surprisingly, it lagged behind the diplomacy of most European states in reputation, expertise, and political influence at home. On the eve of World War I, William Jennings Bryan, Wilson's first Secretary of State, seemed a bizarre parody of a general condition of diplomatic neglect. When the newly-elected President asked him to serve in 1913, the only objection Bryan raised to his acceptance was the possibility that he might be expected to serve intoxicating beverages. According to Graham Stuart,

> From the first moment, his waiting room was overflowing with political friends from all over the country seeking favors for themselves. He was left hardly a moment for Departmental business. . . . He had never been interested in diplomacy; and this made it not only difficult but actually impossible quickly to impart to him a conception of foreign relations.

One of Bryan's first messages to a diplomatic appointee, the Receiver General of Customs in San Domingo, read:

> Now that you have arrived and acquainted yourself with the situation, can you let me know what positions you have at your

disposal with which to reward deserving Democrats? . . . You know . . . how difficult it is to find suitable rewards for the deserving.[2]

(Bryan also indulged his earlier habit of stump-speaking on the Chatauqua circuit, for lecture fees. As the *Nation* magazine wrote, it was "outrageous" to see the "spectacle of the Secretary of State appearing nightly in company with acrobats and vaudeville performers of every kind. We . . . protest at a Secretary of State cutting short conferences with foreign ambassadors to rush off to little towns in West Virginia or Maryland to earn his $250.")

Not just the Secretaryship of State, but important embassy posts abroad were frequently, even typically, filled with amateur diplomats whose chief qualifications were wealth and a meritorious record of campaign contributions to the Administration party. Bryan might parody a condition (there had been competent and intelligent Secretaries of State before his time), but the condition permitted the parody with no disastrous consequences. (Bryan, dismayed and disillusioned by the outbreak of world war and by Wilson's efforts to adapt American policy to these complex conditions, only lasted in office for a year of it.)

The American foreign service was not placed on a firm, professional, career foundation until five years after World War I. However, career diplomacy continued to suffer long after that, until the 1940's, from the parsimony of a Congress, Executive, and public, which tended to interpret its enlargement and improvement as evidence of American departure from its doctrine of isolationism, which itself made diplomacy suspect. Perhaps for this reason, the profession remained outside the normal streams of American life. Most of its practitioners were recruits drawn from a tiny few of America's best colleges and universities. They were a small, exclusive circle of men whose relationship to the mainstream of American politics suffered from their incongruous role

[2] Graham Stuart, *The Department of State.* New York: Macmillan, 1949, p. 230.

as diplomats of a nation which deprecated diplomacy. As Harold
Nicolson wrote, as late as 1955, in criticism of American diplomatic
method and practice:

> The misfortune of the American system is that no foreigner (and
> few Americans) can be quite positive at any given moment who
> it is who possesses the first word and who possesses the last. Al-
> though the Americans in recent years have been in the process
> of creating an admirable service of professional diplomatists,
> these experts do not yet possess the necessary influence on their
> own government and public. The egalitarian illusions of the
> Americans—or, if you prefer it, their "pioneer spirit"—tempts
> them to distrust the expert and to credit the amateur. I am not
> just being old-fashioned when I say that the amateur in diplo-
> macy is liable to be suspicious.[3]

In still another respect, pre-World War II American diplomacy differed in style and purpose from its classic European counterpart. If democratic Americans from the beginning conceived
their nation as qualitatively better than the older states of Europe,
they aimed also for symbolic evidence of the fact. Republican
diplomacy should differ in style and appearance from the aristocratic diplomacy of the European powers. Amateurism and egalitarianism were to be displayed, even in clothing, to affirm the
representative character of a revolutionary political order. In the
early nineteenth century, the drab, Calvinist suits worn by American diplomats, even on ceremonial occasions in Europe, deliberately contrasted with the elegance of European court clothing. For
it was one thing for a diplomat to be an envoy of one king to
another. It was quite something else for him to be a representative
of one people to another.

The old diplomatists of Europe were often shocked by an
American republican diplomat who refused to conform to the
aristocratic court protocol. They were also shocked by the lack of
skills and expertise among their American colleagues. They had,
for the most part, been brought up and trained within the rigorous

---

[3] Harold Nicolson, "The Faults of American Diplomacy," *Harpers*, January 1955, p. 58.

milieu of cultivated Europe. They could speak the same *lingua franca* among themselves; the rigorous code of diplomatic behavior they had established among themselves seemed to undermine the informal amateurism of American representatives. Sartorially, at least, and as confirmation of the triumph of democracy, the American style ultimately triumphed. But in the beginning, simplicity of style and candor in all things were the qualities of American diplomats esteemed by their public at home, a public which was suspicious of elegance and ritualistic complexity.

Elegance was abhorred. If American chiefs of mission worked and lived, while abroad, in a luxury comparable to that of their foreign colleagues, they paid for it out of their own pockets, not out of the United States Treasury. A democratic America, which severely underpaid its government officials at home, could hardly have been lavish with its more distant representatives. If American prestige lay in its democratic suspicion of government and the abuse of power, this was enhanced by contrasting the opulence of "foreign" diplomacy with the more severe restraints of its American practitioners.

(One ironic consequence of this democratic frugality was that a diplomatic career, until recently, was far too expensive for ordinary Americans. Thus it was common for embassies in most important capitals to be run by wealthy men who could afford to pay the representational bills out of their own pockets. While American military command posts were normally given to men who had risen from obscurity, diplomatic command posts were given to men of inherited wealth or to successful bankers and businessmen. The embarrassing story of an American ambassador of modest income trying to make ends meet on a small salary can be found in *Ambassador Dodd's Diaries*, the account of Professor William Dodd's ambassadorship in Nazi Germany during the 1930's.)

In yet a third respect, American diplomacy was to be distinguished in style and purpose from that of the traditional diplomacy of Europe. From the beginning of the Republic, the nature of American democracy itself blurred the meaning of representation in diplomacy. European diplomacy had conceived the diplomat as agent either of monarch or of state to other monarchs or states. The American diplomat played a double, and sometimes bewildering role.

Constitutionally, if not also under international law, the American diplomat represented government and the American chief executive (who according to early constitutional understandings was the sole agent of the American Republic in foreign relations). But he was more than that, for here the Congressional camel pushed its head under the Executive tent. Foreign service officers, chiefs of missions overseas, even the Secretary of State, were all subject to Senatorial confirmation. Congress expressed populist designs on diplomacy. The diplomat was not merely a personal agent of a President. He was also an agent of the American people to other people. If he were, then should he not also carry with him certain typical, ideal qualities of the American as American? That American diplomat was truly representative who represented not merely governmental policy and purpose but also national aspiration and appearance.

Thus American democracy ushered in a new conception of diplomacy. It could be called populist diplomacy. It asserted, in essence, that the profession should conform to, if not also express, the egalitarian and democratic values of American society. It stretched the meaning of representation by demanding that diplomacy accurately mirror the alleged values of the national society itself. Not only should the diplomatic profession exemplify in its workings the procedural values of American society and politics: namely, open diplomacy, public diplomacy, truthful diplomacy. It should also represent, with some degree of sociological accuracy, the egalitarian traits of the ideal America itself. Unless some degree of sociological identity between diplomat and his idealized national culture made him the prototype of the *homo Americanus,* then a dangerous gulf would open between the foreign policy elite and the so-called man in the street at home.

The merits of this novel prescription were offset by its concealed vices. The charm of the ordinary man, and his competence as well, could be an antidote to the highly stratified cultures of the Old World, thus showing what the *homo democraticus,* like the American, could ideally become. A deep popular wish that the diplomatic service should exhibit abroad an undistorted (or at least favorable) image of the real America back home, reflected an optimistic belief that were this favorable image to get through to broad masses of people abroad, it might impress upon them the unique genius of American culture, its unaffectedness, its essential friendliness, democratic hospitality, unsophistication, and, above all, its supposed open honesty. If even a humane European like Goethe could say, "When I enter a peasant's cottage, I leave Europe" (i.e., leave civilization), the egalitarian American would make no such distinction. The image of a democratic America, incorporated in its diplomats, might thus work certain messianic purposes abroad, encouraging in the minds of foreigners everywhere a faith in the kinds of cultural conditions which could bring forth this kind of man. Minimally, it might dispel erroneous notions of what America was really like.

This populist conception of diplomacy contrasted sharply with the traditional diplomacy which had evolved through centuries of Western practice. The established canons of diplomacy stressed uniformities, not national particularities. It stressed, as Harold Nicolson has pointed out in his excellent book, *Diplomacy,* certain general and particular criteria for the character of the diplomat, essentially irrelevant to the unique qualities of the particular culture of the government which he represented. While perhaps resting upon a more universal democratic dogma, the populist claim became particularist and ideological.

The diplomatic profession required of its practitioners certain minimal, homogeneous standards. These were linguistic expertise; observance of particular supranational social customs; negotiatory precision; often, a talent for verbal circumlocution; circumspection; self-control; politeness; and a cast of mind which, as Nicolson wrote, was occupationally trained by experience to see politics and political issues in shades of gray, not black and white. The populist diplomat, if selected chiefly for his cultural and ideological representativeness, might thus fulfill his representational role whether he had these necessary qualities or not. As an American Senator remarked not long ago in opposing the Senatorial confirmation of an experienced career diplomat as Ambassador to Moscow, sheer dedication, not intellectual expertise, could carry the day against all the perfidies of America's diplomatic enemies:

> Only a mind reader could properly analyse the words and actions of those in the Kremlin . . . Personally, I think one realistic, patriotic, anti-Communist American could handle the Russians better than a boatload of Acheson's hold-overs could.[4]

The problem of populism versus traditional expertise could be expressed in the following conundrum: if the American were a diplomat, he could not be successful; if he were a successful diplomat, he could not be American. The nationalistic, populist picture of diplomacy was of a profession distasteful to decent Americans and common to cultures which possessed other undesirable qualities. Was American involvement in the complexities of diplomacy perhaps impossible then because of certain irremediable American virtues? Senator Albert Beveridge, an isolationist-nationalist of the Wilsonian era, put it this way:

> We have few trained diplomats to meet the finished professionals of old nations. So it has come about that, notwithstanding the great ability of our men, we have been beaten, with very few exceptions, in our more important diplomatic encounters.[5]

Thus the familiar stereotype of the diplomat, worldly-wise, experienced, cosmopolitan, affecting outrageous clothing and wines, depicted a way of life alien to the essential simplicities of

---

[4] *Congressional Record*, March 25, 1953, p. 2286. Remarks of Senator Styles Bridges, Republican, of New Hampshire.

[5] Albert J. Beveridge, *The State of the Nation.* Indianapolis: Bobbs-Merrill, 1924, p. 15.

American life. It engendered countless polemical cartoons of the Connecticut Yankee lost in the obscure jungle of elitist politics to which his national experience had never exposed him, or had caused him to despise. As the American humorist Will Rogers once put it, "Americans never lost a war or won a conference."

The Professionalization of American Diplomacy

The antagonism in American diplomacy, then, between populist and professional criteria has posed perpetually troublesome issues. While it has lessened greatly in the past few years, it did not necessarily mean that a more effective caste of diplomats was coming to the fore. The Rogers Act of 1924 placed American diplomacy on a firm professional basis for the first time. The Foreign Service Act of 1946 extended the principle yet further. The so-called "Wristonization" of the Foreign Service and State Department during the Eisenhower Administration fused the civil service functionaries of the Department of State and those of the Foreign Service.

Until the Second World War, the Foreign Service, for all of its more laudable qualities and contrary to the professed aspirations of an egalitarian democracy in world politics, had been quite unrepresentative of American culture. America was a land of many nations, but before 1939 the Foreign Service was predominantly Protestant Anglo-Saxon. America was transcontinental, but the Foreign Service was recruited chiefly from Eastern universities. Culturally, America was Main Street; the Foreign Service, however, drew its officers from the urban, college-educated, cosmopolitan strata of society. Ironically then, in a nation which had traditionally little need or want for diplomatic skills, the old Foreign Service was simultaneously criticized for being unrepresentative of America and for trying to be like the representatives of the international profession of which it was a part.

The sharp, cutting edge of populism has been softened by time and political change. The parochialisms of American political life which once gave rise to it are beginning to disappear. If the diplomat was once suspected of being un-American or aristocratic, we might bear in mind that America's recent rise to great power has blunted the traditional populist animosity to European culture. The populist suspected the European homeland of greater power, subtlety, and influence than its own and the animus came from a deep sense of isolation, an inferiority in social skills, and an ambivalence toward those who had them.

Then, too, the sharp lines which once separated the wealthier Eastern quasi-aristocracy, which furnished the greater part of America's career diplomacy, from the broader American public have been blurred by significant changes in American culture since World War II. For one thing, more people were being educated. If the professional diplomat has frequently been accused of harboring an un-American intellectualism, the great increase in prestige of the life of the mind and of disciplined, professional training has, to that extent, lessened the prior antagonism between intellectuals and anti-intellectuals in American culture.

Finally and particularly, the sociological character of American diplomacy has been greatly changed during the past two decades by numerical increase in the personnel, the breaking of the old Ivy League monopoly on diplomatic training, and the deliberate search for diplomatic careerists from once under-represented regions and once under-represented cultural groups in American life.

The Integrated Diplomat

A third aspect of American diplomacy could be called, for want of a better description, the other-directed face of modern diplomacy. It is frequently invoked by advocates of excellence and effectiveness in contemporary American diplomacy. The professional-traditionalist image stressed technical, negotiatory competence, conformity to the known usages and amenities of a cosmopolitan world, a knowledge of history, literature, and the arts, and an awareness of the ambiguities of encounters among civilized men. The populist image of the diplomat demanded that, in some degree, he reflect the national culture which he represented, either its supposed ideal manifestation or its sociologically real one. But the third and most recent idea was that the diplomat seek to integrate himself into the foreign environment in which he happened to find himself, that, indeed, this capacity for integration was, somehow, the key to effective diplomatic performance.

At first glance, this new, third criterion of diplomacy would seem to resemble the first two. The traditionalist conception had also suggested the need for such adaptiveness, the need to soften the more unique national parochialisms of human nature and to tolerate the perplexing world of cross-cultural relations. The populist conception of diplomacy, too, had a certain resemblance to this new one for it had stressed the common touch of the American democrat, his ability to break through the caste barriers which had long divided the world of culture from the mass of ordinary men. The democratic American, so it was said, had no compunctions about crossing this barrier of race and class.

Yet during the cold war, as America's overseas establishments proliferated and their activities and functions cut deep into other societies, the problem of harmonious integration increased in importance. There are today more than twenty-five thousand civilian Americans overseas, engaged in governmental work which directly or indirectly bears on American national purposes. To them could be added the hundreds of thousands of American tourists who go abroad every year for work or recreation. The sheer mass of overseas Americans created a baffling problem of public relations for a nation which was more experienced in importing than exporting human beings. But the intricate nature of America's involvement in the culture and politics of other nations added an extraordinary new dimension to diplomacy itself. It raised certain questions about the meaning of the term. The limitless variety of activities in which these overseas Americans participated, brought them into continuous contact with nearly every aspect of life in foreign cultures in which they lived. What they sought to do, how "what was done" was perceived and judged locally, necessarily cast reflections upon the larger context of American policies.

It was not merely the increasing mass of overseas Americans which created the problem. There was also a growing uncertainty in America itself about the necessary depth of the institutional and cultural context within which diplomacy should proceed, and a heightened awareness of the psychological and anthropological dimensions of human encounters which the new social sciences provided. Finally, there was a growing uncertainty about the necessary skills and psychological attributes of the diplomat himself. Once diplomacy was defined as the art of negotiation among princes. Now no such narrow and exclusive definitions seemed possible. Traditional systems of politics were collapsing; technological improvements in communications enhanced the ability of the nation-state to penetrate to the core of foreign political societies. The subject matter and the technical complexities of negotiation enlarged as did the realm within which purposeful diplomatic encounters took place. Mass democracy, nationalism, and revolution were to transform diplomacy into an all-embracing process of political and cultural relations. Thus again, the collapse of traditional categories seemed to threaten the meaningfulness of diplomacy itself.

These were problems of living as Americans in a pluralistic universe, where the older patterns of universal culture seemed suddenly swamped by the expansion of the international state system, the universality of conflict within it, and the multiplicity of political cultures with which diplomacy was to deal. Seized with the new task of strengthening the flood-walls against the spread of Communism and Soviet imperialism, American policy, of necessity, added new tasks to the older diplomatic duties. Harlan Cleveland, a political scientist and later a diplomat, described the contemporary role of the overseas American as "institution-building." To those who hold to this way of thinking, the art of overseasmanship should include the task of developing political and economic institutions consonant with values of a free society. This, in turn, should be meshed with the on-going diplomatic purposes of American foreign policy.

Nowhere was this task more difficult or more crucial than among the underdeveloped nations whose regimes and political institutions were fluid, often ephemeral, and laden with danger of subversion and collapse. Within this new context of diplomacy, the free Western world confronted the totalitarian states in a struggle for loyalty and, sometimes, control. In such contexts, the diplomat was to find local regimes and institutions changing constantly. Sometimes they were susceptible to directed change. Sometimes they were intractable. There were also other forces seeking to force change in directions antithetic to Western political values and thus to American security.

Under such circumstances, what was a diplomat? Should he be chosen for manipulative and managerial skills, for his capacity to deal with existing regimes and elites, or for his ability to work with humble men in obscure villages, building durable institutions and transmitting economic skills, and also building a picture of American purposes in world politics? The Russians and Chinese were the new diplomats, with revolutionary purposes. Too often the American found himself associated with the existing order of things, seeking to build upon what existed rather than to subvert or destroy.

The Russian antagonist seemed overwhelming. He was multilingual, accustomed and unashamed to deal with the masses, unconstrained by habit in seeking to carry the message of Communism into the deeper tissues of local societies. How far should the American diplomats imitate him, or his image? The questions were asked ceaselessly; the problem was intractable. The older conventions and usages of diplomacy seemed outmoded contrivances of a vanished world.

What criteria might be established to strike a balance between these three conceptions of diplomacy? Perhaps the notion of balance was absurd, yet clearly, some formula was needed, if only to make Americans aware of the vast complexities of diplomacy in a world where politics was a seamless web of conflict and cooperation. But the danger of the other-directed diplomacy was that if overly concerned with adaptiveness to local cultural conditions, with public relations, and with what other people were thinking, an inner capacity for judgment and purposefulness might well be lost in the jungles of a multi-cultured world.

To sum up, not until the cold war had Americans been forced to deal unremittingly with such a vast array of shifting and obdurate realities which diplomacy, violence, or withdrawal could not mitigate. Until well into the twentieth century, American diplomacy had been concerned with territorial and commercial expansion. Its theater of operations was confined chiefly to the Western Hemisphere. Diplomatic involvement elsewhere had always carried with it the option of withdrawal. "In or out" had always been a feasible set of choices. Set outside the system of world polities first by historical accident and then by conscious choice, American diplomacy had, at one time, been capable of a finite, self-centered realism and a universal moralism. Power politics was the unpleasant business of other nations.

The moralism of American diplomacy had been the more possible for its distance and detachment from those very areas where neither force nor diplomacy could solve political conflict. Then, uninvolved diplomacy could afford to deliver sermons on international morality and law. If American diplomats and Secretaries of State, like Bryan and Hull, delivered many such sermons to the weary diplomats of other countries, the moralism of diplomacy was the more pure for its detachment. A celibate priest can more honestly give advice on matrimonial troubles and the virtues of fidelity than an experienced divorcee, though the credibility of the advice is diminished by the giver's lack of involvement in the problem. Involvement accustoms men to ambiguity, just as it exposes them to the hazards and insecurities they entail. So, too, did diplomatic involvement. How to adapt and maintain the posture of candor, egalitarianism, and openness as well as democratic ideals in this very dangerous world, became the puzzling problem which American diplomacy suddenly confronted.

SUGGESTED READING

Brogan, Denis, "The Illusion of American Omnipotence," *Harpers*, December 1952.

Cleveland, Harlan, et al., *The Overseas American*, New York, McGraw-Hill, 1960.

Jones, Joseph R., *The Fifteen Weeks: February 21-June 5, 1947*, New York, Viking Press, 1955.

Kennan, George, *American Diplomacy: 1900-1950*, Chicago, University of Chicago Press, 1951.

———, "Training for Statesmanship," *The Atlantic Monthly*, May 1953, pp. 40-43.

Kertesz, S. D., "Reflections on Soviet and American Negotiating Behavior," *Review of Politics*, January 1957, pp. 3-36.

McCamy, James, *The Administration of American Foreign Affairs*, New York, Alfred A. Knopf, 1950.

Nicolson, Harold, *Diplomacy*, New York, Oxford University Press, 1952.

———, "The Faults of American Diplomacy," *Harpers*, January 1955, pp. 52-58.

Rubin, S. J., "American Diplomacy: The Case for Amateurism," Yale Review, March 1956, pp. 321-335.

Thayer, Charles, *The Diplomat*, New York, Harper & Brothers, 1959.

THE SEARCH FOR A
NATIONAL PURPOSE

> *. . . civilizations are not built by*
> *tapping people on the knuckles.*
>
> ALBERT CAMUS

UNTIL THIS POINT, we have both observed and used a picture of world politics centered, in a Ptolemaic sense, upon the United States of America. Ptolemy depicted the natural universe as one in which both earth and man stood supreme at the center of a universe whose other, lesser bodies circled them. Sun, moon and stars moved about this enduring point. Within this universe, the nearest things were also most central and most philosophically prominent. So we have regarded America.

THE AMERICAN PTOLEMAIC UNIVERSE

A Ptolemaic outlook on foreign policy, convenient as it may be for special problems of political analysis, confronts the very philosophical difficulties which faced the Ptolemaic world when Copernicus shook man's vision of an earth-centered universe. The

Copernican derangement of man's cosmic self-confidence matches the derangement which we now experience nationally. Today, men with good reason doubt the sufficiency of protection afforded them by the finite territorial states which continue to shelter them. This is a commonly shared condition. In a world of over one hundred states and three billion people, the United States is only one national entity, and its people barely six per cent of the world's swiftly growing population. Foreign policy makers naturally try to relate ongoing enterprises and designs to a touchstone of national interest. This remains their constitutional responsibility. But we easily discern limits to the analytic and philosophic sufficiency of a purely America-centered system both for comprehending world politics, and for justifying and shaping American action within it.

Before considering these limits, however, we recall that the search for popular consent to specific policies is much more than a mere constitutional requirement of national action. This search is also for human resources with which to energize purposes. Policies which lacked adequate approval from dominant groups in American life would never attain their ends. Ironically, then, it still seems easier to gain popular consent to policy by evoking this Ptolemaic picture than it would be were statesmen publicly to point out its insufficiency, publicly to admit both America's lesser role in the universe and to stress the larger human ends which national policy-makers must now necessarily seek to attain.

For at least twenty years, several concepts about the essential center and the nature of the community on whose behalf American foreign policies might be employed have interested and concerned students of foreign policy. One, this older Ptolemaic concept, still pictured the center of concern as a continental America. About this national universe circled a world of movements, events and states; policy, responding to that world, addressed itself to this central reference point, the national community, for justification and for approval. America pursued its interests with power, force, and diplomacy, seeking either to safeguard or to extend the realm within which American authority and influence might prevail, and the nation be safeguarded.

Insofar as this concept informed the actions of American diplomacy, it resembled a traditional statecraft *Realpolitik* of European thought about foreign policy. But there were two uniquely American differences. One was that the American political universe was democratic and liberal, not autocratic or totalitarian. Policies undertaken on its behalf, then, presumably corresponded to the aspirations of free men, rather than merely to those of closed aristocratic classes, monolithic state bureaucracies or totalitarian movements. Corresponding more closely to the general will of the public, policy corresponded, for that reason, more closely to democratic principles themselves.

The second concept was that of the traditional European *Realpolitik*, which portrayed the international universe as one seamless web of states, all equally affected by the nature of the entire system, equally involved in its conflicts and tensions. Within it, shifts of power might affect the paths of movement and the actions of states; but the supposed laws of the system, embodied in the balance of power, acted to prevent its domination by any one power. For most of the nineteenth and twentieth centuries, however, isolationist America acted as though the United States were substantially exempt from such a system. The subjective historical experience of America in the nineteenth century led many Americans to suppose that the laws governing the behavior of states in this system were not necessarily binding upon the United States. America could remain outside the society of nations and the balance of power if it chose to do so. Its acceptance of them was a matter of choice—"in or out"—and this choice might be to reject involvement and commitment.

This belief that the United States was uniquely exempt from constraints and demands of an international society of nations was not, strangely enough, erased even by the sudden experience of involvement in World War II, nor by the cold war. The switch from political isolation to total involvement in world politics which took place between 1940 and 1947, was a switch from strength and relative security in isolation, to temporary preeminence in involvement. In only seven years, America moved from a position of detachment from the society of nations to a position of central involvement and brief supremacy in it. Thus, America's traditional Ptolemaic concept of self, plausible in earlier days of its hegemony within a continental realm, seemed, in the first years of a much broader political and economic hegemony, still pertinent to a world where American influence and power suddenly radiated outward into Europe, Asia, the Pacific, and Africa.

To this day, some Americans continue to think that a desirable system of international politics should be an American-centered one: a network of alliances, alignments, and economic arrangements radiating outward from the Western Hemisphere, and confronting the Soviet-dominated world in a bi-polar contest of global dimensions and apocalyptic possibilities. Since that opposite pole of totalitarian power was repugnant to American political values, then a supreme purpose of American power in world politics was to be that of destroying, transforming, or at least containing its strength. Thus, much of the nationalist spirit which before World War II had been invested in the older idea of an isolated, autonomous American democracy, might easily reconcile itself to this new condition and posture of an America as the center of an enlarged universe of power and influence, acting as deputy of other nations whose survival or recovery depended upon this hegemony. The idea of a paternalist free world, which this American hegemony seemed to make plausible to many men, was by no means a self-evident one. Some Americans, for instance, defined it as an ideal international community within which specific, even rigid conceptions of social and economic organization might prevail—the free-enterprise system, for instance. Others might define it more loosely; the criteria of political and social freedom were susceptible to many variations. But the idea itself was still that the survival in freedom of Western and many non-Western societies depended upon the power and strategic policies of defense which only the United States, in the last resort, could provide. America, so it was said, was responsible for this enlarged realm of political and cultural freedom; American power safeguarded it.

The Reconciliation with Europe

That was one way of looking at world politics in the cold war and the thermonuclear era. Yet as the older order of world politics collapsed, between 1940 and 1945, so also the minds of some urbane and civilized Americans became absorbed in a quite different conception of the desirable nucleus of authority, power, and culture in world politics. They saw the central locale of modern culture and politics not in America alone, but rather in a vastly enlarged nucleus of Western nations, an Atlantic community embracing America, Canada, Britain and the West European democracies. Most of these nations lay athwart the North Atlantic region. For such men, this desirable Western universe perhaps had no necessary center, no Rome to which all roads led. Rather, it found an essential unity in quite diverse historic facts, experiences, and values which the European world commonly had experienced and come to value greatly.

This novel idea of community, in the late 1940's, might have seemed an implausible artifact of wishful thinkers. Twice in twenty-five years, the North Atlantic area had been torn apart by internecine wars unprecedented in their savage destructiveness. The second of these, between Hitler's Germany and the Western democracies, had not been just a war among discrete national entities (as the first had been), but among European political and cultural movements, vested in particular states, which were waging total war upon each other. Under Hitler, Nazi Germany had sought not only to conquer but to transform Europe. It had attacked all of the modern, and many of the traditional, political institutions and ethical values of Europe. The onslaught had commonly been against conservatism, liberalism and socialism. In the name of German cultural supremacy, National Socialism had attempted to destroy the cultural multiplicity and plurality of European civilization. In the name of order, it tried to subdue all of Europe to German control; in the name of totalitarianism, finally, it sought to subjugate Germans and all Europeans to a political movement and process which denied all constitutional restraints upon political action, and which imposed, briefly, upon Europe the limitless ambitions of an ethnocentric romantic movement.

Yet the idea of a North Atlantic community, after World War II, was not wholly implausible. Hitler's attack against Europe, and his ultimate failure, unintentionally accomplished three results: the political collapse of continental Europe, both before his own armies, and before its democratic liberators in 1944-45; a common resistance to totalitarianism throughout nearly all of Europe, and a reconciliation of the antagonisms among socialist, liberal and conservative Europeans, all of whom experienced his atrocities; and third, a brief supremacy of American military and economic power in Western Europe. If a common terror of totalitarianism reconciled Europeans to each other, so also their common condition of chaos in 1945 turned them westward toward America for economic and political aid in reconstruction. Militarily helpless, in the face of suddenly approaching Soviet power, and exhausted in conflict among themselves, the European states in the late 1940's accepted the umbrella of American military guarantees against aggression, and of American aid to restore their economies. Under the shelter of these twin elements of aid, the Atlantic Community idea first took tangible shape. American military hegemony of Europe not only came to serve as shield against Soviet power, but also, implicitly, as protector of Europe against itself, to prevent Western Europe's domination by any one European state. This distant trusteeship, never explicit yet tacitly accepted even by many Europeans who disliked or distrusted America, served as a benign Hobbesian Leviathan, enabling Europe to come to terms with itself; for rather than threatening Europe with terror and punishment, American power at once reduced Europe's fear of Stalinist expansionism and diminished Europe's own fear of itself.

In these surprising circumstances, the idea of Western unity, a persistent theme in European political history, not only revived but flourished. At a moment in time when nearly all European nation-states lay weakened from war and exposed to Soviet incursions, the idea of a Western Europe linked to America seemed both realistic, and a fulfillment of earlier aspirations to unity common among conservative, socialist, and liberal European thought. The link to a multi-European America served also to diminish the national tensions present within Europe. The new community could be deemed historically factual in that its nucleus of power, politics, and culture had, for a very long time, stood for traditional power and authority in the whole modern world. Moreover, America seemed simply an extension of Western civilization. America had been a proving ground for Western concepts of politics and ethics. It could be portrayed not as a new order of things but as a laboratory to which Europeans themselves had gone to experiment with political ideas too novel and grandiose for Europe. This Western idea embodied cumulative traditions of civility, certain aspirations of political freedom, constitutionalism, and Judaeo-Christian religious values.

The concept of such an existing desirable political universe did not deny to America its own specific interests nor assert that American national interests, necessarily and at all times, had to coincide with a transcendent, *Western* set of interests. (Who, in fact, might determine, from day to day, what these might be?) What it meant to those favoring this conception was that American traditions of civility could not long survive if the rest of this Western community were lost. They could point to historic, ethno-cultural, religious affinities between America and its European neighbors and, in practical fashion, to the great resources of industry, manpower, and human skills which this amalgam of Western societies contained. They could point further to the strong European constitutional political forces which, having survived European fascism, were firmly rooted in the social structure of each society, mutually reinforcing the total strength of freedom and civility in them all.

Looking back two decades, we see that America's political reconciliation with Europe commenced with the collapse of Republican France in 1940 and culminated in 1949 with the ratification of the NATO treaty. During this decade, beginning with Hitler's conquest of Western Europe, U.S. foreign policy makers began the design of an order of Western politics which no single intent, no one treaty, no one international act either brought into being or overtly proclaimed. This emerging order, however, was no less real for the absence of a definitive constitutional act. Such an act might, perhaps, have damaged the emerging order. Those engaged in constructing it included many for whom the larger historical implications were not clear and who saw the emerging Western community of nations as necessitated by temporary, strategic, military considerations. Most Americans and many Europeans, too, would have shrunk from the idea of a new community in the making if the choice had been posed unambiguously.

Cold war necessities spurred this process. At no particular moment in time was a Western political community proclaimed in the Western world. But by the 1960's, after two decades of intense involvement in Europe's politics, behavior and custom made it clear that U.S. power and influence were more closely identified by American policy makers with the security and welfare of America's Western European partners, allies, and even nominally neutral states such as Sweden, Ireland, and Switzerland, than with any other bloc of state or national communities elsewhere. NATO was symptomatic of this commitment, rather than its chief symbol. Military priorities for the European theater in World War II; preferential economic and military treatment for Britain in wartime and for Western European democracies in post-war emergency relief and rehabilitation; the Marshall Plan; American attempts, after 1948, to hasten Western Europe's political, military, and economic integration: these all clearly showed America's feeling of involvement in a "Western" society of nations.

Countervailing tendencies were at all times apparent in American policies, setting limits to this merger of American and West European interests and communal concerns. Not the least of these was the consistent thread of political "universalism" in American policies, expressed in American support for the United Nations and its principles of collective security. As the Suez crisis of 1956 showed, there were limits to American support of its Western allies when their policies contradicted explicit provisions of the U.N. Charter. Furthermore, much as American policy makers now pressed for Europe's integration (exhorting its Western allies to merge their economic power and, briefly, during the early 1950's, to merge even their military power in a European Defense Community), America did not ask itself a most important question: what of its constitutional alignment with Europe in a formal North Atlantic Community?

WARTIME ALLIANCES   The shock of aloneness, the isolation with which Hitler's conquest of Europe threatened America in the early 1940's, had made Americans examine their nation's traditional posture of hemispheric isolation. The dangers posed by Europe's collapse in 1940 were not only military. How might the outside world have appeared after 1940, triply divided among the Nazi and Soviet totalitarians and the authoritarian militarists of Japan? America's isolationism until then had been predicated upon a distribution of power in world politics among far more benign rivals. Isolation had been detachment from a distant, conventional system of European civilized states, a system which Americans for a long time had regarded contemptuously as older and less dynamic than its own, yet still capable of converting to democratic conceptions of civility.

America had often lectured this old Europe on its political shortcomings, on its wars, its perpetual failure to reconcile divergent nationalist and ethnic forces, and its need to integrate itself into an economic common market, analogous to that which had made possible America's domestic abundance. But in 1940, Hitler's and Stalin's joint division of Europe raised the specter of a far different constellation of power and cultural force in Europe and its surrounding territories—two new orders confronting America, shackling the whole European orbit of civilized communities to the domination of totalitarian powers.

In 1940, only a utopian could have retained faith in America's capacity to resist indefinitely the ideological encroachment of totalitarianism if the Americas remained the only enclave of constitutional democracy in the world. In a quadripolar world of the United States, Nazi Germany, the U.S.S.R., and a militaristic Japan, hemispheric America might have briefly been spared the dangers of military assault. Through *Realpolitik* alliances with one or several of these regimes, America might have perhaps indefinitely retained its formal independence. Transforming the nation into a garrison state, United States military power might have compared favorably with any one of these other totalitarian powers. But America's philosophical and political strength would have been lost through the conquest, enslavement, and totalitarian *Gleichschaltung* of its European "homeland."

In the 1940 crisis, we recall, the reconciliation of America with Europe began as a reconciliation with England. Roosevelt supported the British resistance to Nazi invasion with the following: arms shipments, Lend-Lease, diplomatic collaboration between himself and Churchill; the Destroyer-for-Bases deal (1940); the Atlantic Charter (1941); convoying supplies in American warships across most of the Atlantic to England, and the decision to wage limited war against German naval vessels in the Atlantic. All these individual acts had, by the fall of 1941, brought Anglo-American purposes into close concert. What doubts Americans had about this commitment to the defense of Britain were resolved by the course of events: the Japanese attack on Pearl Harbor and Hitler's ensuing declaration of war on the United States.

This dramatic reconciliation with Britain unleashed, in time, a great debate within American politics between, on the one hand, a minority of pacifists, isolationists, hemispherists, and their allies in German- and Irish-American circles, and the Administration, leading a dominant, interventionist public, on the other. In 1942, this Anglo-American rapprochement congealed into a powerful strategic wartime alliance. American military strength was focused primarily upon the European theater and the Pacific war against Japan was relegated to a holding operation.

Roosevelt's decision to liberate Europe first, then to defeat Japan in Asia, had far-reaching consequences. The bulk of American military strength was placed in Europe. After the Normandy invasion of June 1944, American power advanced the frontiers of a redeemed Western civil polity to the heart of Central Europe, where they were to remain. In the Far East, largely as a consequence of this basic geographic allocation of power, the war was subsequently won. An overwhelmed Japan was incorporated into the sphere of constitutional democracy. Nationalist China, inadequately aided both politically and militarily, became the neglected child of wartime resource allocation. Large parts of China, overrun earlier by Japanese, fell into Russian hands in 1945. Much of the rest remained in Chinese Communist hands.

In liberated Europe after 1944, American authority and military power facilitated the construction of democratic parties, trade unions, and visible constitutional authorities; not so in China. Here, lack of comparable strength set severe limits upon U.S. influence either to check the spread of indigenous Communist force or to correct the corruption and political weakness of the Chiang Kai-shek regime. Republican China's collapse in 1949 can be seen, in part, as a delayed consequence of a basic, if never explicit, American political decision taken in 1940: namely, to face across the Atlantic, to confront first the crisis of the European order, and to deal with Asia later.

(Many Americans who, in 1940, loudly opposed United States aid to Britain and the Western powers in the war against Germany, were those who, later, indicted the Roosevelt and Truman administrations for their failures in the Far East after the war. There is thus a close, clear, historical connection between the America Firsters of 1940-1941 and the China Firsters of the 1960's. Both of these elements, in their respective eras, were strongest within the Republican Party, weakest within the Democratic Party. At no time were they able to capture control of the top leadership of the Republican Party, which joined with Roosevelt and Truman on the basic issue of setting European priorities on American resources.) Clearly, if U.S. aid programs and the fiscal allocations which made them possible were one test of this basic European orientation of American resources, geographical priorities were apparent. Between 1940 and 1947, a period encompassing the second World War and the early stages of the European aid program, well over $35 billion of U.S. economic and military overseas aid went to Britain and to other European nations. Barely $500 million went to Latin America and only $1.5 billion went to China. Ambitious politicians later were to debate the prudence of this set of priorities and this direction of American purpose. Yet there were reasons enough for it. Americans *were* transplanted Europeans. In time of universal crisis, American affinities proved closest to Europe, not to Latin America or to Asia.

The preoccupation with Europe's liberation and subsequent recovery and defense meant more than the insufficiency of American resources in Asia. It meant also a neglect of traditional Latin-American interests. The idea of Western-hemispheric solidarity, which F.D.R. had made moderately popular in the late 1930's at home and in Latin America, rotted in neglect for some twenty years. In the late years of the Roosevelt New Deal, during the twilight of U.S. isolationism, much had been expected of Roosevelt's Good Neighbor policies, which were essentially to strengthen democracy in the Latin-American republics and to aid economic reform and growth. Perhaps, if the United States had chosen to stay in hemispheric isolationism in 1940, there might have been a cultural and political rapprochment among the countries in the Western hemisphere. The European war and America's shift of attention away from the hemisphere diverted most interest from these problems.

Save for an incongruous array of American business firms, investors, tourists, gamblers, gangsters, and scholars, most U.S. citizens developed no interest in or sense of affinity with Latin Americans. A vast cultural gulf divided them. North America was chiefly Protestant, Latin America was Catholic. North Americans were chiefly Northern European, with strong ties to England, Germany, Ireland, and Central and Southern Europe. Latin America's ties were with Spain and the Mediterranean. The United States was prosperous and powerful; Latin America, weak and poor.

Briefly, Roosevelt's New Deal had sought to fashion inter-American affinities of purpose in the hemisphere. But the Yankee attention span was short and Latin American relations suffered from the neglect. Local tyrants and political gangsters, collaborating with local, powerful, U.S. private economic interests, with rich latifundists and wealthy industrialists, dominated Caribbean politics and those of the northern states of the Southern hemisphere. Concerned with restoring Europe's prosperity and strength, the United States, between 1945 and 1955, devoted little foreign aid and even less intellectual interest to the impoverished lands of the Western Hemisphere. By neglect, not deliberate choice, it tolerated dictatorships which had even less interest in solving the social problems of the continent. Castro's totalitarianism catalyzed America's renewed interest in Latin America in the 1950's but chiefly, and perhaps unfortunately, because Castroism was widely regarded in America with fear.

THE DEBATE ON GOALS

America's turn toward Europe to establish a new trans-Atlantic community was not widely understood or approved by Americans or Europeans at the time, although particular aspects of this policy were, in time, accepted by both. Some isolationists saw in it a surrender of American purpose to the interests of Europe. To them, involvement meant not just the loss of American autonomy but the capture of American resources by Europeans for their own purposes. This point of view was an oversimplification. It assumed American vulnerability to European influence. It overlooked Europe's bankrupt political state and the enormous growth of American influence in Europe. It overlooked the dependence of a fragmented and still devastated Europe on America for military security and it was blind to the decisive role which skillful American diplomacy might play in Europe in diminishing separatist European nationalisms.

American interests obviously did not coincide with those of any one European state, nor even with the totality of interests among those states. Even the intimate ties which bound the United States to Britain during and immediately after World War II did not mean a concert of Anglo-American purpose concerning the politics of Continental Europe or the shape of the post-war non-European world.

What limited America's pro-European orientation and its merging of identity in a nuclear West was a continuing hemispheric isolationist impulse. Conservative nationalists in America set bounds on the nation's involvement in Europe. However, even as they conceived of America as the center and fulcrum of the free world, most of them acknowledged the need for allies in the cold war.

Many of these conservative nationalists saw the cold war as a struggle between American and Communist power and values. Seeing the world crisis thus, integral nationalists conceived America's essential purpose as that of extending the realm of *unique* American versions of politics, culture, and economics. Those nations most receptive to such American values were regarded as "eligible" American allies. Those rejecting them were often regarded as Communists or fellow-travelers. An alliance system founded upon such conceptions of American supremacy would have been difficult to devise and maintain very long. It ignored the nuances of international politics. In Europe, for instance, there were few societies, governments, or influential political parties committed to the values of free enterprise. In Asia and Africa, there were none at all. Yet many conservatives saw the global conflict as between capitalism and communism, just as Soviet Marxists did.

To conceive of it as such was to weaken the very coalition of free nations which had been built up so laboriously. Wishing also to retain American freedom of choice in its defense policies, these conservatives continued to stress the priority of American hemispheric, continental interests over the multiple commitments and activities which the United States government had made to insure the security of forward positions in Europe.

A more significant inhibition upon America's merger with a bloc of Atlantic-European powers sprang from wholly different considerations. American influence in world affairs had been dissociated from the main current of European politics and history for much too long a period to be identified with all the practices, traditions, or historic nationalist ideologies of Continental Europe. Its liberalism pretended to a far broader applicability than did the political theories of most European nations. Among Continental European powers, only Republican France had ever proclaimed comparably universalist and democratic views about its unique culture and politics.

(Nineteenth-century French Republican theories of politics had spread as French colonial power expanded. Unlike the British, Germans, or Italians, French Republicans, in their attitudes towards French colonies, pretended to a political and cultural universality, a Gallic *mission civilatrice*. This purpose to transform colonial subjects into civilized Frenchmen fell far short of its mark by the time French colonialism collapsed in 1940. In a century, it barely managed to penetrate the thin layers of native cultures exposed to it in Africa and Southeast Asia.)

But even to the extent that this civilizing mission of Republican France had proved successful, it bore little resemblance to the more extensive, if more innocent, universalities of American liberalism. French Republicans had assumed that men could be neither civilized nor republican unless they became Gallic as well. American liberalism was quite different. Influenced by America's own revolt from external control, it affirmed the *national* self-determination, of "free men" rising against alien authorities. Furthermore, it held that the proper procedures of revolt should resemble those which Americans themselves had used in 1776: popular consent, arrived at in the open politics of democratically elected representative bodies and political parties. It cherished the idea of a community of democracies grounded in the public will as expressed in frequently recurring free elections. It trusted individual initiative in the free clash of ideas in public market places. The process by which new nations arose according to its theory was essentially Lockean: that is, men voluntarily engaged in the common construction of governments. Free men designated their legislative and executive authorities and held these authorities accountable to the ultimate sovereign, a rational citizenry. American liberalism looked forward to a future society of nations which would be composed of free men in free states.

Americans who retained faith in this ideal shrank from a too close association with the West. Although Western colonial power was beginning to give way against the pressure of Afro-Asian nationalism and social change, an America identified closely with a European or North Atlantic community would still have been identified with the European holding operation. Nations in revolt were constructing their own forms and modes of government to replace European authority and control. To some extent, an anti-European America might help hasten these changes, and thus derive some moral authority among non-Europeans—an authority which might enable Americans to influence the pace and direction which these changes would take. The shock of new independence from Europe certainly called into question the adequacy of Western styles of politics and government in countries where poverty, political anarchy, and little experience in self-rule existed. Little wonder, then, that some Americans, sincerely concerned with the future welfare and form of these new states, were willing to risk great offense to their European friends, if thereby America's advice to these new states, freed from association with the old imperialism, might appear the more credible and sincere.

Although America's pro-Western stance clearly showed a preference for communal association with other constitutional, democratic states which were part of the total culture from which America had come, this was hardly a comprehensive global strategy, or an enduring philosophical basis for American behavior in the cold war. It was difficult to derive from this preference any theory which might legitimize and give purpose to American policies in a rapidly changing world. Soviet expansionism and the ideological doctrines which both underlay and justified it, in a sense simplified this matter of American purpose. If U.S. policies continued to be in essence *responsive*, if their rationale were essentially defensive, they were at least easily understood, although they might be exceedingly difficult to implement. Indeed, this became quite clear in Western Europe during the cold war. When Soviet aggressiveness and brutality periodically hit their peaks, Western unity was most easily maintained. The integrity of the West was to some degree contingent upon this recurrent pressure from the East. Perhaps there was some truth in the axiom (which originated in the West) that Stalin had been the chief founder of West European unity.

America's chief difficulty lay in justifying such a monumental global undertaking to non-Western nations, whose sympathy, passive or benign neutrality, or close affinity of purpose were deemed essential to such a far-flung defensive enterprise. During the Dulles era, one may well have wondered whether the American government's constant exhortation and appeal to non-Western states to lend positive aid to this strategy of containment was either realistic (in its expectations of converting neutrals), or even necessary. The American concern with Soviet expansion was hardly shared in comparable degree by Asian states more exposed to it than America, not to mention those which regarded it as a remote problem, and a distraction from immediate political problems at hand. This was especially true among most of the Afro-Asian nations, which were absorbed in the 1950's in their own revolutions against Western rule, and their own attempts to establish viable political orders. But even in some Western nations, public opinion found containment a sterile and uncongenial doctrine, and viewed American concern with Soviet expansion either as a pathological obsession or a screen for America's own expansionist plans. How could a design for containment, which assigned a paramount role to America, escape the obvious criticism that it was really a design to augment America's own power for her own purposes? If containment were to work, and to persist in time as strategy, it required constant popular legitimation abroad, for the strength which might guarantee its success. Yet the military-strategic connotations of containment made little sense to men or societies remote from direct Soviet military threat, and themselves well aware from historical experiences that such threats were possible, also, from other sources as well.

Wanted: A Supranational Purpose

To justify this power, America also needed a supranational purpose. Could traditional American liberal thought supply it? Where could American statesmen find a purpose to sustain American policy? And even if some overriding philosophical purpose, adequate to the challenge, were to be found, could enough support for it be marshaled within American politics to sustain and harmonize it with American behavior in world affairs? Would the philosophy be "popular" enough to endure?

Wilsonian idealism was compounded of faith in the desirability and viability of democracy, of belief in open, civil societies, of support for national self-determination and universal collective security among such nations. Perhaps it could be utilized.

There were many Americans who were convinced that these purposes should be central to American foreign policy. But such aspirations which other Americans thought unrealistic, could easily
prove to be contradictory themes. For instance, self-determination, irrespective of who was determining what, did not necessarily coincide with democracy, parliamentarism, or civility. As
some newly liberated African nations such as Ghana quickly
showed, the repudiation of democracy and civility by new elites
might easily follow national self-determination. Moreover, in vio-
lation of principles of collective security, such nations as India
and Indonesia might well be aggressive and imperialistic in the
name of national self-determination.

National self-determination contained two contradictory possibilities as a philosophical basis of global, American cold war
aims. One was its philosophical, realistic, permissive pluralism.
The other was a doctrinal orthodoxy, closely associating self-determination with the substantive principles of civilized, constitutional, democratic politics. For example, if one assumes that Castro's revolution has thus far been very popular with most of the
Cuban people, the incongruity of these two conceptions of national self-determination becomes all too clear.

The constant vacillation of American thinking about these
possibilities was accelerated by events in the post-war world.
There were seemingly persuasive reasons to choose the former in
preference to the latter. In a world of heterogeneous states and
diverse social systems (the condition of the free world), America
might well exploit the universal threat of Soviet Marxist imperialism and its compulsion to impose ideological uniformity and
political totalitarianism upon those people who came under its
rule. In its response, America, as guardian of cultural and political
pluralism on a global scale, might profitably speak for a gentler
philosophy. If this were true, American policy might close its eyes
to the shortcomings of all non-Communist states. The various
regimes and cultures threatened by Soviet Communism could be
invigorated by a practical doctrine, a permissive self-determina-

tion. In line with this principle, America might refrain from imitating the Russians and their satellites in reshaping by force the societies which they controlled, in accordance with their own political and philosophical principles. Pluralism, manifest on a global scale, might avoid the pitfalls of doctrinal orthodoxy.

There were prudent arguments for such a policy. There were, to begin with, limits to American power and influence abroad. There was the matter of the appropriateness of open institutions to the new societies. By donning the messianic mantle of Wilson to make the world safe for democracy, America might actually be imposing, by imperialistic means, a deceptive façade of democracy upon a quite different reality. This kind of ideological crusade might be perilous in either success or failure. If success were achieved by force, propaganda, and mass suasion, wouldn't this violate the very pluralism one wished to encourage? And if failure were the result, wouldn't the anger and contempt which all people throughout history have felt for imperialist failures be shown against America, as it was after the Bay of Pigs fiasco? It would surely be ironic if liberalism, imposed by imperialist methods, made its own survival impossible because of the resentment engendered by its forceful imposition. (Squeamish as some American liberals are about America's capacity to impose democratic institutions on other nations, and about the philosophical problems involved in such "political imperialism," there are two instances where U.S.-imposed "democratization" surprisingly took hold and endured, in postwar Germany and Japan. After 1945, U.S. demilitarization and denazification policies in both defeated Axis states profoundly changed the structure of politics in both countries in the direction which policy itself desired.)

But even if this were a risk, how much of a virtue could one make of permissive pluralism? Speaking in its name, one might point out, to present or future subjects of Communist rule, the uncongenial and repugnant aspects of Soviet totalitarianism or its counterparts in other Communist states, particularly the social surgery which, in the name of revolution, forced all societies under its rule into the drab Procrustean bed of state capitalism. One might speak of the harnessing of culture to dreary Socialist necessities; the suppression of political dissent and cultural spontaneity; Soviet Socialism's congenital incapacity to establish a rational popular consensus for state policies, and the official and quite cynical claim that history legitimized the Communist party's monolithic rule over whole societies. Could not America, cherishing cultural, ethnic, and political diversity, refrain from imposing its own version of freedom upon others and, in the name of such diversity, act accordingly to diminish the appeal and power of Soviet Communism?

In Behalf of Pluralism

Was this possible? In a recent essay on America's national purposes, Professor William Langer of Harvard unwittingly, perhaps, posed the difficulty—America's vacillation between espousing the diverse values of a politically plural world and pressing for those of a constitutional, democratic one. Langer wrote:

> The United States . . . has *no thought of imposing the democratic system upon other nations.* [Italics mine.] It has long since abandoned the fond belief that it could, by its own influence and effort, make the world safe for democracy. For it now recognizes that many nations are for the present stopped by tradition, by poverty, by illiteracy and by many other factors, from rapidly transforming their present politico-social systems and abruptly adopting what for them must be an alien order. . . . In the free world of today there are almost as many variations in social and economic systems as there are countries. Such variations are not only acceptable, but unobjectionable, for in the last analysis no nation or people should be obliged to conform to patterns imposed by others.

Yet, in the following paragraph, he says:

> Americans . . . also believe that over the long term free institutions can survive only in the setting of a community of free nations. It must therefore be a prime objective of American

policy *to encourage, support and defend* [italics mine] those
forces which, in the present-day world, are working in the direction of freedom, equality, and representative government.[1]

Unless one drew a tedious semantic distinction between
"imposition" and "support of" freedom and democracy and representative government, which of these two quite contradictory
themes was it to be, or should they be regarded as a perpetual
contrapuntal theme of policy? A permissive pluralism might urge
that Americans regard the world of international politics as one
composed of quite heterogeneous, diverse political societies, whose
diversity was to be maintained. A political realist might find the
first of Professor Langer's paragraphs quoted above in accord
with his own particular way of looking at the world, since both
doubted the immediate possibility of establishing any significant
overriding political values among divergent political systems.

The suggestion of a permissive pluralism had no little intellectual merit. To accept it was also to adopt a quite empirical
approach to the vast complexities of politics. This was the empiricism upon which policy could rationally be built. Even those
who might, for sentimental reasons, prefer Langer's (let us call it
Wilsonian) second theme, could easily be made to admit the
pitfalls of accepting, as American purposes, goals which simply
lay far beyond known human capacities. As F. S. C. Northrop
pointed out:

> The most important development after World War II was the
> resurgence of the common people of Africa, Israel, Islam and
> Asia. This resurgence . . . bespeaks more than the insistence of
> the masses of mankind upon the Lockean-Jeffersonian-Lincolnian
> kind of right to run their own affairs. The resurgence is cultural
> and spiritual as well as material and instrumentally secular. Con-
> sequently they are insisting not merely on running their own
> affairs, and hence, democratically throwing out the traditional
> Hindu maharajahs, as in India, but also in doing so in the light

[1] William Langer, "The U.S. Role in the World," *Goals for Americans,
The Report of the U.S. President's Commission On National Goals.* New
York: Prentice-Hall, 1960, pp. 300-301.

of their own unique spiritual and cultural traditions. This means that, notwithstanding their acceptance and insistence upon what amounts to the classical United States Lockean-Jeffersonian-Lincolnian philosophy—that is, the right to run their affairs themselves—a United States foreign policy based on carrying Christian civilization and the American way of life to the world is doomed to generate the neutralism it has in fact generated, and likely to be self-defeating. In addition to their deep respect for and acceptance of the Lockean-Jeffersonian-Lincolnian component of the United States culture, the masses of men throughout the world have an equal pride in and respect for the different spiritual traditions of their own particular religions and institutions. Hence, only a national foreign policy based on (a) the Lockean-Jeffersonian-Lincolnian natural rights of *all* men philosophy and (b) ideological, religious and cultural pluralism can hope to succeed in the contemporary world.[2]

A pluralist attitude such as Northrop's might enhance a much needed empirical outlook on world politics in American statesmanship. Policy-makers who were conscious of great diversity in the world about them might better escape the traps laid for too zealous, overly doctrinaire men. An awareness of diversity and ambiguity in human affairs might prevent the moralizing and sermonizing which made Cordell Hull and John Foster Dulles sound, to foreign ears, like patronizing clergymen.

Unfortunately, Northrop's pluralism raised special difficulties. It was possible to be unduly sensitive to the multiplicity of politics and culture in other nations. By taking the world for what it seemed at any given time, by being tolerant of qualities in others which would be despicable in oneself, America risked tarnishing her own political principles. It was as risky and offensive to others to act as though Americans alone were talented enough to appreciate liberal political values as it was to impose them forcibly on others. To remain silent in the face of a Trujillo or a Castro left the field open to others who were quite well aware that universally formulated values appealed to the growing numbers of men every-

<hr>

[2] F. S. C. Northrop, "Neutralism and U.S. Foreign Policy," *Annals of the Academy of Political and Social Science*, July 1957, p. 58.

where who no longer regarded their small national universes as closed systems of political morality.

In adopting Northrop's view or Langer's first theme, then, America risked an ethical relativism which, though lauding the principle of national self-determination, stood otherwise silent before the qualitative differences among the many political and social systems in the non-Communist world. It was possible that such self-imposed detachment would lead to a paralysis of will and judgment when there was a conflict between such systems (as there was in the Suez crisis in 1956) or within one (as there was in Cuba and in the Dominican Republic in the early 1960's). Ethical relativism, moreover, could easily harden into a *Realpolitik* arrogance which denied the relevance of any yardstick of American policy to such crises save that of power or specific interests. Thus there would be no ethical issues but only current, U.S., strategic interests.

Surely the absence of any universally accepted consensus about common-law rules of behavior between nations or about optimal conditions of civility within them did not mean that ethics were totally absent or irrelevant. They existed, playing significant parts in all international crises, often decisive ones. During World War II, Stalin, to show how little he thought of the Catholic Church's influence on European politics, asked a Western statesman, "How many divisions has the Pope?" He lived long enough to appreciate that Catholic power could not be measured by conventional military standards.

George Kennan, urging Americans to acknowledge the moral and ethical diversity of world affairs, once wrote:

> Let us face it: in most international differences, elements of right or wrong, comparable to those which prevail in personal relationships, are—if they exist at all—simply not discernible to the outsider. Where is the right or the wrong in the Kashmir dispute? I am glad to say that it is not my task to seek it. . . . Morality, then, as the channel to individual self-fulfillment— yes. Morality in governmental method, as a matter of conscience

and preference on the part of our people—yes. But morality as a general criterion for measuring and comparing the behavior of different states—no. Here other criteria, sadder, more limited, more practical, must be allowed to prevail.[3]

The difficulty here can be seen by the logical extension of Kennan's thought. Pluralism and ethical relativism exhibit perplexity or waiver of judgment about all the actions and purposes of other states, insofar as they do not directly bear upon one's own. There is something appealing about this way of looking at things to persons of a melancholy cast of mind or to those whose job it is, like the diplomat, to confront disillusion daily. But as the touchstone of national purpose, at a time when traditional barriers to communication among peoples were crumbling, such waiver of judgment could be calamitous.

Pluralism and ethical relativism avoid judgment of the actions and purposes of other states at a time when the infractions of certain, necessary common-law principles of international behavior not only risk nuclear war, but sabotage the very rudimentary procedures—like the U.N. Charter's proscription of aggression—which might diminish its likelihood. Kashmir was one of innumerable instances where the relevance of a transcendent ethics was obscure; but this in itself was significant to the matter at hand. Was the question of whether Kashmir belonged rightfully to Pakistan or India, both constitutional polities, comparable, say, to the great issue in 1939, of whether Hitler or Poland should control Danzig? Or, to press the issue further, was it comparable also to the Nazi government's struggle with the peoples of Eastern Europe which followed?

Shunning value judgments except as they might pertain to the immediate necessities of American *raison d'état* or except as these arose from clearly perceived American interests abroad, pluralism and relativism pointed to the "reality" of an ideologically plural world. This point of view assumes, however, that ideolo-

[3] George Kennan, *Realities of American Foreign Policy*. Princeton: Princeton University Press, 1954, pp. 36-37, 49.

gies and interests in world politics arise from and pertain chiefly to discrete national cultures or states, one hundred or more Balkanized moral universes, each with its specific standards and canons of morality. But it is no longer true that ideologies and ethical norms are confined to territorial states or that they are carefully insulated from each other. The most vigorous ideologies of the twentieth century have not owed their origins to state entities, even though such entities might, and often did, become their theaters of fulfillment or betrayal. American liberalism, unique as some of its features appeared to North America because of its long habitation there, has no more been an exclusive product of America than Marxism has of the Soviet Union or Russian steppes.[4]

In the 1930's, thoughtful Americans saw Fascism's universal features too clearly to assume that they could condemn native fascists like Gerald L. K. Smith since their theater of operations lay within the confines of the United States, but abstain from censuring Hitler, since this was "foreign" and did not directly affect American interests. A too-tolerant pluralist had very little to say about universal human conditions save, perhaps, that coexistence was necessary among all existing territorial polities.

If the United States shrank from expressing moral judgment on the internal characteristics of other states or on their international behavior, would it not quickly lose, by default, whatever moral influence it possessed in the broader international society? To assume in realism's name that, in a world of more than one hundred states, one hundred flowers might spontaneously bloom, each according to its unique political laws, was also to overlook the mutual antagonisms which such global permissiveness promised. It also ignored the unreality of this picture of the world. For contemporary, ideological coalitions and communities of purpose

---

[4] Some environmentalists, like Frederick Jackson Turner, had sought to suggest otherwise of American democracy, accounting for its development as a result of the interaction between settler and frontier. Little credence is today given this aspect of Turner's thesis. See Henry Nash Smith's *Virgin Land*. Cambridge: Harvard University Press, 1953.

cut across frontiers; and the strength of governments in world politics (a quality which realists, and others, stressed) was now due, in large measure, to such communities of purpose. Treaties and *Realpolitik* maneuverings of statesmen might reflect a government's existence, but could not really give life to it.

In short, to overlook the significance of transnational appeals of democratic freedom and of Socialist totalitarianism except to the degree that these appeals strengthened states which made use of them overlooked an obvious fact of life; namely, that both totalitarianism and democracy arose from universal philosophical propositions to which realism could not address itself, because realism's touchstone was merely the assumed power, interests, and needs of specific nation-states or national cultures. Not to address American policies to these, or to other ethical standards or propositions of universal or transnational character, risked abandoning the fate of nations to others like the Communists, who had neither such fine sensibilities about intervening in the internal affairs of peoples nor self-doubts about remolding the philosophies of men.

A Context for Survival

The other, Wilsonian proposition of Mr. Langer poses difficulties because it asserts that since free institutions can survive only in a context of free nations, American democratic purposes in world politics both transcend national interests and safeguard them. This recurrent, idealistic theme, which, in earlier Wilsonian and Jeffersonian contexts of American history had been, rhetorically at least, aggressive, was now, in contemporary contexts, defensive. Even Langer spoke of "survival," not "triumph."

How extensive must such a community of free nations be? What were its essential peripheries? Could such peripheries be drawn along perceivable geographic lines as the frontiers of the Roman Empire and other great, extensive political communities were?

This became a serious problem for American policy makers in 1959, when Castro's Cuba became the first totalitarian state in the Western hemisphere linked, ideologically at least, to the Communist system of states. Though Perón's Argentina had manifested totalitarian symptoms, it had not been Communist and had no ideological affinities with non-hemispheric political systems save that of Franco's Spain.

How was "support and defense of those democratic forces" to affect American policies which assisted regimes possessing little ideological affinity for representative government or individual liberties (as did American aid to Poland, Franco's Spain, Yugoslavia, China, Saudi Arabia, and Egypt)? Economic or military aid to such states *might* be justified as a means to the end of greater American security. Through such aid, for instance, American military bases might be established to perform defensive functions deemed essential to cold war military strategies. In this way, also, the United States might seek to keep non-democratic states such as Saudi Arabia and its material energy products within the non-Communist orbit.

All these considerations had their defenders and much to recommend them as temporary expedients. The question was, however, like all such temporary means to ultimate goals, how did one establish the danger point at which means began to corrupt ends? To be more specific, at what point in cold war security considerations, multiplying as Communist military power increased, would American policy-makers simply lose interest in the internal character of regimes so long as these seemed to be pulling their own share of the military or economic weight in a protracted conflict?

Batista's Cuba and other Caribbean authoritarian tyrannies were classic instances where, at least in the context of Western hemispheric politics, the point was reached in the 1950's. Fulfilling military commitments to U.S. defense establishments and fulfilling their economic quotas to private American business interests, these regimes seemed perfectly acceptable to important

American policy-makers until, like Jiminez' regime in Venezuela and Batista's in Cuba, they were overthrown in popular insurrections. The same mistake was not made subsequently with regard to the infamous Trujillo regime in the Dominican Republic. In fact, the United States finally took the lead in isolating the Dominican Republic from the Western hemisphere's international system.

Wilson and other American reformist liberals had not espoused national self-determination as just a worthwhile principle of American foreign policy. Indeed, they had placed this quite high in the catalogue of American priorities. When Roosevelt, at his Atlantic Charter meeting with Churchill in 1941, included in their joint declaration the statement that all nations had the right "freely to choose" their own forms of government, this declaration was not a disavowal of interest about the political consequences of such choice. Freedom, for instance, did not include freedom to disavow political freedom or to waive permanently the right to the free, popular exercise of political choice in the future, as the German people had in their plebiscites of 1933. To Wilsonians, freedom had meant, at the least, a constitutional condition within a nation-state, whereby government was permanently to be based upon recurrent, systematic, popular consent through free elections. In this sense, freedom also meant freedom for citizens in fully organized, political parties to choose rationally among alternative public policies. And this, in turn necessitated, even in modern mass societies, a wide variety of conditions and institutions, such as a free press, freedom of assembly, freedom to organize political parties and voluntary associations, so long as these respected the constitutional rules of the game. Freedom also involved legal protection of the rights of constitutional opposition in political parties.

The ways in which such utopian principles fitted themselves into America interests and foreign policies was what was at stake here. Was this Wilsonian purpose a clarion call to reform the world which, in so doing, would necessitate slighting, or at least subordinating, the other interests of a free society? During the 1950's, when the United States had become the fulcrum point of a large coalition of states resisting the encroachments of Communism, this became a paramount issue for those concerned about foreign affairs. Then, realism clashed with utopianism in the academic as well as the political arena.

To such philosophic realists as Professor Hans Morgenthau of the University of Chicago, realism necessarily involved repudiating Wilson's universalist goals. These people saw power as the outstanding political fact in the real world. In world politics, this power was embodied in states and national entities. The most significant processes of world politics were the shifts and realignments of states-with-interests. To continue their argument, American power was only one among a number of significant elements within this total system. The purposes for which such power was to be expended constantly referred to these interests. To assume that the affairs of the world were conducted in any other way was to risk the evaporation of national power in fruitless, moral crusades with the subsequent demoralization engendered by failure. It also risked expending American power on behalf of international objectives, like a transcendent system of collective security, which were not operative, not a part of the collective common law of states, or not seriously respected by states, particularly when vital interests were at stake.

In such a world of constantly shifting power and influence, said the realists, the United States had to acknowledge the finiteness of its political influence and the perpetual need to join in common tasks with states whose political systems and ideologies were alien, or even antithetic, to Jeffersonian democracy. Finally there was the need to husband national power to achieve the kinds of basic economic and security bulwarks which an on going democratic society demanded, mundane and ideologically uninteresting as these might be.

To sum up, the higher morality of transcendent, universal purposes might temptingly suggest that all politics were grounded upon human rationality, and that such rationality could lead men commonly to acknowledge the need for the very international institutions and practices which liberalism espoused. But to the realists, politics were grounded in power and acknowledging this meant that the only reasonable referent points for national policies were national interests and a recognition of the limits of American influence in the total complex of world politics. They thought that such abstract, ideological goals as the attempt to "make the world safe for democracy" were not only bound to fail, but that granting them such a conspicuous place in the hierarchy of national purposes seriously endangered the actual security of the United States.

But there was an internal contradiction in this realist doctrine. To realists, utopianism was errant in that it ignored both power and interests or, at worst, employed idealism to attain impossible goals. But in denigrating the American utopian tradition in world politics, this view also deprecated the moral authority and ethical influence which this tradition had long held. Such authority and influence could be viewed as a quite special, often indispensable, element of national power. Surely this was true of the ideology which Soviet leaders used to legitimize both their own rule and further extension of the Communist orbit. An assault upon the Wilsonian tradition was, ironically, an assault upon one element of American liberal principles which had immeasurably added weight to United States influence in the world, at least since World War I. Not even a realist could deny the political influence of Woodrow Wilson during World War I, or that this influence had sprung from an authentic, philosophical commitment.

During the war and the post-war period of European revolution, Wilson had been the voice of Western liberalism. In the brief, yet surprisingly successful contest between Western liberalism and the traditions of Western civility on the one hand, and Bolshevism on the other, Wilson's was the only persuasive Western voice to speak authoritatively to the political conditions which confronted the peoples of Central and Eastern Europe. Much as one might reduce this element of philosophical authenticity to one of a number of elements of national power, how could its authenticity and influence be sustained in the long-range contest for the minds of men if, realistically, one merely regarded it as an instrument for something with far less widespread appeal—the narrower interests of a unique American polity?

Such doubts about American purposes in world politics and about the scope of the community on whose behalf these energies were to be expended were attributable to the collapse of the traditional, Ptolemaic mode of looking at world politics. Clinging to that continentalist tradition would make purpose dangerously parochial and would diminish the authenticity of America's voice in world affairs. This, in turn, would diminish American influence in the larger issues of world order and organization. In their own way, the new realists of the 1950's had tried to solve the theoretical dilemma posed by the collapse of America's traditional hemispheric security. In asserting the primacy of national interest and national power, they were, in a sense, Copernicans. However, their proposed substitute for a now bankrupt, ethnocentric view of world politics, turned out to be but an updated version of the tidy, traditional, eighteenth-century model universe, composed of states-with-interests, orbiting among themselves according to supposed quasi-mechanical laws.

This conception of world politics, however well it suited the classic, bygone world of the European society of nations, was clearly as insufficient as the nativist utopianism which it sought to replace. Realism simply could not cope with the fact that the older, Western political order of things had permanently collapsed, and that in its wake remained, outside the Soviet orbit, a pseudo-order of nation-states in dangerous turmoil and flux. The escalating destructive power of some of these states, and the Soviet Union as well, had long since passed the threshold where states and nations both could, in theory, disappear, unless national power and the disintegrative tendencies of revolutionary movements were subject to the constraints, usages and international controls of a supranational order.

THE PHILOSOPHICAL VACUUM

This uncertainty of American purpose exposed a most perplexing problem. Was it possible that the nature of contemporary America and its political system ruled out the possibility that American philosophical purposes could be developed and sustained at all in world affairs? American political theory, notably its liberal voice, had described the political order of America as essentially Lockean, best designed to permit within its realm a constant free jockeying among political interests, a constant search for mutual accommodation among the conflicting political pressures of a free society. In contrast to Marxism, there was here no overriding theory of history and no doctrinal certainty that things would turn out in specified ways. There was no commonly accepted, analytic yardstick by which to judge the ultimate significance of major political changes within other national polities. And finally, there was no overriding philosophy to guide American purposes abroad. There was only an overriding rationale of power which stressed the constant augmentation of American economic and military strength to match or exceed that of the U.S.S.R. and its satellites.

Perhaps then the faithful constancy with which the American Congress annually appropriated, without protest, billions of dollars for defense, yet often balked at trivial appropriations for other foreign policy purposes, could be attributed less to a superstitious confidence in the sufficiency of military power as such (whose nihilistic capacities everyone was aware of), and more to a deeper skepticism about America's capacity to sustain any more philosophical missions in world affairs.

The annual augmentation of military power was acceptable to nearly all segments of American society. First of all, it seemed a self-evident response to Soviet military power. Secondly it was the classic, conventional response to shelter an individual polity against possible armed attack. Also, the domestic consensus about defense and military strength conveniently deferred consideration of quite uncomfortable philosophical problems which, if faced directly, might shake the fabric of American society. The vast range of non-military policies and undertakings in the outside world—foreign aid, educational and scientific exchanges, foreign information programs—were favored by the Congress and the public on the grounds that they supplemented, and were in fact intrinsic parts of, a cold-war defense program. In other words, they contributed to the defense of a territorial America against both subversion and attack. Thus the public consensus about defense could, to some extent, permit America to engage in substantial international programs which a few Americans justified on quite different grounds.

Indeed, after nearly two decades of the cold war, it was a curious feature of America's comprehensive strategies in world politics that their philosophic rationale was based, not on assessment of American purposes in world politics, but rather upon an assessment of Soviet aims. George Kennan's theory of containment (see Chapter 9), the first coherent theory to generate purposeful designs for action in the cold war, remained the only plausible one. It had proved a cogent, intellectual framework not only for understanding Soviet aims but for American responses to them.

According to this theory, America and her allies might prevent the further enlargement of the Soviet empire without major war through patience, firmness, and military strength. Its growth thus checked, Soviet power might, in time, either wane or mellow as the initial revolutionary fervor and the terror and suspicion of Soviet leaders gave way to more civilized habits and more humane aspirations. Regardless of the soundness of Kennan's strategic analysis, what is important to note here is that his remained the only comprehensive formulation of American purpose in world politics to govern the broad political and strategic actions of the

West. It meant that the basis of broad policy was fixed less upon long-range American goals and purposes (or those of the West as a whole) than upon the real or apparent nature of Soviet doctrine, expectations, and intentions. As an American writer put it recently, the West and America, instead of dealing with Russia "in terms of a world policy, persists in the attempt to deal with the world in terms of a Russian policy, this being in essence the policy of containing Russia all over the world." [5]

The contrast was between doctrinaire Soviet purposefulness in world politics and the pragmatic, problem-oriented, situational American responses to the world crisis. The ritualistic language of Soviet leaders, heralding Communism's historically determined triumph, might veil profound strategic disagreements and political conflict within the Communist world. As many scholars of Soviet politics pointed out, it might also serve to obscure prudent, even conservative purposes of Soviet managerial leadership which, since Lenin's death, had been all too aware of the risks of making Soviet foreign policy the captive of a world revolutionary process. For such a process, if permitted to get out of hand, might result both in Russia's losing political control of its course and, possibly, in cataclysmic thermonuclear war. Still the philosophical contrast between Soviet purposefulness and American pragmatism was there for all to see.

Possible Alternatives

Faced with this contrast between totalitarian doctrine and Western (American) "situationalism," one might conclude that the West, and America in particular, should devise equivalent doctrinaire ideologies to match in influence those they were designed to check. Another possibility is that, in time, history itself and the protracted exposure of Communist leaders in Russia and China to the ambiguous realities of a complex world might under-

---

[5] Robert Tucker, "Russia, the West, and World Order," *World Politics*, October, 1959, p. 4.

mine or transform "Socialist" dogma, thus modifying Soviet practices to the point where they might no longer seriously threaten
the vital interests of the West and America.

So long as the West (and America chiefly) remained firm in
its posture of containment, willing to negotiate where negotiation gave promise of justice and durable order; so long as it maintained its internal prosperity and improved the excellence of its
culture, the latter possibility might become an eventuality. Then
Russian civilization, along with that of the entire Communist bloc,
might some day be won over to the humane, pragmatic, liberal
values which the West at its best exemplified. To quote George
Kennan once more,

> The first dictate of progress toward a better world is, it seems to
> me, that America must become more receptive and more out-
> going. The second is that it must take a tighter control of its own
> life and evolve a greater sense of purpose with regard to the
> shaping of its own development.[6]

These two responses, though commonly concerned with the
defense of the free world without major war, displayed a primary
common difficulty. They were preoccupied with *Soviet* purposes,
Soviet theories of history, *Soviet* revolutionary ideology. If America
and the West were to maintain their influence in world politics
and, hopefully, to extend it to confront the purposes of the Communist world, did not their capacity to attract popular support
depend upon some statement of purpose? Whatever one thought
of Marxism or its contemporary expressions, it was not devised as
an ideological weapon which one political system might use to
defend itself against other political systems. Even the bowdlerized
version of Marxism which remained as doctrine after Stalin's time
was never totally divorced from its original messianic intent. To
suppose that it now served *merely* as an ideological superstructure
to hold together a vast, shaky imperium, overlooked the appeals
of Soviet Communism within the U.S.S.R. to new elites. Even

---

[6] Kennan, *op. cit.*, p. 110.

more, it overlooked its appeals to many people in non-Western societies experiencing the early pains of industrialization.

Aside from the sticky question of whether official American attempts to synthesize a countervailing sense of purpose to inform America and the West would be acceptable to important and quite diverse elements in a democratic mass society (see below), there was an equally important problem. Would such a reactive attempt have much appeal beyond the existing frontiers of America or the West as a whole? It was painfully tempting to lock horns with the Russians by permitting the peoples or elites of uncommitted countries to decide on such national purposes. But such definitions attuned to the ephemeral interests of malleable societies and interpreted by their equally unstable leaders might result in unparalleled organizational catastrophe.

It was true, as had often been alleged, that Soviet-American ideological competition for the loyalties of new elites in under-developed countries had prematurely hastened independence for countries poorly prepared for it, and, in some instances, unfavorably affected the definition of what specific economic and constitutional priorities in these countries should be. Without much doubt, the American-sponsored Volta Dam for Ghana was more to be commended as a device for keeping Soviet influence over Kwame Nkrumah at a tolerable level than for any positive, economically defensible purposes or for encouraging democracy in that country. As had been the case in Egypt, foreign-aid programs could strengthen unpalatable regimes by giving them additional power over their people.

It was possible that this matter of national purpose was intrinsically insoluble, but there did seem to be some easily defined, existing goals. Important elements of the American liberal tradition, like the Wilsonian, had become part of world politics. There were two reasons for this. The first, and the one most clearly identified with Woodrow Wilson, had been largely institutional in its approach to the transcendent problems of the world society. It saw America's responsibilities as encouraging the establishment of *other* Lockean politics with the same constitutional conditions of *political* freedom and establishing supranational organizational systems which, though perhaps lacking in sovereign authority, demonstrated prototypes of the institutional forms of parliamentary government. America should try, within such institutions, to broaden a sense of international community of purpose and to develop capacities for peaceful change and international legislation as a substitute for war.

This was the formal, sometimes formalistic, Wilsonian side of the American liberal tradition, and though American liberals were among its strongest supporters, they had by no means been its inventors. The second, non-Wilsonian aspect of American liberalism which affected foreign policy was an essentially paternalistic or humanitarian egalitarianism. It was concerned with extending the supposedly egalitarian welfare values of American liberalism to less fortunate societies or with combating poverty, disease, and ignorance or alleviating them by spurring economic development, and so forth.

The roots of the latter concern may be seen in the attitudes of many New Deal reformers of the 1930's whom World War II "liberated" from a preoccupation with domestic economic reform. Roosevelt made it explicit in his enunciation of the Four Freedoms during the war.

Different as they were in emphasis, there was clearly no philosophical antagonism between these two liberal purposes. For the first was in essence organization-minded, concerned with the constitutional aspects of a future international community of nations. The second drew upon strong humanitarian impulses within American society which were, essentially, less concerned with institutional, legal problems than they were with the basic material and educational needs of human beings. It could be argued plausibly that neither internal democracy within states nor a viable order among democratic polities could be established or long endure if it were grounded upon illiterate and impoverished mass societies (see section on the U.S.I.A. in Chapter 9). It could also be argued that, if the price of overcoming such poverty and ignorance were that of permanently crippling the capacities of new societies to develop in political freedom, then this price, possibly, was too great to be paid, at least by American funds. In theory, the Gordian knot had to be cut by some fine Damascus steel. However difficult the formula was to find, at least the two indispensable component elements were easily recognized.

As a group of American senators reported on their experiences during an African tour in the fall of 1961,

> We believe that if the long-range interests of the United States are to be served by the creation of free and independent states which respect the fundamental rights of the individual, American aid can in good conscience be provided only to governments which respect those basic rights and freedoms.[7]

But the risk inherent in the termination of U.S. aid was that its withdrawal might further accelerate the very undesirable political tendencies it had been designed to offset. Maximally, there was danger of accelerated Soviet penetration of such countries, and their possible alignment with the Soviet bloc. Minimally, the danger was that, bereft of adequate, external capital and other assistance, yet pressed for economic and social development, regimes such as Kwame Nkrumah's might become police-states and might *force* such necessary changes by totalitarian domestic methods.

A more difficult problem, however, was the relationship between these two manifestations of American liberal purpose in world politics and the nature of the constitutional, democratic polity within which they had come to fruition. Could any concept of transcendent national purpose in world politics overcome the inherent philosophical, institutional, and cultural characteristics of American society?

[7] See "Study Mission to Africa; Report of Senators Albert Gore, Philip A. Hart, and Maurine B. Neuberger," U.S. Eighty-seventh Congress, First Session, Senate Foreign Relations Committee. Washington: Government Printing Office, 1962.

Viewed from afar, the Soviet problem of promulgating Socialist principles in world politics was not only philosophically
simple but, in the context of a one-party state, it was also apparently easy to obtain the necessary popular support for it. This
could be done through mass propaganda, elitist training, and, if
necessary, political force. If ever since Lenin's time, the interests
of Soviet society had successfully been manipulated to square with
the on-going purposes of the Socialist state, as defined by highly
indoctrinated party cadres, so too, the interests and purposes of
the Russian people were synchronized with the supposedly revolutionary objectives of the Soviet Union in world politics.

To be sure, there had been startling changes since the early
1920's in Soviet leaders' prophecies about the nature of the historical process which would lead inexorably to the universal triumph of Socialism. What was left was the perpetual enunciation
of future victory, a victory necessitated by inexorable "laws of
history."

(The original apocalyptic promise was that the Bolshevik
Revolution was the first stage of a more generalized revolution
in the more advanced European countries. Hence, it was regarded
by Lenin and other Bolsheviks as essentially Western-oriented.
Stalin's heresy was to parochialize the vision and to concentrate
upon Socialism in one country. However, in Stalin's later days and
subsequently, the "historical direction" of the spread of revolution changed 180° eastward, into the former colonial areas.)

No such laws of history governed American policies in world
affairs, rationalized them, or found any significant support within
any part of the American public. In fact, such concepts of historic
inevitability in American culture were to be found only among
fundamentalist religious sects, not notable for their grasp of, or
involvement in, the contemporary world. Not unnaturally, perhaps, in the 1960's such fundamentalist sects proved important
recruiting grounds for fanatical, right-wing political movements
which sought to dichotomize the political crisis as one between

a messianic, apocalyptic Christianity and a messianic, apocalyptic Communism, with their chief seats of influence in America and Russia respectively.

It seemed that a free society was intrinsically unable to devise equivalent absolutist certainties. There was a hollow ring to the rhetoric of any American statesman or politician who could speak about the inexorable march of humanity towards democracy, freedom, and international order after the events of the past forty years. Just as there were no necessary reasons for the triumph of democracy, there were no necessary reasons for the collapse of Soviet totalitarianism, due to its inner contradictions. In justifying his doctrine of containment Kennan revealed the difficulties which any skeptical humanist might have about the unavoidable consequences of political action. In 1947, he wrote:

> Soviet power . . . bears within itself the seeds of its own decay, and . . . the sprouting of these seeds is well advanced. . . . [If] anything ever were to occur to disrupt the unity and the efficacy of the Party as a political instrument, Soviet Russia might be changed overnight from one of the strongest to one of the weakest and most pitiable of national societies.[8]

Of this prediction, Kennan himself was to say that it "cannot be proved. And it cannot be disproved." On such slender reassurances, a global American strategy became founded.

The Inner-Directedness of Democracy

There was a theoretical obstacle to settling this national purpose problem in the original Lockean philosophical basis of American political order. This doctrine drew a radical distinction between foreign and domestic affairs. Foreign policy was chiefly a defense or extension of the communal, collective interests of American society. Representative governmental processes were designed chiefly to permit government to express what the public

[8] Kennan, *American Diplomacy, 1900-1950.* Chicago: University of Chicago Press, 1951, p. 125.

and its organized elements of power wished-done. For this reason, American liberalism stressed, above all, the substantive value of the procedures of democracy. That foreign affairs, at least in peacetime, were subject to such powerful democratic restraints from agencies of the public, meant also, as we saw in Chapter IV, that although most Americans accepted the idea of national interest, its substance was not self-evident.

Certainly very few Americans viewed their nation as an agency for any transcendent mission in world affairs, and even among those important few who did, there was still the question of what this mission might be. Perhaps at any given time in recent American history, it would have been possible to discern at least in Congress a broad consensus among powerful groups of both political parties respecting certain immediate, broad goals of policy. But the nature of the consensus seemed to change from decade to decade, as conditions in the external world also changed. An existing balance of power within American politics limited the maneuverability of policy-makers. It was difficult to advocate national missions in world politics which could not *easily* be reviewed by the lawmakers and citizens of a democratic society who held their *own* various conceptions of shifting national interests and purposes. Note the constant review of American foreign aid programs in Congress and in the press.

It is difficult to imagine the philosophical framework within which a conscientious congressman could equate federal "foreign aid" and federal "domestic aid." When a dam was to be built with American funds in Egypt, for Egyptians, on what grounds did one justify the cost to Americans who might benefit from a dam constructed in their area. It was all well and good to establish the rationale for foreign aid by linking it to military defense programs, and making it the agency which kept communism far away from, say, Senator McClelland's impoverished Mississippi constituents. If one sought to substitute quite different purposes than merely *defensive* ones, there was trouble. As one group of American legislators noted,

Year after year, members of Congress are subjected to increasing criticism for helping foreign nations solve power, water, and other development projects while postponing similar ventures in the United States. It is obvious that at some point the U.S. will reach a limit beyond which its aid cannot be increased. While that limit is related to our capacity to provide assistance, far more important is the relationship between what we provide and the results achieved. When the Congress, under its authority to appropriate funds "to pay the Debts and provide for the Common Defense and General Welfare of the United States," decides to build a dam in Africa rather than in the U.S., it does so because it believes that decision serves a national interest. In the words of the Act for International Development, Congress believes the "survival of free institutions in the U.S. can be best assured in a worldwide atmosphere of freedom" and that it is "a primary necessity, opportunity, and responsibility of the United States" to demonstrate that "economic growth and political democracy can go hand in hand to the end that an enlarged community of free, stable, and self-reliant countries can reduce world tensions and insecurity." [9]

Inexorably, so it seemed, one returned to the Wilsonian theme. Strategic and defensive rationalizations of American aid programs would be backed by a domestic consensus only so long as they seemed correlated with negative, defensive responses to Soviet initiatives. Thus fear could motivate policies and enhance solidarity. But fear devised only patchwork expedients. If the survival of free institutions in the U.S. were the primary concern of policy-makers, and if their survival depended upon "an enlarged community of free, stable, and self-reliant countries," how could this latter object be made acceptable to men in other countries when its reference point remained an American national interest? And, to accentuate this difficulty, how could the concept of a future world of free, stable, and self-reliant countries make sense to Americans unless it were couched in terms consistent with specific, on-going interests of a national community as seen from within it? After all, the achievement of any really bold program to

[9] Eighty-seventh Congress, Second Session, "Study Mission to Africa," *op. cit.*, p. 14.

strengthen free institutions abroad required not merely continual outlays of American resources, but also some overriding conviction that *this* objective was the essential thing. Minimally, it had to keep the periphery of freedom from shrinking further.

PHYSICIAN, HEAL THYSELF

To the problems already posed by the question of national purpose we can add two new ones. First, what was America's capacity to sustain or develop a sense of common purpose with other peoples in a cold war which obviously could not be settled by military means. The other problem was the possible effect of the cold war on the nature of the Western values in America. Here Byron's ironic verses about freedom fighters comes to mind:

> *When a man hath no freedom to fight for at home,*
> *Let him combat for that of his neighbours;*
> *Let him think of the glories of Greece and of Rome,*
> *And get knocked on the head for his labours.*

> *To do good to Mankind is the chivalrous plan,*
> *And is always as nobly requited;*
> *Then battle for Freedom wherever you can,*
> *And, if not shot or hanged, you'll get knighted.*[10]

It is pointless to worry about the perimeters of the free world if the meaning of freedom were forgotten in America. The rivalry between the totalitarian world and the West would be decided not so much by events on the perimeters, but by what happened at home. The problem is how certain essential qualities of freedom in one's own society might relate to traditional or emergent ones elsewhere which are considered worth defending or establishing.

What has made this problem so infinitely complex is how any one could set acceptable criteria of freedom within the Communist world which Western policy might wish to become reality.

[10] Byron, "Stanzas" (to Thomas Moore, November 5, 1820, first published, 1830).

In the early 1960's, there have been at least a few Marxist theoreticians in the Soviet world who have thought that the fulfillment of Marxism's historical mission requires a new emphasis upon "humanism." The Polish Marxist, Adam Schaaf, was one. Is it hypocritical to hope that some of the most unpleasant features of Stalinist totalitarianism remain a part of Soviet practice, to serve as object lessons to those outside the Communist world and as negative yardsticks beside which the virtues of the Western world might shine the brighter?

Considering first the problem of political freedom in the West and, notably, in America, it is easy to see that the cold war has created and intensified certain unpleasant, social, organizational, and economic trends in American life. A certain perspective of judgment is needed here as an antidote to political hypochondria. After fifteen years of cold war, America has remained the center of political and constitutional stability in the non-Communist world. Within the United States, political fanaticism, either from the undemocratic left or right, has stayed within bounds. A climate of political moderation, bordering perhaps upon torpor during the Eisenhower administration, has at least simplified the strategy of the free world. So long as America remains constant in its broad range of external commitments, notably those which hold out for a Western defense community, so long can the necessary patterns of order and cooperation remain within the West.

Here, the pre-eminence of American power within the coalition is necessary, for among America's chief partners in the cold war there are some, like France, whose internal political order has been, to say the least, threatened constantly by civil war. There are others like West Germany, whose democratic institutions have barely been tested, and who could hardly be regarded as central to the common, defensive purposes of the West, partly because of the unresolved issue of German reunification. This inherent American constitutional stability and the firmness with which America has remained committed to clear, defensive guarantees has kept the Western alliance together. Even West European neutralists who wished to dissociate their own nations from an American strategic alliance and from the risks of living under an American thermonuclear umbrella, have been hardly able to contemplate the consequences of the American military and strategic withdrawal into the Western hemisphere which they proposed and which would have exposed their ensuing national helplessness. Thus, it has been impossible to speak of any meaningful free-world coalition at all, unless one assumed that it was grounded upon a politically stable America. This meant an America relatively untroubled by major internal discords, and which fulfilled the broad kinds of political commitments it had undertaken. The free world could not sustain a major seismic event within the United States and an ensuing polarization of American public opinion. Such essential stability of political purpose and the accompanying economic stability seem to require, in essence, a public, American calm.

Bearing in mind these broad perspectives, it is possible to see that during the cold war, the matter of freedom in American life has itself become increasingly ambiguous. To be sure, throughout the entire period, the American public has made few discernible *material* sacrifices. During the 1950's, for instance, scarcely ten percent of the American gross national product was expended on the cold war. During the same period of time, in fact, the private affluence of Americans grew. A humane conscience might be shocked by the staggering contrast between the resources allocated to defense in all its ramifications and to "peaceful uses." But few could seriously believe that a tax of such small total magnitude in and of itself really pinched. If America were to be a garrison state, which few wanted, it would at least be an upper-income garrison state.

It was more important that individualism seemed caught in the meshes of an increasingly complex organizational system which the cold war involvement seemed to make more complex. These systems, private and governmental both, interlaced American society. Within them, and seemingly of necessity, private and public power seemed on the way to attaining a degree of concentration which, half a century ago, would have amazed even radical Trust Busters. Within these systems of power, concomitantly, knowledge and specialization of expertise were fragmented.

To be sure, America has remained far from the condition of a totalitarian state. There have been no constraints on the free expression of public opinion. Mass media, however much it resembles a cartel, still disseminate diverse ideas to those who trouble to watch, read, or listen. The two-party system remains strong. The courts are open, the judiciary is free, and religious and cultural diversity flourish in a climate of thought made possible by rising educational standards. Finally, the quality of American political leadership can hardly be said to have declined, either in or out of government.

Despite all of these things, the problem remains. As one thoughtful commentator on the American scene wrote, if Americans can establish no meaningful sense of belief in or identification with these vast, private institutions of power upon which they depend, both for their livelihood and for the services they provide, then a positive attitude toward them can persist only so long as these continue to serve individual economic interests. "Beyond the façade of extreme organization . . . lies a reality of anti-social individualism, which is further masked by the protective tyranny of public opinion."[11] As Hans Morgenthau wrote, "A public with no constant dedication to public affairs at home will hardly feel such dedication to affairs abroad."

Much as the "new corporatism" in America has sought to infuse "loyalty" in its employees and to induce proper habitual preferences in its consumers, the matter of power remains. Who is truly free or equal vis-à-vis agencies of the garrison state, like General Motors or its thousands of large subcontractors? How can a democratic public deal rationally with such sacrosanct entities

---

[11] Philip Green, "National Purposes and New Frontiers," *Commentary*, June, 1961.

of power, deciding what proper influence they should have within American society at the very time when their stability and organizational health is so essential to the conduct of cold war strategies? The very fact that overriding cold war perils require tight concentration of decision-making power places a premium upon managerial expertise and the power to funnel American resources this way or that, in accordance with the "dialectics" of cold war, peaceful co-existence.

Here, already, one can see the constant tension between an ethic of democracy which distrusts power and wishes to divide and limit it and make it perpetually responsive to the popular will, and a more urgent ethic of responsibility which, in the cold war context, makes ever greater power indispensable for national survival and for rational strategies and policies. If, for instance, one sees a constant need to augment American economic and technological power to keep pace with that of the totalitarian world and thus maintain the perimeters of freedom, then how can one seriously object to the enormous, ramifying systems of control and organization deemed necessary to undergird and focus that power? "Keeping up with the Russians," at least after Sputnik, has involved a vast acceleration of government-sponsored scientific research and progress. Federally subsidized research in both basic and applied sciences has become a significant factor in the universities, radically redirecting the nature of intellectual life and the kinds of intellectual pursuits which a new generation of American students and scholars would pursue.

Such an ethic of responsibility is not necessarily incompatible with a democratic or liberal ethic, but not necessarily compatible, either. The ethic of responsibility is synonymous with an ethic of necessity in these circumstances. To accept it would narrow and constrict the range of democratic choices in public policy. For new necessities seem constantly to arise out of a cold war context, requiring vast new programs and activities which might easily have far-reaching, permanent effects upon the character of American institutions and American life.

Some of these cold war necessities might seem to be desirable on their merits, under any circumstances: the necessity, for instance, for racial equality and constitutional guarantees of civil rights to American Negroes in a new context of world politics where white men are a minority and where Soviet propaganda makes perverse use of America's shortcomings. Others are the need for "excellence" in American education at a time when Soviet academic attainments have been higher; the need to maintain and even improve rates of American economic growth *because of* Soviet ones, which have been far higher; the need to maintain high levels of employment and business activity, since a U.S. recession or depression might ingloriously fulfill Soviet predictions about the inherent instability of the American economy. Such necessities could be found acceptable on grounds wholly unconnected with the cold war.

Several of them, notably, the need for accelerated action on civil rights, call for things long overdue and postponed. Such needs could be justified in the context of traditional American liberal values. When the ethic of cold war necessity coincides with a prior ethic of democracy, the coincidence could spur action to a pace perhaps impossible in normal times. There is, perhaps, much irony in the fact that in the 1960's, a prudent concern for the sensibilities of African diplomats has helped to hasten the conferral of long overdue rights to American Negroes in access to housing, restaurants, and various other public facilities. But why should one complain, so long as it happened?

The ethic of necessity and responsibility has also made less happy demands. The logic of military, strategic, and technological competition with the U.S.S.R. has diverted much of America's resources—material, human, and intellectual—into enterprises by means which have quite radically altered America's economic organization. The extent of American economic involvement in military necessities has built powerful resistance to a peacetime conversion of the American economic system. To this extent the American government's search for workable systems of international disarmament has been hampered. Whole regions, such as Southern California, have become fixed in a hothouse cold war economy with the *raison d'être* of human occupation and industrial organization chained to the demands of military production.

Other exigencies of protracted conflict have worked ceaselessly to remold the nature of American private institutions. Various disciplines in state and private universities have been locked into federal programs of research and development of weaponry and its ramifications. New programs, spurred by protracted competition between the United States and the U.S.S.R., place high premiums upon technological, scientific, and organizational innovations. The warlike compulsion to engage the enemy with resources similar to his, or better, has forced upon America a certain symmetry and centralization of organization and internal development. As we have seen, the need for continuity of political purpose and national strength places a high value on stability of public mood and upon expert judgment. It has also placed a premium on decision making systems which could act swiftly in crisis (enhancing America's dependence upon machines to compute its power) to make many of its administrative decisions, and to program its tactical and strategic plans. The logic of thermonuclear age strategy might press demands upon the American public which, like certain crash civil defense proposals, portend vast transformations in American ways of living.

The new corporatism of which these organizational changes are symptomatic surely possesses an inner justification, but one which no longer holds out promise that the problems of world politics could be alleviated or overcome by the means which it provides. The East-West arms race offers little hope that America could recover ever again the spectacular eminence of power she possessed in the 1940's, or recover the security she had not two decades ago.

Surely it is questionable whether a new sense of public purpose can be engendered within the ever increasing, organizational complexities of the cold war. There are many reasons why it could be inhibited by it. The elusive values of freedom and democracy had arisen in a climate of American national optimism, enthusiasm, and individualism. As Whitman had written, ". . . the American compact is altogether with individuals." Neither organizational nor social engineering, whatever their immediate utility in the military contest, would supply the means to what Henry Wriston called "the central goal," "a renewal of faith in the infinite value and the unlimited possibilities of individual development." Neither can they address themselves to the fundamental issues which fifteen years of cold war have posed between America and Russia. Among these are ones which address themselves *both* to the ways in which nations ideally should arrange their internal ordering and management, and to the ways in which nations should arrange their relationships with each other. To speak to these issues has required of Americans, possibly, that they acknowledge the great power of these enormous corporate entities, that they remain skeptical of their inherent value, and that their sense of national purpose be derived, not only from the traditions of freedom which they have cherished, but from the unique and terrifying organizational crisis which all men have faced personally and which has threatened all men, in common, with destruction.

For, in truth, the central issue of human survival in freedom is one which Americans might profitably consider their overriding purpose. Out of their unique national experiences with individual freedom and with power; out of their historical experience both with national freedom in isolation and now with deep, responsible involvement in world crisis, they could speak with some authority about the regulation of power in the interests of *both* freedom and survival to others who might listen. Both in earlier isolation and in cold war involvement, the American nation gave birth to and maintained a viable constitutional order, consonant with ideals of human freedom. Americans might now affirm as their object a search for an international order consonant with such ideals. Marxism, even as it has betrayed its original, authentic commitment to human freedom and the human personality, can not address itself any more to problems of human freedom *nor* speak sense to the organizational crisis which has threatened all nations with destruction. But American liberalism might. Woodrow Wilson said once, "We are citizens of the world; and the tragedy of our times is that we do not know this." In sober awareness of this, perhaps, we might find our national purpose.

SUGGESTED READING

Bowles, Chester, *The New Dimensions of Peace*, New York, Harper & Bros., 1955.

Emerson, Rupert, *From Empire to Nation: The Rise to Self-Assertion of Asian and African Peoples*, Cambridge, Mass., Harvard University Press, 1960; esp. "Nationalism and Democracy" and "Self-Determination."

Feis, Herbert, "Europe *vs.* Asia in American Strategy," *Yale Review*, March 1954, pp. 351-3.

Fromm, Erich, *Can Man Prevail? An Inquiry into the Facts and Fictions of Foreign Policy*, Garden City, Doubleday and Co., 1961.

Green, Philip, "National Purposes and New Frontiers," *Commentary*, June 1961.

Khrushchev, Nikita S., "International Situation of the Soviet Union," in Harold K. Jacobson, *America's Foreign Policy*, New York, Random House, 1960, pp. 247-55.

Kissinger, Henry A., *The Necessity for Choice: Prospects of American Foreign Policy*, New York, Harper & Brothers, 1961.

Knorr, Klaus, ed., *NATO and American Security*, Princeton, Princeton University Press, 1959.

Niebuhr, Reinhold, "Reflections on Democracy and Communism," *Columbia University Forum*, IV (3), Summer 1961, pp. 10-18.

Roberts, Henry L., *Russia and America: Dangers and Prospects*, New York, Harper & Brothers, 1956.

Stillman, Edmund, and William Pfaff, *The New Politics: America and the End of the Postwar World*, New York, Coward-McCann, 1961; esp. Chs. 8 and 9.

Tucker, Robert C., "Russia, the West, and World Order," *World Politics*, XII (1), October 1959, pp. 1-23.

Whitaker, Arthur P., *The Western Hemisphere Idea—Its Rise and Decline*, Ithaca, Cornell University Press, 1954.

Bibliography

Almond, Gabriel, *The American People and Foreign Policy*, New York, Harcourt, Brace, 1950.

Aron, Raymond, *The Century of Total War*, Boston, Beacon Press, 1955.

Barghoorn, Frederick, *The Soviet Image of the United States*, New York, Harcourt, Brace, 1950.

Beard, Charles, *The Idea of National Interest, an Analytical Study in American Foreign Policy*, New York, Macmillan, 1934.

Beloff, Max, *Foreign Policy and the Democratic Process*, Baltimore, The Johns Hopkins Press, 1955.

Boorstin, Daniel J., *America and the Image of Europe*, New York, Meridian Books, 1960.

Bowles, Chester, *The New Dimensions of Peace*, New York, Harper & Brothers, 1955.

Bundy, McGeorge, *The Pattern of Responsibility*, Boston, Houghton Mifflin Co., 1951.

Butterfield, Herbert, *Christianity, Diplomacy, and War*, New York, Abingdon-Cokesbury Press, n.d.

Carleton, William, *The Revolution in American Foreign Policy*, New York, Random House, 1957, rev. ed.

Cleveland, Harlan, et al., *The Overseas American*, New York, McGraw-Hill, 1960.

Cook, Thomas Ira, and Moos, Malcolm, *Power Through Purpose. The Realism of Idealism as a Basis for Foreign Policy*, Baltimore, The Johns Hopkins Press, 1954.

Corwin, Edwin S., *The President: Office and Powers, 1787-1957*, New York, New York University Press, 1957.

Dahl, Robert, *Congress and Foreign Policy*, New York, Harcourt, Brace, 1950.

DeConde, Alexander, *Isolation and Security: Ideas and Interests in Twentieth Century American Foreign Policy*, Durham, N.C., Duke University Press, 1957.

Emerson, Rupert, *From Empire to Nation: The Rise to Self-Assertion of Asian and African Peoples*, Cambridge, Mass., Harvard University Press, 1960.

Fromm, Erich, *Can Man Prevail? An Inquiry Into the Facts and Fictions of Foreign Policy*, Garden City, Doubleday & Co., 1961.

Graebner, Norman, *New Isolationism: A Study in Politics and Foreign Policy Since 1950*, New York, Ronald Press, 1956.

Handlin, Oscar, *The Uprooted*, Boston, Little, Brown, 1951.

Hero, Alfred, *Americans in World Affairs*, Boston, World Peace Foundation, 1959.

Herz, John, *International Politics in the Atomic Age*, New York, Columbia University Press, 1959.

Hilsman, Roger, *Strategic Intelligence and National Decisions*, Glencoe, Ill., Free Press, 1956.

Jaspers, Karl, *The Future of Man*, Chicago, University of Chicago Press, 1961.

Jones, Joseph R., *The Fifteen Weeks (February 21-June 5, 1947)*, New York, Viking Press, 1955.

deJouvenel, Bertrand, *Power: The Natural History of Its Growth*, British Book Centre, 1953.

Kennan, George, *American Diplomacy: 1900-1950*, Chicago, University of Chicago Press, 1951.

Kissinger, Henry A., *The Necessity for Choice: Prospects of American Foreign Policy*, New York, Harper & Brothers, 1961.

Knorr, Klaus, *NATO and American Security*, Princeton, Princeton University Press, 1959.

Knorr, Klaus, and Baumol, William J., *What Price Economic Growth?* Englewood Cliffs, N.J., Prentice-Hall, 1961.

Koenig, Louis W., *The Invisible Presidency*, New York, Rinehart, 1960.

Langer, William and Gleason, S. E., *The Challenge to Isolation 1937-1940*, New York, Harper & Brothers, 1952.

Lefever, Ernest, *Ethics and United States Foreign Policy*, New York, Meridian Books, 1957.

Lippmann, Walter, *Essays in the Public Philosophy*, Boston, Little, Brown, 1955.

Lippmann, Walter, *U.S. Foreign Policy: Shield of the Republic*, Boston, Little, Brown, 1943.

Lubell, Samuel, *The Future of American Politics*, Garden City, Doubleday & Co., 1956, rev. ed.

McCamy, James, *The Administration of American Foreign Policy*, New York, Alfred A. Knopf, 1950.

McLean, Joseph E., ed., *The Public Service and University Education*, Princeton, Princeton University Press, 1949.

Marshall, Charles B., *The Limits of Foreign Policy*, New York, Henry Holt, 1954.

Millis, Walter, and Murray, John Courtney, S. J., *Foreign Policy and the Free Society*, New York, Oceans Publications, 1958.

Mills, C. Wright, *The Power Elite*, New York, Oxford University Press, 1956.

Morgenthau, Hans J., *In Defense of the National Interest*, New York, Alfred A. Knopf, 1951.

Myrdal, Gunnar, *An International Economy: Problems and Prospects*, New York, Harper & Brothers, 1956.

Nef, John U., *War and Human Progress: An Essay on the Rise of Industrial Civilization*, Cambridge, Harvard University Press, 1950.

Nicolson, Harold, *Diplomacy*, New York, Oxford University Press, 1952.

Niebuhr, Reinhold, *Moral Man and Immoral Society*, New York, Scribner's, 1932.

Niebuhr, Reinhold, *The Irony of American History*, New York, Scribner's, 1952.

Niebuhr, Reinhold, *The Children of Light and the Children of Darkness*, New York, Scribner's, 1944.

Potter, David M., *People of Plenty: Economic Abundance and the American Economy*, Chicago, University of Chicago Press, 1954.

Roberts, Henry L., *Russia and America: Dangers and Prospects*, New York, Harper & Brothers, 1956.

Spykman, Nicholas, *America's Strategy in World Politics*, New York, Harcourt, Brace, 1942.

Stillman, Edmund, and Pfaff, William, *The New Politics: America and the End of the Postwar World*, New York, Coward-McCann, 1961.

Tannenbaum, Frank, *The American Tradition in Foreign Policy*, Norman, Okla., University of Oklahoma Press, 1954.

Tocqueville, Alexis de, *Democracy in America*, New York, Oxford University Press, 1947.

Toynbee, Arnold, *The World and the West*, New York, Oxford University Press, 1953.

Whitaker, Arthur P., *The Western Hemisphere Idea: Its Rise and Decline*, Ithaca, Cornell University Press, 1954.

Wolfers, Arnold and Martin, Laurence W., eds., *The Anglo-American Tradition in Foreign Affairs, Readings from Thomas More to Woodrow Wilson*, New Haven, Yale University Press, 1956.

INDEX

INDEX

About the Author

PAUL SEABURY, Associate Professor of Political Science at the University of California at Berkeley, previously taught at Columbia University, where he received his Ph.D., and during 1951 was visiting lecturer at the Free University in Berlin. In 1961-2 he held a Guggenheim fellowship, and spent the year as a Visiting Scholar at the Brookings Institution. He is the author of *The Wilhelmstrasse: A Study of German Foreign Policy During the Nazi Regime* (1954) and of *The Waning of Southern Internationalism* (1957).

A NOTE ON THE TYPE

This book is set in Electra, a Linotype face designed by W. A. Dwiggins. This face cannot be classified as either modern or old-style. It is not based on any historical model, nor does it echo any particular period or style. It avoids the extreme contrasts between thick and thin elements that mark most modern faces, and attempts to give a feeling of fluidity, power, and speed.

6⅙
4 P,